D0315704

FR-21698

The French National Front

The Extremist Challenge to Democracy

Harvey G. Simmons

Westview
PRESS

A Member of the Perseus Books Group

Copyright © 1996 by Westview Press, A Member of the Perseus Books Group

Published in 1996 in the United States of America by Westview Press, 5500 Central Avenue, Boulder, Colorado 80301-2877, and in the United Kingdom by Westview Press, 12 Hid's Copse Road, Cumnor Hill, Oxford OX2 9JJ

A CIP catalog record for this book is available from the Library of Congress
ISBN 0-8133-2891-8.   ISBN 0-8133-8979-8 (pbk.)

The paper used in this publication meets the requirements of the American National Standard for Permanence of Paper for Printed Library Materials Z39.48-1984.

10   9   8   7   6   5   4   3   2

Contents

Preface   ix

Introduction   1

    Notes, 6

Part One
History

1   Out of the Ashes: Postwar Fascism in France   11

    The Fascist International, 14
    The Extreme Right in France, 15
    De Gaulle and the Extreme Right, 20
    Notes, 22

2   From Poujade to de Gaulle   27

    Jean-Marie Le Pen, Poujadist, 31
    Algeria and the Extreme Right, 36
    Le Pen in Algeria, 37
    Le Pen and the Fall of the Fourth Republic, 41
    Crossing the Desert, 46
    Notes, 48

3   From Tixier-Vignancour to the National Front   53

    The Student Revolution of May 1968, 56
    The June 1968 Election, 58
    Le Pen and Ordre Nouveau, 59
    The Birth of the National Front, 62
    Ideas and Policies, 63
    The 1973 Election and After, 65
    Notes, 67

4 Into the Limelight: 1981–1986   71

Breakthrough, 72
The Left, the Right, and the National Front, 77
Immigration and the Campaign, 79
The 1986 Election and Cohabitation, 80
The National Front Electorate, 83
The National Front in the National Assembly, 84
Notes, 86

5 Sinking Roots: 1987–1995   89

The 1988 Presidential and Legislative Elections, 92
Le Pen and the Scandal of the Rhyme, 94
The Scarves Affair, 95
Dreux Again, 95
Immigration, 96
Carpentras, 99
The Gulf War, 100
The National Front and the Media, 103
The National Front and the Balladur Government, 105
Election Mania, 107
The de Villiers Phenomenon, 108
The Front and Local Politics, 111
Notes, 114

Part Two
Analysis

6 Anti-Semitism   123

Divided Loyalties, 125
Doubting the Holocaust, 126
The Jewish Conspiracy, 127
Anti-Semitism and Divisions in the Front, 130
Anti-Semitism and Party Tactics, 132
The Centrality of Anti-Semitism, 134
Notes, 136

7 Immigration and Racism   143

Immigration in Perspective, 144
Attitudes Toward Immigrants, 145
Identification and Numbers, 146

Immigration and Policy, 147
The Extreme Right and Immigration, 149
Immigration After 1945, 150
Turning off the Tap, 152
Against Immigration, 153
The Socialists and Immigration, 157
The National Front and Immigration, 159
The Social Costs of Immigration, 160
On National Identity and Racism, 161
The Front and "Anti-French Racism," 163
Notes, 164

8 Electorate   169

The Extreme Right and Poujadism, 170
Front Voters: Extreme Right or on the Extreme
    of the Right? 172
Analyzing the Front Vote, 175
Front Voters, Immigration, and Security, 177
Local Factors, 180
The Nature of the National Front Vote, 181
Notes, 183

9 Party Organization   187

Power at the Top, 190
Associated Organizations, 191
Party Finance, 193
The Pro-Front Press, 197
Factions in the Front, 198
Notes, 202

10 The New Political Discourse of the Extreme Right   207

GRECE, 209
Doctrine, 212
Club de l'Horloge, 215
Political Discourse, 216
The Vocabulary Battle, 217
Racism and Antiracism, 223
AIDS, 224
The Front's Conspiracy Theory, 225
The Extreme Right, 228
Notes, 230

11 Metaphors of War: Women and the National Front   237

Joan of Arc: Virgin and Warrior, 238
Women Defending the Home Front, 240
Women and Biology, 241
Women and the Family, 242
Women, Equality, and the Natural Order, 244
Women and Social Policy, 245
Women in the National Front, 247
Notes, 248

Conclusion   251

Notes, 258

Postscript   261

Notes, 266

Appendix A: The National Front at the Polls   267
Appendix B: Political Bureau, February 1994   268
Bibliography   269
About the Book and Author   275
Index   277

Preface

I began research for this book on the French National Front some years ago after I had written about mental retardation policy and mental health policy. Having taught European politics for many years at York University, I was surprised that in the early 1990s academics (with some exceptions) continued to fret about the European left while ignoring the significant, and dangerous, rise of the extreme right. My purpose, therefore, was to write a clear, straightforward account of the most popular and dangerous extreme right political party in Western Europe, the French National Front.

Along with other extreme right parties, the National Front loudly proclaims its allegiance to democracy, refuses the extremist label, and demands to be included among the mainstream parties of the right. However, thinly concealed behind a rhetorical fog of coded language and slogans, the Front's ideology is pervaded by anti-Semitism, racism, and hostility to parliamentary democracy. In addition, Jean-Marie Le Pen, the Front's charismatic leader, has surrounded himself with ex-Vichyites, ex-fascists, or fundamentalists of the far right whose commitment to democracy and tolerance is open to question.

In the June 22, 1995, *New York Review of Books*, Italian author and scholar Umberto Eco discussed the revival of the extreme right and put forward a model of "Ur-Fascism." Eco, like many other people, is troubled by the ambiguities of the contemporary extreme right: It disclaims any relation to prewar or wartime fascism, yet its ideology echoes many of fascism's principal themes. "Ur-Fascism," said Eco, "is still around us, sometimes in plainclothes. It would be so much easier, for us, if there appeared on the world scene somebody saying, 'I want to reopen Auschwitz, I want the Black Shirts to parade again in the Italian squares.' Life is not that simple. Ur-Fascism can come back under the most innocent of disguises."

The purpose of this book is to discover what lies behind the plainclothes of the French National Front. Part 1 uses the mechanism of a brief political biography of Jean-Marie Le Pen to provide a history of the French extreme right from 1945 to 1995. Although the revival of the extreme right is a Europeanwide phenomenon, one cannot understand the amazing success of the French National Front without knowing something of the French context. Part 2 consists of a series of analytical chapters on various aspects of the Front: anti-Semitism, immigration and racism, electorate, organization, political discourse, and women and the Front.

The book concludes in an ambiguous fashion: The Front may not be an old-style fascist party, yet its ideology and the political beliefs of its leadership pose a serious threat to democracy. If the Front should ever win national office in France, it could undermine the foundations of the Fifth Republic. Whatever it is, therefore, the Front is a dangerous political party.

This book is based almost entirely on secondary sources. Except for two trips to France when I did research on the pro-Front press at the Bibliothèque Nationale, most of my work was conducted at the library of the London School of Economics during a sabbatical year and at the York University library. Recently, I was fortunate in being able to purchase copies of the pro-Front weekly *National Hebdo* in downtown Toronto and thereby to keep in touch with what Front leaders and sympathizers had to say about issues of the day.

I wish to thank the London School of Economics for its courtesy in providing me with a library card and use of a computer, all in the space of twenty minutes when I first applied. Also, Scott Library at York University is a wonderful place for research: The staff are always pleasant and helpful, the facilities are commodious, and, best of all, through the efficient interlibrary loan service one can obtain books or journals from around the world. Add to that the resources of the Robarts Library at the University of Toronto, and one has available in metropolitan Toronto a vast array of resources for research on European politics.

Above all, I made great use of *Le Monde*. I especially want to thank Lili Minski of the periodical room: She always made sure that, once the microfilm had arrived, I was supplied with copies of *Le Monde* and any additional French popular or scholarly journals I needed for research.

Finally, as always, I thank Eileen.

Harvey G. Simmons

Introduction

The specter of right-wing extremism is haunting Europe. Although the extreme right seemed to disappear along with Nazism and fascism after World War II, it never completely vanished. In the late 1940s and 1950s, tiny groups of fascists or ex-Nazis met to discuss common problems, publish newspapers or periodicals, and organize extreme right movements or political parties. However, Europe was basking in the long economic boom that followed World War II, parliamentary democracy had been restored, and anti-Semitism and authoritarianism were politically unpopular. In these circumstances the extreme right seemed doomed to permanent exile on the periphery of the political system. Yet over the past four decades, extreme right parties have emerged in almost every Western European country and, since the fall of the Berlin Wall, in Eastern Europe and the former Soviet Union as well.

The largest and most influential of these parties is the French National Front (NF). Its leader, Jean-Marie Le Pen, won 15 percent of the vote in the April 1995 presidential election, and the Front elected more than one thousand members to municipal councils and three mayors in the local elections that followed in June. Not only has the Front become the third most popular political party in France, but also its anti-immigration campaign has led to a tightening of France's immigration laws and increased policing of immigrant ghettos. The NF's barely concealed racism has contributed to growing public hostility to Muslim and African immigrants.

There is a good deal of ambiguity about the true nature of the National Front. While the Front rejects socialism, liberalism, and fascism and is skeptical of Enlightenment values of autonomy, rationality, and egalitarianism, its ideology is an odd pastiche of elements from the history of fascism and the extreme right, with references to prewar anti-Semitism, Vichy, fundamentalist Christianity, neofascism, racism, and the philosophy of the French new right. To complicate matters even more, all this is overlaid with protestations of support for democracy and democratic values. The Front itself claims that "it is not a structure inherited from the past" but is rather "a new and original political expression whose roots extend into the depths of our history and values."[1] But which history? The history of the Republic? Or of Vichy? And what values?

The essential problem, therefore, is to determine on what side of the amorphous boundary that separates the extreme right from fascism the Front falls. Is it, as some would argue, a neofascist party in disguise?[2] Or is it "a full-fledged participant in and beneficiary of the democratic process"?[3]

From one perspective, it can be argued that the National Front is a democratic party like the other French political parties. Le Pen himself tirelessly claims to be a "Churchillian democrat," and except for a violent rampage by NF deputies in the National Assembly in 1987, there is no evidence that the party openly endorses antidemocratic behavior. Although the NF has attracted its share of skinheads and thugs over the past decades, and although it is often accused of provoking violence in demonstrations, its record is mixed. No doubt NF militants have occasionally attacked reporters and political opponents, but the Front increasingly tries to project a pacific image, and it claims to eschew violent confrontations.

From another angle, however, there appears to be a large fascist potential in the NF. A number of people on the NF's political bureau have historical associations with wartime fascism or with neofascism, and many of them are anti-Semitic and racist. The pro-NF press expresses virulently racist, anti-Semitic, and thinly veiled antidemocratic sentiments.[4] NF cadres prefer authoritarian government or monarchy to democracy.[5] Bruno Mégret, the party's second in command and Le Pen's likely successor, has consistently expressed views that border on anti-Semitism and racism. Above all, from the beginning of Le Pen's career, he has associated with, and appointed to top party positions, neofascists, anti-Semites, and racists of all stripes.

On the face of it, the Front leadership appears only weakly committed to democratic values and traditions. In a television interview during the 1988 presidential election campaign, Le Pen was asked if he condemned South African apartheid. He replied, "The definition of democracy in a country is not limited only to the exercise of the right to vote. . . . Let's have the courage to say that the level of security, of employment and the social level are part of the definition of democracy."[6] There are echoes here of communism—and of fascism as well. Did Le Pen mean to imply that in some cases it might be necessary to sacrifice democracy to maintain public order and security and an acceptable level of employment and social provision? Le Pen's words recall the Maurrasian dictum that the maintenance of order in the state takes precedence over other priorities, such as democracy or individual justice: "Order, it is said, is superior justice."[7]

Repeatedly, Front leaders have suggested that under certain circumstances the democratic rules of the game could be violated. In 1993 Bruno Mégret observed that France no longer lived within a democracy and that "victory can't come progressively as in a normal democratic regime, but quickly, as happens when totalitarian regimes collapse or are overthrown and when the destiny of civilization is at stake."[8] In early 1994 Le Pen stated that, if the ineffectiveness of power (referring to the presidency of François Mitterrand) "became a rule . . . then it is clear that nature, which fears a vacuum, will bring about other political forms than those which exist."[9] After scoring 43.05 percent of the vote on the first round of the 1995 municipal election for the city of Vitrolles, just outside Marseilles, Mégret was interviewed by Olivier Biffaud of *Le Monde*. Mégret stated that if elected mayor, he would apply the Front's policy of "national preference," that is, giving preference in housing and social welfare to French citizens over non-French immigrants.[10] The intention of implementing the policy would be to "incite foreign families who do not live in Vitrolles not to want to come here, and to incite those who do live here to leave."[11] When Biffaud asked him what national preference would mean in the actual management of a commune, Mégret replied: "You know quite well that currently, that policy is illegal. . . . If one wants to stay within the law, it [the national preference policy] can only be done covertly; in the same way that certain city authorities, like the ex-mayor, do it to favor foreigners." Biffaud then asked, "You would practice an underground national preference?" And Mégret replied, "I can't say any more to you."[12] In short, the second in command of the National Front, expecting to assume public office, explicitly promised to disobey the law once he had been elected—and all in the name of discriminating against non-French nationals in housing and welfare.[13]

The ambiguous nature of the Front can be further illustrated by a close look at the implications of Le Pen's often-repeated jibe that he says out loud what ordinary French people think to themselves. On one level Le Pen merely claims that he is frank about his opinions and beliefs, whereas orthodox politicians are not—in this Le Pen is merely following well-worn populist lines. But the statement also implies that the majority of French are afraid to express their honest opinions about politics and society.

Why?

Because, according to the Front, powerful lobbies or oligarchies have deliberately circumscribed the terms of political debate in France, thereby delegitimizing views and opinions that, if the public only knew, are widely shared by many citizens. Thus, the leader who says out loud what others only say to themselves destroys the barriers established by "occult" elites to prevent the public from knowing the truth. According to the NF's 1993 election program, "The 'politician's Establishment' has taken away the voice of the people and confiscated it for its own profit. Increasingly servile to foreign powers on the outside and to lobbies on the inside, and with the complicity of a media power, which is under orders, it systematically gags those who are trying to make the voice of truth heard."[14]

Who are these "lobbies" that muzzle the Front and that give orders to the media? They are the "all-powerful oligarchy," the "*mondialistes* [worldists]," the "media class," the "anti-French racists," the "lobbies under orders." These terms are codewords for Jews, Freemasons, antiracist organizations such as SOS-Racisme (SOS-Racism), and the Communist and Socialist Parties; that is, the sempiternal enemies of the extreme right—Charles Maurras's "confederation" of Jews, Protestants, Freemasons, and *métèques* (wogs).

This persistent, vituperative hostility toward Muslims, North Africans, and Jews raises questions about the Front's commitment to one of the basic assumptions of democracy: equal treatment under the law of all citizens. After all, what conclusion should be drawn from the fact that Le Pen consistently praises every known present and past dictator or authoritarian leader (with the exception of Adolf Hitler and Benito Mussolini), including Francisco Franco, Augusto Pinochet, Juan Perón, Antonio Salazar, Saddam Hussein, and Anastasio Somoza?[15] And what does Le Pen mean when he says that some people "have more rights than others"?[16]

As we look to the future, it is difficult to avoid the conclusion that an NF government would destabilize democracy. Once an NF government attempted to implement anti-Semitic or racist measures, inevitably there would be demonstrations, riots, and other forms of protest. Given the party's commitment to law and order and a strong state and the traditionally violent manner in which the extreme right reacts to criticism, an NF government likely would not hesitate to use extreme force to repress such protests.[17] In 1986, for example, during a National Assembly debate on terrorism, Le Pen referred to the "large number of immigrants" that France received and he noted: "In identical circumstances a government as democratic as that of the United States put an entire population of Japanese in camps after 1941. It is a truism that one can't count on foreigners obeying the law in our own country."[18]

The NF might even use resistance to its policies as an excuse to install an authoritarian or a dictatorial regime. When questioned on television in 1984 about his sympathy for Spanish dictator Francisco Franco and Chilean general Augusto Pinochet, Le Pen noted that it was "sometimes necessary" for the army to take power "to evade civil war" or "to save the people" since the army was charged with watching over the people.[19] Nor should one forget that Le Pen himself was sympathetic to the attempt by army generals and the forces of Algérie Française (French Algeria) to overthrow the Republic in the early 1960s.

According to *Le Monde* journalist Alain Rollat: "The denunciation of immigration and insecurity, which have ensured the electoral emergence of the National Front, in effect only represents the surface of a far-reaching societal project inspired by a totalitarian logic at the service of a clearly defined objective: 'to restore order in France.'"[20]

When it became clear that proportional representation might be dropped after the 1986 election, Le Pen said: "If the national representation of the National Front is reduced, there is always the risk that provocations and violent initiatives might materialize."[21] A month later, he threatened: "In depriving my 2.7 million voters of representation in the National Assembly, the Minister of the Interior, Mr. Pasqua, is opening the way to tempting my voters to violence. It is necessary that we have the possibility of being elected. Lacking legal methods, extremist methods are legitimated: this is clearly evident."[22]

For the NF, politics is not a process involving compromise or the give and take of ideas; politics is a "battle," and "our movement is an army."[23] According to an internal party document: "The very essence of politics rests on the antagonism friend-enemy. . . . The object of political discussion, therefore, is to destroy the enemy. Never concede anything positive about the adversary. . . . Diabolize the adversary. . . . 'Many enemies, much honor.'"[24] Defined in this fashion, politics becomes a desperate zero-sum game in which compromise is almost impossible and each side in the political struggle must use every available instrument to gain power. Of course, the use of military language to characterize politics may be a rhetorical device intended to inspire party militants to greater efforts and to reinforce party solidarity, but how deeply committed to democracy is a political party that defines the essence of politics in such absolutist terms?[25]

In November 1992 Roger Holeindre, one of the leading figures of the Front, warned that if the twenty or so leading members of the Front lowered their guard, "there would be a real Nazi party in France."[26] This remark implies that if it were not for the efforts of the NF's top leaders, the Front could easily swing toward fascism. In light of this evidence, one must treat with some skepticism the Front's claim that it is an orthodox political party like any other. What follows, therefore, is an attempt to show how the Front's history, leadership, and coded language belie its democratic pretensions and to expose the Front for what it really is—a danger to democracy.

Notes

1. Front National, *300 mesures pour la renaissance de la France* (Paris: Éditions Nationales, 1993), pp. 12–13.

2. Peter Fysh and Jim Wolfreys, "Le Pen, the National Front, and the Extreme Right in France," *Parliamentary Affairs* 45, 3 (July 1992):325.

3. James G. Shields, quoted in ibid., p. 310.

4. In 1990 Dr. Bernard Lefebvre, formerly a member of the antigovernment Comité de Salut Public (Committee of Public Safety) in Algeria, wrote in the NF publication *Le Glaive,* "When our country's families are submerged by too many foreign families, when our fathers' religion is vilified and foreign relations are triumphant and protected ... then we shall be in great peril and the time will have come for men of arms to execute the mission of last resort." Quoted in Jean-Yves Camus, "Political Cultures Within the Front National," *Patterns of Prejudice* 26, 1–2 (1992):12.

5. In 1990 NF militants were asked the following question: "In your opinion, what would be the best political system for France today?" Ten percent chose a popular democracy, 16 percent chose a monarchy, 38 percent chose an authoritarian government, and 32 percent chose a republic. In the same survey, 75 percent of NF cadres placed the party on the extreme right end of the political spectrum, and 77 percent placed themselves on the extreme right. *Le Monde,* March 8–9, 1990.

6. Quoted in *Le Monde,* May 8, 1987.

7. Charles Maurras, *Mes idées politiques,* rpt. (Paris: Albatros, n.d.), p. 113.

8. Quoted in *Le Monde,* September 26–27, 1993.

9. Quoted in *Le Monde,* January 18, 1994.

10. *Le Monde,* June 23, 1995. L'Association des Maires de France (The Association of Mayors of France) released a communiqué shortly after Mégret's remark noting that French law stipulated that foreigners had the same rights as citizens with regard to "protection of the individual" and "social security."

11. Quoted in *Le Monde,* June 18–19, 1995.

12. Quoted in ibid.

13. When Mégret lost his bid for the mayor's seat, he complained that his loss was "the result of a campaign of hate, lies, blackmail, physical threats, attacks on offices and vehicles, of the recruitment of schoolchildren, of an unprecedented mobilization of the media with the complicity of the con-man Bernard Tapie." Quoted in *Le Monde,* June 20, 1995.

14. Front National, *300 mesures,* p. 9.

15. In the mid-1970s Le Pen praised Léon Degrelle, the former Belgian Nazi, as a "monument of the Second World War." Degrelle never renounced any of his convictions and often appeared in public in a Nazi uniform. Gilles Bresson and Christian Lionet, *Le Pen* (Paris: Seuil, 1994), p. 313.

16. Quoted in *Le Monde*, June 17, 1995. In a speech attacking Catholic bishops who denounced racism, Le Pen said, "The duty of charity doesn't preclude a hierarchy between those who have more rights than others." Quoted in *Le Monde*, June 17, 1995.

17. As Alain Rollat pointed out, "If M. Le Pen some day . . . found himself in a position to apply his totalitarian program, the damage would be such that, very quickly, his 'restoration of order' would inescapably bring about movements of resistance. Immigration or not, no civilized society these days could support the establishment of personal power founded on the rejection of the other and the cult of the scapegoat." *Le Monde*, February 4, 1992.

18. Quoted in *Le Monde*, October 10, 1986.

19. Quoted in *Le Monde*, February 15, 1984.

20. Alain Rollat, *Les hommes de l'extrême droite* (Paris: Calmann-Lévy, 1985), p. 117.

21. Quoted in Guy Birenbaum, *Le Front national en politique* (Paris: Balland, 1992), p. 110.

22. Quoted in ibid., p. 111.

23. *Le Monde*, March 30, 1990.

24. Quoted by Edwy Plenel, in *Le Monde*, March 30, 1990.

25. Yvan Blot, a member of the NF's political bureau, cited Julien Freund, who "has shown . . . that politics is the management of conflict and of 'friend-enemy relations.'" Yvan Blot, *Les racines de la liberté* (Paris: Albin Michel, 1985), p. 234. German philosopher Carl Schmitt argued in the 1920s against universalistic notions of a common humanity or membership in a common political community by defining politics as the ability to distinguish between friend and enemy. Carl Schmitt, *Parlementarisme et démocratie* (Paris: Seuil, 1988), pp. 140ff. See also Stephen Holmes, *The Anatomy of Antiliberalism* (Cambridge, Mass.: Harvard University Press, 1993), pp. 40ff.

26. Quoted in *Le Monde*, November 7, 1992.

THE FRENCH
NATIONAL FRONT

PART 1
History

———

1

Out of the Ashes: Postwar Fascism in France

Rare are those who, these days, dare to say publicly that they are fascists. And almost as rare are those who in the depths of their soul recognize themselves as such.

—*André Fontaine, in* Le Monde, *April 2, 1949*

Jean-Marie Le Pen was born on June 28, 1928, in La Trinité-sur-Mer in the Department of Morbihan in Brittany, the far northwestern area of France, where agriculture and fishing have been traditional activities for centuries.[1] Le Pen's mother came from a farming family, and his father owned a fishing boat. In 1942, when Le Pen was fourteen, his father drowned after his fishing boat struck a mine. Soon thereafter the young Jean-Marie Le Pen left home to work as a fisherman with his maternal grandfather. In 1984 Le Pen claimed that as a fifteen-year-old, in June 1944 he had tried to join a Resistance group but had been turned back by members of the Free French forces in the area. Yet there are a number of inconsistencies in his story, and except for one witness who later joined the National Front (NF) and claims to have seen Le Pen and a friend in the area, no one else remembers Le Pen.[2] In high school after the war, Le Pen proved to have all the qualities of a born leader: He was amusing, articulate, and always in trouble. According to one classmate, Le Pen was "an agitator, an agitator at any price, he waited and always looked for some kind of occasion to use."[3] Big and strongly built, Le Pen also became a brawler who enjoyed provoking arguments and fistfights. At the age of nineteen, after being graduated from a Jesuit school in Brittany, he enrolled in the Paris Law Faculty, traditionally a hotbed of extreme right-wing agitation.

In *Les Français d'abord* (The French first), Le Pen wrote that on arriving in Paris, he was "apolitical, areligious, but on the right."[4] Shortly afterward he traveled to East Berlin, then the capital of the Communist German Democratic Republic. Nearly four decades later, he recalled: "I was overwhelmed. . . . The story of the taking of Berlin by the Red Army; the rapes, pillage and massacres, inspired me with revolt and revulsion. . . . I am afflicted with this vision . . . that the Communists . . . are an implacable force of repression and tyranny."[5]

After he enrolled in the Law Faculty in 1947, Le Pen's debating skills, energy, and bravado helped him become vice president and then president of the Corpo de Droit (Law Student Corporation), a right-wing faction of the Union National d'Étudiants Français (National Union of French Students, or UNEF). Le Pen spent much of his time propagandizing for the UNEF, debating and quarreling with fellow right-wing students, and brawling in demonstrations and street battles against the left.[6] His activities in the UNEF soon brought him to the attention of the ex-Vichyites who frequented extreme right circles in the late 1940s and early 1950s. In 1951, at the age of twenty-three and at the height of the cold war, Le Pen was asked to direct the security service of Jacques Isorni, leader of the extreme right Union Nationale des Indépendants Républicains (National Union of Independent Republicans, or UNIR), who was then contesting a seat in the legislative elections. Isorni was a leading right-wing lawyer and a former advocate for Vichy leader Marshal Pétain and pro-Nazi intellectual Robert Brassilach during their treason trials. In the 1960s Isorni was to support the extreme right terrorist Organisation de l'Armée Secrète (Secret Army Organization, or OAS), which tried on three occasions to assassinate President Charles de Gaulle. However, in 1951 the UNIR was obsessed with rehabilitating the memory of Vichy and the honor of Marshal Pétain, who had died in July 1951 shortly after being released from prison.[7]

Le Pen eagerly joined Isorni's campaign—after all, Marshal Pétain was one of Le Pen's heroes. "Until 1945, I kept a photo of Marshal Pétain and retained my admiration for him. Nor did I renounce the authors of my youth just because they were in prison like Maurras, or among the executed, like Robert Brassilach."[8] However, the UNIR received only 280,000 votes in the 1951 election and sent only four deputies to the National Assembly. A few years later, wracked by personal quarrels and fatally undermined by Isorni's ambition to join one of the major political parties, the UNIR disappeared.[9] Although it failed to become the political spearhead of the extreme right, the party provided the young Le Pen with valuable experience in political organizing.

By 1953, having failed to complete his degree and too impatient to continue as a student, Le Pen enlisted in the famous Third Paratroop Regiment of the Foreign Legion.[10] At this time the French were fighting a bitter rear-guard action against the communist army of Ho Chi Minh in a doomed attempt to keep Indochina in the French Union, and the legion was in the forefront of the battle.

As was to be the case in the United States more than two decades later, the Indochina War created deep divisions in French society. The Communists, the Socialists, and the moderate center advocated a French withdrawal from Indochina, while the mainstream and extreme right supported nothing less than a military victory over the communist National Liberation Front. Each side saw the Indochina War through the lens of its own ideology. For the Communists, the war was being fought in the interests of French capital. For the Socialists, the war was the last gasp of an outmoded colonialism. For the right, the war was a battle between the forces of democracy and freedom, represented by France, and the forces of brutality and totalitarianism, represented by Ho Chi Minh. Le Pen saw Indochina as a battle in the war against communism.

Luckily for Le Pen, he arrived in Indochina just in time to miss a paratroop drop on Dien Bien Phu, the ill-fated valley fortress that had been subjected to a murderous artillery bombardment by the Vietminh army led by the legendary General Vo Nguyen Giap. Unable to withstand the assault, the legionnaires defending Dien Bien Phu were forced to surrender in spring 1954. The defeat drove home to the French government the futility of any further military action and led Premier Pierre Mendès-France to declare a cease-fire and sign the 1954 Geneva Accords, which divided the peninsula into a communist North and a noncommunist South Vietnam. According to Le Pen's biographer, Roger Mauge, the farseeing Le Pen realized as early as 1954 that the battle for Indochina was the first phase of a two-stage campaign by the communists to deprive France of its colonies. During a battalion meal, seated amid legionnaires from all over Europe, including former members of the German Wehrmacht, the young Le Pen had the temerity to proclaim that the next war would be in Algeria. After a brief silence, one of the legionnaires said: "In Algeria? Why not in Paris? Lieutenant, in case you don't know it, Algeria is France. And if there is a rising in Algeria, it will be crushed."[11] After some argument from the tenacious Le Pen, his commander told him to "shut up." Le Pen kept his peace, but his predictions were borne out when, on November 1, 1954, the Algerian National Liberation Front (FLN) attacked a number of police posts in Algeria, signaling the beginning of a colonial war that was to last for eight years.

In addition to sharpening his geopolitical skills in Indochina, Le Pen saw enough to confirm him in his visceral hatred of communism. Watching the starved and abused legionnaires who had been prisoners of the Vietminh march by, and witnessing the way in which, after the armistice, the victorious communists exacted revenge on those who had supported the French, Le Pen observed: "I returned from Indochina with a concrete revelation about the Communist enemy, its terrible methods, the pitiless manner of liquidating its adversaries, its technique of psychological warfare, its destruction of man from within. . . . The Indochina humiliation and the first murderous encounters in the Algerian War decided my political engagement."[12]

While completing his tour of duty in Indochina, Le Pen heard about a rising young right-wing politician named Pierre Poujade and speculated about the influence Poujade might have on the politics of the Fourth Republic. "We have been betrayed here in Indochina by governments which have been accomplices of the enemy. Entire populations helped us, but Paris delivered them to a dictatorship which reduced them to slavery. It is in Paris that it is necessary to fight."[13] According to Mauge, Le Pen devoted an issue of the Foreign Legion magazine *Caravelle,* which he edited, to the rise of Poujadism and confided to a friend that he was going to enter politics "like Poujade."[14] Le Pen's political career was about to begin.

The Fascist International

While Le Pen was studying in Paris and serving in Indochina, a skeletal fascist organization was kept alive by small groups of die-hard adherents in a myriad of clandestine organizations scattered across Europe. Among these organizations was the Odessa group organized by Otto Skorzeny, leader of the German commando unit that had rescued Benito Mussolini from the partisans during World War II and briefly installed him as the head of the fascist "Salo Republic" at the end of the war. Around Odessa floated an array of Nazis, fascists, and French ex-collaborators nostalgic for the heady days of Adolf Hitler and Mussolini and hurling imprecations against "international capitalism served by the Jew and Stalin."[15] Although the fascists kept a low political profile after 1945, the coming of the cold war and mounting anticommunism led fascist leaders, including Oswald Mosley from Great Britain, Georges Albertini (the former aide-de-camp to the French fascist Marcel Déat), and Guy Lemonnier, to organize a preparatory conference for a fascist international in Rome. In October 1950 a youth congress was organized and a European committee was formed.[16] Finally, in May 1951 the first full congress of the so-called Mouvement Social Européen (European Social Movement, or MSE) took place in Malmö, Sweden, attended by sixty delegates from Western Europe. The MSE enunciated the familiar themes of wartime fascism: the need for a strong central government based on plebiscites, emphasis on physical strength and spiritual regeneration, and reorganization of the economy along corporatist or organic lines.[17] The congress also proposed establishing an education system that would "make *strong* men and women" and would "spiritually regenerate man, society and the state."[18]

Like the Trotskyists who argued that it was impossible to build socialism in one country, the postwar fascists maintained that fascism had to be international, or it would be nothing at all. After all, Alfred Fabre-Luce asked, why should internationalism be the exclusive monopoly of the left when it equally well could be adopted by fascists?[19] The Nazis had been wrong to propose uniting Europe under the German heel; international fascism should henceforth base itself on the principal of equality among nations. Europe should form an intermediary power bloc between the two wartime superpowers, the United States and the Soviet Union, carving out what the congress called a "European empire," excluding Great Britain. Obviously, the North Atlantic Treaty Organization and military integration with the United States were rejected.[20]

Beyond redrawing the map of Europe, the postwar fascists had grandiose plans to rebuild the foundations of Western society. Under international fascism, a new civilization would emerge that rejected the enslavement of "men and peoples, bureaucratic dictatorship," and the liberal-capitalist principles of supply and demand.[21] Much of this was a rehash of older fascist themes, although the issue of anti-Semitism proved highly troublesome. Some neofascists wanted to reduce the level of or even eliminate anti-Semitism from fascist doctrine because of the worldwide revulsion against the death camps or, in some cases, because of a genuine change of heart. Others, like René Binet, wanted to retain anti-Semitism as a central feature of postwar fascist doctrine. Whatever their views, however, legal restrictions on the expression of fascist opinions and the hostility of public opinion forced the postwar fascists to mitigate the extreme edges of their doctrine until memories had dimmed, resentments had cooled, and the fascist message could be put forward without equivocation.[22] As extreme right historian François Duprat put it, "Only the necessities of the moment imposed this [moderate] tone."[23]

The Extreme Right in France

Whereas the Allied armies had completely crushed the German and Italian military machines and eliminated Nazism and fascism as political movements, in France the Occupation, the Vichy experience, and the restoration of a French government under the leadership of General de Gaulle had thinned the ranks of the extreme right but had left the core unaffected. In the 1930s the French extreme right had engaged in street battles with Communists and Socialists, disseminated anti-Semitic propaganda, expressed hostility to the Republic, and looked with admiration at the discipline and military might of Nazi Germany and fascist Italy. When the

French army collapsed before the German invasion in May 1940, the extreme right explained the French defeat in terms of the moral decay of capitalism and democracy and the machinations of a Jewish conspiracy led by Léon Blum, the Socialist premier of the 1936 Popular Front government. Many extremists welcomed the German victory of 1940 and justified their collaboration with the Nazi occupiers by explaining that Germany was the last line of defense of Western civilization against the imposition of Soviet communist hegemony over Western Europe.

But more than tortured logic explained the enthusiasm for collaboration: The extreme right had fallen in love with Nazism. The Nazis had accomplished what the French extreme right could not—they had slain the Republic, the "slut," as Charles Maurras called it, and in doing so, they had destroyed the hated parliamentary democracy of the Third Republic. The division of France into a northern zone under German occupation and a semi-independent southeastern zone under the jurisdiction of the Vichy government presided over by Marshal Pétain and Pierre Laval gave the extreme right a golden opportunity to rid society of gross materialism and rampant individualism and to build a new state based on the simple virtues of *travail, famille, patrie* (work, family, country)—the Vichy slogan. In the enthusiasm to defend Vichy against its enemies, the extreme right joined wholeheartedly with other Vichyites in the effort to crush the Resistance within and the enemy without. Some joined the hated Vichy Milice, which specialized in hunting and torturing resisters, while others enlisted in the German SS Charlemagne armored division for the battle on the eastern front.

With the Allied landings in Normandy in June 1944, however, the hunters became the hunted as the Resistance emerged to dispense rough justice to collaborators and Vichyites alike. One historian sympathetic to Vichy estimated that forty thousand collaborators were executed without trial or after summary trials; extreme right historian François Duprat stated that fifteen thousand were killed.[24] However, serious scholars estimate that approximately nine thousand collaborators of all kinds were killed, the majority in action against the Resistance just before or during the June 1944 Allied landings in Normandy and the remainder as a result of death sentences handed out by courts or tribunals hastily set up in 1944–1945.[25] Some of the more notorious collaborators, such as former Vichy premier Pierre Laval or fascist intellectual Robert Brassilach, were tried and executed by the provisional government established immediately after liberation. One of the most famous of the fascist intellectuals, Pierre Drieu la Rochelle, chose to commit suicide in 1945 rather than face a court trial.

For a while after the "settling of accounts" in 1944–1945, the extreme right disappeared from view. But as early as 1946, ex-Vichyites, fascists, and other members of the extreme right began to emerge from hiding and to rally the troops. Small in numbers, the extreme right threw itself into journalism, publishing pamphlets, newsletters, reviews, and, sometimes, weekly newspapers. Among the most energetic in fanning the flames of right-wing extremism was the egregious René Binet. He called for the "purging of the French race of elements which sully it: the negroes, the Jews and the Mongols; the conquest of the Communist trade union, the Confédération Générale du Travail (General Confederation of Labor, or CGT) and the construction of a national socialist revolution."[26]

A tireless pamphleteer and organizer, Binet was a whirlwind of activity, creating and then disbanding one fascist organization after another. In 1948 he created the Mouvement Socialiste d'Unité Française (MSUF), whose symbol was the "solar wheel, an old Celt symbol, and the baton, representing violent action against Communist and reactionary traitors."[27] This symbol and the Celtic cross are still used by extreme right and neofascist organizations in France. *Unité* (Unity), an MSUF publication, called for European unity against both the United States and the Soviet Union and, referring to an "African invasion," advocated returning all North African Arabs to their home countries.[28] In an ephemeral newspaper published in 1951, Binet wrote: "Culture is born of a people, of a race; it belongs to the people, it determines its survival. But it is a product of the race. . . . No race has the power to impose its culture on others. No race can, without perishing, incorporate a culture which is not in conformity with its genius or which is not born out of it."[29] This neoracist argument, which justified excluding immigrants from France because of the putative insuperable differences between cultures rather than because of the racial superiority of the French race, was a precursor of similar arguments put forward by the National Front in the 1970s, when it opposed non-European immigration and advocated the deportation of immigrants from North Africa.[30]

However, not all members of the extreme right were as crude as Binet. One of the leading figures on the postwar extreme right was Maurice Bardèche, graduate of the École Normale Supérieure and friend and brother-in-law of the anti-Semitic and racist intellectual Robert Brassilach. Bardèche had been a professor of literature at the Sorbonne and at the University of Lille during the war and in the immediate postwar period emerged as a theoretician and spokesman for the neofascist right.[31] Bardèche defended his decision to support collaboration and Vichy in terms of the threat posed to the West by the Soviet Union. "I thought that the German victory was desirable," Bardèche wrote, "because the capitulation, the defeat of Germany would be a catastrophe for us all and because it would be a victory for Russia."[32] During the 1950s, Bardèche devoted himself to whitewashing the Nazis, attacking the Resistance, and defining a "pure" fascism adapted to postwar European conditions. Above all, Bardèche wanted to distinguish between fascist theory, of which he approved, and the unfortunate deviations from that theory forced on Hitler and Mussolini by circumstances beyond their control.[33]

According to Bardèche, Hitler never had a chance to implement pure fascism during the few years of peace that preceded the war because mobilization for all-out war forced the adoption of extraordinary measures that detracted from the building of a fascist state. For Bardèche, the Third Reich was an example of fascism manqué, a fascism that had failed to develop its potential because of aggression from the Soviet Union and the Allies. Faced with the problem of explaining the German and Italian defeats, however, Bardèche criticized the excessive personalization of power under Hitler and Mussolini, contending that their failure to maintain contact with regime elites undermined their authority. "Let us warn of a serious and permanent danger of fascism: it is too often bound to the health of a man, to his intellectual equilibrium, to the sureness of his judgment."[34] Pure fascism, Bardèche said, was hard to pin down; it was ineffable and dynamic. Yet the core doctrine was based on a link between socialist economic principles and nationalism. "The first proclamation of all *national socialism*," Bardèche maintained, was that "there was no privilege, no power, no property which can oppose itself to the nation. Nice words are not enough: sometimes one needs a brutal arbiter to impose the rights of the nation and the necessities of social justice."[35] But fascism demanded more than a strong hand at the helm; it assumed a particular kind of personality, a new fascist man.

"The man who dreams about fascism is young and is, above all, a soldier. . . . We want men to be men and have the qualities of men; the noble qualities, the animal qualities of men: courage, generosity, respect for promises, fidelity of man to man, needing discipline and faith." The fascist man is "a young savage who only believes in qualities which are needed in the wild . . . and who rejects civilization in which he sees only hypocrisy and imposture."[36]

Bardèche touched here on a recurrent theme in fascism—machismo—the vaunting of the so-called masculine virtues as essential to fascism. For fascism, the essence of man is found in action, battle, and war. The hunter-warrior is the true fascist—which means, of course, that women serve as wives and mothers. Women are the backdrop, the admiring audience who make possible and witness the heroism of the warrior. For Bardèche, whereas capitalism is self-regarding and egoistic, emphasizing the accumulation of wealth for private purposes, fascism puts the economy at the service of the state and of national values such as patriotism, heroism, and self-sacrifice. Capitalism emphasizes the here and now; fascism celebrates the past and in rituals and all aspects of culture attempts to validate the present in terms of the past.

None of this was new, but Bardèche realized that if fascism was to survive, the doctrine had to be renovated and renewed. The problem lay in "the absence of a precise doctrine . . . [as well as the] excessive particularism of fascist organizations, each with its own saint [and] the inheritance of the contradiction which is the most dangerous idea of fascism: the myth of the providential chief." According to Bardèche, "Neo-fascism must define itself and its principles ought to take precedence over muscles."[37] Above all, fascism had to be somehow detached from the history of Hitler and Mussolini, cleansed of its association with anti-Semitism and racism, and reborn as a philosophy suitable for the postwar period. Thus, Bardèche wrote in 1961, "as a political system, fascism is no more responsible for the extermination of the Jews than nuclear physics, as a scientific theory, is responsible for the destruction of Hiroshima."[38]

Although Bardèche's ideas were undoubtedly attractive to a large fraction of the extreme right, others looked for inspiration to the writings of Charles Maurras, the leading intellectual on the prewar extreme right and founder of the Action Française (AF). At its foundation in 1899, the AF was nationalist, anticapitalist, antiparliamentary, and, for a year or so, in favor of the Republic. However, Maurras became disillusioned with the Republic and argued that only the restoration of the French monarchy could evoke the respect for government that was necessary to hold together and legitimize the state.[39] Although Maurras never fudged his opposition to the Republic, in a 1953 volume of collected essays he hypocritically tried to dilute his anti-Semitism with escape clauses and glib sarcasm:

From the very first steps I took in Paris during the morning of December 2, 1885, I was struck, moved, almost wounded by the material spectacle of these beautiful streets and these grand boulevards which were decked from the ground floor to the rooftops with a multitude of foreign signs filled with these names in K, in W, in Z that our print workers call wittily, Jewish letters. *Were the French still at home in France?*

Anyone who tried to ask this question awakened in me confused feelings of approval and of adhesion. . . . The Jewish question is not to be confused with [immigration,] although it touches on it. I hope that you are not going to yell about pogroms? Nor of crematoria? Nor about legal castration? Nor of Mendel's laws?

In the middle of the Occupation, we publicly said to anthropology professor and philo-boche [philo-German] Montandon that we were not for the little racist sauce of his "bone deep antisemitism." It wasn't a question of saying *"Death to the Jews"* who have the right to live like all creatures, but *"Down with the Jews"* because they have climbed too high here.

Our state antisemitism consisted of taking it [French nationality] away and forbidding them from having it because they had taken too much in the first place of French nationality, while they have one indelible one, and they in fact always keep it. Let it be enough for them! . . . Justice means only that those Jews who have rendered important services during peacetime or war to the country should not be frustrated. Their person has acquired a title to our nationality, it ought to be used in a personal capacity.[40]

After the war those who followed Maurras split into two groups. One, centered around the journal *La Nation Française,* disavowed the anti-Semitic aspects of Maurrasian thought. The other, associated with journals such as *Rivarol* and *Aspects de France* (the journal's acronym, AF, deliberately echoed that of Action Française), retained the anti-Semitic theme.

Yet despite the proliferation of extreme right and neofascist groups, mainly located in Paris, in the 1950s the movement was still weak and ineffective.[41] According to François Duprat, the extreme right

> never became anything more than an assembly of a few powerless people with good intentions, without an audience and without a future. They worked within a confined space and polemics with neighboring movements occupied them more than struggling on the terrain occupied by their ideological adversaries. Lacking central ideas, their propaganda was striking in its lack of realism. . . . To cry "U.S. Go Home," when [the extreme right] was anti-Russian and when 150 Soviet divisions could be unleashed at any moment on Western Europe, upset the average right-wing Frenchman.[42]

Thus, the immediate postwar period was a bad time for the extreme right. The German defeat, the Liberation, the restoration of parliamentary democracy, and the installation of General de Gaulle at the helm of government abetted the myth that wartime France was united in resisting the occupying Germans. The fact that the majority of French citizens had accepted Vichy and the Occupation and that a significant minority had actively supported Marshal Pétain and the Germans was swept under the carpet—to everyone's mutual advantage. Anxious to pose as full-fledged members of the Allied camp and to share in hoped-for political (and economic) benefits, the French did not want to hear from those who, far from renouncing their previous allegiances, inconveniently insisted on reminding the nation that some of them at least had not disavowed their loyalty to Pétain and Vichy.

De Gaulle and the Extreme Right

Despite the fact that he had fought against Vichy from the very beginning, and that it was thanks to the victorious Allies that he had been installed as the leader of the Provisional Government in 1945, General de Gaulle's ardent nationalism, contempt for the politicians of the Fourth Republic, Catholicism, and anticommunism made him the magnetic point toward which the entire French right wing turned after 1945. As the premier of the Provisional Government in 1944, and then of the Fourth Republic in 1945, de Gaulle attempted to mitigate wartime passions by reintegrating into the French political system political pariahs of both the left and the right.[43] He accepted the return of Communist leader Maurice Thorez from Moscow, where he had fled in the early days of the war, and dropped the desertion charge against him. And de Gaulle commuted Pétain's death sentence to life imprisonment.

However, in January 1946, unable to impose his will on the governing coalition of Communists, Socialists, and the Mouvement Républicaine Populaire (Popular Republican Movement, or MRP) de Gaulle resigned from government and began to attack the "poisons and delights" of the Fourth Republic parliamentary system. In April 1947 he created the Rassemblement du Peuple Français (RPF) and "called on everyone [to support the RPF] without worrying about the origin of their ideas, sentiments or even [political] labels."[44] What could be better calculated to appeal to ex-Vichyites and Pétainists, who felt themselves guiltless of any crime except backing the wrong side during the war? Moreover, de Gaulle's attacks on the Fourth Republic struck a deep chord on the extreme right, where antiparliamentarism and the desire for strong authority were defining characteristics. "The day will come," de Gaulle said, "when, rejecting sterile games and reforming the ill-built framework within which the nation has gone astray, and the State dishonors itself, the immense mass of the French will gather themselves around France."[45]

The creation of the RPF came at a time when France was racked by strikes, shortages, and economic upheaval. In fall 1947 production of coal declined, there was a poor harvest, and rising food prices and scarcity of bread and sugar ignited riots in Verdun and Le Mans. President Vincent Auriol observed: "The unrest is close to panic. . . . The government appears to lack the means to get its authority respected."[46] In the eyes of the left, de Gaulle's attacks on the Fourth Republic and his proposals for a strong presidential system seemed deliberately aimed at destabilizing the system. In December 1947 the Christian Democratic journal *Ésprit* devoted an entire edition to the theme *La Pause des Fascismes est Terminée* (The Pause in Fascism Is Over). The *Ésprit* journalists echoed a common theme during this time: that de Gaulle might consciously or unconsciously be preparing for a coup d'état or a revolution that would install a fascist-type dictatorship. According to Emmanual Mounier, one of the founders of the "personalist" Christian Democratic movement, "Fascism is a foreign word. In French it translates literally as 'rassemblement.'"[47] The clear implication was that de Gaulle's RPF could turn into a fascist organization.

The October 1947 local elections had seen de Gaulle's new RPF win an astounding 38 percent of the vote, giving it a solid base on which to build support for the coming legislative elections. But what explained the Gaullist success? Writing soon after the election, one of France's leading political scientists, François Goguel, saw the specter of fascism lurking behind de Gaulle. According to Goguel, "Even hardened Pétainists, who hadn't pardoned de Gaulle for having put Pétain on trial, [voted for the Gaullists]" and did so because de Gaulle was a *"faute de mieux,"* a second-best alternative to a party farther to the right. Goguel further maintained, "One can see in the RPF a step in the precise direction of fascism."[48] For Goguel, the situation looked like the 1930s all over again, with parliamentarism threatened by the Communists on the one side and right-wing authoritarianism on the other.

"In a country like France where the struggle against democracy has for the past century taken the form of antiparliamentarism, where protests against the existence of parties have always emanated from the partisans of personal, monarchical or dictatorial power, it is clear that a program [for a presidential system] includes a very serious risk if not of fascism, at least of sliding into fascism."[49]

Few dreamed in 1947 that a scant eleven years later de Gaulle would have an opportunity to practice exactly what he preached—or that from the ruins of the Fourth Republic would emerge a strong, highly stable (and nonfascist) presidential system. Nor did anyone at the time pay much attention to the tiny group of extreme right and neofascist militants fighting over tactics and doctrine.

Yet if a prerequisite for the rise of fascist movements is general political, economic, and social instability, then the first years of the Fourth Republic should have provided an excellent opportunity for fascism's renascence. But fascism had been so thoroughly discredited by World War II and the ideology's supporters compromised by their support for the Nazi occupiers that, despite the premonitions of Mounier or Goguel, fascism was never a real threat in the late 1940s. Despite de Gaulle's authoritarian manner and contempt for political parties, his commitment to democracy was never really in doubt. Moreover, as provisional head of state, as first premier of the Fourth Republic, and then as leader of the RPF after 1947, de Gaulle became a rallying point for elements of the right that might otherwise have been sympathetic to a renewed or revised fascism. Even after de Gaulle retired from active politics in 1953, it was not the neofascist right that benefited from his absence, but a surprising new movement that seemed to emerge from nowhere, led by a stationery salesman named Pierre Poujade.

Notes

1. By far the best biography of Le Pen is Gilles Bresson and Christian Lionet, *Le Pen* (Paris: Seuil, 1994).

2. Ibid., pp. 26ff.

3. Ibid., p. 32.

4. Jean-Marie Le Pen, *Les Français d'abord* (Paris: Carrère/Laffon, 1984), p. 39.

5. Ibid., p. 40. Le Pen's soul vibrated in sympathy with the Germans, but it seems to have been unaffected by the more horrific tales of Nazi depredations.

6. According to police records of the time, on April 29, 1948, he was charged with assault and causing bodily harm; on November 6, 1949, with assault while drunk; and on March 25, 1950, with assault during a brawl in a café. Serge Dumont, Joseph Lorien, and Karl Criton, *Le système Le Pen* (Anvers, Belgium: Éditions EPO, 1985), p. 23.

7. Pétain was released from prison for health reasons on June 8, 1951, and died on July 23, 1951. Isorni then campaigned tirelessly to get the government to move Pétain's remains from the Isle d'Yeu and to get a revision of the treason verdict imposed in 1945. On the extreme right and Vichy, see Henry Rousso, *The Vichy Syndrome* (Cambridge, Mass.: Harvard University Press, 1991).

8. Quoted in Dumont et al., *Le système*, p. 28. Charles Maurras was an anti-Semite and racist ideologue of the extreme right during the 1930s and 1940s; Brassilach was a supporter of Nazism and an anti-Semite. In October 1941, he was reported to have said of the Jews, "One must kill them all, even the young children." Quoted in Zeev Sternhell, *Ni Droite Ni Gauche* (Paris: Seuil, 1983), p. xi. If Le Pen in fact had read Brassilach and counted the man among his heroes, it is hard to see how Le Pen could put Brassilach only "on the right" when he considered himself a fascist. Le Pen, *Les Français*, p. 39.

9. It was later to reemerge as the Centre National des Indépendants (National Independent Center, or CNI) and to play a key role in the politics of the Fourth Republic.

10. According to Roger Mauge's hagiography of Le Pen, the 1950s were an era when everyone expected the cold war to burst into flame. "Viewed from the Latin Quarter, when one is a young man of the right, this true war had begun, it was called the Indochina War. There, young men like Le Pen fought against the 'cocos' [communists] but with real bullets." Roger Mauge, *La vérité sur Jean-Marie Le Pen* (Paris: Éditions France-Empire, 1988), p. 72.

11. Bresson and Lionet, *Le Pen*, pp. 95–96.

12. Le Pen, *Les Français*, p. 45.

13. Mauge, *La verité,* p. 97.

14. *Ibid.*, p. 99. For a fuller, and accurate, account of Le Pen's activities in Indochina, see Bresson and Lionet, *Le Pen*, pp. 81–104.

15. Jean Plumyène and Raymond Lasierra, *Les fascismes français: 1923–1963* (Paris: Éditions du Seuil, 1963), p. 199.

16. Marie-José Chombart de Lauwe, *Complots contre la démocratie: Les multiples visages du fascisme* (Paris: Fédération Nationale des Déportés et Internés Résistants et Patriotes, 1981), pp. 29ff. According to François Duprat, the MSE was destroyed by René Binet, a violent, dictatorial, and deeply anti-Semitic fascist. In trying to dominate the MSE, Binet forced Maurice Bardèche, a leading postwar fascist theorist, out of the organization and alienated a large number of its members. François Duprat, *Les mouvements d'extrême-droite en France depuis 1944* (Paris: Albatros, 1972), pp. 51–52.

17. Pierre Milza noted that fascism attracted as much by its aesthetics as by its theory. And he quoted Brassilach, who noted that "only revolutionaries have understood the meaning of myths and of ceremonies. . . . If February 6 [1934, when the extreme right tried unsuccessfully to invade the National Assembly] was a failed

plot, it was an instinctive and magnificent revolt. It was a night of sacrifice which remains in our imagination with its odors, its cold wind, its pale, running figures, the groups of people on the edge of the pavement, its invincible hope for a national revolution, the precise birth of social nationalism in our country." Pierre Milza, *Fascisme français: Passé et présent* (Paris: Flammarion, 1987), p. 218.

18. Quoted in ibid., pp. 282ff.

19. Quoted in Hans Jaeger, *The Reappearance of the Swastika* (London: Gamma Publications, January 1960), mimeograph, p. 21.

20. Ibid., p. 38.

21. Duprat, *Les mouvements*, p. 49.

22. According to Pierre Milza: "Without doubt because the postwar period in Europe was caught between memories of brown totalitarianism and the threat of red totalitarianism, a frontal assault against democracy had little chance of attracting the masses. Thus, the toning down of certain themes, and thus the prudence imposed by representatives of the MSI and other neo-fascist organizations concerning racism and anti-Semitism." Milza, *Fascisme français*, p. 282.

23. Not everyone toned down the fascist message. René Binet mimeographed one thousand copies of the *Européen Combattant* in March 1946 and distributed them secretly and against government regulations. Eventually, Binet's efforts to revive the fascist press earned him a prison term. Duprat, *Les mouvements*, pp. 21–24.

24. Duprat, *Les mouvements*, p. 21; see also p. 17. Robert Aron, *Histoire de la Libération de France* (Paris: Fayard, 1959).

25. Jean-Pierre Rioux, *The Fourth Republic, 1944–1958* (Cambridge: Cambridge University Press, 1987), p. 32.

26. Quoted in Milza, *Fascisme français*, p. 284.

27. Chombart de Lauvwe, *Complots*, p. 14.

28. Algazy, *La tentation*, p. 77.

29. Quoted in Duprat, *Les mouvements*, p. 53.

30. Pierre-André Taguieff developed a critique of this argument in a number of articles beginning in the early 1980s. See, for example, Pierre-André Taguieff, "De l'anti-socialisme au national-racisme: Deux aspects de la recomposition idéologique des droites en France," *Raison Présente* 4 (1988):15–54.

31. Duprat, *Les mouvements*, p. 35.

32. Quoted in Algazy, *La tentation*, p. 202.

33. On this point, see Ariane Chebel d'Appolonia, *L'extrême-droite en France de Maurras à Le Pen* (Brussels: Complexe, 1987), pp. 341ff.

34. Maurice Bardèche, *Qu'est-ce que le fascisme?* (Paris: Les Sept Couleurs, 1961), pp. 49–50.

35. Ibid.

36. Ibid., pp. 78, 79.

37. Ibid., pp. 101–102.

38. Ibid., pp. 53–54.

39. Richard Griffiths, "Anticapitalism and the French Extra-Parliamentary Right, 1870–1940," *Journal of Contemporary History* 13, 4 (October 1978):721–740.

40. Charles Maurras, *Votre bel Aujourd'hui* (Paris: Fayard, 1953), pp. 457–458. One consequence of retroactively depriving French Jews of their nationality was to make them eligible for roundups by Vichy police and for deportation to extermina-

tion camps. Susan Zuccotti, *The Holocaust, the French, and the Jews* (New York: Basic Books, 1993), Chapter 5.

41. The amnesty laws of 1946, 1947, 1951, and 1953 freed large numbers of ex-collaborators who had been imprisoned by the postwar government. Many of these ex-Vichyites immediately joined the ranks of the extreme right.

42. Duprat, *Les mouvements*, p. 43.

43. It was de Gaulle who facilitated the return from the Soviet Union of the Communist leader Maurice Thorez and ensured that the state dropped the charges of desertion pending since 1940.

44. Quoted in René Chiroux, *L'extrême droite sous la Ve République* (Paris: Librairie Générale de Droit et de Jurisprudence, 1974), p. 46.

45. Quoted in ibid., p. 46.

46. Quoted in Rioux, *The Fourth Republic,* p. 126.

47. Emmanual Mounier, "Le Pause des Fascismes est terminée," *Ésprit* 140 (1947):798.

48. François Goguel, "Conjoncture politique du néo-gaullisme," *Ésprit* 140 (1947):886.

49. Ibid., p. 886.

2

From Poujade to de Gaulle

We are governed by a bunch of people without a country and by pederasts.
—Pierre Poujade, quoted in Pierre Birnbaum, Un mythe politique

France is governed by pederasts: Sartre, Camus, Mauriac.
—Jean-Marie Le Pen, quoted in Stanley Hoffmann, Le mouvement Poujade

After de Gaulle retired from active politics in 1953, a multiplicity of small, undisciplined, and divided parties emerged alongside the larger Communist and Socialist parties and the MRP. With no single party able to command an absolute majority of seats in the National Assembly, the traditional pattern of French party politics reasserted itself: Coalitions formed and collapsed, governments rose and fell, and the Fourth Republic began to sink into disrepute. However, in 1956 an entirely new political party burst on the scene and immediately caught the public's attention. Pierre Poujade's Union de Défense des Commerçants et Artisans (Shopkeepers' and Artisans' Defense Union, or UDCA) was a populist, single-issue movement founded on a narrow sociological and ideological base—and doomed to disappear within two years. But while it lasted, the Poujadists sent shock waves throughout the French political system. During the 1956 election campaign, to the slogan of *Sortez les sortants,* "Throw the rascals out," the Poujadists added the vague demand that the National Assembly be dissolved and a new session of the Estates General (last called during the French Revolution) be convened to let the French express their grievances. Although Poujade was quoted as saying that his propaganda "had as much intellectual content as a scream," his party struck a responsive chord among farmers and small shopkeepers fed up with what they felt was an intrusive state and a corrupt party system.[1]

Poujadism appeared as a reaction against the modernization of the French economy. Modernization in the French context meant a continuing depopulation of the countryside as rural masses moved to the burgeoning industries located near or in the cities (every year after 1950 the rural population fell by 1 percent of the total active population); a spurt in industrial production, which leapt 70 percent from 1949 to 1957; and the beginnings of a modern retail sector with the establishment of supermarkets and retail chains such as Uniprix.[2] On every index of economic growth—from the total increase in the gross national product (GNP), the per capita GNP, and the percentage of the workforce in the industrial and service sectors, to the indices of industrial and agricultural production—the French economy was expanding at a rate somewhat slower than West Germany but faster than Great Britain.[3] But while those who worked in industry or the service sector benefited from the boom, farmers and small shopkeepers suffered. From 1954 onward, thirty thousand farms disappeared each year, or three out of every ten farmers. At the same time, increasing taxes bore heavily on small shopkeepers who had profited from postwar shortages and inflation.[4]

In the mid-1950s the symbol of the new face of French modernity was Premier Pierre Mendès-France, elected in 1954 thanks to support from urbanites, service sector workers, and middle-class groups in the modernizing sectors of the economy. The polar opposite to Mendès-France was Pierre Poujade, who drew most of his support from rural areas that had suffered the largest decline in population and from those sectors of the population—vintners, artisans, and small shopkeepers—whose livelihoods were threatened and revenues undermined by a fall in purchasing power and by the growth in chain stores, cooperatives, and supermarkets.[5]

Pierre Poujade was the son of an architect who had been a prewar member of the extreme right Action Française. Before the war, Poujade had joined the youth wing of the fascistic Parti Populaire Français (French Popular Party, or PPF) led by Jacques Doriot, but Poujade eventually fled from occupied France to Vichy and then to North Africa to a Royal Air Force training camp. After being demobilized in 1945, Poujade became a book salesman and was elected a town councillor under the Gaullist RPF label in 1953.[6]

At this time tax evasion was endemic in France, especially among small businesspeople who were highly skilled at concealing the size of their revenue from the state.[7] Unable to accurately determine small business revenues, French tax inspectors had developed an ingenious system of estimating revenue or income by the outward signs of wealth.[8] To thwart the inspectors, Poujade organized an opposition movement among small shopkeepers and businesspeople threatened by economic modernization, opposed to high taxes, and angry at the corruption of national politics.

Poujade also drew support from traditional extreme right supporters, who saw in him a "poor man's de Gaulle," a leader who "could attract mass support to the antiparliamentary, ultra-nationalist cause."[9] Poujadism blossomed at a time when Premier Mendès-France had begun to implement measures modernizing education, providing loans for municipal housing, and reducing the privileges of the *bouilleurs de cru,* the home distillers of France.[10] A dedicated opponent of alcoholism, Mendès-France became well known in Western Europe and North America as the milk-drinking French premier. But his opposition to alcohol, his attacks on the home brewers, and the zeal of government tax inspectors enraged small businesspeople and farmers, who flocked to Poujade's movement.

In the early 1950s Poujade proved himself an adept organizer, speaking at mass meetings and getting his supporters elected to professional organizations to propound antitax policies. During 1954 and 1955, Poujadism picked up steam as its leader encouraged people to withhold their taxes, withdraw funds from state banks, and take to the streets in antitax demonstrations. By 1955 the Poujadists had moved to direct action, blocking roads to prevent tax inspectors from entering towns and cities to carry out their work.[11]

But there was more to Poujadism than merely its antitax, antiestablishment position: From the very beginning Poujadism echoed some major themes of the extreme right. A 1955 pamphlet published by the Groupement de Défense des Intérêts Agricoles et Viticoles (Agricultural and Wine Growers' Defense Group), associated with the Poujadists, warned that the state was "under the yoke of politicians, international trusts, stateless bands which live off the work of others."[12] These references to international trusts and stateless bands were anti-Semitic codewords. Anti-Semitism was a constant theme in Poujadist propaganda.[13] In *J'ai choisi le combat* (I chose combat), published in 1955, Poujade used the fact that Mendès-France did not drink alcohol and opposed the wine lobby to allude to the fact that he was a Jew: "If you had a drop of blood of the Gauls in your veins, you would never have dared . . . to have yourself served milk at an international reception. . . . No Mendès! Under Mendès, our apprentice Mendès, when one is the son of the ancient soil of France, one is not made for slavery. . . . Better if you pack your bag and get out! The French didn't ask you to come here. . . . They are not keeping you here."[14]

At a December 1955 election meeting, small groups of people punctuated Poujade's talk with cries of "The Jews to Jerusalem!" When mentioning the name of former minister Jacques Chaban-Delmas, Poujade observed: "He is no more Chaban than you or I [his name had been Delmas]. . . . It's part of the national folklore of the Fourth Republic. Although, when I say that, I am treated like a terrible racist—but I don't care, I am not called Levy, I am called Poujade. But if I go to Israel or Patagonia, I will always be called Poujade, the idea of being called Moscovitch wouldn't occur to me."[15]

When Poujade warned that a strong government was needed to prevent the loss of the colonies in Indochina and Algeria, one member of the audience yelled, "On condition that there aren't any Jews." Poujade responded: "That depends on you, it is necessary to have a strong state."[16] Poujade kept up a constant fire of criticism and slander against Mendès-France. Poujade took to calling him *Mendès les fuites* (Mendès the escaper or leaker), a play on words referring to the extreme right canard that Mendès-France had abandoned France in 1940 by fleeing to North Africa and to a 1954 police operation trumped up by Commissioner of Police Jean Dides and designed to implicate Mendès-France and Minister of the Interior François Mitterrand in a plot to leak defense secrets to the French Communist Party.[17] At a party meeting in early January 1956, speakers not only attacked the press and the government but also expressed antiparliamentary and racist sentiments. A Poujadist spokesman referred to "Issac Mendès."[18]

Some of Poujade's close associates were rabid anti-Semites. The leader of a Poujadist farmer's organization asked: "By whom are we governed? By people who don't dare say their name: Mendès-Portugal, from a family of Portuguese Jews and married to an Egyptian Jew; Salomon Hirsch Ollendorf, called Grandval, and Soustelle Ben Soussa. It is necessary to unmask them and smash their faces in."[19] The Poujadist journal *Fraternité Française* sketched the genealogy of Premier Mendès-France and commented, "That's terrific for France, as the song says."[20]

When asked about anti-Semitism, Poujade replied: "I have shaken up a few 'Israelite' ministers because they were ministers, not because they were Israelites. . . . I never denied that Mendès-France had the right to direct operations if he had the mandate. . . . I attacked equally violently Pinay and Bidault and the Vatican didn't complain."[21] To the accusation of racism, Poujade commented: "What is racism? It is the exaltation of one race. That cannot be among us. France is a crucible in which all the races are mixed and where all the races sought asylum."[22] A journalist observed to Poujade at a 1956 press conference that if one strictly adhered to the party statute that one had to be a third-generation French citizen to be elected to a leadership post, the great Third Republic leader Léon Gambetta would have been excluded from the movement.[23]

Antiparliamentarism was another theme the Poujadists shared with the extreme right. During the election campaign, Poujade insisted that the Poujadists' only objective was to force the government to convene a meeting of the Estates General. In an interview with the *Journal de Genève* in December 1955, Poujade said that those elected from his movement had as their "only mission, to paralyze the National Assembly as long as the Estates-General were not convened."[24] During the campaign, the Poujadists went beyond the usual heckling or occasional disruption of election meetings that was a typical feature of French election meetings and tried to prevent socialists and left-wingers from speaking. According to English scholar Philip Williams, "Everywhere the Poujadist campaign was slanderous, violent and utterly negative, except over North Africa where the movement expressed the most extreme colonialist views."[25] The Poujadists particularly targeted former Minister of the Interior François Mitterrand, whom they pelted with a barrage of vegetables and fruit throughout the campaign. No wonder Mitterrand responded by calling the Poujadists "closet fascists."[26]

Another Poujadist theme that echoed the prewar extreme right was a contrasting of the solidarity, selflessness, and patriotism of the wartime soldier with the self-serving, divisive, and corrupt behavior of citizens in democracy. One 1956 election poster warned, "The Country Is in Danger," and added: "We French farmers have spilled our blood every time that the country was threatened. Today it faces the most serious time in our history. In presenting ourselves to the public we are looking neither for places nor honors. Our only goal is to clean house and to let the people speak through the convocation of the Estates-General."[27]

Jean-Marie Le Pen, Poujadist

On his return to Paris after army service in Indochina in late 1955, Le Pen took the helm of a tiny group of extreme right students associated with the Law Faculty, the Jeunes Indépendants de Paris (Young Independents of Paris), and decided to run for election in the fifteenth district of Paris. Although he and his young colleagues put enormous energy into the 1956 campaign, it quickly ran short of funds. Then, thanks to ex-Police Commissioner Jean Dides, Le Pen was introduced to Poujade. After some discussion of election tactics, Poujade asked Le Pen and his friends to help organize a protest "against Parliament and decadence."[28] But when Jean-Maurice Demarquet, Le Pen's comrade-in-arms from Indochina, exclaimed that they were not shopkeepers, Poujade replied: "That's not the issue. I'm a veteran of free France, a patriot like you. It's necessary that everything change. The state has become bed of dogshit, it can't continue. The tax police controls and torments us. It's the Gestapo! France isn't France anymore."[29]

Poujade then invited Le Pen and Demarquet to accompany him to the city of Rennes in Brittany, where Poujade was scheduled to speak.[30] Just before going on stage, Poujade told Le Pen that in view of his Breton origins, he might want to address the crowd. Poujade later recalled turning to Le Pen and saying:

"Tell me, are you a Breton?"

"Yes."

"And you want to be a lawyer, so you know how to speak?"

"I was the head of the law union."

"Good, when the speaker before you finishes, go the microphone and say something."

"But what should I say?"

"Work it out yourself. Say anything: Say, 'hello,' tell them what you are doing with me."

And then, to Poujade's surprise, Le Pen took off on a flight of oratory. "To listen to him, I was Joan of Arc, I was Dugesclin [the fourteenth-century Breton warrior], I was Brittany. And the people roared. And the louder they roared, the more it suited him. . . . And at the end of it all, he turned to me and said: 'Pierre, I give you *my* people.'"[31]

Soon after, Le Pen was appointed a "national orator" by Poujade and was asked to speak throughout France.

In January 1956 the Poujadists won 2.6 million votes and sent fifty-three members to the National Assembly, among them Jean-Marie Le Pen, at twenty-seven the youngest deputy in the legislature. Poujade himself foolishly had not contested a seat and tried to run the party from outside the National Assembly.

In the National Assembly the Poujadists called themselves Groupe d'Union et de Fraternité Française (Group for Union and French Fraternity), the use of the word *fraternity* referring to the motto of the Republic but also implying a movement that crossed party lines to include everyone in broad agreement with its goals. Initially, the Poujadists made a splash, and the young Jean-Marie Le Pen quickly made a name for himself. Uncowed by his position as a neophyte deputy, violently attacked and criticized by the Communists and Socialists, Le Pen proved a formidable debater. When the Communists in the National Assembly began to hurl cries of "fascist" and "Nazi" against him, Le Pen replied: "You will not silence me. Your allies [referring to the Vietnamese Communists] did not silence me with their machine guns."[32]

Almost immediately after entering the National Assembly, Le Pen was chosen to lead the fight against left-wing attempts to unseat Poujadist deputies accused of electoral fraud. He attacked the Communist deputies as traitors, disrupted debate with slanging matches, and staked out a position as an ardent defender of French Algeria, proposing that the government execute captured guerrillas, censor the press, and suppress criticism of the army.[33] Years later Le Pen recalled that immediately after entering the National Assembly, he began to make headlines and appear in political cartoons.[34]

In the eyes of the left, Poujadism was fascism renascent. The Ligue Internationale Contre le Racisme et l'Antisémitisme (International League

Against Racism and Anti-Semitism, or LICRA) launched an appeal to all "Republicans" to boycott Poujadist activists because of "the fascist and racist danger represented by the Poujadist movement."[35] After English cartoonist Vicky portrayed Poujade as "Poujadolph," the cartoon was reproduced in the French weekly magazine *L'Express.* Poujade rejected the fascist label, and the Poujadist deputies at first refused to take seats on the extreme right side of the National Assembly.[36] "Incapable of finding a good argument," Poujade said, "they [the critics] can only use an old, worn-out slogan: 'fascists.' Nevertheless, it's a little violent to be insulted and calumnied daily by pale wogs [*pâles métèques*]."[37]

But was Poujadism fascist? According to Pierre Milza: "All in all, the Poujadist movement wasn't fascist. . . . There was in the Poujadist revolt, spontaneous, anti-state, anarchistic aspects which linked it to a long tradition of protest and popular 'emotion.' Poujadism was more in the line of traditional anti-authority folk heroes and country bumpkins rather than Hitler or Mussolini."[38] However, Milza also said that the "second generation" of Poujadists leaned toward neofascism, and were prevented from realizing their fascist potential only because of internal divisions on the extreme right and the absence of a political-economic crisis similar to the one that had prepared the way for Nazism in Germany in the 1930s and Italian fascism in the 1920s.

According to Joseph Algazy, Poujadism was full of ambiguity and ambivalence. It could be defined as fascist to the extent that it was nationalistic, corporatist, extremist, xenophobic, racist, and anti-intellectual and followed a cult of the leader. But because it was opposed to the cult of the state as well as to any idea of the state taking over or absorbing civil society, because it did not "transform violence into a religion and only used violence on occasions and was not organized along rigid lines," Algazy argued, "it cannot be counted as fascist."[39] In a major work on Poujadism, Stanley Hoffmann confessed, "One doesn't quite know whether it is Jacobinism, classical xenophobic antiparliamentarism or at the limits of fascism." Hoffmann also pointed out that Poujade expressed not so much racism as "the old idea—Maurrasian—that the Jew remains a stranger because he refused to mingle with the French, and that, therefore, it is he [the Jew] who is racist."[40]

Whatever the true essence of Poujadism was, extreme right intellectuals asked why Poujade had been able to capitalize so handsomely on the discontent of the petit bourgeois shopkeepers and businesspeople, while the extreme right remained at the margins of French politics. A stab at answering this question appeared in "Le Poujadisme," a series of essays in *Défense de l'Occident,* the journal of an extreme right movement with the same name, headed by neofascist intellectual Maurice Bardèche. According to Bardèche, the French were tired of talk, sick of politics, and receptive to action—and Poujade was, above all, a man of action. Bardèche was impressed by Poujade's American-style door-to-door campaigning. Preferring to sit together with five or six people in a café rather than speak before large crowds, Poujade entered into direct contact with his would-be supporters, impressing them with his dynamism and conviction.[41] It was not enough to sit on the sidelines and snipe at the politicians, Bardèche argued; one had to dirty one's hands in everyday politics. For Bardèche, therefore, the UDCA was more than a mere flash party or protest movement; it was a new phenomenon in French politics.

Bardèche was particularly impressed with the spontaneity of the Poujadists. Unlike leaders whose movement flowed from their charisma, Poujade had been created by the movement. "Poujade is neither a madman, a conductor of the masses, a prodigious actor playing dictator to the world, a technician of personal power, nor the president of a military junta chosen by his peers to restore order. It is the spectacle of injustice which made him a chief, it is action which made him a spokesman, it was events which made him the chief of the party. . . . He has become the chief he didn't want to be."[42]

Bardèche claimed that Poujade was the spontaneous emanation of the people themselves, a figure who, without necessarily willing it, could not help but speak for the crowd of which he was the symbol. Moreover, according to Bardèche, the lack of organization among the Poujadists and their refusal to organize along the lines of a modern mass party with an executive, branch organizations, and regular meetings echoed the French Revolution's "idea societies," whose members argued, "One wants us to organize in order to get rid of us."[43] By avoiding organizing along the lines of orthodox political parties, the Poujadists had entered into a direct and mystical contact with their leader. Where an antidemocrat would have built a hierarchical and authoritarian party and tried to persuade the French that his program was the best, "the Poujadists think that they are the 'Sovereign' and, communing with the Republican mystique, behave like one of the popular societies which made the revolution."[44]

Although Bardèche never used the word *fascist* in association with the Poujadists, doubtless he saw the UDCA as protofascist, prefiguring a new form of French fascism. The spontaneous and unmediated connection of leader and masses, the emphasis on action, and the loose organization are all fascist characteristics, and they attracted Bardèche. Poujade's leadership style was particularly appealing to Bardèche because, unlike the orthodox political parties, which elected their leaders, there were no elections and no pretense of elections in the UDCA. "Poujade's authority replaces anonymous power. . . . At the risk of displeasing him, it is necessary to say it: democracy doesn't exist."[45] In Poujade, Bardèche saw a man who had no ideas of his own, who was nothing more than an echo chamber for the discontents and frustrations of the social class he represented. As Poujade himself put it: "I was neither a deputy nor an inspector of finances. I didn't know a thing about charts, opinion polls or statistics. I was only a reflection of opinion, a loudspeaker, a flag-carrier."[46]

Moreover, Bardèche argued, Poujade was not opposed to the Republic; rather, in calling for a convening of the Estates General, he wished to return to the "real Republic," to "true democracy against the falsification of democracy."[47] For Bardèche, any leader in true contact with the masses was inevitably pushed to oppose democracy, a "system"[48] whose leaders "thwart and deprive [people] of their power . . . betray and sell out at every point in their history."[49] In this way Bardèche carefully stretched the Poujadist picture onto a fascist frame—and sketched a model of party organization and leadership that, when the time came, Le Pen did his best to avoid.

For the fact was that the spontaneous, unstructured, and personal nature of the Poujadist organization was a fatal weakness. Lacking political experience, trying to practice an absurd apoliticism by refusing to play the political game within the legislature, and unwilling to follow Poujade, the Poujadists soon fell to quarreling with their leader, who literally hectored them from the corridors of the National Assembly.[50] When Poujade called on his parliamentary group to oppose French participation in the British-French-Israeli Suez campaign, one-third of the Poujadists refused to follow his orders. Among the rebels were Le Pen and his friend Jean-Maurice Demarquet. Poujade, realizing that he was rapidly loosing control over his troops, belatedly attempted to win a seat in the National Assembly in a 1957 Paris by-election. But he was soundly beaten by an ardent supporter of Algérie Française, the movement to crush the Algerian independence movement and keep Algeria within the French orbit. The final blow came when Poujade instructed his deputies to oppose de Gaulle's investiture as premier in the last days of the Fourth Republic, only to find that the Poujadists voted unanimously for the general.

As the war dragged on, Le Pen and Poujade drifted apart. Whereas Le Pen wanted Poujade to support the cause of French Algeria and to endorse insurrection in the event of government negotiations with the Front de Libération Nationale (National Liberation Front, or FLN), Poujade warned against "the beginnings of a mobilization which once more violates Constitutional principles [Poujade was referring to the stirrings of revolt against the Fourth Republic, which evoked the fall of the Third Republic and the rise of Vichy]."[51] Intent on maintaining unity among his quarrelsome rank and file, Poujade did not want to rock the boat by taking unconstitutional positions. Many years later Le Pen was to argue that Poujade should have taken a much tougher position on Algeria and on the Fourth Republic because he had a lot of support in Algeria among the French *pieds-noirs* settlers [black feet—because of the rich black soil on their farms], and amongst the Muslim masses, because the most developed of the Muslims were artisans and traders. . . . But as soon as he might have assumed certain responsibilities, he fled his national destiny. From all the evidence, he ought to have been the inheritor of the defunct Fourth Republic. In fact, he breathed a deep sigh of relief when he learned that General de Gaulle was ready to enter the fray. The idea of being in power frightened him and he did not feel up to the measure of his destiny. Every time that one tried to lead him toward it, he wriggled out of his responsibilities. That is why I decided not to fight for this providential man who fled from providence.[52]

According to Poujade, however, Le Pen was pulling the party toward the extreme right rather than trying to maintain its original image as a "national" movement outside the usual left-right struggle. "Le Pen wanted to transform the group into a political party. For me, the deputies—we called them 'delegates'—had a specific mission: 'In the legislature you are like commandos parachuted into enemy territory. You don't have to discuss the mission: the system is evil; it's necessary to tear down the dump.'"[53]

In retrospect, Le Pen was right: Poujade's tactics were self-defeating, while Le Pen's idea of using the Poujadists as a rallying point for the extreme right might have saved the movement from complete extinction. But Poujade refused to budge. In September 1956, after nine months in the National Assembly, and increasingly at odds with Poujade, Le Pen volunteered to join the First Paratroops of the Foreign Legion in Algeria.[54]

Certainly, it was thanks to Poujade that Le Pen won his spurs in parliament. It was in the National Assembly that Le Pen honed his debating skills and learned from Poujade that one could win a devoted following by speaking frankly and directly to the public and by claiming to act as its tribune. It was from Poujade that Le Pen first learned to boast that he said out loud "what millions of French were thinking to themselves."[55] And it was from Poujade that Le Pen learned that a loose party organization, lack of a coherent party doctrine, and an incoherent leadership were recipes for political disaster. But in 1956, with his brief political career behind him, Le Pen was off to Algeria to defend French soil against "terrorists and murderers."[56]

Algeria and the Extreme Right

In 1954 Premier Mendès-France had reached an accord with the communist forces of North Vietnam, dividing the country at the seventeenth parallel between a communist north and an authoritarian south. Although French troops were now withdrawn from former Indochina, France's colonial trauma was far from over as guerrilla attacks by the Algerian FLN against French police stations and army units sparked the beginning of the Algerian War in 1954. Soon Algeria became the focus of a political debate that in its intensity and violence far outstripped the controversy over Indochina.

Algeria had been a French colony since 1830, and by the mid-1950s the population was composed of more than 1 million people of French nationality and 8–9 million Muslim Algerians. The French dominated the managerial sectors and the government; and while 20,000 French owned 2.7 million hectares of land, 630,000 Moslems worked 7.3 million hectares. According to Raymond Aron writing in 1960, "Modern Algeria is a French creation from which only a minority of the Moslem population has profited."[57] To economic inequality was added political inequality. In 1947 the French had established two electoral colleges with equal numbers of French and Muslims. In effect, this meant that one French voter was equal to eight Muslim Algerians. An attempt to rectify this injustice by establishing a single electoral college and universal suffrage in 1954 came too late to stem the revolutionary tide.

The French government reacted to the FLN attacks by sending increasing numbers of troops to Algeria and escalating the armed struggle. The battle was particularly brutal, with both sides engaging in torture and mutilation of combatants and civilians. The FLN exploded bombs in cafés and bus stations, killing and wounding men, women, and children indiscriminately, while the French *pieds-noirs* in Algeria and die-hard elements in France called for more troops and for total victory over the FLN.

In France the Communist Party, which at first supported the Socialist schemes for reforming the Algerian political system, eventually turned toward outright support for the FLN. In turn, the Socialists were forced by public opinion and by the hostility of the French Algerians to renounce any talk of negotiations. In the meantime the extreme right became increasingly vociferous in its support for the Algérie Française position and violent in its opposition to the left and to the Fourth Republic, which was accused of betraying Algeria.

Le Pen in Algeria

Although Le Pen hoped to join the fighting in Algeria, the nationalization of the Suez Canal by President Gamal Abdel Nasser of Egypt in July 1956 provoked an Anglo-French invasion. Le Pen's unit was sent to join the French invasion forces, and in early November 1956 Le Pen found himself on the banks of the Suez Canal rather than in Algeria. Le Pen was given the unpleasant task of burying the Egyptian dead, whose corpses were scattered along the banks of the canal. Le Pen performed the task with efficiency and sensitivity, ensuring that the dead Egyptians were buried wrapped in a shroud, their feet bare and their heads turned in the direction of Mecca.[58] Le Pen watched from the sidelines as the Suez campaign ground to a halt and the Anglo-French and Israeli invaders were forced to withdraw under pressure from President Dwight Eisenhower and Soviet first secretary Nikita Khrushchev. Once again, as in Indochina, Le Pen felt the humiliation of being on the losing side in a battle that he believed was in France's national interest. For Le Pen, French submissiveness to the superpowers proved that when forced to choose between French national interests and office, French politicians chose office every time.

From Egypt Le Pen was sent to Algeria, where he was appointed intelligence officer to the Tenth Airborne Division. Exactly what occurred during the three-month period from January to March 1957 when Le Pen was involved in questioning Algerian suspects and prisoners remains a matter of controversy. Records show that on April 1, 1957, the commissioner of police of Algiers reported the case of Abdenour Yahiaoui, who claimed that "during his arrest, two electric wires were connected to his earlobes and Lieutenant Le Pen himself operated a hand-driven transformer. In the presence of the same officer the young Yahiaoui was struck with a blackjack; he was bound naked on a bench, feet and hands tied, where he was forced to ingest some water. Finally, he was imprisoned for five days in a 'tomb,' a hole dug in the earth, with no amenities and closed in by barbed wire."[59]

At a dinner in Paris in 1957, Le Pen and his longtime friend and army colleague Jean-Maurice Demarquet were reported to have said:

> We were given a police mission and we accomplished it using the most efficient means possible, which demanded using illegal methods. There is a place for human feelings in the struggle against terrorism, but there is no place for the rules of classic warfare, still less for those of civilian legality. If it is necessary to use violence to discover a nest of bombs, if it is necessary to torture one man to save a hundred, torture is thus inevitable and, in the abnormal conditions in which we were asked to act, it is just.[60]

In an interview with the newspaper *Combat* on November 9, 1962, Le Pen was asked: "There has been a lot of talk about the [brutality of both sides in the] Battle of Algiers." Le Pen responded: "I know it, I have nothing to hide. I tortured because it was necessary to do it."[61] A former secretary-general of the Algiers police, Paul Teitgen, testified that Le Pen "was a torturer in Algeria."[62] However, in 1985 Le Pen brought a libel case against two newspapers that published accounts from his purported victims. They claimed that Le Pen had beaten prisoners, using electric shock and a blowtorch to extract information. One witness claimed to have seen Le Pen murder a prisoner named Moussa by shooting him through the head. The libel case against the satirical weekly *Le Canard Enchaîné* failed not because the court ruled that Le Pen had in fact engaged in torture, but on the technical grounds that because Le Pen had publicly justified torture, he could not claim to be libeled by being accused of something he supported:

> As a result of the testimony and documents involved in this debate, during the first months of 1957 serious violence was perpetrated by the French military acting within the framework of anti-terrorism. Second, it is established that Lieutenant Le Pen, present in Algiers during that time, had knowledge of acts of torture practiced by certain interrogators. . . . Mr. Le Pen constantly approved and justified this violence. The testimony that he has proposed and his filmed documents whose object is to recall the atrocities imputable to the National Liberation Front [the Algerian FLN], are of no significance. Lieutenant Le Pen cannot therefore claim injury to his honor because he cannot at the same time approve the conduct of those who committed acts which are imputed to him and affirm that this imputation dishonors them.[63]

According to Le Pen, however, he was the victim of a campaign of defamation and denigration instigated by the Communist Party and the left-wing intelligentsia. "If I had committed reprehensible acts I would have been tried and judged. On the contrary, I was decorated by General Massu, commander of the division."[64] However, in 1985 Jean-Maurice Demarquet told Alain Rollat of *Le Monde* that "it is absolutely clear that Le Pen was himself part of teams that personally tortured. Personally!" When Rollat noted that Demarquet had been stationed in Constantine 125 miles away, while Le Pen had been stationed in Algiers, Demarquet replied that Le Pen had personally told him about having tortured, "in detail."[65] In a 1987 interview Le Pen claimed that he had "only [been] ordered to arrest people, to conduct round-ups and identity checks. . . . With regard to Algeria, everyone claims to have been tortured by Le Pen just as everyone claims to have been tortured by Barbie."[66]

Nevertheless, the evidence is mixed on whether Le Pen himself tortured Algerians or whether he gave orders to others to torture Algerian prisoners.[67] Whatever the truth of the matter, during his stay in Algeria, and for a long time afterward, Le Pen took a hard-line position on defeating the FLN and keeping Algeria within the French orbit. In doing so, he drew on a variety of arguments: the historical commitment of France to Algeria since 1830; the obligation to protect French citizens, who made up one-ninth of the population, against "terrorists"; the importance of the Saharan oil reserves, which France lacked; the need to prevent Algeria from falling within the Soviet orbit; and the necessary role that France would have to play in assisting the technical, economic, and social progress of Algeria. In a 1971 interview he repeated arguments that were common among certain elements of the French military in the 1950s—namely, that France's mission was to modernize and "civilize" the colonies and that it should be willing to pay the cost, no matter how large, first in military support and then in economic assistance.

> I was a partisan of assimilation [of Algeria into France]. . . . I think that African and North African nationalism are a reactionary historical element and that giving power to nationalist military oligarchies or to a nationalist and "progressive" bourgeoisie is a reactionary move in a world which is shrinking and where education and the conditions of life are deeply changing conditions.
> . . .
>
> To tell the truth, the military was the most socialist. What is extraordinary is that the right was socialist to the point of science fiction and the left was extraordinarily reactionary. Of course, they talked about the equality of races and humanity, but amongst themselves in socialist or communist meetings they said: "Enough of those wogs, there isn't any more work, this is costing us a fortune, and, besides, our kids are sent to fight down there."[68]

Moreover, Le Pen argued, if France had retreated from Algeria, it would have been "reduced to a little hexagon in the little Asiatic peninsula that is Europe."[69] To these arguments, Le Pen added a racist twist:

> Our defeat left the doors open to the "barbarians" who are flocking to us. . . . We fought for assimilation between France and Algeria, in order not to be assimilated ourselves. French Algeria was the best means for resolving the problem of our century, the problem of the races. . . . We have increased the demographic decadence of the white race. By retreating to our hexagon we have undergone a defeat: that of biological vitality. . . . It is necessary to respect ethnic traditions: each group, whites, Jews, Arabs must respect the rules of the game.[70] But one must recognize that some aren't "favored by nature." . . . And when I see the Arabs with their shabby look, I ask if there isn't some kind of biological determinism at play.[71]

When Le Pen wrote, "We could have made a national revolution to forge new, different men," he was echoing one of the major themes of orthodox fascism.[72] Beyond a radical reshaping of the political and economic systems, fascism aims at reshaping human nature itself. The new fascist man is forged out of the white heat of battle, where his devotion to country, his self-sacrifice, and his heroism lift him above the petty concerns of day-to-day living and the materialism of modern life. The new fascist man thus becomes the model for the citizens of a "new order."[73]

Two other aspects of Le Pen's argument are also worth noting. First, by implying that the essence of socialism consists of using state power to achieve economic or social ends, Le Pen committed the logical fallacy of composition, that is, taking the part for the whole. Thus, Le Pen claimed that the French military in Algeria was the "most socialist" because it wanted to use the state to build a modern society in Algeria, as if everyone were socialist who argued for the use of state power for national goals. Second, the accusation that the Socialists were reactionary is an early example of the NF's rhetorical trick of taking a word or phrase from one's opponents (in this case the term *socialism*), reversing its meaning (from socialism - progressive, to socialism - reaction), and then using the redefined word or phrase against one's opponents: for example, accusing the Socialists of holding up progress in Algeria because of their reactionary policies.[74]

Le Pen and the Fall of the Fourth Republic

Having quit the Poujadists, Le Pen and Demarquet resumed their seats in the National Assembly in 1957, sitting as independents. Le Pen also renewed his ties with the extreme right, focusing his energies on veterans' organizations nostalgic for French Indochina and anxious to keep Algeria French. One of Le Pen's friends suggested they adopt the term *Front National* for the new organization, but Le Pen objected: "There aren't enough of us for that, and we haven't the structure."[75] Le Pen proposed that the organization call itself the Front National des Combattants (Fighters' National Front, or FNC). As its symbol, the FNC adopted a sword, the emblem of Le Pen's Foreign Legion regiment, in front of a tricolored flame. The sword was later replaced by an urn when the National Front was established in 1972.[76]

In March 1958, while attending an election meeting in support of an Algerian Muslim who supported French Algeria, Le Pen began to heckle the rival candidate. After a brief exchange, Le Pen leaped onto the platform and slapped the candidate. The candidate's security guards quickly threw Le Pen to the ground, beat him, and kicked him in the right eye. Subsequently, Le Pen took to wearing a piratical-looking black band over his injured eye. Contrary to legend, it was not this eye that went blind but his left eye, which eventually developed a nontreatable cataract and was replaced by a glass eye.[77]

Meanwhile, the French army high command in Algeria was increasingly at odds with Fourth Republic politicians over the Algerian War. The generals suspected the politicians of engaging in secret negotiations with the Algerian rebels and warned the government that they would accept nothing short of complete victory over the FLN. Behind the scenes, however, leading right-wing politicians in league with certain army generals were plotting the overthrow of the Republic. Finally, on May 13, 1958, the army high command informed the government that it had assumed full powers in Algeria and would no longer take orders from Paris. France had reached the point of civil war.

While the crisis developed into stalemate, with neither side able to move decisively against the other, rebel generals secretly drew up a plan, code-named "Resurrection," to invade Paris with a combined air and armored assault.[78] During these crucial weeks in May 1958, France hovered on the brink of invasion and civil war as the Fourth Republic government unsuccessfully tried to reassert its authority over the rebel generals. However, Le Pen and his friend and fellow deputy Jean-Marie Demarquet were delighted by the crisis and on May 14, 1958, led a march to the Tomb of the Unknown Soldier at the Arc de Triomphe. After observing a minute of silence, the two deputies, accompanied by local politicians, led a crowd of two thousand down the Champs-Elysées in the direction of the bridge that leads from the Place de la Concorde, across the river Seine, to the Palais-Bourbon, the home of the National Assembly. On the way the crowd yelled, "Long live France!" "French Algeria!" and "Throw the Deputies in the Seine!" Reaching the bridge to the Left Bank, however, they met a wall of police vans and a line of police. To cries of "Down with the regime! Down with the Republic!" the crowd unsuccessfully tried to storm police lines. It was pushed back by the Compagnies Républicaines de Sécurité (Republican Security Force, or CRS), the heavily armed, paramilitary riot police used by the government to deal with strikes and demonstrations. The demonstrators soon abandoned their attempt to cross the bridge, and the march broke up.

This event provokes comparison with a march that had taken place twenty-four years earlier, when on February 6, 1934, extreme right demonstrators tried to cross the Seine from the Place de la Concorde and storm the Chamber of Deputies. The police guarding the bridge at the Place de la Concorde at that time opened fire and killed fifteen demonstrators. The 1934 riot occurred when the Third Republic was threatened by a renascent Germany and wracked by internal political and social dissension. Although the rioters came from a variety of feuding right-wing organizations, they were united in their hatred for communism and socialism, their disgust with what they argued was a corrupt and self-serving political system, and their antipathy toward foreigners and Jews.[79] Of course, Le Pen's 1958 march was a much less dramatic reenactment of the 1934 incident, and the marchers were dispersed without incident. Nonetheless, the Fourth Republic had been fatally wounded by the army revolt, and its death throes had begun. The question was whether the Fourth Republic would give way to a new republic, an authoritarian dictatorship, a civil war, or anarchy.

During those heady days in May 1958, anything seemed possible. Driven to a fever pitch of excitement by the prospect of the Fourth Republic's collapse, Le Pen and Demarquet flew to Lisbon on May 21, 1958, and then to Spain and to Algiers, where the two deputies were forced by the police to reenter the aircraft and return to Spain. Exactly why Le Pen and Demarquet were expelled when other extreme right deputies were allowed to enter Algeria is unclear. Later, when asked to explain why he had been expelled from Algeria, Le Pen, inflating his importance, replied, "We were known and [General Raoul] Salan [a leader of the army rebels] knew that if we entered into direct contact with the Algerian people, that would cause problems."[80] According to Jean Chatain, the reason for the expulsion had to do with rivalries among the various factions of the extreme right that were involved in the plot to overthrow the Fourth Republic.[81]

Once back in Madrid, however, Le Pen and Demarquet contacted the famous Otto Skorzeny, ex-commando and leader of the Odessa Nazi organization. Skorzeny took them to dinner, where he introduced Le Pen and Demarquet to former dictator of Argentina Juan Perón. While in Madrid, they were given permission to return to Algeria on condition that they reenlist in the paratroopers for six months. But hearing that de Gaulle was on the verge of returning to power, Le Pen and Demarquet decided to return to Paris, where, they believed, the fate of Algeria would be determined. According to Roger Mauge, Le Pen again demonstrated enormous prescience by contradicting those who thought de Gaulle would save French Algeria: "It's going to finish very badly."[82] According to Le Pen, he realized that de Gaulle would give up Algeria because of an incident that had occurred when Le Pen was touring France in 1957, drumming up publicity for the FNC:

> I met a man named Demichel who was the biggest importer/exporter dealing with the USSR, and who has since been unmasked as a key Soviet agent for Europe. In July 1957, Demichel said that if I agreed to support the return of General de Gaulle, I would have lots of money, if not, I wouldn't. I concluded that the East was betting on the return of de Gaulle. And as I wasn't as naive as the French deputies, having read General de Gaulle's speeches, I knew who were his intermediaries with the Arab world, and I knew they had nothing to do with the groups supporting French Algeria. . . . The whole bunch of them made me suspect de Gaulle from the start.[83]

Under threat of invasion and possible civil war, the leaders of the Fourth Republic asked de Gaulle to defuse the situation by taking over as premier. De Gaulle accepted on condition that his only act would be to dissolve the National Assembly in order to write a new constitution, which would be submitted to the country by referendum. The National Assembly then voted to appoint de Gaulle premier by a vote of 339 to 224: Le Pen voted against de Gaulle—as did François Mitterrand. With de Gaulle in command, the army returned to its barracks and the French Algerians to their homes on the assumption that Algeria would remain French.

After spending the summer with colleagues drafting the Fifth Republic constitution, de Gaulle submitted it to the nation on September 28, 1958. Le Pen and the FNC advocated a "yes" vote. Two months later in the November legislative elections, Le Pen ran for the National Assembly on a pro–de Gaulle platform for the Centre National des Indépendants (CNI) and rode the Gaullist wave to victory, winning 44 percent of the vote on the second round of the election.

Over the next two years, however, it became apparent that France could not sustain the permanent drain of blood and resources required to keep Algeria French. In 1960, therefore, de Gaulle began negotiations with the FLN on Algerian independence. Le Pen and the supporters of French Algeria were humiliated; once again France was selling out to "terrorists." Then in January 1960, furious at the looming possibility of negotiations with the FLN, armed French Algerians, under the benevolent eye of the military, set up barricades in Algiers. The barricades were topped with flags decorated with the Celtic cross, the symbol of French neofascism. It looked as if May 1958 might repeat itself. Once again Le Pen sided with the rebels, calling on students in Paris to strike and hinting at the possibility of an insurrection: "I am in complete solidarity with the men who are being killed in Algiers to remain French. . . . I am sorry I am not in Algiers, but Paris has an old insurrectional past which might perhaps revive in order to sweep away all that."[84] But General de Gaulle was made of sterner stuff than the politicians of the Fourth Republic. The police put small-fry agitators like Le Pen under house arrest for a brief time, while loyal army units crushed the rebellion and restored order.

Shortly afterward, in May 1960, Le Pen went to Algeria to participate in local elections, but he was again expelled and forced to return to France. Meanwhile, supporters of French Algeria began to marshal their forces for another attempt at overthrowing the government. This time Le Pen was invited to a meeting of the conspirators in a Paris apartment. On entering, Le Pen was immediately queried by General André Zeller, one of the plotters: "Le Pen, we have decided to take power. De Gaulle is betraying Algeria. Are you with us?" According to Robert Mauge, Le Pen then asked: "Of course, you are going to begin with a surprise occupation of the Elysée [the office of the French president]?" "Oh, no. . . . We aren't touching the Elysée." "Then you are going to occupy the National Assembly, the television and radio stations?" "No, not at all, we're taking power in Algiers. We aren't touching Paris." At that point, Mauge reported, Le Pen understood that the plot would never succeed.[85]

Mauge clearly implied that if the plotters had answered Le Pen's queries positively—that is, if their intention had been to take over the presidential palace and the media—Le Pen might have joined with them in trying to overthrow the Fifth Republic.[86] This assertion completely contradicts

Mauge's claim that Le Pen had always been "resolutely 'legalist,'" never even imagining that the "destiny of France could be influenced other than through the election route."[87] Le Pen explained his actions as follows: "French Algeria was lost. I stayed out of the putsch since the objective which the putschists seemed to have—to give back a French Algeria to General de Gaulle, who didn't want it—was incoherent and weak."[88] In a 1971 interview Le Pen stated that at the end of 1960, he and his colleagues thought that the only way to reverse de Gaulle's policy was to take over power in Paris and "eliminate" the chief of state.[89] Both Mauge's account and Le Pen's remarks clearly imply that Le Pen backed out not because of any democratic scruples but because he thought the plot would fail.

In any event, the attempted coup took place on April 22, 1961—and was almost immediately crushed.[90] On April 25, 1961, General Zeller was arrested in Algiers, and on May 20, 1961, the French government reached an agreement with the FLN on Algerian independence. Now that the tide had turned against the proponents of French Algeria, the situation in Algeria deteriorated. Die-hard elements formed the Organisation de l'Armée Secrète, dedicated to disrupting the peace process and assassinating those accused of having betrayed French Algeria. By 1962 the OAS had moved its operations to France. Bombs were set off in the Arab quarter of French cities, attempts were made to assassinate loyalist army and police officers, and Communist Party offices and buildings were targeted.

While Le Pen argued fiercely in the National Assembly and in public against the "policy of abandonment," events in Algeria were moving inexorably against the die-hards.[91] On April 8, 1962, de Gaulle's referendum on Algerian independence received massive approval: 17.8 million voting for and only 1.8 million against independence. The following September de Gaulle narrowly survived an assassination attempt when twelve OAS terrorists fired 150 shots at his speeding limousine. Confronted with the possibility of leaving a power vacuum if he should be assassinated, or becoming a president whose legitimacy was only narrowly based, de Gaulle decided to submit to the nation a constitutional referendum establishing direct election of the president through universal suffrage. Le Pen strongly criticized the move. However, the October 1962 referendum won a majority of 62 percent, and de Gaulle then called for new legislative elections in November 1962. By this time Le Pen and the CNI had entered into opposition, and Le Pen fought the election on an anti-Gaullist, pro-European platform. But the CNI lost 78 of its 122 seats in the election, and Le Pen, with only 15.9 percent of the vote on the second ballot, was one of those swept away in the Gaullist tidal wave. Le Pen was out of the National Assembly, France's colonial history was at an end, and to all appearances the French extreme right was dead. Now began the period that Le Pen refers to as "the crossing of the desert."

Crossing the Desert

For the next few years Le Pen and his friend Pierre Durand ran a public relations and research company called Société d'Études et de Relations Publiques (Research and Public Relations Company), which soon turned into a record publishing company specializing in historic recordings of figures such as Charles de Gaulle, Marshal Pétain, André Malraux, Winston Churchill, and Adolf Hitler. The collection was called "Men and Events of the Twentieth Century." In 1965 a recording of songs of the Hitler era led to Le Pen being sued for "apologizing for war crimes." The basis of the accusation was a statement on the record jacket:

> Here are the songs of the German revolution. The arrival in power of Adolph Hitler and the National Socialist Party was characterized by a powerful, popular and democratic mass movement which triumphed after regular elections—circumstances which are generally forgotten. In this, the oratorical propaganda of Hitler's chiefs, and the political songs expressing collective passions played an essential role. This record recreates this spirit with the help of original documents of an inestimable historic value.[92]

Whereas a recording by Le Pen's company of events concerning anarchism had been accompanied by an editorial disclaimer of support or apology for anarchists, the record jacket containing the Nazi songs contained no such disclaimer. In 1968 Le Pen was given an eighteen-month suspended sentence and was fined Fr 10,000 for "justifying war crimes."[93]

During the 1960s, the passions occasioned by the Algerian War had begun to cool. The *pieds-noirs* who had flocked to France after Algerian independence soon found work in France's booming economy, and the OAS was on the run from the police and on the road to extinction. It had become clear that terrorism and violence could not reverse a policy supported by the vast majority of French citizens. The restoration of normalcy also meant that former OAS leaders could devote their energies to the drive for unity on the extreme right. Moreover, with Algeria removed from the political agenda as a major issue, the presidential election scheduled for 1965 could allow the extreme right to disseminate its message to circles previously closed to its influence.

By the mid-1960s the extreme right had begun a slow evolution away from violent action and extremist language. In the 1950s organizations such as Jeune Nation (Young Nation) had specialized in attacks on Communists and peace groups. On one occasion in 1954 Jeune Nation militants had murdered a truck driver delivering issues of the Communist Party newspaper *L'Humanité*. Jeune Nation's program was the usual poisonous fascist brew of strident nationalism, antiparliamentarism, anticapitalism, anticommunism and antisocialism, and, of course, racism and anti-Semitism. Jeune Nation called for "a total eviction of the 'wogs'" from France, "revision of naturalizations and the annulling of rights for undesirable foreigners."[94] It also demanded that women be confined to the sacred tasks of wife and mother. Dissolved by the government in 1958 because of the organization's violence, Jeune Nation reemerged in September 1960 by publishing a review called *Europe-Action* and then establishing a movement with the same name.[95] It attracted adherents from a variety of extreme right and neofascist organizations, including the right-wing Fédération des Étudiants Nationalistes (Federation of Nationalist Students). Many of these groups followed a cult of violence, invading meetings of left-wing groups and beating people with clubs or iron bars or setting off bombs in front of buildings occupied by Communist or left-wing militants.

But Europe-Action leader Dominique Venner, after being released from jail in 1962, where he had been imprisoned for plotting against the state, began to argue against perpetrating violence and for using all available legal means for putting the "nationalist" case to the public during the presidential election campaign. He faulted the extreme right for acting impulsively and for being indiscriminate in its choice of leaders. Now was the time to change, he maintained.

Although the ranks of Europe-Action included ex-OAS members and other extreme right militants, the organization began to advocate discussion, propaganda, and electoral politics as the best means for gaining influence and disseminating its message. Venner argued that Algerian independence had led to a major change in public opinion and had relieved France of the burden of being a colonial power. "Henceforth when a person of European origin is murdered in Africa," Venner wrote, "he will be a victim, rather than, as it used to be, an oppressor."[96] France should now concentrate on defending the "superior western civilization" from the threat posed by immigration from the outside and materialist and atheistic socialism and communism from inside. This battle had to be fought at the European level; old-style nationalism, which thought in World War I terms of a France defending its integrity against hostile powers, had to give way to a "common European nationalism" threatened by multiple external and internal enemies.[97] Europe-Action's publications therefore emphasized the persecution of whites in Africa and crime among Algerians in France in an attempt to illustrate how the nonwhite races threatened French society. "Even if the election is lost in advance, that is of little importance. What counts is the possibility of publishing propaganda, the possibility for the national opposition to no longer be a museum piece, but a politically active organization."[98]

It had finally dawned on the extreme right that, whatever the other attractions of violence, it did not win elections.[99] The presidential election of 1965 was to be a testing ground for the new tactics of moderation.

Notes

1. Gordon Wright, *France in Modern Times* (New York: Rand McNally, 1960), p. 542.

2. Jean-Pierre Rioux, *The Fourth Republic, 1944–1958* (Cambridge: Cambridge University Press, 1987), pp. 320ff.

3. Ibid., p. 335.

4. Christopher Flockton and Eleonore Kofman, *France* (London: Paul Chapman, 1989), p. 5.

5. Stanley Hoffmann, *Le mouvement Poujade* (Paris: André Colin, 1956), pp. 13ff.

6. Poujade was more than the simple stationer of legend. Annie Collovald, "Les Poujadistes, ou l'échec en politique," *Revue d'histoire moderne et contemporaine* 36 (January-March 1989):122.

7. "Personally, at that point," said Poujade, "I had never had any trouble with the tax people. . . . They left me in peace. But I was aware that this tranquility was precarious. The hundreds of small clients who I supplied had less chance than I because they had been in business for a long time. The tax people sniffed around them, suspected them. Then began the harassing, the unnecessary checks, the fines and the settlements." Pierre Poujade, *À l'heure de la colère* (Paris: Albin Michel, 1977), p. 99.

8. In the 1950s in France, more than 75 percent of shopkeepers, artisans, and small businessmen did not pay income tax, preferring to let tax inspectors estimate their income by assessing property and goods. This led to enormous conflict between the state and the commercial sector. John C. Cairns, *France* (Englewood Cliff, N.J.: Prentice-Hall, 1965), pp. 68–69.

9. Philip Williams, *Crisis and Compromise* (Hamden, Conn.: Archon Books, 1964), p. 167.

10. Of the Radical Socialist Party, it was said that the party was neither radical nor socialist. In North American terms it was somewhat similar to the American Democratic or Canadian Liberal Parties.

11. Hoffmann, *Le mouvement Poujade*, pp. 41–42.

12. Quoted in ibid., p. 154.

13. Pamphlet published in ibid., p. 154.

14. Pierre Poujade, *J'ai choisi le combat* (Saint-Céré: Société Général des Éditions et des Publications, 1955), pp. 114, 115, 116. In the 1930s anti-Semites mocked Jewish premier Léon Blum because he preferred water to wine. According to the *Journal des débats:* "The citizens of Aude thinking, along with the proverb, that nasty people drink water—that's proven by the Flood—submitted the unfortunate Blum to a test that he underwent heroically. But Mr. Blum didn't drink. He would have died." Quoted in Pierre Birnbaum, *Un mythe politique: "La République juive"* (Paris: Fayard, 1988), p. 182.

15. Quoted in Hoffmann, *Le mouvement Poujade,* p. 181.

16. Quoted in ibid., p. 183.

17. If Mendès-France had not escaped from a Vichy jail, he might well have suffered the same fate as his Jewish colleague, former Third Republic cabinet minister Georges Mandel, executed by the Vichy Milice; or he might have been handed over to the Nazis. After his escape, he served with the Royal Air Force.

18. *Le Monde,* January 20, 1956.

19. Quoted in Hoffman, *Le mouvement Poujade,* p. 226.

20. Quoted in ibid.

21. Quoted in *Le Monde,* January 20, 1956.

22. Quoted in ibid.

23. *Le Monde,* January 20, 1956.

24. Interview reported in *Le Monde,* December 21, 1955.

25. Williams, *Crisis,* p. 164.

26. *Le Monde,* December 13, 1955.

27. Quoted in Hoffmann, *Le mouvement Poujade,* p. 154.

28. Quoted in Roger Mauge, *La verité sur Jean-Marie Le Pen* (Paris: Éditions France-Empire, 1988), p. 107.

29. Quoted in ibid.

30. Some years later Le Pen recalled that it was Poujade's interest in the question of the nation and in France's relationship with Algeria that led him to join the Poujadists. Personal interview with Jean-Marie Le Pen conducted by Professor Hartmut Elsenhans, Paris, March 6, 1971. Transcript supplied to author courtesy of Professor Elsenhans.

31. Quoted in Gilles Bresson and Christian Lionet, *Le Pen* (Paris: Seuil, 1994), p. 117.

32. Quoted in Bresson and Lionet, *Le Pen,* p. 135.

33. On March 8, 1956, he attacked Prime Minister Guy Mollet and demanded that the government execute "the condemned murderers in Algerian prisons. . . . Control the press, information and the defamatory campaigns which undermine the army and the nation." Quoted in Jean Chatain, *Les affaires,* p. 62.

34. Jean-Marie Le Pen, *Les Français d'abord* (Paris: Carrère/Laffon, 1984), p. 46.

35. *Le Monde,* January 15–16, 1956.

36. In an interview in *Libération* on February 14, 1984, Poujade said: "When we arrived at the Assembly we were arbitrarily stuck on the extreme right: equally arbitrarily we could have been put on the extreme left. Personally, I wanted to sit on the staircase"—which, in effect, is what he wound up doing.

37. *Le Monde,* January 15–16, 1956.

38. Pierre Milza, *Fascisme français: Passé et present* (Paris: Flammarion, 1987), p. 307.

39. Joseph Algazy, *La tentation néo-fasciste en France, 1934–1965* (Paris: Fayard, 1984), pp. 129–130.

40. Hoffmann, *Le mouvement Poujade,* p. 226.

41. See special edition of *Défense de l'Occident,* edited by Maurice Bardèche, "Le Poujadisme" (May 1956):9.

42. Ibid., p. 10.

43. Ibid.

44. Ibid.

45. Ibid., p. 25.

46. Poujade, *J'ai choisi*, p. 20.

47. Bardèche, "Le Poujadisme," p. 26.

48. A popular book critical of the Republic in the 1950s was Jean Maze, *Le système* (Paris: Segur, 1951).

49. Bardèche, "Le Poujadisme," p. 35.

50. Poujade's attack on traditional politics sometimes took a bizarre form, as in December 1956 when he appealed to the voters to abstain during the first round of an upcoming legislative by-election and was supported in this by none other than the Poujadist candidate, Armand Rivereau. *Le Monde*, December 30–31, 1956.

51. *Le Monde*, March 10, 1956.

52. Le Pen, *Les Français*, p. 46.

53. Quoted in Gilles Bresson and Christian Lionet, *Le Pen* (Paris: Seuil, 1994), p. 145.

54. Poujade and Le Pen were never on good terms after Le Pen's resignation. During a May 1992 television interview, Poujade said that Le Pen had been with the combatants in Indochina not "in the mud" but "in the brothels of Saigon." In 1993 a court ruled that, although Poujade was merely repeating information "notoriously admitted by public rumours," it held him guilty of defamation and fined him Fr 23,000. *Le Monde*, March 27, 1993.

55. Serge Dumont, Joseph Lorien, and Karl Criton, *Le système Le Pen* (Anvers, Belgium: Éditions EPO, 1985), p. 35.

56. Quoted in Bresson and Lionet, *Le Pen*, p. 140.

57. Raymond Aron, *France Steadfast and Changing* (Cambridge, Mass.: Harvard University Press, 1960), p. 99.

58. One friend noted that what struck him at the time was the ceremony with which Le Pen went about his task: "This respect for the dead, the family rituals, had a Barrèsian side to it [after Maurice Barrès's philosophy of honoring the dead as representing the continuity of the nation]." Quoted in Bresson and Lionet, *Le Pen*, p. 156.

59. Quoted in Chatain, *Les affaires*, p. 66.

60. *Le Monde*, May 3, 1957.

61. Cited in Chatain, *Les affaires*, p. 67.

62. Quoted in Alain Rollat, *L'Effet Le Pen* (Paris: La Découverte, 1984), p. 27.

63. Dumont et al., *Le système*, pp. 43, 44, 45.

64. Le Pen, *Les Français*, p. 48. Roger Mauge devoted an entire chapter to defending both Le Pen and the troops of the Foreign Legion from accusations of torture. Mauge, *La verité*, pp. 130–151.

65. Interview with Demarquet by Alain Rollat, in *Le Monde*, October 16, 1985.

66. *Le Monde*, December 17, 1987. Klaus Barbie was a Gestapo chief in the city of Lyon during the war and was accused of having tortured and killed, among others, Jean Moulin, the French Resistance hero. Barbie was finally extradited from Bolivia, where he had been in hiding since the end of the war, and after a long delay was brought to trial in France. His case reignited old quarrels between Vichy supporters and members of the Resistance.

67. Bresson and Lionet reported conflicting accounts of Le Pen's actions in Algeria: Some Algerians arrested by Le Pen and many of his colleagues say he did not engage in torture; other Algerians identify Le Pen as having tortured them; and at least one Foreign Legion colleague claims to have been astonished by Le Pen's "brutality" during interrogations. Bresson and Lionet, *Le Pen*, p. 173.

68. Elsenhans interview.

69. Le Pen, *Les Français*, p. 49.

70. Notice that Jews and Arabs are not considered by Le Pen to be "white."

71. Gregory Pons, *Les rats noirs* (N.p.: Jean-Claude Simeon, 1977), pp. 50–5l. In a 1984 television interview Le Pen denied saying anything at all to Pons, who, he claimed, had spent exactly three minutes in his office before he showed Pons the door. However, Le Pen admitted that he had not gone to court over the issue, although he had done so over a number of other remarks attributed to him. Le Pen, *Les Français*, p. 227.

72. Quoted in Dumont et al., *Le système*, p. 48. The term *national revolution* was used by Vichy to describe its political project.

73. Roger Griffin argued that the idea of the "new man" is part of the "palingenetic myth," the myth of a rebirth that will occur "after a phase of crisis or decline." The core of fascism resides in this kind of myth. Roger Griffin, *The Nature of Fascism* (London: Pinter, 1990), pp. 32–33.

74. Le Pen's use of twisted logic pales before the French Socialist government's equally perverse attempt to use socialist principles to defend its conduct of the Algerian War in 1956–1957 and its participation in the British-French-Israeli invasion of Suez in 1956. Harvey G. Simmons, *French Socialists in Search of a Role* (Ithaca: Cornell University Press, 1970).

75. Quoted in Bresson and Lionet, *Le Pen*, p. 186.

76. Bresson and Lionet, *Le Pen*, p. 186.

77. Ibid., p. 196.

78. Milza, *Fascisme français*, p. 313.

79. *Le Monde*, May 15, 1958.

80. Chatain, *Les affaires*, pp. 74–75.

81. Ibid.

82. Mauge, *La verité*, pp. 160–165.

83. Elsenhans interview.

84. Quoted in Chatain, *Les affaires*, p. 76.

85. Mauge, *La verité*, pp. 171–172.

86. In reporting on the meeting, Mauge did not say that Le Pen was so shocked by the first question that, to play for time and gather his wits, he decided to seek further information. Nor did Mauge say that Le Pen's first response was that he would have nothing to do with such a plot. Nor did Mauge suggest that on leaving the meeting, Le Pen expressed relief at not being involved or pressured into joining the plot. No matter how one reads this passage, the impression conveyed is that under different circumstances Le Pen would have been tempted to join the conspirators. Even more curious, Mauge then devoted the next two full pages to Le Pen's deep commitment to the Republic, adducing as evidence the books Le Pen read as a child as well as the Breton blood in his veins. Ibid., pp. 171–172.

87. Ibid., p. 173.

88. Le Pen, *Les Français*, p. 50.

89. Elsenhans interview.

90. Mauge, *La verité*, p. 173.

91. Le Pen, *Les Français*, p. 50.

92. Quoted in Mauge, *La verité*, p. 185.

93. See ibid., pp. 185–186; and Algazy, *La tentation*, p. 73.

94. Milza, *Fascisme français*, p. 319.

95. Ibid., p. 328.

96. *Le Monde*, February 28, 1965.

97. *Le Monde*, September 3, 1965.

98. *Le Monde*, February 28, 1965.

99. According to Milza, Europe-Action aimed to disencumber nationalism and fascism of antiparliamentarism, chauvinism, and anti-intellectualism. "In other words, it was necessary to do better than the Third Reich, and to do that it was necessary to refine the doctrine baptized 'nationalist revolution' in order to prevent it from being assimilated to national socialism." Milza, *Fascisme français*, p. 329.

3

From Tixier-Vignancour
to the National Front

We are the national opposition, the social right, the popular right. . . . A new adventure awaits people at this point in history. . . . In this fight we aren't alone, with us there is the immense and glorious cohort of those who fell in the rice paddies and in the jellaba.

—Jean-Marie Le Pen, *in* Le Monde, *November 9, 1972*

For almost one hundred years, no political party in France dared label itself as on the right, until in 1972, the National Front decided to define itself as the social, popular and national right.

—Jean-Marie Le Pen, *in* Le National, *March 1976*

On learning that President de Gaulle planned a referendum on universal suffrage, Le Pen realized the impact it would have on French politics and the new importance that presidential elections would assume in national politics. Initially, he seems to have considered entering the race himself, but since he was only thirty-five years old at the time, he abandoned the idea. Le Pen's choice was Jean-Louis Tixier-Vignancour. "Tixier-Vignancour incarnated French Algeria, whose sympathizers composed our electoral base."[1] For a while Pierre Poujade thought about running, but eventually he threw his support behind Pierre Marcilhacy, a senator with no party allegiance.[2]

Tixier-Vignancour, or "TV" as he became known, was one of the stars of the extreme right: a skilled lawyer and an excellent speaker with a long history of commitment to extreme right and neofascist causes and movements. Tixier-Vignancour had been educated at the elite Lycée Louis le Grand, where he was a classmate of Pierre Mendès-France and Edgar Faure, both to become premiers in the Fourth Republic. Tixier-Vignancour passed the bar in 1927, did his military service, and then returned to Paris, where he was active on the extreme right, participating in the street battles between left and right that raged through the Latin Quarter in the 1930s. He served for one term as a deputy under the Third Republic. Mobilized during the war, he led a checkered career, acting for five weeks as the head of radio and cinema under the Vichy government but then resigning his post.[3] After various adventures and prison terms in Vichy, German, and Allied prisons, he was freed in 1945.

In 1949 he participated in the establishment of Jeune Nation but left shortly afterward.[4] In 1952 he became a supporter of the fascist monthly *Défense de l'Occident* (which was the basis for the extreme right organization Occident), established by Maurice Bardèche, and then participated in the launch of the neofascist European Social Movement. After floating from one group to another, he founded his own party, the Rassemblement National (National Assembly).[5] The group's only success was to elect Tixier-Vignancour to the National Assembly in 1956, where he allied himself with the Poujadists.[6] During the Algerian War, he devoted himself to the cause of French Algeria and served as defense lawyer in some of the most famous treason and terrorism trials of the 1960s.[7]

Unquestionably, Tixier-Vignancour's candidacy was Le Pen's brainchild, and he called the shots during the campaign. Le Pen's goal was quite clear: to bring the different factions of the extreme right together into a serious and credible political party and to use the 1965 campaign as a way to acquaint the country with the new, moderate face of the extreme right.[8] In 1964 Le Pen and Tixier-Vignancour established the "TV Committee," which included on its executive committee a cross section of the far right, from die-hard supporters of French Algeria to longtime members of the extreme and neofascist right. One journal described the executive committee as consisting of "those nostalgic for Vichy, the descendants of Action Française, Catholic fundamentalists, ultras of French Algeria, the residue of Poujadism, embryonic fascists, and representatives of the liberal right."[9]

As always, Le Pen proved himself an ingenious and energetic organizer.[10] Greatly impressed by American-style campaign methods, Le Pen distributed key chains with pictures of Tixier-Vignancour, ballpoint pens with his initials, ashtrays in the shape of France, and scarves with Tixier's colors. Le Pen's record company turned out recordings of the candidate's speeches, and he produced a film entitled *Seven Years of Misfortune*—a reference to de Gaulle's seven-year tenure as president. Drawing on his experience in the 1950s when he established "union and defense" committees grouping together Poujadists from various occupations, Le Pen established TV Committees to support his candidate's campaign. He then imitated his summer 1957 public relations success—visiting the beaches of France in a cavalcade of cars, trailers, and vans under the slogan "The French Algeria Caravan"—by organizing another tour of the beaches. "I was in charge of organizing his [Tixier-Vignancour] campaign. I gave it a tone and a dynamism which disturbed the political class and those who were in power."[11] A May meeting of the TV Committee in Paris drew four thousand participants and led to clashes between Tixier-Vignancour's security force, composed of members from Occident, and the police.[12]

However, within the campaign camp there were increasing tensions as Europe-Action and Occident began to jockey for position. Eventually, Le Pen fell out with Pierre Sidos, leader of Occident, who pulled his organization out of the campaign and was replaced by Dominique Venner and Europe-Action. Despite all this frantic activity, Tixier-Vignancour's energy was being sapped by tuberculosis. And although Tixier-Vignancour was admired for his skills as a courtroom lawyer and his beautiful voice, he turned out to be a flop on television and in large halls.[13]

Although the major focus of Tixier's campaign was "to tell the truth about the loss of Algeria," he also criticized the "managed economy," praised economic liberalism, and put his campaign under the sign of "God and country."[14] Tixier claimed to represent the "national opposition" and to be the "candidate between de Gaulle and Moscow."[15] But his campaign was mainly negative: He evoked nostalgia for Algeria; opposed the seven-year term for the president of the Republic; and evoked Vichy by asking that the remains of Marshal Pétain be buried at his home in Douaumont.

Finally, to everyone's surprise, and Le Pen's fury, believing against reason that he had a chance of coming in second to de Gaulle on the first ballot of the election (and of winning the election on the second ballot), Tixier-Vignancour suddenly abandoned the radical rhetoric of the extreme right and began to court the moderate right.[16] Next, he tried to shed the extreme right label and pin it on de Gaulle. *TV Demain* (TV Tomorrow), a publication of the Tixier-Vignancour campaign, wrote: "In our opinion the principal candidate of the extreme right could be General de Gaulle. One has only to refer to his authoritarianism, to his personal conception of power, to his contempt for parliamentarism, to his persnickety nationalism, to his mystical worship of the state."[17]

Tixier-Vignancour even began to invoke the name of Jean Moulin, the great Resistance hero who had been tortured to death by Klaus Barbie.[18] Despite Tixier-Vignancour's prediction that he would win 25 percent of the vote, he received only 1.2 million votes on the first ballot (much of it from repatriated French Algerians), a little more than 5 percent.[19] Even more disappointing than the vote was the fact that Tixier-Vignancour then called on his supporters to vote for François Mitterrand, who was pitted against de Gaulle on the second round of the presidential election.[20] Mitterrand, in turn, did nothing to discourage Tixier-Vignancour or other members of the extreme right from throwing their support to him in order to defeat de Gaulle. Asked on television about extreme right support, Mitterrand replied, "If I'm being asked to choose between votes, that's not my business."[21] Disgusted with Tixier's maneuvering, Le Pen quit the campaign.

What accounted for Tixier-Vignancour's failure? One problem was his message. Tixier-Vignancour was still fighting the battle for French Algeria when the issue had largely faded from public view. Doubtless, too, his illness and problems with the media handicapped his campaign. Another problem was the entry during the campaign of Jean Lecanuet, a moderate candidate who attracted anti-Gaullist right-wing votes that might otherwise have gone to Tixier-Vignancour.[22] In addition, most voters on the far right supported de Gaulle as the candidate best placed to defeat the left-winger Mitterrand.[23] Tixier-Vignancour's flirtation with moderation hurt as well: Although his reputation had been established as a leading figure on the extreme right, his moderate campaign alienated potential voters. Finally, de Gaulle's continued presence on the French political scene had rendered the extreme right helpless.

Far from forcing the squabbling factions of the extreme right to submerge their differences in the presidential campaign, the disappointing showing of the candidate of the extreme right exacerbated those differences.[24] For Le Pen, the continued infighting ended his attempt to forge a single movement and a new political party out of the fragments of the extreme right.

After withdrawing from the Tixier-Vignancour camp, Le Pen returned to his recording business. In 1966 he and some of his friends established the Cercle du Panthéon (Pantheon Circle), a study and social group that met in a restaurant owned by Roger Holeindre (nicknamed "Popeye"), a veteran of Indochina and Algeria and a former member of the OAS.[25] By now the extreme right had nearly disappeared from the French political scene.

"Profoundly divided, without doctrine, practicing a dangerous and often sterile electoral game," according to Roger Chiroux, the extreme right "was in bad shape."[26] It was to take another fifteen years before the extreme right could find a leader who, in the person of Jean-Marie Le Pen, far exceeded Poujade in the ability to transform, interpret, and utilize the doctrines of the extreme right in the service of a highly sophisticated and efficient party organization.

The Student Revolution of May 1968

In May 1968 France was wracked by one of the most spectacular events in its history—the student revolution. What began as a student protest against crowded classrooms, poorly situated campuses, and bewildering changes in curriculum soon sparked a nationwide general strike. Throughout the country workers occupied factories, often against the wishes of their trade union leaders, while white-collar workers, civil servants, and a vast cross-section of employees and workers walked off the job. By May 20, 1968, 10 million students and workers were on strike, and the entire government, including President de Gaulle, was aghast at the extent of the problem and baffled about a possible solution.

The fact that the May 1968 strike is often referred to as a revolution shows the extent to which the events assumed almost mythic proportions, for the strikers challenged all the received assumptions of French society. The flavor of the times can be conveyed by some of the graffiti: "Make love, not war," "It is forbidden to forbid" (signs in France often begin with "*Il est interdit de . . .* "), and: "Be a realist—ask for the impossible." In the Sorbonne, occupied during the first week of the events, students engaged in nonstop discussions about the university, democracy, and society.

The extreme right was absolutely confounded by the 1968 revolt. Some members tried to join the students on the barricades, imprudently brandishing the Celtic cross—and were promptly ejected.[27] Others sided with the government against "Bolshevism."[28] Although prior to the May events, Occident had engaged in pitched battles with Communists, peace groups, and leftists in Paris, the movement was so massive as to render even the most violent extreme right groups helpless. The extreme right was also thrown into confusion because it shared some of the ideas of the student radicals, particularly their opposition to de Gaulle and their yearning to replace the values of a bourgeois, materialistic society with finer, higher values. Pierre Pujo of Action Française wrote that his organization went even farther than student leader Daniel Cohn-Bendit by calling into question the very principles of democracy, while "the anarchists only questioned its effects."[29] For the extreme right, the May 1968 events were everything it had hoped for—except that the revolt sprang from the student left. Nonetheless, extreme right leaders and intellectuals imagined how the May events would have looked if only the extreme right had been its author. Pujo contended that "liberalism as well as socialism are incapable of assuring the true autonomy of the universities, a real defense of the workers, an authentic decentralization; in a word, democracy destroys the authority of the state as well as liberty. . . . Public order demands a monarchy at the summit."[30]

Maurice Bardèche, always anxious to paste any news clipping about cracks in the Republic into his ideological scrapbook, thought he glimpsed signs of fascism in the student revolt. "This lost energy, this energy which cannot be used, this energy which our society is not capable of using for anything, youth was going to use for its own liberation, for the liberation of those who were as weak as it is, the oppressed, the eternal minors. . . . It represented violence: it was violence."[31]

According to Roger Mauge, for Le Pen the May 1968 events were "stupefying." Walking through the Latin Quarter during the crisis, Le Pen and Pierre Durand, his associate in their public relations firm, "were torn between astonishment and satisfaction at seeing their old adversary General de Gaulle . . . thwarted by a few thousand demonstrators. What famous generals and hundreds of thousands of *pieds-noirs* could not do, shake the throne, three thousand students uttering inanities through the voice of Cohn-Bendit, who isn't even French, did."[32]

Le Pen described his reaction to 1968 as "nausea. It was a gesture of despair and disenchantment. It was at that moment that it was necessary to straighten things out, even at the risk of a confrontation between left and right."[33] Although Le Pen noted that there were only a few tiny groups of young "nationalists" in the Latin Quarter at the time, he was looking toward the future. "It took the creation of the National Front in 1972 for me to leave my political retreat and with a handful of the brave and the faithful, to pit all my forces against those who owned the political 'thing,' and to reconquer stray spirits and anaesthetized consciences."[34]

The June 1968 Election

Uncharacteristically, President de Gaulle was unsure how to handle the May 1968 revolt. However, on the advice of Prime Minister Georges Pompidou, President de Gaulle dissolved the National Assembly and called for elections in June 1968. The tactic of meeting the challenge of the general strike by calling for new legislative elections worked: The Gaullists won an overwhelming victory, capturing 293 of the 486 National Assembly seats. Le Pen was pushed aside by the Gaullist wave, winning only 1,947 out of 37,143 votes in his constituency in Paris.

Less than a year later, however, in spring 1969, the roller coaster of French politics swooped around again when de Gaulle unwisely called for a referendum on regionalization and Senate reform—and threatened to resign if the referendum was defeated. During the campaign, the extreme right called for a "no" vote. On April 27, 1969, 53.18 percent of the voters rejected the referendum proposal. At midnight, as promised, President de Gaulle resigned.

De Gaulle's sudden disappearance from the political scene removed one of the main sources of division on the extreme right. According to Maurice Bardèche: "The negative and purely sentimental policy which led us to prefer anyone to de Gaulle had its source in the historical lie that he represented and in the permanent danger constituted by the presence as head of State of a man who was a traitor in the past and who was a source of disequilibrium in the present."[35]

Two months later former Prime Minister Georges Pompidou beat Senator Alain Poher on the second ballot of the presidential election to become the second president of the Fifth Republic. On both the first and second ballots of the election, 88 percent of the extreme right voted for Pompidou.[36] Although Pierre Sidos, former member of Occident and leader of the neofascist Oeuvre Française, tried to get himself nominated for the election, he was able to get only 67 of the required 100 signatures from local mayors (of whom there were more than 36,000 in France in 1969) or national politicians. When the Constitutional Council subsequently rejected Sidos's appeal against being denied a place on the ballot, he accused its Jewish members of discriminating against him.[37] According to Roger-Gérard Schwartzenberg, the 1965 election demonstrated that a two-ballot presidential system gave an advantage to moderate candidates and proved a disadvantage to candidates on the extreme ends of the political spectrum. As long as the French presidential system forced the country to choose on the second ballot between only two candidates, there was no chance at all for the extreme right (or the extreme left, for that matter) to win an election.[38]

Le Pen and Ordre Nouveau

Undaunted by his defeat in the 1968 legislative election, Le Pen continued to work at uniting the disparate factions of the extreme right into a single party. Every group, grouplet, or movement of the extreme right, no matter how loathsome its views, was the object of his interest. Le Pen was, as he put it, obsessed with unifying the right. "A major reason for the weakness of the French right," he wrote, "came from the fact that it did not defend interests, but only ideas."[39] Clearly, Le Pen had a grasp of the conditions for political success that escaped his colleagues: Rather than dissipating energies over fruitless and obscure doctrinal quarrels, the extreme right, Le Pen realized, had to build a party on the basis of discrete, concrete interests. "I had tried it with Tixier-Vignancour; getting people to agree on specific actions, avoiding useless differences; to create a dynamic around common actions, to get people to work together, to do their best to know each other and to appreciate each other."[40]

By the early 1970s Le Pen had turned his attention to regrouping the various factions of the "national opposition."[41] As Le Pen put it: "Everything that is national is ours."[42] One group particularly attracted Le Pen's attention because of its dominant position on the extreme right: Ordre Nouveau (New Order).

Ordre Nouveau has been called the "most important, the most dynamic and the most dangerous" neofascist movement in France in the postwar period.[43] Ordre Nouveau was established on December 15, 1969, after a series of discussions among the leaders of various extreme right and neofascist groups and after the leaders rejected one suggestion that the new group call itself the "Phalange" (an obvious reference to Spanish and Italian movements of the same name).[44] The group was hardly new, being a direct descendant of Occident and Jeune Nation, both of them violent neofascist movements that drew most of their support from Paris students (most of them male).[45] According to a study of 1,000 members of Ordre Nouveau conducted by François Duprat in 1970, 60 percent of its members were twenty-five years old or less and 80 percent less than forty years old. Fifty-two percent of the members were either high school or university students, and 14 percent were employees. In 1972 Ordre Nouveau published its own figures, which showed that 71 percent of its 3,200 members were less than thirty years old, 44 percent were high school or university students, and 81.5 percent were men.[46]

The new organization set for itself the grandiose objective of "becoming a great party like the Italian Movimento Sociale Italiano [MSI] . . . of becoming a majority and not a minority."[47] By this time two schools of thought about taking power had established themselves on the extreme right: one that questioned the efficacy of violence and advocated working through the orthodox channels of electoral and parliamentary politics; another, a die-hard group, that advocated street violence, inflammatory propaganda, and outrageous publicity stunts in order to destabilize the political system and, it was hoped, bring about an authoritarian government. In the late 1960s and early 1970s the second school still dominated on the extreme right.[48]

In February 1970, following a tried-and-true tactic that held that when an organization was small (at that time Ordre Nouveau had about two hundred members), the best way to attract publicity was to commit an outrageous act that would provoke the left, bring on the police, and make headlines, Ordre Nouveau invited delegates from the German, Italian, Portuguese, Spanish, and Swedish neofascist parties to a mass meeting in Paris. The tactic succeeded. Civil rights and left-wing organizations rose in outrage and threatened to prevent the meeting, while the authorities, fearing a riot, banned it. The result was that by focusing attention on a tiny, unknown group with hardly any following, the authorities and the left opposition helped Ordre Nouveau recruit new members and make itself widely known.

Three months after the group's initial meeting was banned, more than three thousand people attended a May 1970 meeting of various extreme right organizations, including Ordre Nouveau. Guarded by police and by Ordre Nouveau security forces wearing badges with the Celtic cross, the speakers denounced Marxism and capitalism. Heroes of the extreme right were mentioned, including Primo de Rivera, the former leader of the Spanish Phalange; Robert Brassilach; Maurice Bardèche; and, of course, members of the OAS.[49] There were cries of "France for the French," and the audience demanded that existentialist philosopher Jean-Paul Sartre be shot. Many of the delegates greeted with the Hitler salute a representative of the youth movement of the Italian neofascist MSI.[50] Ordre Nouveau called for the formation of a large nationalist party to "defend the West." One Ordre Nouveau leader, François Brigneau, a former member of a fascist militia in Vichy and editor in chief of the extreme right weekly *Minute,* declared, "It is necessary to build a revolutionary party as white as our race, as red as our blood and as green as our hopes."[51] The national secretary of Ordre Nouveau, Jean-François Galvaire, said that "it may be necessary to settle accounts and perhaps erect execution posts."[52] It was necessary, he said, to "'cleanse' France of leftists."[53]

But the biggest obstacle in the way of gaining any influence beyond the narrow confines of the extreme right lay in Ordre Nouveau's addiction to violence. This was due partly to the preponderance of young male students in the organization and partly to the importance of the cult of violence in extreme right ideology. Since the extreme right saw its ultimate objective as the destruction of capitalism and democracy and the establishment of a corporate state directed by an elite at the head of a single party or mass movement, it was difficult to argue that such revolutionary goals could be achieved through democratic means. But some militants were coming around to the view that violence simply did not work. After all, they argued, the best that Ordre Nouveau and similar organizations had achieved was to convince the public that the extreme right stood for violence, thereby alienating the vast majority of the electorate and permanently consigning the movement to the periphery of French politics. The time had come to try something different.

At the organization's June 1972 congress, looking for some way to break out of the "political ghetto where we find ourselves," Ordre Nouveau decided to present "nationalist candidates in the [1973] election under the label 'National Front for a New Order.'" Criticizing "the living fossils who always invoke Nazism," "the royalist sects," and the "last survivors of national-socialism," the movement proposed a new approach. In view of "rising social discontent . . . a large number of French are much more amenable to radical solutions." Ordre Nouveau claimed that: "the only law for a revolutionary is the law of effectiveness: for him, the end really justifies the means and everything ought to be subordinated to the victory of the cause." As a model, Ordre Nouveau took the MSI, which had practiced an "opening to the right" and in alliance with the monarchists had won 8.7 percent of the vote and fifty-six seats in the Italian legislature in the May 1972 elections.[54] It was suggested that Ordre Nouveau follow the MSI model and try to establish alliances with other organizations. To accomplish this, the organization would have to have

total discipline . . . . Every political party must have a true core of steel, a unified and effective center for direction. . . . The Nationalist Revolution is not a
game. . . . It is total and absolute commitment. . . . It is necessary to accept the
formula of the PPF [the Vichyite fascist party led by Jacques Doriot]: "You owe
everything to the Party, the Party owes you nothing." We no longer say that
"power lies at the end of a gun," nor "that power is in the ballot box." We
know that we must take this Power . . . to save the Nation. We are ready to
take on this task by every means. . . . The Revolution consists in totally destroying the old regime and realizing completely the New Order. We are true
revolutionaries because we have decided that this is an absolute necessity,
whatever it costs. Reversing the decadent regime and its servants, transforming
from top to bottom a society collapsing under its defects and its vices[,] we will
build a new world, a world free of exploitation of the worker, a world of
beauty, courage and justice.[55]

For Ordre Nouveau democratic elections were a necessary, and temporarily tiresome, means for taking power.

The Birth of the National Front

To rally the forces of the extreme right, leaders from Ordre Nouveau and
other extreme right organizations met on October 5, 1972, to establish the
National Front.[56] Its central office was composed of six members: Alain
Robert, a veteran of Occident and Ordre Nouveau; François Brigneau, an
obsessively anti-Semitic journalist; Roger Holeindre, a journalist and extreme right activist; Pierre Bousquet, formerly a member of the Waffen-SS;
and Le Pen and his friend Pierre Durand, director of Le Pen's public relations concern. On October 8, 1972, Le Pen was elected president of the NF.
As its symbol, the NF took an urn in which burned a tricolored flame
(copied from the Italian MSI) and the slogan "With us before it is too late."
According to Le Pen, the NF would constitute the heart of the "national,
social and popular opposition."[57]

Soon after the birth of the NF, the extreme right embarked on a radical
recasting of its image.[58] At the first public meeting of the National Front,
on November 7, 1972, a journalist noted that, despite the presence of Ordre
Nouveau members at the meeting, "one would hardly know that they were
there" because of the absence of helmets, weapons, or the Celtic crosses
that were their usual accoutrements. "From all the evidence, the National
Front, even if it leaned on the militant support of the Ordre Nouveau at the
beginning, seems careful to dissociate itself from an image which might risk
disquieting the electorate."[59]

In a December 20, 1972, radio interview, Le Pen was asked about the
presence of Ordre Nouveau in the National Front. "I am not a member of

Ordre Nouveau, although it has one-third representation in the National Front. . . . I can tell you this, however, in no case will the National Front take the initiative, nor accept that its local sections take an initiative which will lead the election battle into violence or the employment of instruments that I reject."[60]

Le Pen had been convinced for a long time that violence led nowhere. One former member of the OAS told journalists Gilles Bresson and Christian Lionet that he had talked with Le Pen about the OAS in 1961 and that Le Pen had said he had reservations about its methods: "Reservations about tactics, not morals."[61] The failure of the OAS to change de Gaulle's Algerian policy and the fact that the organization's tactics isolated the extreme right from mainstream opinion clearly had demonstrated that the route to political power lay in winning elections. The National Front would try the parliamentary road to power. Le Pen described the new party's main objective as beating the Communists and the Gaullists in elections, and he stated that if forced to choose on the second ballot between the left and the Gaullists, he would support the noncommunist left.[62]

Ideas and Policies

Although the National Front soon reverted to the bickering over personalities and ideology that had always plagued the extreme right, Le Pen and his colleagues tried to present a coherent program to the country. Le Pen was particularly insistent that the new party not shirk the right-wing label. "For almost one hundred years in France," he noted, "there was no political party which dared claim to be Right, until in 1972, the National Front decided to define itself as the national, popular and social, right."[63] What did being on the right mean in 1972? "First and above all, a negative reflex; a reaction of defense: refusing the left, its system, its objectives and its program." Being on the right meant an "attachment to traditional values . . . and to our national culture." This meant "a feeling for the land, fidelity to the country, the feeling of sacrifice, love of family, esteem for work well done, a taste for order, authority, hierarchy, attachment to individual liberties, admiration for glory, tenderness for the weak and the oppressed."[64]

The right was committed to private property, distrusted the "Moloch-State," and wanted to limit the state to its essential functions of "arbiter." All this was part of the traditional doctrinal baggage of the right, but Le Pen also claimed as the heritage of the right "respect for nature, pre-eminence of the quality of life . . . decentralization."[65] What is noteworthy here is that from the very inception of the National Front, Le Pen proved highly skilled at incorporating into the Front's doctrine themes that had emerged on, and were associated with, the left. For example, after the May 1968 events provoked widespread criticism of technology and the deleterious effects on society of industrial civilization, Le Pen argued that this fear of "dehumanization" and questioning of progress "offered great hope to the right,"[66] which traditionally had warned against the dangers of materialism and the decline of religion and moral values. Le Pen tried to interpret these issues in extreme right terms, warning against the invasion of the country by uncontrolled immigration and the threat it posed to the "employment, security and the health of the French, and to the independence and national defense of France."[67]

This position was supposed to represent the acceptable face of the extreme right. Nevertheless, for anyone who had paid attention to Le Pen's statements or who had followed the extreme right over the previous few years, there was another, more brutal side to the message. Some years before, during the summer of 1969, there had been fifteen attacks against cafés and rooming houses frequented by North Africans. Stickers bearing the message "Hitler was right" had been found after each attack. When asked about these pro-Hitler sentiments, Le Pen had responded:

Young people need order and purity. At a time when atheism has made formidable progress, there is a resurgence of the need for a moral order whose focus is as great as the decline in morals. Today, young people want certitudes, not problems. From this perspective, the SS with its uniform is like a kind of priest with his cassock. Although he disappeared in the apocalypse of fire, bombs and blood, Hitler's soldier has become a martyr for these young people looking for purity, even if it is the purity of evil. But although the danger of dictatorship persists, Nazism is a dead movement: it is too typically Germanic.[68]

In internal propaganda the Front called immigrants degenerates, delinquents, and criminals. In this the Front was echoing a theme that had emerged in the right-wing newspaper *Minute,* which consistently accused Algerian "riff-raff" of exploiting social security and raping French women.[69] Furthermore, the Front demanded that immigrants who violated the law be expelled immediately from France, and it referred to foreigners and immigrants as a "wild minority."[70] Shortly before the 1973 legislative elections, the NF put forward a program entitled "Defend the French." In contrast to the 1972 party program, which had been aimed at the party faithful, the 1973 election platform was moderate: The NF stood for proportional representation (PR), a European confederation including Great Britain, extension of social services to young people, and defense of private religious schools.[71] The Front even contemplated abortion on authorization of a medical committee.[72] In a letter to *Le Monde,* Le Pen added some details, including the fact that "the National Front is leading a campaign for a tough regulation of foreign immigration and in particular of immigration from outside Europe. It asks, like other modern countries, that immigration be submitted to qualitative and quantitative criteria. This policy aims simultaneously to protect French workers and the dignity of foreign workers who the country really needs."[73]

The 1973 Election and After

Despite promises that the National Front would run candidates for nearly all of the National Assembly's 430 seats, the NF could nominate only 104 candidates. Of these, 13 were Ordre Nouveau leaders, while 20 of the 31 candidates in Paris were Ordre Nouveau members. Among them were some of the most fanatical members of the extreme right in France.[74] The new party did very poorly at the polls, winning only 2.5 percent of the vote and failing to elect a single NF candidate to the National Assembly. Although Le Pen had hinted a few months before that the NF might support the left on the second ballot, on March 6, 1973, he called on voters "to bar the route, at all costs, to the communists."[75] Although the first response of Ordre Nouveau to the defeat was to return to its violent tactics, at the first NF congress in April 1973 Le Pen urged caution. "We must guard against political or physical activism. We must guard against sectarianism."[76] And Le Pen urged that the federated organizations that composed the NF fuse into a unitary structure.[77] Ordre Nouveau rejected Le Pen's suggestion.

At the May 1973 third national congress, Ordre Nouveau stated that "The justification for the National Front is to be a point of assembly, a point of convergence for all national and nationalist opinion. . . . Through its favorable image and its unifying goals, the National Front is the tool best adapted to lead the political battle."[78] In other words, Ordre Nouveau would continue to participate in the Front as long as the Front remained a point of assembly, that is, a federal organization. When Ordre Nouveau scheduled a June meeting under the slogan "Call a Halt to Uncontrolled Immigration," Le Pen protested that too close an identification with an anti-immigration stance would hurt the Front, and he urged its leaders to cancel the meeting. When the meeting degenerated into a violent confrontation between Ordre Nouveau and left-wing movements, the minister of the interior took the opportunity to disband both Ordre Nouveau and the Communist League. There then ensued a heated battle between Le Pen and Ordre Nouveau for control of the National Front. In fall 1973 Le Pen succeeded in evicting Ordre Nouveau from the party.

The death of President Georges Pompidou in April 1974 meant that the presidential election followed hard on the heels of the legislative election. This turn of events also gave Le Pen, who had entered the race for the NF, little time to prepare. Because public attention focused on the conflict between the major contenders, Le Pen's candidacy was generally ignored. His program was summed up in one sentence: "A strong state for a free and fraternal France, capable of evoking respect for its laws defending the French against the threat external threat and subversion."[79] Le Pen's message clearly referred to the Soviet threat from the outside and the internal threat from the Communist Party. Nothing was said about the question of immigration. As part of the official presidential campaign, Le Pen had the right to appear on television. During his programs, he attacked "legal abortion" (contradicting the NF proposal for a medical committee put forward the year before) and the decline in the authority of the family, and he claimed that immigration contributed to a lowering of wages for manual workers.[80]

In view of the disastrous showing at the polls, what did the future hold for the extreme right? Right-wing analysts were pessimistic. According to political scientist Roger Chiroux writing in 1974, it was hard to distinguish between the extreme right and mainstream parties of the right. Whether it was the threat posed by the Communist Party to traditional religious values and to the state; the decline in morals; hostility to progressive priests; support for capitalism (the National Front now wished to reform capitalism, although it rejected neofascist corporatist or anticapitalist ideas); antipathy to socialism or the Soviet Union and world communism, only nuances of opinion separated the extreme from the mainstream right. The major difference seemed to lie in the "way in which problems were presented; the tone used, the polemical vigor [of the extreme right], the provocative air, the personalization of its attacks."[81] With decolonization gone from the political agenda and the evolution of French foreign policy toward a hard anti-Soviet line, the extreme right seemed to have reached a dead end.

Nevertheless, neofascists such as Maurice Bardèche pinned their hopes on a national crisis provoked by the left that would institute "pillage, terror, murder and authoritarian legislation," thereby eliciting a defensive reaction from the right and establishment of a "national opposition." Or there might be a "progressive and happy" evolution of public opinion toward a realization of the dangers from the "Jewish International," which, along with declining confidence in parliamentary democracy, would lead the country in a "healthy direction," that is, toward fascism.[82] On the other side of the political spectrum, questions were also being raised about the nature of French democracy. Writing in *Le Monde* in fall 1973, Professor Roger-Gérard Schwartzenberg noted that the public seemed indifferent to violations of basic liberties and to growing government authoritarianism. The Pompidou government had initiated fifteen hundred to five thousand mainly illegal telephone intercepts; it had dismissed the head of French radio and television because he had complained of government interference, and the authorities seemed indifferent in the face of "racist campaigns against 'uncontrolled immigration.'" All this, combined with the oil crisis occasioned by the Yom Kippur War and growing inflation, could lead to an undermining of public morality, alienation of vulnerable economic classes, and even fascism. According to Schwartzenberg, under the Fifth Republic people were accustomed to thinking of themselves as subjects rather than as participants in the democratic process. Habituated to a charismatic leader who would take decisions in the name of the public, the average citizen had come to rely on authoritarian leaders rather than on his or her own resources and energies to solve political problems. In these conditions, Schwartzenberg warned, what kind of Arturo Ui might begin his "resistible rise" to power?[83]

During the latter part of the 1970s, three of the six extreme right leaders who had formed the National Front, Pierre Bousquet, François Brigneau, and Alain Robert, left after it became clear that Le Pen intended to become the undisputed leader of the NF and that he intended to rid the extreme right of its antidemocratic, revolutionary image. For a brief period the National Front competed with the newly formed Parti des Forces Nouvelles (New Forces Party, or PFN) of Brigneau, Robert, and other extreme right leaders for the allegiance of extreme right supporters. But whereas Le Pen had decided that the extreme right could emerge from its ghetto only by staying clear of entangling alliances with the mainstream right, the PFN threw its lot in with Valéry Giscard d'Estaing during the 1974 presidential election and then fell apart when key members sought to improve their political fortunes by joining mainstream parties of the right. The NF experiment seemed to have ended in failure.

Notes

1. Quoted in Gilles Bresson and Christian Lionet, *Le Pen* (Paris: Seuil, 1994), p. 257.

2. Serge Dumont, Joseph Lorien, and Karl Criton, *Le système Le Pen* (Anvers, Belgium: Éditions EPO, 1985), p. 59.

3. Roger Martin du Gard observed Tixier-Vignancour in the corridors of the Chamber of Deputies in July 1940, "attacking the Jews and lying in wait for the distant and unfortunate Léon Blum in order to insult him again." Roger Martin du Gard, *Chroniques du Vichy, 1940–1944* (Paris: Flammarion, 1975), p. 68.

4. The extreme right historian François Duprat mentioned Tixier-Vignancour along with Pierre Sidos and Albert Heuclin as the founding members. Other founding members were Jacques Sidos, Jacques Wagner, and Jean Marot. François Duprat, *Les mouvements de l'extrême-droite en France* (Paris: Albatros, 1972), p. 56.

5. Tixier-Vignancour was a member of the board of directors of Jeune Nation. Joseph Algazy, *La tentation néo-fasciste en France, 1934–1965* (Paris: Fayard, 1984), p. 127.

6. Philip Williams, *Crisis and Compromise* (Hamden, Conn.: Archon Books, 1964), p. 161.

7. Roger Mauge, *La verité sur Jean-Marie Le Pen* (Paris: Éditions France-Empire, 1988), p. 177.

8. Dumont et al., *Le système*, p. 59.

9. *Le Nouveau Candide*, December 3, 1964, cited in Algazy, *La tentation*, p. 21. Members of the committee were a cross-section of the extreme right, and four of them, Pascal Arrighi, Roger Holeindre, Jean-Marie Le Pen, and Jean-Pierre Reveau, were to become NF deputies in the 1986 election.

10. François Duprat, who was a member of Europe-Action during this period, noted that Le Pen, "different from the others, had a great talent for organization and had decided to establish a true electoral machine." Duprat, *Les mouvements*, p. 128.

11. Le Pen, *Les Français d'abord* (Paris: Carrère/Laffon, 1984), p. 54.

12. A new version of Occident was established in 1964 (an earlier organization with the same name had given rise to Jeune Nation) by dissidents from the Fédération des Éstudiants Nationalistes and was led by Pierre Sidos. The Sidos brothers (Pierre and Jacques) had a history of violence and had long been active on the extreme and neofascist right.

13. Mauge, *La verité*, p. 178.

14. Fondation Nationale des Sciences Politiques, *L'Élection présidentielle des 5 et 19 décembre 1965* (Paris: Armand Colin, 1970), p. 72.

15. Ibid., p. 71.

16. Dumont et al., *Le système*, p. 70.

17. Cited in René Chiroux, *L'extrême-droite sous la Vème République* (Paris: Librairie Générale de Droit et de Jurisprudence, 1974), p. 103.

18. Duprat, *Les mouvements*, p. 131.

19. The French president is elected after two ballots held two weeks apart. If no candidate wins a majority on the first ballot, the top two candidates contest the second, with the candidate with the most votes winning the election. See Chiroux, *L'extrême-droite*, p. 119, on Tixier-Vignancour's electorate.

20. "My only goal was to force General de Gaulle to run on a second ballot. . . . This has happened and I am happy. . . . I will do everything to ensure his defeat." Quoted in Dumont et al., *Le système*, p. 71.

21. Quoted in Emmanuel Faux, Thomas Legrand, and Gilles Perez, *La main droite de Dieu* (Paris: Éditions du Seuil, 1994), p. 34.

22. "An important fraction of the extreme right" supported Lecanuet. Chiroux, *L'extrême-droite*, p. 104.

23. According to one calculation, about 60 percent of the extreme right electorate voted for de Gaulle. Chiroux, *L'extrême-droite*, p. 102.

24. Ibid., p. 93.

25. Le Pen had first established the Cercle du Panthéon in 1959, but it had soon disappeared.

26. Chiroux, *L'extrême-droite*, p. 137.

27. Francis Bergeron and Philippe Vilgier, *De Le Pen à Le Pen* (Bouere: Éditions Dominique Martin Morin, 1986), p. 74.

28. Algazy, *L'Extrême droite en France (1965–1984)* (Paris: L'Harmattan, 1989), p. 56.

29. Quoted in Chiroux, *L'extrême-droite*, p. 151.

30. Ibid.

31. Quoted in ibid., p. 143.

32. By this Roger Mauge meant that Cohn-Bendit was doubly culpable since he was both Jewish and of German nationality. Mauge, *La verité*, p. 188.

33. Quoted in Dumont et al., *Le système*, p. 78.

34. Le Pen, *Les Français*, p. 55.

35. Quoted in Dumont et al., *Le système*, p. 83. For the extreme right, de Gaulle was a traitor because in 1940 he had refused to recognize the armistice signed between Vichy and the Germans.

36. Alain Lancelot and Pierre Weill, "L'évolution politique des électeurs française, de février à juin 1969," *Revue française de science politique* 20, 2 (April 1970):273, 277.

37. Algazy, *L'Extrême droite*, p. 75.

38. Schwartzenberg, cited in Chiroux, *L'extrême-droite*, p. 207.

39. Interview with Professor Hartmut Elsenhans, Paris, March 8, 1971.

40. Ibid.

41. In 1970 Le Pen enrolled as a student in the Faculty of Political Science, taking a course with the famous political scientist Maurice Duverger. Duverger recalled that Le Pen was on his best behavior, and one of his fellow students, Pierre Ceyrac, later to become a high official of the Moonies and a member of the NF, remembered that some of Le Pen's interventions were "remarkable . . . and even impressed Duverger." Quoted in Bresson and Lionet, *Le Pen*, p. 298.

42. Quoted in Mauge, *La verité*, p. 190. Among these groups were Occident, Jeune Révolution (Young Revolution), Group Union Droit (Union Law Group), Jeune Europe (Young Europe), and Fédération d'Action Nationale et Européenne (European and National Action Federation).

43. Algazy, *L'Extrême droite*, p. 88.

44. Among the founding members were Louis Battu, Gérard Boulanger, Jacques Chasse, Jean-Claude Nourry, Alain Robert, Jean-François Galvaire, Philippe Asselin, François Brigneau, François Duprat, Gabriel Jeantet, Claude Joubert, and Paul Leandri. The full name of the organization was Centre de Recherche et de Documentation pour l'Avènement d'un Ordre Nouveau dans les Domaines Social, Économiques et Culturels (Research and Documentation Center for the Coming of a New Order in Cultural, Economic, and Social Areas).

45. Algazy, *L'Extrême droite*, p. 115.

46. François Duprat, *Les mouvements d'extrême-droite en France depuis 1944* (Paris: Albatros, 1972), Appendix XII.

47. Algazy, *L'Extrême droite*, p. 90.

48. For an account of the opposing arguments, see Alain Rollat, *Les hommes de l'extrême-droite* (Paris: Calmann-Lévy, 1985), pp. 49ff.

49. *Le Monde*, May 15, 1970.

50. In January 1995 the MSI rejected anti-Semitism and racism and disavowed its fascist heritage.

51. *Le Monde*, May 15, 1970. This reference was to the MSI colors. The NF took over the MSI symbol but exchanged the green for blue.

52. Quoted in *Le Monde*, May 15, 1970.

53. Quoted in Rollat, *Les hommes*, p. 51.

54. Ordre Nouveau, quoted in Dumont et al., *Le système*, p. 93.

55. Quoted in Rollat, *Les hommes*, pp. 53, 54, 55.

56. According to Gilles Bresson and Christian Lionet, the idea for the National Front was first raised at a December 19, 1971, dinner whose guests included Roger Holeindre, François Brigneau, Maurice Gaït (a former Vichyite youth official), and Claude Joubert (a former member of the OAS). Bresson and Christian, *Le Pen*, p. 237.

57. *Le Monde*, November 9, 1972.

58. Rollat, *Les hommes*, p. 57.

59. *Le Monde*, November 9, 1972.

60. *Le Monde*, December 22, 1972.

61. Quoted in Bresson and Lionet, *Le Pen*, p. 236.

62. *Le Monde*, December 22, 1972.

63. Le Pen, *Les Français*, p. 67.

64. *Le Monde*, December 27, 1972.

65. Ibid.

66. Ibid.

67. *Le Monde*, December 27, 1972.

68. Quoted in *Le Monde*, November 23–24, 1969.

69. Bresson and Lionet, *Le Pen*, p. 296.

70. According to Joseph Algazy, older people might have thought the National Front program was thirty years old because its principles fit the old Vichy slogan "*Travail, Famille, Patrie* [Work, Family, Country]." Algazy, *L'extrême-droite*, p. 118.

71. *Le Monde*, February 2, 1973.

72. Bresson and Lionet, *Le Pen*, p. 364.

73. *Le Monde*, February 27, 1973.

74. Among those nominated were Pierre Bousquet, Roger Holeindre, François Duprat, Alain Robert, José Bruneau, and François Brigneaux.

75. Quoted in *Le Monde*, March 6, 1973.

76. Quoted in Bresson and Lionet, *Le Pen*, p. 365.

77. Ibid.

78. Quoted in Rollat, *Les hommes*, p. 59.

79. Quoted in ibid., pp. 370–371.

80. Bresson and Lionet, *Le Pen*, pp. 366–371.

81. Chiroux, *L'extrême-droite*, pp. 217, 245ff.

82. Quoted in ibid., pp. 261–262.

83. Roger-Gérard Schwartzenberg, "Le malaise français et le virus du fascisme," *Le Monde*, November 27, 1973.

4

Into the Limelight: 1981–1986

Jean-Marie Le Pen is the greatest mystifier I have ever known. Always a little bit of truth, but a cartload of lies.

—Françoise Bernard, quoted in Edwy Plenel and Alain Rollat,
La République menacée

Don't worry about Le Pen, I know him, he's nothing, just a small-town politician. . . . It's a political force like the others. Don't be afraid of the National Front.

—François Mitterrand, quoted in Emmanuel Faux et al.,
La main droite de Dieu

The extreme right has fallen apart. It no longer has any electoral importance. . . . It is today nothing more than an historical relic.

—Jean-Christian Petitfils, L'Extrême droite en France

By 1981 the National Front's fortunes had fallen so low that Le Pen failed to get 500 political notables to sign the nomination petition needed to get his name on the ballot for the May presidential elections.[1] Unwilling to support Rassemblement pour la République (Assembly for the Republic, or RPR) candidate Jacques Chirac, Le Pen called on the electorate to vote for Joan of Arc.

But if 1981 was Year Zero for the extreme right, it was annus mirabilis for the left. In the May 1981 presidential election, Socialist leader François Mitterrand narrowly beat Valéry Giscard d'Estaing, winning 51.8 percent of the vote to Giscard's 48.2 percent. A month later, rashly promising a "break (*rupture*) with capitalism," the Socialists and their left radical allies won a clear majority of the seats in the elections for the National Assembly.

The Communists suffered a serious setback, winning only forty-four seats and losing forty-two.

With a secure majority in the legislature and with Mitterrand in the presidency, the united forces of the left embarked on the most radical program of economic and social change in France since the immediate postwar period. The government nationalized thirty-six private banks and some of the leading electronics, chemical, glass, and textile companies and increased substantially the level of old-age pensions, child allowances, and housing subsidies.[2] By extending the government's control over the commanding heights of the economy and by pouring money into the economy, the left hoped to stimulate production in key industries, increase the number of jobs, and raise tax revenues.

As early as the first year of the government's tenure, however, Socialist reflationary policies drove the value of the franc to unsustainable heights, forced interest rates to a record level, and led to increased inflation. Under immense pressure from foreign markets, the government was forced to devalue the franc. But the trade deficit continued to increase, investment fell, and the government moved from a surplus position of Fr 2.9 billion in 1980 to a deficit of Fr 61.2 billion in 1982. Even more damaging for a Socialist government was the increase in unemployment by 17.2 percent from 1980 to 1982. To control inflation and restore confidence in the economy, the Socialists made a U-turn in 1982–1983, embarking on a program of public expenditure cuts, wage and price controls, and further devaluations within the exchange-rate mechanism. By 1983 the increase in gross domestic product was down to 0.7 percent compared to 1.8 percent in 1982, and unemployment had risen from 5.2 percent in 1976–1980 to 8.6 percent in 1983.

In the midst of economic crisis, the Socialists found themselves embroiled in controversy over immigration policy. Mitterrand's 1981 campaign proposal to give immigrants the vote in local elections had been widely condemned by the entire French right and even by some factions on the left. According to psephologist Eric Dupin: "The French have never liked immigrants, and for a long time have nourished a particular hostility toward those who came from the Maghreb. . . . It isn't the 'crisis' that has created racism and xenophobia. . . . Economic difficulties have simply reactivated latent feelings in French society."[3]

Breakthrough

Then suddenly, the National Front made a surprising breakthrough. In 1983 NF secretary general Jean-Pierre Stirbois and three NF colleagues were elected to the Dreux municipal council in an election that caught the attention of the country and revived the flagging fortunes of the National Front.

Dreux is a small city located east of Paris with a largely working-class population of thirty-five thousand, of whom 25 percent are foreign-born. According to former Socialist mayor Françoise Gaspard, Dreux had provided a home to successive waves of immigrants, including Italian and Spanish refugees from fascism during the 1930s, Bretons searching for work in the 1950s and 1960s, and immigrants from North Africa, Turkey, Spain, and Portugal.[4] Although earlier waves of immigrants often found steady work in nearby factories or industries, by the 1970s economic stagnation had led to growing unemployment. At the same time, recent immigrants were housed on the outskirts of the city in enormous, poorly maintained housing estates, isolated from the rest of the population, which, in turn, was often ignorant of the immigrants' existence except when youths from the estates ran into trouble with the law. According to Gaspard, who grew up in Dreux, "Merchants with stores on the Grande Rue told me that they had never heard of the Les Bregeronnettes [housing estate] less than two miles away as the crow flies."[5]

By 1990, sixteen years after the government had ended the free flow of immigrants, the number of foreigners in Dreux had doubled. Sixty-seven nationalities were represented, with Moroccans, Turks, Portuguese, and Algerians making up the majority. Exactly how many of these possessed French nationality was not clear, although many of the Algerians certainly were French citizens. But Gaspard claimed that Dreux was not drastically different from a myriad of French cities and towns that had become home to increasing numbers of immigrants and that faced social problems because of rising unemployment and economic change.

Although Mayor Gaspard had vigorously campaigned to integrate immigrants into society and had succeeded in making the city generally free of racial tension and ethnic conflict, Stirbois had been assiduously campaigning for years in working-class areas, stirring up opposition to the immigrants. His message was simple: Immigrants caused unemployment and undermined law and order According to Stirbois, the Socialists coddled immigrants, while the mainstream right—namely, the RPR, led by Chirac, and the Union pour la Démocratie Française (Union for French Democracy, or UDF), a coalition of centrist parties whose titular head was former President Valéry Giscard d'Estaing—avoided the issue. Only the National Front had the courage to tackle the issue head on by developing specific policies aimed at coping with the immigrant "problem."

Stirbois was not new to Dreux, having run for office there almost continually since the 1978 legislative election, when he campaigned on a platform devoted almost exclusively to the dangers of immigration and the need for increased security. A veteran of extreme right organizations, and no stranger to violence, Stirbois was accompanied by militants wearing combat boots and hoods. When questioned about the gear, Stirbois replied: "My supporters wearing boots and helmets? It was cold. . . . Should our people have to go barefoot?"[6] In the 1978 election he won a derisory 2 percent of the vote. A year later Stirbois was back again, campaigning in the 1979 cantonal elections, turning up at opponents' meetings with his thugs and throwing eggs at the assembled candidates. Again he focused on immigration and security, and again he lost.

Undaunted, both Stirbois and his wife, Marie-France Stirbois, unsuccessfully ran for office during the 1982 cantonal elections. During the campaign, a mimeographed pamphlet mysteriously appeared in the constituency. Purporting to be a copy of a letter from an Algerian living in France to his friend "Mustapha," who still lived in Algeria, it read: "Dear Mustapha. By the grace of all-powerful Allah we have become the lords and masters of Paris. I wonder why you hesitate to join us. . . . Your presence here is indispensable, and who knows if you might not be elected to our future council of émigrés. Come soon. Lots of us await your arrival, because Mitterrand has promised to grant us the right to vote very soon now. We kicked the French out of Algeria. Why shouldn't we do the same thing here?"[7]

No one took responsibility for this "letter."[8] This time Stirbois won 12.6 percent of the vote, and his wife, who ran in a neighboring canton, won 9.6 percent. Meanwhile, the mainstream right saw that anti-immigrant sentiment was mounting. Alain Juppé, an associate of RPR leader Jacques Chirac (and currently prime minister under President Chirac), claimed that there was a link among "clandestine immigration, delinquency and criminality." A pamphlet put out by three mainstream right parties stated, "It is necessary to stop this invasion."[9] The Giscardian mayor of Toulon (which elected a National Front mayor in 1995) said that his city should "refuse to be the trash can of Europe."[10] In the March 1983 election for the Dreux municipal council, the Socialist list headed by Mayor Gaspard won by only eight votes.[11] The losers appealed to the courts, and new elections were ordered for September 4, 1983. By this time Stirbois had changed his tactics. He now appeared at election meetings and rallies without the provocatively garbed militants of previous elections, and the radical rhetoric had been toned down. But if the tune had changed, the song was the same: Immigrants were the source of all France's economic and social problems. Stirbois called for a halt to immigration, attacked "laxity," and warned "immigrants from outside the Mediterranean: return to your huts."[12]

In the first round of the Dreux by-election, Stirbois received 16.72 percent of the vote. Now wild rumors began to circulate: Eight hundred Turks were about to arrive in Dreux because the mayor had built a factory for them; the mayor had authorized the construction of a mosque in one of the housing estates; the mayor was hiding a baby that she had with a Moroccan. A journalist from the left-wing weekly *Le Nouvel Observateur* recounted how salesmen began to appear in a poor quarter of the city peddling expensive tape recorders, hi-fi sets, and jewelry: "Good day madame, are you interested? No? Too bad! Your neighbor (Mohammed, Miloud or Yusef) has two of them. I'm not kidding: thanks to Madame Gaspard, the Arabs around here earn more than the French."[13]

After Stirbois's surprisingly good showing on the first ballot, the mainstream right suddenly discovered that the National Front was not the pariah it had thought. Whereas ex-RPR cabinet minister Simone Veil, one of France's most popular politicians, said she would abstain on the second ballot if she voted in Dreux, RPR national leader Jacques Chirac quoted political theorist Raymond Aron, who said, "Four National Front members on the opposition list in Dreux is not the same as four Communists in the Cabinet," an obvious reference to the Communist ministers in the 1981 Socialist government.[14] Politicians from the mainstream right argued that there were excellent reasons for concluding a temporary election alliance with the National Front. As one deputy from the Giscardian UDF put it: "If I were a Dreux voter, I would not abstain. To do so would make oneself an objective ally of the communists and socialists."[15]

With the RPR and the UDF inviting Stirbois to join their list for the second ballot, the joint list of the right won the election in September with 54.33 percent of the vote. Stirbois was elected to the municipal council and subsequently became the assistant mayor of Dreux. Although the Dreux election took place on a local political stage, the tergiversations of the traditional right-wing parties in negotiating with the Front and Stirbois's ultimate success attracted the attention of the national media. Le Pen observed that the "excellent results" meant that the NF was the "third element of the opposition. . . . Immigration and insecurity are not problems specific to Dreux but for a long time will be problems felt by people in hundreds of cities."[16]

Despite the intense media coverage and the enormous controversy provoked by the election, Stirbois's 1983 election victory should have come as no surprise. The NF victory was the culmination of years of politicking, propagandizing, organizing, and intense self-criticizing. In local council elections the previous March, Le Pen had won 11.26 percent of the vote on the first ballot and 8.54 on the second, an impressive score for the extreme right. However, Dreux was different. According to *Le Monde,* Dreux was "a success of national importance."[17]

Most observers agreed that the key to Stirbois's success in Dreux lay in his hard-line attacks on North African immigrants and on the "laxity" of French immigration policy. But, as Le Pen himself put it, the NF had been talking about the "problem" of immigration for ten years. Why, then, did the NF's message on immigration suddenly find a receptive audience? There were a number of reasons.

The 1981 Socialist victory had thrown the mainstream right into opposition for the first time in twenty-five years. Desperate to counterattack, many elements on the mainstream right were willing to conclude election alliances with the extreme right if it made the difference between defeat and victory. The National Front, for its part, eagerly sought these alliances in order to present itself as a legitimate component of the French right-wing opposition. *Le Monde* journalist Alain Rollat claimed that the admittance of Front candidates to the joint election list in Dreux had "legitimated the electoral pretensions of a formation which aspires to become the indispensable support for the two main parties of the opposition."[18]

In the mid-1980s the Front benefited as well from the rising popularity of the right. From 1981 to 1986 the percentage of French voters classifying themselves as on the right increased from 31 to 36 percent, while among those who supported the Gaullists and Giscardians, there was an increasing percentage who supported neoconservative and even reactionary positions.[19] During this time, liberal and neoconservative ideas popularized by Ronald Reagan and Margaret Thatcher had begun to win a following in France, with the result that the Front's policies looked less extreme in 1983 than a few years before, when Socialism had been so popular.

With anti-immigrant sentiment growing and the Socialist economic program in trouble, the Socialists had to backpedal on the idea of granting immigrants the right to vote in local elections.[20] Government spokesmen now stated that immigrants would not be given that right. In 1982 the Socialists decided not to release a brochure on immigrants for fear of an adverse reaction.[21] As one observer put it, "Mr. Le Pen is in the process of winning, not at the ballot box, nor in the public opinion polls . . . but more quietly, the extreme right is progressing within people's heads."[22]

The French were becoming increasingly cynical about politics and politicians. In a 1984 poll 62 percent of respondents expressed themselves as dissatisfied with the way in which "politicians treat the important subjects which concerned the life of the French," while 82 percent were convinced that politicians did not speak the truth.[23] In these circumstances it is not surprising that some portions of the electorate turned toward the National Front, which, never having been in power, could not be accused of having compromised its ideals.[24]

The Front also picked up support from people whose jobs or careers were at risk amid rising inflation and unemployment and who were disoriented by the radical changes that had occurred after the Socialist victories in 1981.[25] According to Françoise Gaspard, the Dreux election provided the voters with "the opportunity to issue a warning to the government in power. . . . The tactics and rhetoric of the new majority had at first sur-

prised and soon irritated many, even among its own electorate. Frenetic reforms had failed to improve the daily lives of citizens, especially since early
hopes of a major redistribution of wealth had given way . . . to austerity
under Jacques Delors's stabilization program."26

In addition, the election system provided the Front with opportunities
that were lacking in a first-past-the-post system. For municipal elections the
French use a complicated mix of a two-ballot list system and PR.27 Since a
party's fortunes depend to a certain extent on the number of allies it can recruit to its list, municipal elections provide a chance for small parties like
the NF to attach their fortunes to like-minded larger parties. Proportional
representation also favors small parties because each political party gets the
same percentage of seats in the legislature as the percentage it wins in the
election. Once a party crosses a certain minimum threshold of votes, it is
sure to win a seat. Thus, whereas winning less than 20 percent of the vote
in an American- or a British-style election would be no cause for celebration (or alarm), in France the 16.72 percent of the votes cast for the
National Front on the first ballot in the 1983 Dreux election provided a
springboard for the NF candidate to win a seat on the municipal council on
the second ballot.

The Left, the Right, and the National Front

In late 1994 three young French journalists, Emmanuel Faux, Thomas
Legrand, and Gilles Perez, published *La main droite de Dieu* (The right
hand of God), which argued that President Mitterrand deliberately boosted
the fortunes of the National Front in order to split the mainstream right.
On June 22, 1982, for example, after having received a letter from Le Pen
protesting the fact that French television did not cover NF conventions,
Mitterrand notified the minister of communications of this lapse. Seven
days later Le Pen was invited to appear on the evening television news. The
following September Le Pen appeared several times on radio and television.
By 1983 Le Pen was on his way to becoming a media star and a sought-
after guest on political interview programs. Of course, his appeal as a media
personality was enhanced by his consummate skill as a debater and self-
publicist. According to Faux, Legrand, and Perez, "Contrary to all logic,
the media rise of Jean-Marie Le Pen preceded his electoral success: recogni-
tion before legitimacy."28 Although Mitterrand defended his decision to
give Le Pen airtime as in conformity with the principle of political "pluralism," this pluralism did not extend to minor parties and personalities on the
extreme left. Close associates of Mitterrand stated that the president's policy of advancing the fortunes of the National Front was a deliberate ploy
aimed at splitting the mainstream right. One Socialist friend of Mitterrand

said: "Without Le Pen, the left would not have stayed in power for 10 years. Mitterrand is a wonderful tactician—a champion. It's the rule, you know, to divide one's enemies. If you are on the left, you can't disagree with that."[29]

Although Mitterrand was not averse to giving Le Pen airtime in order to advance the Socialist cause, the mainstream right had its own strategy for dealing with the extreme right. Since 1945 the mainstream right had always discounted the threat from the extreme right, secure in the knowledge that whatever party or movement popped up, it soon fell to quarreling and, ultimately, collapsed. Of course, the mainstream right carefully nurtured this self-destructive impulse by offering to disillusioned or ambitious members of the extreme right the tempting possibilities of office, privilege, and power if they joined the mainstream. Nor was the mainstream right averse to using the extreme right for shady operations when doing so suited its purposes. There is some evidence that under Giscard the government security services used members from Ordre Nouveau to burgle Communist and Trotskyite offices in the 1970s, and Giscard d'Estaing did rely on Ordre Nouveau for his security service during the 1974 presidential election.[30]

However, the willingness of the mainstream right to establish an election alliance with the NF candidate in Dreux, and the growing criticism of the Socialist's immigration policy, helped legitimize Le Pen and the National Front in the eyes of the public. According to Françoise Gaspard, the NF succeeded because "for the first time since the war [a part of the right] accepted an alliance with the extreme right."[31]

In November 1983, a few months after the Dreux breakthrough, the National Front again contested a local election, this time in the Paris suburb of Aulnay-sur-Bois. The NF candidate, Guy Viarengo, entered the race with a program under the slogan "*Ras-le-bol* [Fed up to the teeth]": "Fed up with lack of security, unemployment, fiscal billy-clubbing, communist frauds . . . and the politics of lies and the ruin of the left." Viarengo received 9.32 percent of the vote, but the moderate success of this campaign convinced Le Pen that the NF could attract votes through what Alain Rollat called a "neo-poujadist rejection of left-wing politics . . . as well as anti-parliamentarism."[32]

In January 1984 Le Pen announced that the NF would enter the European elections scheduled for the following June. By now the NF's victory at Dreux had focused national attention on the party and particularly on its controversial leader. During the early part of 1984, Le Pen was interviewed on the radio three times; on February 13, 1984, he appeared on the popular *The Hour of Truth* television program. Accused by journalists of being a racist and anti-Semite, Le Pen referred to himself as a "Churchillian democrat" and warned against the threat posed by two hegemonies: "Soviet hegemony, but also the hegemony deriving from the demographic explosion of the Third World and in particular in the Arab-Islamic world which currently is penetrating our country and progressively colonizing it."[33]

Asked how he responded when he heard or read anti-Semitic remarks, Le Pen replied: "Listen, I have said it several times, but I will repeat it. If anti-Semitism consists in persecuting Jews because of their religion or their race, I am certainly not an anti-Semite. . . . But I don't believe I am obliged to like the Veil law [on abortion], to admire Chagall's paintings or to approve Mendès-France's policies."[34] Of course, Le Pen's response was duplicitous—anti-Semitism can take a number of forms that fall far short of actual persecution; insulting or racist remarks like those that appear in the pro-Front press, for example, count as anti-Semitism, but the panel did not take Le Pen up on this. In any case Le Pen's appearance on national television was considered a success, and a subsequent poll showed that the number of people intending to vote for the NF had doubled, from 3.5 percent to 7 percent.[35]

Immigration and the Campaign

The Front's first election program, in 1973, devoted only six lines to immigration policy: "The National Front demands that an end be put to the absurd policy which allows uncontrolled immigration in disastrous moral and material conditions for those concerned and for our country. . . . The establishment of foreign areas or cities in France [is] an explosive element and one that puts at risk the unity and the solidarity of our people."[36] One year later, during the presidential election campaign, Le Pen attacked abortion, nationalization, bureaucracy, and the "fiscal inquisition." He also called for restrictions on the right to strike in the public sector; defense of the family, law and order, and moral values; and reform of the electoral system through the return of proportional representation. The Front did not raise the question of immigration, and it was hardly mentioned in the right-wing press.[37]

By the late 1970s, however, the issue of immigration policy was becoming controversial, and Le Pen and the NF began to develop an anti-immigrant campaign. On March 12, 1978, Le Pen wrote an article for *Le Monde* entitled "Against Immigration." "For some months," he said, "the National Front has mounted a very active campaign against immigration, and it has based its electoral activities on this problem." According to Le Pen, the solution to unemployment was to immediately stop all immigration and repatriate 2 million foreign workers to their countries of origin. Putting "France and the French first," said Le Pen, was the essence of the National Front's program. These two themes—the linking of unemployment to immigration and the claim that the National Front was the only party to put French interests first—were to become the centerpieces of the

National Front program and have remained so ever since. Over the years the message has been elaborated and refined, but its essence is based on a simple syllogism:

- There are 3, 4, 5, or 6 million immigrants in France (the figures vary).
- Immigrants are the source of every problem from acquired immune deficiency syndrome (AIDS) to unemployment.
- Therefore, to solve these problems, immigrants must be encouraged or forced to emigrate.

Alluding to Hitler's concept of *Lebensraum,* or "living space" (*éspace vital*), Le Pen remarked: "The nation is becoming empty [he was referring to the declining birthrate]. Nature fears a vacuum and this vacuum will be filled. It is already in the process of being filled by immigration. So what is at stake is the independence of France, even its existence. As far I am concerned, I propose a family policy that will allow France to survive."[38] In a *Le Monde* interview he was asked: "Your campaign is based on the 'hexagonal slogan' [the hexagon refers to France], 'The French above all!' Isn't that paradoxical in a European election? In your opinion, is this election only concerned with domestic politics?" In reply, he commented that for three years the Communists and Socialists in government had set about changing society and that people wanted to use the European elections as a vehicle for expressing their opinions about domestic policy.[39]

Driving home the putative link between immigration and security, Le Pen said, "Insecurity has been considerably aggravated by immigration."[40] The problem was, he claimed, that many immigrants who had been unemployed in their own countries had come to France knowing "perfectly well that they would not find work" and then resorted to thefts, the drug trade, and "attacks on old women."[41] The solution was not more policemen but people who respected the law and authorities who imposed harsh penalties.

The 1986 Election and Cohabitation

In 1985 the Socialists were in a quandary. Since the mechanics of the French two-ballot electoral system meant that a party that won a plurality of the vote or a bare majority overall could still win a disproportionately large number of seats in the National Assembly, public opinion polls indicating a victory for the right in the upcoming elections seemed to threaten the end of the Socialist government. Something had to be done to stave off catastrophe.

The response from President Mitterrand was effective and cynical: He decided to change from a two-ballot, first-past-the-post electoral system to one based on proportional representation. At one stroke this completely altered the nature of the election game. Under PR, political parties are awarded the same proportion of seats in the legislature as they win in the election. In the French multiparty system, where the average voter can choose among an array of left, right, and center parties, this means that each party does everything it can to sharpen its image and to convince the voter that it and it alone represents the left, right, or center in French politics.

PR calls for a completely different election strategy from what is practiced under a two-ballot system. The two-ballot system puts a premium on alliances and on the blurring of differences between parties. Proportional representation drives parties apart and puts a premium on the drawing of sharp distinctions among them. The implementation of proportional representation meant that Giscard's Republican Party and Chirac's RPR would compete against each other for the support of mainstream right voters. Mitterrand was also well aware that under proportional representation a minor party like the National Front would win more seats in the legislature than under the two-ballot system. But against this, he set the great advantage that the extreme right and mainstream right would spend their time quarreling with each other, that the vote would split three or four ways on the right, and that the Socialists, who had fallen in the public opinion polls, were certain to win more seats than if the election were held under the two-ballot, single-member constituency system.

The mainstream right reacted angrily at what seemed an obvious attempt by the Socialists to snatch its chestnuts out of the fire and deprive the mainstream right of certain victory. The National Front, however, was overjoyed with the change in electoral system. Having won around 10 percent of the vote in recent elections, the party would win few, if any seats, under the two-ballot system.[42] But under PR 10 percent of the vote would win the party about 10 percent of the seats (which meant forty seats) in the legislature. After a heated debate in the National Assembly, where a member of the Giscardian UDF accused the Socialists of committing "the original sin" of wanting to escape from popular sovereignty, the electoral law was passed and implemented.[43]

The subsequent election campaign was marked by a low level of controversy between the Socialists and the mainstream right parties, especially as the Socialists had largely abandoned the anticapitalist rhetoric of the previous years. In view of mounting economic difficulties during the early 1980s, the Socialists had backpedaled from their promise to "break with capitalism" and had begun to praise individual initiative, private enterprise, and the market. Of course, the Socialists had not converted to neoliberalism, but during the latter part of their term the government had promoted private enterprise, abandoned lame duck industries, made financing more flexible, and installed modern management methods in hospitals and the social security system. The Socialists even won the praise of the *Wall Street Journal,* the *Financial Times,* and *The Economist* for their new economic policies.[44]

Opinion polls conducted during the election campaign showed that as disillusioned as the French might have been about the Socialists and their grandiose schemes for curing the ills of French society, French voters were not about to abandon Socialist social welfare policies and embrace Thatcherite (in this case, Chiracian) ideas on the efficacy of the market. Although a majority of voters favored reducing the level of state intervention in the economy, letting businesses freely set prices, and reducing taxes for social security and social welfare, 69 percent opposed reducing taxes on large incomes. Large majorities opposed reducing the duration and levels of unemployment benefits, eliminating the minimum salary, limiting social security benefits, or eliminating social security compensation for minor illnesses. As one observer put it, "Liberalism for businesses—Yes; liberalism for social actors: No!"[45]

As the campaign progressed, it became clear that the mainstream parties of the right were in a difficult situation. Although popular sentiment was running in their favor, the fact that the Socialists had moved to the right prevented the opposition from painting them as wholeheartedly and disastrously committed to outmoded ideas on nationalization and statism. At the same time, the mainstream right endeavored to create some distance between it and the National Front. Of course, the mainstream right might have reacted to the electoral threat from the Front by parroting its ideas on immigration and security, but in turn Le Pen would have responded, as he had in the past, that the voters might as well support the "original rather than the copy." Thus, the Gaullists and Giscardians emphasized issues such as employment, the economy, or cohabitation (referring to the question of how a Socialist president would get along with a centrist prime minister) and ignored immigration and security, two issues with which the National Front was closely associated.[46] In winter 1985–1986 centrist leader and former Prime Minister Raymond Barre said that "immigration should not be a stake in the electoral game," and Jacques Chirac stated that he would not form an alliance with a racist party. At the same time, however, catching the mood of Front supporters, the mainstream right accused the Socialists of laxity toward criminals and illegal immigrants, while an RPR spokesperson, responding to Raymond Barre's statement that France was a multicultural society, said, "Multiracial France exists, but our country is not inclined toward pluriculturalism."[47]

The results of the 1986 election confirmed the polls: The Socialist list won 30.8 percent of the vote, the Communists won 9.7 percent, and the combined forces of the mainstream right won 42.1 percent of the vote and took 286 seats in the National Assembly, just short of a majority. With support from some of the smaller right-wing parties, RPR leader Jacques Chirac became prime minister. The Front won 9.8 percent of the vote and 35 seats in the National Assembly. The National Front's 2.7 million votes confirmed its position as a major party on the French scene, and its 35 seats in the National Assembly gave the extreme right, for the first time since 1945, a nationwide forum in which to express its views.

The National Front Electorate

Surveys of NF voters confirmed the findings of previous years. The NF electorate was predominantly male, with 53 percent of its vote coming from male voters. NF voters were also young: The NF and the left were tied with 39 percent of their vote coming from people eighteen to thirty-four years of age. Moreover, the profile of NF voters looked more like that of the Socialists than of the mainstream right: 24 percent identified themselves as either middle-level professionals or employees, 26 percent as workers, and 21 percent as inactive or retired. In contrast, the Gaullists and Giscardians drew 36 percent of their support from inactive or retired people and only 16 percent from workers and 19 percent from middle-level professionals or employees.

However, there was one feature that distinguished the Socialist/Communist electorate from the right-wing (including the National Front) electorate: the voters' relation to state employment. Of those salaried employees who voted Socialist, 44 percent worked for the state; of the salaried employees who voted for the NF, only 23 percent worked for the state.

Two additional features distinguished the electorates of the mainstream right from that of the National Front. The first was the voters' relationship to the Catholic Church. Whereas 51 percent of mainstream right voters were either regular or occasional practitioners of the Catholic faith, fully 59 percent of those who voted for the National Front identified themselves as nonpracticing Catholics. The second, and most important, factor was the disproportionate weight Front voters accorded to immigration and insecurity as the most important issues of the day. Sixty percent of National Front voters, as opposed to 7–16 percent of non-NF voters, stated that immigration influenced their vote; and 50 percent of NF voters stated that insecurity motivated their vote, compared to 10–31 percent for other parties.[48]

According to one French psephologist, the NF was supported by an "electorate of rejection and despair," an electorate "literally obsessed by the twin themes of immigration and insecurity."[49]

The National Front in the National Assembly

During the first few months of the 1986 legislature, the NF deputies (whose parliamentary group was called the Rassemblement National) zealously followed the rules and customs of the National Assembly.[50] But as time passed, some of them began to resort to insulting and unparliamentary language. NF deputy Jean-Claude Martinez, a university professor and expert on tax policy, when reporting the education budget to the legislature explained that the "failure of national education" resulted from "the [sexual] coupling of teachers and unionists, the perverts of national education and the flops from teaching." He referred to "teaching establishments as places of perversion" and to some of the personnel as "pathogens having escaped radiation."[51] During a speech on February 13, 1987, about AIDS, National Front deputy Dr. François Bachelot, assistant secretary general of the National Federation of Electro-radiologists, warned "Africans" that "they couldn't do everything in their sexual life" and "Israelites" to beware of "circumcision and . . . razors."

Why would the civil servants, journalists, lawyers, and professionals who composed the NF parliamentary group use such language? According to Guy Birenbaum, "moderns" such as Jean-Claude Martinez, Dr. François Bachelot, and Bruno Mégret used extremist language as "a kind of initiation rite, which demonstrated the reality and the force of their membership [in the extreme right]."[52] By contrast, "ancients" such as Le Pen or journalist Roger Holeindre had spent most of their political life within the extreme right and did not have to prove their credentials or play to populist sentiments. The newly elected NF deputies felt compelled to signal that they, like their leader, were not part of the prevailing elite culture and would not conform to the traditional rules of political discourse. Thus, the vulgar directness of the Front discourse was meant to distinguish Front deputies from those of the mainstream political parties and to demonstrate that Front deputies could speak in terms that the ordinary citizen could understand.

This argument had been put forward in more theoretical terms by Yvan Blot in 1985. According to Blot, it is important to distinguish between "technocratic" or "serious" language and "demagogic" or more popular language, which is generally thought to be inferior. Contrary to popular belief, however, Blot argued that a denigration of populist language reveals "contempt" for human nature because "feelings, sentiments and passions are not necessarily dishonorable." At the right time and place, therefore, there is nothing wrong with using populist language to "demystify" the opposition when one is addressing "man in his totality."[53] This kind of logic removes any limits whatsoever on the use of emotional, vulgar, or populist language—as long as one takes account of man in his totality.

But on one occasion Front deputies crossed the line that separated extremist language from violent action. On the evening of October 9–10, 1987, the National Assembly was practically empty, with only eight members from the government present. This was not unusual since French deputies, like their counterparts in legislatures throughout the Western world, have great demands placed on their time: They must serve on parliamentary committees, maintain contact with their constituencies, and, in the case of France, where deputies are permitted to hold local political office, attend to their municipal duties. On this occasion the Chirac government had tacked onto a bill dealing with the drug trade two amendments condemning incitations to racism and criminalizing justifications of crimes against humanity. The NF members, enraged by this move and seeing that on this particular evening they outnumbered government deputies, went on a rampage, running behind deputies' desks and turning the keys that actuated the electronic voting system. When Paris RPR deputy Françoise de Panfieur tried to stop National Front member Pierre Descaves, he brusquely shoved her aside. At the same time, two members of the National Front pushed their way toward the president of the Assembly and harassed him as he attempted to control the situation.

For ten hours during that night and early morning, there was pandemonium in the National Assembly as Le Pen and his colleagues heaped insults on the other deputies and deluged the president of the chamber with amendments denouncing abortion, the "Katyn massacre," "Budapest," and the "massacre of the harkis."[54]

The following day even the normally supportive *Le Figaro* strongly condemned the NF's tactics, noting that "the degrees of difference between democracy and dictatorship are limited in number, and in attacking the first one can arrive very quickly—consciously or not—at apologizing for totalitarianism."[55] Le Pen responded: "In the face of the political class which betrays the will of the people, the National Front puts itself forward as the defender of the interests of the French people. ... Beyond questions of procedure, the National Front is conscious that by its actions in the National Assembly it acts in the name of the people, with the people and for the people."[56]

Had the unacceptable face of the Front suddenly appeared from behind its mask of moderation? There were no further incidents of this kind provoked by the Front, but then the legislature lasted only a scant two years. Exactly how the Front deputies might have behaved if the term had been four or five years is impossible to say. Clearly, however, the disrespect demonstrated by this incident was well in keeping with the extreme right ideology of hostility to parliament. Whatever the Front's intentions may have been at the time, the NF hardly made an impact on the National Assembly before being rudely evicted from office.

Notes

1. He collected only 434 signatures. Gilles Bresson and Christian Lionet, *Le Pen* (Paris: Seuil, 1994), p. 398.

2. Peter A. Hall, "The Evolution of Economic Policy Under Mitterrand," in George Ross et al., *The Mitterrand Experiment* (Oxford: Basil Blackwell, 1987), pp. 54–72.

3. Eric Dupin, *Oui, non, sans opinion* (Paris: Interéditions, 1990), p. 219. Dupin pointed out that regardless of economic class, a clear majority of French were opposed to foreigners. Moreover, xenophobia increased as one moved from the professions to the working class.

4. Françoise Gaspard, *A Small City in France* (Cambridge, Mass.: Harvard University Press, 1995), pp. 44ff.

5. Ibid., p. 60.

6. Quoted in ibid., pp. 109–110.

7. Quoted in ibid., p. 117.

8. This same technique was used against Jewish Socialist leader Léon Blum. In 1925 an anti-Semitic writer using the pseudonym Jacob Nathan Hourwitz wrote a letter purportedly from the Soviet Union advising Blum to practice "vivesection on reactionaries" as well as cannibalism. Pierre Birnbaum, *Un mythe politique: "La République juive"* (Paris: Fayard, 1988), p. 274.

9. Quoted in Edwy Plenel and Alain Rollat, *La République menacée* (Paris: Le Monde Éditions, 1992), p. 91.

10. Quoted in ibid.

11. The 1983 municipal elections were run under a proportional representation law introduced by the Socialist government—which meant that a minority party such as the National Front now had a better chance than before to elect a member to a municipal council.

12. Quoted in Bresson and Lionet, *Le Pen*, p. 399.

13. Quoted in Gaspard, *A Small City*, p. 124.

14. Quoted in Serge Dumont, Joseph Lorien, and Karl Criton, *Le système Le Pen* (Anvers, Belgium: Éditions EPO, 1985), p. 191.

15. Gilbert Gantier, UDF deputy from Paris, quoted in *Le Monde*, September 7, 1983.

16. *Le Monde*, September 7, 1983.

17. *Le Monde*, September 5, 1983.

18. *Le Monde*, September 14, 1983.

19. Piero Ignazi, "Un nouvel acteur politique," in Nonna Mayer and Pascal Perrinneau, *Le Front national à découvert* (Paris: Presses de la Fondation National des Sciences Politiques, 1989), pp. 67–69.

20. In a 1983 opinion poll, 51 percent of those polled agreed that returning immigrant workers "back from where they came" was the best solution to unemployment. *Le Monde*, September 9, 1983.

21. Gaspard, *A Small City*, p. 178.

22. Edwy Plenel, in *Le Monde*, September 10, 1983.

23. Cited in Mayer and Perrineau, *Le Front national*, p. 75.

24. Writing in 1992, Alain Rollat asked: "What happened in France in 1982–83 that was so extraordinary that the National Front suddenly captured the attention of so many voters . . . ? Nothing." For Rollat, the sudden surge of the NF was due to disappointed hopes after the enormous Socialist victory in 1981 and the temporary disarray of the mainstream right following that victory. *Le Monde*, February 4, 1992.

25. According to psephologist Jérôme Jaffré: "Behind the tension over immigration is hidden the drama of unemployment and the consequences of the crisis which exacerbates the reactions of part of the electorate disoriented by the helplessness of the political class, whether right or left, to resolve its problems. In the National Front electorate the themes of unemployment and purchasing power therefore assume growing importance." *Le Monde*, May 26, 1987.

26. Gaspard, *A Small City*, p. 155.

27. Alistair Cole and Peter Campbell, *French Electoral Systems and Elections Since 1789* (Aldershot, England: Gower, 1989), pp. 187ff.

28. Faux et al., *La main*, p. 20.

29. Bastien Leccia, quoted in ibid., p. 27.

30. See Dumont et al., *Le système*, pp. 109–110; and Pierre Milza, *Fascisme français: Passée et présent* (Paris: Flammarion, 1987), p. 343.

31. Quoted in *Le Monde*, September 14, 1983.

32. Alain Rollat, *L'Effet Le Pen* (Paris: La Découverte, 1984), p. 96. Le Pen himself entered a legislative by-election in Brittany in early December 1983. He received 12.50 percent of the vote.

33. *Le Monde*, February 15, 1984.

34. Le Pen, *Les Français d'abord* (Paris: Carrère/Laffon, 1984), p. 221.

35. Ignazi, "Un nouvel acteur politique," p. 65.

36. Quoted in Dumont et al., *Le système*, p. 102.

37. Simone Bonnafous, *L'immigration prise aux mots* (Paris: Kimé, 1991), p. 42.

38. Quoted in Pierre-André Taguieff, "Un programme révolutionnaire," in Mayer and Perrineau, *Le Front*, p. 217.

39. *Le Monde*, June 8, 1984.

40. Le Pen, *Les Français d'abord*, p. 122.

41. Ibid., pp. 122–123.

42. In the 1985 cantonal elections, run under a two-ballot system, the mainstream right rejected an election agreement. As a result, the Front was unable to elect a single candidate to any of the 1,460 seats at stake.

43. *L'Année politique* (1985):94.

44. Elie Cohen, "Les socialistes et l'économie," in Elisabeth Dupoirier and Gérard Grunberg, *Mars 1986: La drôle de défaite de la gauche* (Paris: Presses Universitaires de France, 1986), p. 92.

45. Pascal Perrineau, "Glissements progressifs de l'idéologie," in Dupoirier and Grunberg, *Mars 1986*, p. 43.

46. Jean-Louis Missika and Dorine Bregman, "La campagne: La sélection des controverses," in Dupoirier and Grunberg, *Mars 1986*, pp. 111–114.

47. Quoted in ibid., p. 143.

48. Jérôme Jaffré, "Front national: La relève protestaire," in Dupoirier and Grunberg, *Mars 1986*, pp. 210–229.

49. Pascal Perrineau, "Front national: L'écho politique de l'anomie urbaine," *Ésprit* 3–4 (March–April 1988):26.

50. Guy Birenbaum, *Le Front national en politique* (Paris: Éditions Balland, 1992).

51. Quoted in ibid., p. 99.

52. Ibid., p. 102.

53. Yvan Blot, *Les racines de la liberté* (Paris: Albin Michel, 1985), pp. 24, 22–23.

54. Katyn referred to a massacre of Polish army officers during World War II by the Soviet army, a crime initially attributed to the Nazis; Budapest referred to the Soviet repression of the 1956 Hungarian uprising; and the massacre of the harkis referred to the purported massacre by the Algerian National Liberation Front of Muslim soldiers who fought with the French during the Algerian War.

55. *Le Figaro*, October 12, 1987.

56. *Le Monde*, October 14, 1987.

5

Sinking Roots: 1987–1995

There will be a "before- and after-Toulon." This [National Front] victory marks a major change in French politics since World War II because it is the first significant victory on our territory of a political tendency which has ambiguous relations with the Republican consensus forged at the Liberation.
—Fabien Roland-Lévy, in Le Parisien, June 6, 1995

If the fight against the National Front is to take place on the level of words, it is necessary to stop referring to "national preference" when one really is talking about racial discrimination.
—Philippe Bernard, in Le Monde, June 24, 1995

No sooner had the National Front taken its thirty-five seats in the 1986 National Assembly than the presidential election of 1988 loomed on the horizon. Because there was a good possibility that the new president would dissolve the National Assembly and call for new elections, and because Prime Minister Chirac had abandoned proportional representation and returned to the previous two-ballot system under which the Front fared poorly, the NF's foothold in the legislature was very tenuous. However, having won 11 percent of the vote in the 1984 European elections and 10 percent in the 1986 elections, the NF realized that its swing votes could spell the difference between victory and defeat in close races between right and left.

At the same time, the solidification of NF support had thrown the mainstream right into a quandary. If it moved too closely toward the Front, the right risked alienating its own supporters; if it completely rejected the Front, NF voters might abstain or even vote for the Socialists in future elections. For a while in the late 1980s, there were persistent rumors that informal contacts had taken place between Le Pen and some RPR leaders, particularly the RPR minister of the interior, Charles Pasqua, with a view toward an election pact.[1] Although RPR spokespersons denied these rumors, in 1987 former NF deputy Marcel d'Ormesson said that "we [it is unclear to whom d'Ormesson is referring] wanted to make Jean-Marie Le Pen the popular leader of a conservative and national right." When asked whether he thought that the leaders of the mainstream right had been ready to reach an understanding with Le Pen, despite the fact that both Chirac and Raymond Barre had explicitly rejected such links, d'Ormesson replied, "Absolutely." The ultimate objective, he said, was to make Le Pen into the head of a "large conservative party." But, he added, NF secretary general Jean-Pierre Stirbois and his associates were completely opposed to cooperating with the mainstream right.[2] According to Yann Piat, a former NF deputy, the RPR tried to tempt some National Front deputies to join it by voting for NF amendments in the National Assembly and by inviting some of them to dine with RPR government ministers at the headquarters of the conservative newspaper *Le Figaro*.[3] But these attempts came to nothing and the RPR ultimately rejected the idea of integrating the NF within a broad right-wing alliance.[4]

By spring 1987, with the campaign for the 1988 presidential election well under way, Prime Minister Jacques Chirac was trying to ignore the Front altogether. In early May 1987 when asked to comment on the election and the role of the Front, Chirac said: "I have no intention of getting involved in an argument. I am faced with too many serious, difficult and important problems. . . . Let others who have nothing else to do, argue. As for me, I am working."[5] But as the date for the presidential election approached and he continued to lag in the polls, Chirac began to make overtures toward Front supporters. In a March 1988 speech in Marseilles, Chirac adopted Front terms and language, accusing the Socialists of displaying laxity in their dealing with "clandestine" immigrants and of failing to stem the increase in crime and delinquency. Contrary to Le Pen's claim that there was no real difference between the Socialists and the mainstream right, Chirac tried to convince the voters that a second-round presidential battle between Mitterrand and Chirac would offer the electorate a real choice between right and left.[6] One month later, however, Chirac tacked in a different direction, implicitly criticizing the Front by launching a strong attack against "inequalities, exclusion and injustice." "I have never stopped struggling against all forms of racism, against this deviation which is so foreign to our national spirit and so contrary to all of General de Gaulle's ideas."[7]

While Chirac maneuvered, Charles Pasqua drummed home the tough message for which he had become famous. As minister of the interior in Chirac's 1986–1988 government, Pasqua had implemented policies making it easier to deport illegal immigrants and giving the police wide powers to stop and question suspected illegal immigrants. Moreover, the Chirac government had toyed with the possibility of changing France's immigration law from one in which nationality was acquired by birth on French soil (*jus soli*) to one in which nationality could be acquired only through naturalization or through birth to a French citizen (*jus sanguinis*). Although the government ran into resistance on this issue and ultimately handed it over to a study commission, Pasqua associated himself with a tough line on immigration policy. A few weeks before the 1988 presidential election, Chirac emphasized that France "ought not to allow entry to anyone or anybody, no matter why."[8] Referring to Charles Pasqua by name, Chirac promised that "the actions undertaken by Charles Pasqua will continue for seven years [the length of a presidential term]."[9] According to *Le Monde:* "Mr. Chirac didn't state that the Minister of the Interior would spend seven years in this position, but he clearly implied that he would be reappointed after an eventual victory. . . . In Marseilles, is a vote for Chirac . . . a vote for Pasqua?"[10]

In addition to borrowing the Front's ideas on immigration, Pasqua echoed many Front themes. In March 1988 he said, "When I see the media pity the terrorists who have begun a hunger strike instead of pitying the victims; when I look at those who have murdered old people and at child murderers, I regret that the death penalty has been abolished."[11] And a month later he remarked:

> There is no shame in saying that we want a strong France, with large families, respect for moral values, and the end of attacks on children which are the outcome of pornography. I must add that the Gaullist movement has supported direct democracy since its origin, even more than parliamentary democracy. It is the only way of bringing about major reforms. . . . Yes, there are a few extremists in the National Front, but basically, the National Front has the same preoccupations, the same values as the majority. It merely expresses them in a more brutal and noisy way.[12]

While Chirac temporized and Pasqua threatened, a third faction in the RPR resolutely opposed any ideological or political compromise with the extreme right. This group included younger party members such as Jacques Toubon, RPR secretary general, who insisted that there would no local or national election alliances with the National Front, and RPR cabinet minister Michel Noir, who asked, "Are we ready to lose our souls in order to win the elections?"[13]

Presidential hopeful Raymond Barre, a centrist former prime minister under Giscard from 1976 to 1981, also tried to ignore the Front. As the 1988 election approached, however, his attempts to appeal over the head of Front leaders to Front voters became increasingly blatant. While stating that under no circumstances would he bring the National Front into government, Barre assured Front supporters that "you are attached to several fundamental values concerning the future of the country. You don't hesitate to express your fidelity to patriotism in an era when this value has been besmirched. You don't hesitate to express your attachment to the national idea . . . to underline that our society must respect several principles, without which laxity and anarchy would rule."[14] Barre also stated that he approved of the Vichy slogan *"Travail, Famille, Patrie"* but, he added, "within a free France."[15] And he chided Front voters for giving the impression they were partisans of racism and xenophobia.[16]

The 1988 Presidential and Legislative Elections

In the first round of the April 1988 presidential election, President Mitterrand won 34.09 percent of the vote; Jacques Chirac, 19.94 percent; Raymond Barre, 16.54 percent; Jean-Marie Le Pen, 14.39 percent; and the three extreme left candidates, including the Communist Party candidate André Lajoinie, 11.3 percent. According to the rules of the French election system, the top two candidates, Mitterrand and Chirac, would now face each other on the second runoff ballot. However, Le Pen's 4.3 million votes far exceeded poll predictions and was the largest vote for any extreme right candidate since 1945. According to Le Pen, "It was an earthquake."[17] Moreover, in view of a comparatively low score on the first ballot, Chirac desperately needed the support of a good portion of the NF vote if he was to come within striking distance of Mitterrand.

At the same time, the NF had to make a difficult choice. Should the Front ask its voters to support Chirac, the hated leader of the RPR, and open itself to the accusation of betraying its principles? Should the party throw its support to Mitterrand, the detested Socialist, and be accused of opportunism? Or should it advocate abstention? Behind the scenes the party was split. On one side was a hard-line faction led by Jean-Pierre Stirbois, who argued that a Chirac defeat would "re-enforce the National Front, which would then appear as the only political force whose goal was to break with socialism."[18] On the other side was a faction that hoped for an alliance with the mainstream right. Le Pen determinedly tried to maneuver between these two.

On the morning after the first ballot, Le Pen shocked the party executive by saying, "It is necessary to vote for Chirac,"[19] explaining that the RPR was ready to make concessions if the NF threw its support behind Chirac on the second ballot. After a heated debate, however, the leadership rejected Le Pen's proposal, pointing out that the NF could not suddenly endorse a man whom the NF had vituperatively criticized during the campaign.[20] Having rejected Chirac, however, the NF had to avoid giving the appearance of implicitly endorsing Mitterrand. On May 1, 1988, at the end of a long speech criticizing both leaders, Le Pen remarked that the choice between Mitterrand and Chirac was between the "frying pan and the fire."[21] And Le Pen concluded, "Not a vote for the left." In other words, Le Pen was advocating abstention. According to Yann Piat, "Everyone understood. Mitterrand could sleep peacefully. Chirac was the one who should be alarmed. The majority of NF voters would vote either for the God of the socialists, or go fishing."[22] In fact, a poll taken after the election showed that 65 percent of those who voted for Le Pen on the first ballot voted for Chirac on the second, while 19 percent voted for Mitterrand.[23] Despite the fact that a majority of NF voters rallied to Chirac on the second ballot, Mitterrand won the election with 54.02 percent of the vote to Chirac's 45.98.

After the election Mitterrand dissolved the National Assembly and called for new legislative elections. Because proportional representation had now been replaced by the traditional two-ballot, single-member constituency system in 1986, the Front's thirty-five seats in the National Assembly were now under threat.[24] But if the National Front could not hope to retain its seats, NF votes could well determine the outcome of left-right battles on the second ballot of legislative elections.

To counter this threat, the RPR and the UDF (grouped together in an electoral alliance called the Union du Rassemblement et du Centre [Union of the Assembly and the Center, or URC]) decided to refuse any election alliance with the Front. They also agreed not to run candidates against each other on the first ballot of the legislative elections, but rather to jointly support deputies from the 1986–1988 legislature who were up for reelection.[25] This tactic was confirmed in May 1988 when the RPR minister of the interior, Charles Pasqua, announced that there would be no local or national alliances with the National Front. In deciding against any overt cooperation with the NF, the mainstream right took an enormous risk since it knew that the National Front might run candidates on the second ballot, especially in the south around Marseilles, where the NF was quite strong, thereby splitting the right-wing vote and ensuring a left-wing victory. Le Pen was furious: If the mainstream parties refused to cooperate with the Front, he would bring the temple pillars crashing down on everyone's head. "There will be other elections. They [the leaders of the mainstream right] have only to continue like this and they will end up like lemmings. Lemmings are animals which, for reasons we don't understand, throw themselves into rivers and drown. It's a form of idiopathy, a sickness whose origin is unknown. Chirac and [Jacques] Lecanuet are idiopaths."[26]

Nevertheless, the mainstream right held fast—until the first ballot confirmed its worst fears. The voters had split almost evenly between the right and the left, with the National Front holding the fate of the right in its hands. Now, according to Daniel Vernet in *Le Monde*, echoing the words of Michel Noir, the RPR had to choose "between losing its soul and losing its seats."[27] The RPR chose to lose its soul. Between the two rounds of the election, the RPR withdrew eight of its candidates in the Marseilles area, while the National Front reciprocated by withdrawing eight of its candidates in Marseilles. As a result, Le Pen, Bruno Mégret, and Jean-Pierre Stirbois, among others, remained as the sole flag bearers of the right against the left on the second ballot.[28]

Despite these maneuvers, and despite receiving 2.4 million votes (9.5 percent, about the same as the party had received in the 1986 legislative elections), the Front managed to elect only Yann Piat, from Var, to the National Assembly. Le Pen, Mégret, and Stirbois were all defeated, although by narrow margins.[29] The combined forces of the left won 49.2 percent of the vote and sent 304 deputies to the National Assembly; the URC received 40.5 percent of the vote and sent 270 deputies to the National Assembly. The Front blamed its defeat on an "unjust, wicked and antidemocratic" election system.[30]

Le Pen and the Scandal of the Rhyme

Despite the fact that the NF had made little headway in the legislative election, Le Pen was not about to relinquish the headlines. After a tranquil summer, Le Pen burst onto the public stage with an outrageously anti-Semitic remark. During a September 1988 speech to the National Front's summer school, Le Pen rhymed the name of the Socialist government's Jewish minister of public services, Michel Durafour, with the word *crématoire*— "Durafour-*crématoire*." *Crématoire* means "oven," so Le Pen was playing on both the meaning and the sound of the two words. Immediately, there was widespread condemnation in the press and the media; but Le Pen referred to the furor as a "tempest in a teapot" and refused to apologize to a "political opponent who violently attacked me."[31] According to Yann Piat, the remark was "deliberate, [and] aimed at breaking the cover of media silence."[32] However, Le Pen's anti-Semitism had begun to alienate members of his own party, including Yann Piat, the NF's only deputy in the National Assembly, and François Bachelot, formerly Le Pen's personal physician.

After roundly criticizing Le Pen for the remark and for his management of party affairs, Bachelot was summoned before the NF's political bureau for a disciplinary hearing in September 1988. Le Pen accused Bachelot of shooting him in the back, of wanting to replace Le Pen at the head of the party, of betraying him to the enemy, and of giving out information on his health. Before leaving the meeting, Bachelot replied, "M. Le Pen, the absence of any ideological explanation demonstrates to me that you have reached the level of your incompetence."[33] Piat, too, was forced to resign for deviating from party policy. During her brief term in office, she had criticized Le Pen over the rhyme incident, and in the National Assembly she had voted for a minimum salary bill that included immigrant workers. This was completely contrary to the NF "national preference" policy of refusing noncitizens access to social benefits. With Piat's resignation, the National Front lost its last remaining deputy in the National Assembly.[34]

The Scarves Affair

In September 1989 the principal of the Gabriel-Havez school in Creil expelled three young Muslim girls because they insisted on wearing the chador, or Muslim scarf, to school. By October the affair had become headline news throughout France. The left split between those who opposed letting the girls wear the scarves on the grounds that granting students the right to wear clothing with religious significance would undermine the secular tradition of the public school system and those who supported the girls' right to wear the chador in the name of tolerance and pluralism. The dispute split both right and left and threw together, although for different reasons, people from opposite sides of the political spectrum. For example, Le Pen and Elisabeth Badinter, a well-known essayist and wife of Socialist minister of justice Robert Badinter, supported the headmaster's decision to ban the scarves; Danielle Mitterrand, the president's wife, and Alain de Benoist, theoretician of the extreme right Groupement de Recherche et d'Étude pour la Civilisation Européenne (Research and Study Group on European Civilization, or GRECE) think-tank, opposed the decision. Le Pen opposed the scarves because it symbolized for him the refusal of Muslims to integrate into French society, while Badinter opposed the practice because it was contrary to the laic traditions of French schools and was a sign of the subjugation of women to Islamic fundamentalism. Danielle Mitterrand supported wearing the scarf in the name of multiculturalism, while Alain de Benoist argued that, in the name of the "right to difference," people should be allowed to choose their own cultural values and symbols.

Amid this confusion, many on the extreme right used the scarves affair as an illustration of the danger that Islam posed to French society. In *Le Figaro-Magazine,* Louis Pauwels noted that Muslims "dreamed of 'Islamicizing' our society," and he warned that giving immigrants the right to vote would "aggravate the ghetto situation, as in England." He noted with glee the confusion on the left, torn between its traditional support for the secular school against the intrusion of religion and its desire to support "without distinction" all the Muslim movements in France because, Pauwels said, the Socialists hoped to get the support of Muslims once they were given the right to vote. According to Pauwels, except for the National Front, no one hitherto had realized the importance of the "crisis that we are now undergoing."[35]

Dreux Again

Almost at the same time, another series of events focused media attention on the NF. In fall 1989 the RPR deputy for the Dreux area resigned his seat to move to the Senate; a by-election was then scheduled for December 1989. The NF candidate was Marie-France Stirbois, the widow of Jean-Pierre Stirbois, who had been killed in an automobile accident in 1988.

With the left and mainstream right divided over the scarves affair and traditional party lines blurred, the voters were confused. The Socialist candidate kept a low profile, minimizing his party allegiance, while the RPR candidate echoed NF themes on immigration and security. As one ex-Socialist voter commented to the former Socialist mayor of Dreux, Françoise Gaspard, "Sure, I voted National Front, because I am fed up with you jerks . . . and one way or the other you should know it!"[36] For many voters, the National Front seemed to be the only party that took a consistent stand on crime, delinquency, housing, and unemployment.[37]

By this time the NF's electoral strategy had been honed to fine point. Stirbois conducted a low-key and methodical campaign no different in style from the mainstream parties—except for one curious event. During the campaign, a slick-looking pamphlet from the "National Association for the Integration of Third World Immigrants, Seine-Saint-Denis Sector, Paris" appeared in Dreux. It asked people to inform the "association" of any vacant dwellings in their neighborhood so it might provide better housing for immigrant families in the area. The pamphlet claimed that this policy had been approved by deputies from the Communist, Socialist, Gaullist, and Giscardian parties, "despite the retrograde and racist opposition of the Le Pen group."[38] Obviously the pamphlet was intended to portray every party except the National Front as "soft" on immigrants. However, the provenance of the pamphlet was never discovered, nor was anyone able to locate the National Association for Integration.

With the mainstream parties in disarray, and Stirbois running a textbook-style campaign, the NF candidate won a resounding 42.5 percent of the vote on the first ballot and trounced the other candidates on the second ballot, winning 61.3 percent of the ballot. According to Stirbois, the NF victory was part of the struggle against the foreign "invader," and she compared the situation of the extreme right in France in the 1980s to that of the wartime Resistance against the Nazis.[39] Once again the National Front had a deputy in the National Assembly.

Immigration

During the campaign, the mainstream right had tried unsuccessfully to cut the ground out from under the NF by taking a hard line on immigration and security. In view of the results, however, the question was whether the mainstream right should persist with this strategy or moderate its policies and hope to attract Socialist voters. The mainstream right's difficulties were compounded by the fact that immigration had now moved from seventh place in 1989 to second place in 1990 among those issues of most concern to the French public. After some discussion, the mainstream right decided to stick to a hard line on immigration in order to convince the voters that the NF was not alone in taking their concerns seriously. At the same time, the mainstream right had to prevent the NF from exploiting any divisions between the RPR and those who supported Giscard. To this end a joint meeting of the principal parties of the mainstream right was convened in April 1990, and agreement was reached on a common approach to immigration. According to the agreement, "The question of immigration is basic for the future of France." The parties stated:

1. We affirm that France can no longer be a country of immigration.
2. Integration can only succeed if it follows completely new paths.
3. France ought to lead the fight for development.[40]

None of these principles was remarkable, nor was there any suggestion at the meeting that the nationality law be changed from one that granted French citizenship to children born on French soil (*jus soli*), although Giscard d'Estaing proposed that once prospective citizens reached the age of majority, they would have to actively request French nationality rather than having it automatically conferred on them.[41] However, there were clear indications that Giscard was willing to adopt the NF's vocabulary in an attempt to win the support of NF voters. In April 1990, using Front-style language, Giscard stated, "We accept neither xenophobia nor francophobia."[42] Following the meeting both Chirac and Giscard increasingly resorted to extremist, even racist rhetoric. In June 1991 Chirac stated that France suffered from an "overdose" of immigrants, and he expressed sympathy for the "French worker" who suffered from the "noise and smell" from immigrants.[43] In September 1991 Giscard referred to immigration as an "invasion," and he proposed that France "return to the traditional conception of the acquisition of nationality, that based on the right of blood."[44] Those aspiring to French nationality, he stated, should reside in France for at least ten years, possess sufficient resources to take care of the person's own or family needs, and be able to speak French. Ignoring the fact that, except for the period from 1804 to 1851, French nationality laws had been based on *jus soli*, both Giscard's language and his policy proposals demonstrated how closely he had moved toward the Front's position on immigration.[45]

In the 1980s, with Islamic fundamentalism sweeping across the Middle East and North Africa, the Front had begun to focus on Islam as the defining characteristic of the North African community and as the single most important reason North Africans could never assimilate into French society. In April 1988 Le Pen began to warn of the "military risk" posed to France by a "core of the foreign population. . . . An increasingly powerful, irresistible wave from the underdeveloped countries threatens us. . . . As long as we are alive, France will never be an Islamic Republic."[46] Some months later Le Pen paid tribute to the city of Lyon, which was the capital of the "resistance against the German occupation and which is today facing an Islamic occupation."[47] He demanded that France declare "war on terrorists."[48] Front immigration expert Jean-Yves Le Gallou opposed the construction of mosques on French territory because there was an irreconcilable contradiction between being Muslim and being French: Muslim Arabs "had to choose between France and Islam."[49] In a December 1989 interview published in *Le Figaro-Magazine,* Le Pen stated that "the foreign communities on French soil are practically inassimilable. Integration is at an impasse."[50] For this reason, he said, immigrants who had entered France after 1974 (the date when free immigration from Algeria had been suspended), "even if they have been 'regularized,'" would have to expect that their presence in France would be called into question.[51] The shocking implications of the proposal that French citizens of North African background (Le Pen obviously was not referring to European immigrants) might find their citizenship revoked and be expelled from the country was overlooked by most observers.[52] Then in November 1991 Bruno Mégret of the NF raised the stakes in the anti-immigrant campaign by setting forth "fifty measures on immigration."[53]

The heart of the proposal was to substitute *jus sanguinis,* or race, for *jus soli,* or residence, as the basis for acquisition of nationality. Mégret claimed that these measures could be seen as part of the ecological movement since they were aimed at preserving the French "species" against "cross-breeding [*métissage*]."[54] According to historian Marc Ferro, the source of the analogy between animal species and nations could be found in pre-Nazi and Nazi ideology with "the glorification of the *Volk* as the identifying mark of the nation. . . . The importation of this notion into the French nation and ideology is something new."[55] The importance to the NF of blood as a metaphor for racial purity was underlined by the suggestion that all non-Europeans wishing to visit France be tested for AIDS and that they leave a deposit of Fr 100,000 prior to entering the country. Once again Mégret repeated the NF's call for a retrospective investigation and possible revocation of the citizenship of all those who had acquired French nationality since 1974.

As Robert Solé pointed out in *Le Monde,* in French history only the Vichy government had adopted the "scandalous" policy of retroactive challenging citizenship.[56] Mégret also proposed a national preference policy that would discriminate against non-European immigrants in every sphere of activity: French citizens would be given priority in securing employment, in obtaining public housing, and in gaining access to social services. Goods would be labeled "made in France by the French." There would be quotas imposed on the number of immigrants in classes, ethnic ghettos would be "dismantled," the construction of mosques would be suspended, and the opening of Koranic schools and Islamic centers would be regulated. Once illegal and "clandestine" immigrants were identified, guarded "lodging centers" would be established near airports and seaports to house immigrants prior to their expulsion on chartered boats and airplanes. As Jean Madiran, director of the pro-Front daily *Présent,* pointed out, "Deporting clandestine immigrants would imply massive round-ups of dozens or hundreds of thousands of people, concentrating them in camps, which no one would admit were concentration camps, and then expelling them via an aerial bridge."[57] Finally, Mégret's proposals contained anti-Semitic swipes against "cosmopolitanism," which threatened French national identity and would be banished from the educational system through censorship of school texts.

Mégret's plan provoked a storm of criticism, which in turn provoked a violent reaction from Le Pen. He referred to the critics as "cretins" and "poor imbeciles," while also implicitly trying to mitigate the criticism by calling Mégret's plan an internal party document. Giscard d'Estaing, who had previously propounded the notion of *jus sanguinis,* rather than *jus soli,* as the basis for citizenship, criticized the proposal for retrospective examination of naturalization as "contrary to French tradition."[58] Even the extreme right monarchist Action Française criticized this proposal as "risking creating useless tensions."[59]

Carpentras

On the evening of May 8 or 9, 1990, a person or group of people overturned gravestones and exhumed coffins in a Jewish cemetery in Carpentras. In the days following the incident, Le Pen and the National Front were accused of contributing to the rise of anti-Semitism and to the Carpentras incident. Some people argued that Le Pen's appearance on the popular television show *L'Heure de Verité* (The Hour of Truth) on the evening of May 9, 1990, had provoked the profanation. However, investigators could not determine whether the incident happened on the evening before or on the evening of Le Pen's interview.

One commentator wrote of a "Carpentras machine," arguing that, faced with the inexorable rise in popularity of Le Pen and the Front, the mainstream parties tried to use Carpentras as an instrument to destroy Le Pen and the National Front.[60] Whatever the circumstances of the case, however, the desecration was condemned by representatives from all sides of the political spectrum, including Le Pen himself, who stated that the National Front shared the emotions "evoked by the profanation of the Carpentras cemetery . . . and extends its fraternity to the families of those who were profaned. Who more than French patriots can be shocked by an action aimed at the dead and their peaceful resting places . . . since the country is the land of our fathers, the land of the dead and because we are believers and patriots and believe in the respect due to the body."[61]

That Le Pen was in fact shocked by the profanation is not surprising considering the extreme right's view that the dead consecrate French soil and are, in the words of Maurice Barrès, "this voice of our ancestors." "The dead! . . . When each of us looks over his shoulder, he sees a succession of indefinable mysteries, which in more recent times have come to be called France. We are the sum of a collective life that speaks in us. May the influence of our ancestors be permanent, the sons of the soil vital and upstanding, the nation one."[62]

Despite Le Pen's remarks and the lack of any evidence linking the incident to the National Front, a public opinion poll found that 66 percent agreed with the proposition that Le Pen and the NF were partly responsible for the Carpentras incident, while 55 percent of those polled thought that the NF was anti-Semitic.[63] However, Le Pen began to accuse "French politicians" of having "programmed an operation" aimed at diverting attention from government scandals and corruption. As time passed and the authorities proved unable to identify the perpetrators, the incident faded from the headlines.

In late 1995 the Carpentras affair resurfaced when a public prosecutor announced new leads concerning the perpetrators. For a long time rumors had circulated in Carpentras that the exhumation of the body and the desecration of the cemetery had been part of a witchcraft ritual conducted by six young people from the area.[64]

The Gulf War

Until recently the extreme right's perspective on the Middle East and on Palestine has been through the lens of anti-Semitism. As early as 1890 Édouard Drumont suggested that one way to rid France of Jews would be to send them all to Palestine.[65] According to anthropologist Georges Montandon, an "expert" on ethnicity in the 1930s and 1940s, if Palestine became a Jewish state, then all Jews outside Palestine could be treated as foreigners, and there would be no reason for them to assimilate to other countries—such as France.[66] After the creation of the state of Israel in 1948, continued hostility between Israel and its Arab neighbors elicited mixed reactions from the French extreme right. At one point the fiercely anti-Semitic newspaper *Rivarol* suggested that if the French Algerian putschists of 1961 had been led by men of the calibre of Moshe Dayan or Yitzhak Rabin, they might have succeeded in defying de Gaulle and keeping Algeria French. However, during the 1967 war Maurice Bardèche had accused Israel of practicing genocide against the Palestinians.[67] By the 1970s the National Front was accusing Israel of being a springboard for an international Jewish conspiracy and of manipulating the United States and Great Britain for its own ends. Israel, according to Le Pen, was an "artificial state created by the oil interests of the United States and Great Britain."[68]

It is a testimony to Le Pen's dialectical skills that he was able to oppose French participation in the 1990 Gulf War and yet maintain his image as an ardent supporter of the French military. Le Pen defended his position on a variety of grounds: his desire to preserve the blood of the sons of the nation, his opposition to the risking of French lives to defend Kuwait's interests and its "emirs enriched by petrodollars," and the lack of a "reason to go so far to combat 'Arabism or Islam' when one does nothing against it here."[69] But there is another explanation for Le Pen's stand.

The Israelis were extremely wary of the nuclear threat that Iraq posed, and they had already bombed an Iraqi nuclear reactor in 1981. Now Saddam Hussein threatened to shower Israel with short-range missiles tipped with poison gas in the event of a U.N. attack on Iraq, despite the fact that Israel was not a party to the conflict. In these circumstances someone opposing military intervention against Iraq could be seen as taking sides against Israel. Of course, Le Pen never gave this as a reason for supporting Iraq, but the pro-Front anti-Semitic *Présent* and *National Hebdo* supported Le Pen's position. According to ex-deputy Jean-Claude Martinez, a member of the Front's political bureau, "The American intervention was done to assure Israel's survival and Israeli domination over the region."[70]

Le Pen attempted to justify his opposition to the U.N. intervention in terms of his conception of nationalism. "We want the Arabs to be masters in their own house," he said, "and the Arabs should understand that France wants to be master in its own house."[71] For the Front, every nation had an absolute right to determine its own internal affairs—which implied, for example, that no Arab country could criticize any future NF government if it moved to expel immigrants.

Finally, there were pro-Iraqi sympathizers in the fundamentalist wing of the National Front. Their support was motivated not by any particular sympathy for Saddam Hussein or for his regime, but by Iraq's replacement of Israel as a major arms supplier to the Falange in its battle against the Muslim forces in the Lebanon. For people like Bernard Antony of Christian-Solidarity, the Falange was a bastion of Christianity in the battle against Islamic fundamentalism.[72] Anti-Americanism also played a role, especially among the fundamentalists and the "Horlogers." As the Front's

1993 election program put the matter: "In the Middle East, France renounced its role of protecting the Christian communities. In 1979, our government helped to put in place the Iranian regime. So many withdrawals earned us the contempt of the Arabo-Muslim world, while as a consequence we watched a re-enforcement of Anglo-Saxon influence in this region of the world as shown by the sad Gulf War."[73]

By opposing the war (the NF put up posters that read, "Mitterrand = War, Le Pen = Peace"), Le Pen could pretend to play the role of a statesman ready to step onto the world stage.[74] According to Bruno Mégret in *Le Figaro*, "He [Le Pen] is a man of measure, reflective, who doesn't let himself be carried away by the media waves of so-called international opinion."[75] On numerous occasions in late summer and early fall 1990, Le Pen tried to get Iraqi permission to visit Baghdad, where he hoped to emulate Kurt Waldheim, secretary-general of the United Nations, and bring home hostages held by the Iraqi regime. When Saddam announced that he was going to free 330 French hostages in October 1990, Le Pen told *Le Figaro* that he thought he had "played a large role" in obtaining their freedom. Finally, in late October, as part of a delegation of right-wing parties from Europe, Le Pen met Saddam and returned to France with 53 European hostages. According to Le Pen, "I had the kind of reception given to Chiefs of State, journalists in Baghdad told me, because I had the privilege of being received the day of my arrival whereas, as a general rule, foreign delegations have to wait 48 hours."[76]

Supporting Iraq was also an ingenious way for Le Pen to counter accusations that the NF was viscerally anti-Arab and drive home the message that far from being racist, French nationalism meant supporting all nationalisms, including Arab nationalism. Nor was Le Pen's opposition to the war completely out of step with public opinion, for polls showed that the French were ambivalent about the issues involved. When asked if they agreed with the statement "No cause, no matter how just, is worth a war, it is always better to negotiate and find a compromise even with an aggressor like Saddam Hussein," 83 percent of those polled agreed. Yet when asked if in the eventuality of hostilities, France should participate in military operations with the Western countries, 61 percent agreed. However, Front supporters proved to be the least bellicose of all. When asked if they agreed with the proposition "Even if the Western countries are right, in no case should there be a military intervention against Iraq," 67 percent of Front sympathizers agreed, followed by 64 percent of Communist sympathizers.[77]

Whatever Front supporters may have thought about the issue of the Gulf War when it first arose, by fall 1990 most Front supporters shared Le Pen's opposition to war.[78] A public opinion poll in October 1990 found that 67 percent of NF sympathizers agreed with the proposition "Even if the Western countries are right, it is not necessary to intervene militarily against Iraq."[79]

The National Front and the Media

Relations between the National Front and the non-NF press have never been good. As the 1993 legislative election approached, they worsened. This was no accident, for over the years Le Pen has carefully orchestrated the Front's attitude toward the press, courting it when the polls were favorable to the NF and lambasting it when the polls were bad or when the press responded critically to one or another aspect of the Front's activities. Although Le Pen is a superb television performer, and his abilities as a debater have boosted his image before the public, the National Front has been extremely irritated by the hostility of newspapers such as *Le Canard Enchaîné, Libération, Globe,* and *Le Monde.* The NF has responded in a typical fashion. The pro-Front press engages in insulting, personal, and, when relevant, anti-Semitic or racist attacks on journalists. At the same time, it insinuates that there is a mysterious power or force behind the press "ordering" critical coverage of the Front. Le Pen himself accuses journalists of bias, hints that their criticism is inspired by Jewish journalists, and suggests that an NF government would pass legislation imposing greater objectivity on the media.

In autumn 1985 Le Pen featured prominently in the news both because of accusations surrounding the Lambert affair and because he apparently had paid no taxes on assets of Fr 3.5 million or on his chateau, whose estimated worth was between Fr 10 and 15 million. Infuriated, Le Pen went on the attack. At a speech given at the NF's fifth annual "Blue-White-Red" festival, he said, "I dedicate your reception to Jean-François Kahn, to Jean Daniel, to Ivan Levaï, to [Jean-Pierre] Elkabbach, to all the liars in the country." Referring to these journalists as "anti-France," Le Pen said that some "had the excuse of only recently learning French," and he referred to himself as the victim "of snakes of calumny and hate."[80]

All the journalists named were Jewish, so the references to their being "anti-France" and only recently learning French fit the usual pattern of anti-Semitism by insinuation. At the same time, Le Pen promised "to take the initiative to lay down precise professional ethics as well as a professional organ from within the field, to make the [journalists] respect [ethics] as is the case for the majority of the liberal professions."[81] A few days after this speech, *Le Monde* journalist Alain Rollat was insulted and abused by twenty NF militants at a talk on Le Pen. Led by Michel Collinot, an NF member of the European Parliament, and Roland Gaucher, director of *National Hebdo,* Rollat was called a "communist, Freemason and Jew," all of which constitute insults for NF militants. Rollat was characterized in *National Hebdo* by Collinot as "a communist agent, hideous, hands already red with the blood of national militants." Collinot accused Rollat of "leading a campaign to get *beurs* [French of North African origin], leftists, pals [a reference to SOS-Racisme], fellow travelers (although Rollat only travels for Gorbachev) to kill" NF militants.[82]

On occasion, NF supporters went beyond mere verbal insults and threats and physically assaulted journalists. In early 1988, for example, a journalist's camera was smashed, and another journalist was kicked after an NF meeting in Nice.[83] In February 1993 a journalist was attacked at the Front's Blue-White-Red fair by five people from Groupe Union et Défense (Union and Defense Group, or GUD), an extreme right student organization with links to the Front's youth movement.[84] The following year a journalist with *L'Évènement du Jeudi* was attacked during a demonstration organized by the National Front's youth movement.[85]

The Front's attitude toward the media is not unremittingly negative. Depending on the circumstances, the press may be courted and NF militants restrained from expressing their antipathy. During what was called the "third, or soft, phase" of the NF's public relations strategy in 1990, a journalist who was manhandled by a member of the NF's security staff received an immediate apology from the usually pugnacious Roger Holeindre, while the offending militant was transferred to different functions.[86] But the wheel turned full circle again in 1992 when a French television station broadcast a documentary on the NF that infuriated Le Pen. He accused the press of being manipulated by mysterious forces. "Somewhere," he said, "there must be a clandestine orchestra leader "[87] He then warned that he could not assure the safety of the author of the documentary if he attended NF meetings. A few days later at the annual Blue-White-Red NF festival, stickers appeared with the message "When you meet a journalist, slap him. If you don't know why—he knows."[88] That evening at the festival a journalist was punched in the face and called a "dirty Jew" by a gang of young people. A lighting technician was knocked unconscious, and other journalists were spat on. In a radio interview Bernard Antony, an NF member of the European Parliament and a member of the NF's political bureau, said: "I am going to be accused tomorrow of having threatened these journalists [the authors of the documentary]. I would like to say the truth. I struck one of them and I regret having struck only once. In fact, if I find them again, I will hit them, I promise, because they are thugs. . . . They are absolutely abject beings."[89]

On the eve of the 1993 legislative elections, the Front's attacks on the media became more strident. At a meeting at the Salle Coubertin, Le Pen accused the media of treating the National Front like a dog that only gets crumbs from the table, and the audience booed as he criticized the editor of *Le Monde,* whom Le Pen quoted as saying that it might be necessary to use "other means" to stop the rise of the National Front. He accused the media of having taken a decision to "deprive the National Front of the right of expression."[90] Reporting on the meeting, a headline in *Présent* read, "France Ravaged and Corrupted by Its Politico-Media Class."[91] A few days later, as part of a dispute with *Le Monde* about references to collaboration with the Nazis during World War II, Roland Gaucher, editorial director of *National Hebdo*, referred to the "bunch of bastards of *Le Monde*," including its editor Jacques Lesourne.[92]

Finally, before the annual NF Blue-White-Red festival in September 1995, the pro-Front newspaper *Présent* characterized television journalists as "cutthroats, frauds and hired picklocks." At the festival a cameraman was manhandled, and television journalists were shoved and booed. Only the intervention of the NF security force prevented the journalists from being seriously injured.[93]

The National Front and the Balladur Government

Almost a year after the NF had garnered 12.5 percent of the vote on the first ballot of the March 1993 elections, a public opinion poll showed that support for the National Front was slipping. Only 19 percent of those polled agreed with the ideas put forward by Le Pen and the NF, and a record 79 percent disagreed. In addition, 73 percent of those polled thought that Le Pen and the Front represented a danger to democracy, while 23 percent thought they did not—these results, too, were records. But 61 percent of the respondents approved of Le Pen's position on immigrants.[94] It is this continued high level of hostility toward immigrants that explained both the new RPR government's policy and the slippage in Front support. The Front was badly hurt when Prime Minister Édouard Balladur appointed Charles Pasqua as minister of the interior soon after the March 1993 election. Pasqua had already earned a reputation as a hard-liner on immigration policy as minister of the interior in the 1986–1988 Chirac government, so it came as no surprise in April 1993, just a month after the election, when Pasqua sent to the National Assembly a package of bills drastically restricting the conditions under which immigrants could become French citizens.

Whereas in the past children born in France to immigrant parents automatically became French nationals on their eighteenth birthday, the new bill stipulated that children between the ages of sixteen and eighteen had to inform the authorities of their intention to acquire French nationality. If such a person applied for French nationality between the ages of eighteen and twenty-one, and if he or she had previously been subject to an expulsion order or had been condemned for using or trafficking in drugs, then French citizenship could be refused. In addition, a prison sentence of six months for a variety of infractions could render such a person ineligible for French nationality. Foreigners who married someone French would have to wait two years before acquiring French citizenship. Ostensibly, this was to prevent so-called white marriages, contracted by one of the partners solely to obtain French nationality. Mayors were to be given the power to suspend for eight days a marriage between a foreigner and a French resident "if there exist serious indications that the marriage was intended to achieve a result foreign to the matrimonial union."[95] A series of additional measures were proposed restricting the acquisition of French nationality by Algerians.

Pasqua also asked the National Assembly to pass a series of measures making it more difficult for non-European foreigners to enter and work in France. The police were also given wide latitude to stop and question those suspected of being illegal immigrants. The right to asylum was also restricted. In June 1993 these measures passed the National Assembly by an overwhelming majority, with 480 deputies voting for and 88 Socialist and Communist deputies voting against the measure.

Meanwhile, the Front could only grind its teeth as Pasqua implemented one after another of the Front's proposals, rejecting only the most extreme. Georges-Paul Wagner in *Présent* complained that with everyone agreeing that "it is necessary to expel clandestine immigrants and foreign delinquents, and that it is even necessary to get immigrant workers to return, what is the point of this discrimination, this ghetto in which the Front is kept? . . . What is the point of presenting Pasqua as a guardian angel for doing what is reasonable, while pointing at Le Pen like a devil?"[96]

But, Wagner added, the government had not gone far enough. The "only remedy" was to "give the French preference in jobs and in housing."[97] Although the mainstream right did not endorse the NF's policy of national preference, in view of the tough immigration law passed by the Balladur government in summer and fall 1993, it was reasonable to ask whether the National Front had not in fact won an (im)moral victory.

With the Front losing support in the polls and with its electoral support in decline in legislative and local by-elections, in fall 1993 Front spokespersons began to hint darkly that the regime was headed toward catastrophe and that the Front had to be ready to save the system from complete collapse. According to Bruno Mégret: The victory [of the Front] will not come about progressively as in a normal democratic system. . . . But it will come suddenly as always happens when totalitarian regimes collapse and are reversed and when the destiny of a civilization is at stake."[98] Although it is unlikely that the Front really expected the Fifth Republic to collapse in ruins like the Soviet Union, the implication that radical changes were afoot and that the Front was prepared to undertake drastic action underlined the ambiguity of the Front's commitment to the normal processes of parliamentary democracy.

Election Mania

In the space of four years, from the beginning of 1992 to the end of 1995, the French were called to the polls five times: There were cantonal and regional elections in 1992, European elections in 1994, and presidential and municipal elections in 1995. (In September 1995 there were also senatorial elections, but only members of the legislature and municipal councillors were eligible to vote.) Abstention rates were at an all-time high (30.8 percent in the 1993 legislative election and 21.63 in the 1995 presidential election), which meant that the biggest party in France was the abstentionist party. Although there was growing disaffection for politicians and the party system because of high unemployment and the high-profile political corruption trials of the late 1980s and 1990s, an added element must have been voter fatigue because of the continual election campaigning for local, regional, national, and European office. Whatever the reasons for the abstention rates, however, the election results revealed that important changes had taken place in voting behavior and the party system.

In 1992 Denis Jeambar and Jean-Marc Lech spoke of a "divorce between politics and the social. . . . The social problematic which sustained the confrontation between left and right has given way to ethics and ecology. Morals have become the basis for evaluating politicians."[99] Jeambar and Lech noted a declining correlation between class or religion (or similar sociological characteristics) and the vote, and they observed that voters' choices were increasingly shaped by issues and messages emanating from parties and candidates and less by elections as "a ritual for the expression of symbolic loyalties."[100] Put another way, psephologists were now arguing that French voters behaved like consumers in the marketplace: They came to the electoral arena with few preconceived ideas or loyalties and made their choices on the basis of the perceived quality of the candidates and the policies they put forward. If this is indeed the case, it helps explain why the French electorate has been increasingly fickle, with large numbers of voters either refusing to vote or moving to parties and movements of the extreme left or extreme right.

In 1994 and again in 1995 Pascal Perrineau, director of the Centre d'Étude de la Vie Politique Française (Center for the Study of French Political Life), calculated the percentage of the electorate that had voted for "peripheral parties," that is, the Communist, ecology, and minor parties on the left and the National Front and smaller parties on the extreme right. In the 1993 legislative elections 40 percent of the voters supported these peripheral parties; in the April 1995 elections the figure was 38 percent.[101] According to Perrineau, this demonstrates the degree to which the party system has broken up and fragmented. One sign of this fragmentation is the emergence of Philippe de Villiers and his Mouvement pour la France (Movement for France) as competition for Le Pen and the National Front.

The de Villiers Phenomenon

In the 1990s, like American voters who in 1992 flocked in the millions to Ross Perot, or Italian voters who supported Silvio Berlusconi, large numbers of French voters swung toward populist, antiestablishment personalities emerging on the margins of the party system. In the 1994 European election, for example, Bernard Tapie, the controversial Marseilles businessman and Socialist maverick, headed an election list that won 12.03 percent of the vote and thirteen seats in the European Parliament. In that same election Philippe de Villiers, a member of Giscard's Republican Party, headed an anti-Europe list that won 12.33 percent of the vote and thirteen seats in the European Parliament. These scores put Tapie and de Villiers in third and fourth positions, behind the Gaullists and Socialists, but ahead of the National Front, the Communists, and smaller groupings of left and right. However, Tapie ran afoul of the law and was sentenced to jail in 1995 on corruption charges, which thus removed him from electoral politics. By contrast, de Villiers won a disappointing 4.74 percent of the vote on the first round of the 1995 presidential election.

From the moment he appeared on the scene, de Villiers posed a serious problem for the National Front. Born in 1949 in the Vendée (an area in the west of France that rose against the French Revolution and has historically been a right-wing stronghold), de Villiers attended the elite École Nationale d'Administration and, from 1976 to 1978 he served as a top civil servant in Jacques Chirac's government. In 1987 de Villiers was elected a deputy for the Republican Party and then won a seat in local politics. In May 1992 he launched his *Combat pour les Valeurs* (Combat for values) movement, whose major themes were opposition to the Maastricht Treaty, an end to immigration, an end to political corruption, and improved security. In November 1994 de Villiers resigned from the Republican Party to form his own party, Mouvement pour la France.

Although Le Pen saw de Villiers as poaching on his territory, the NF had a hard time deciding on what attitude to take toward de Villiers and his upstart movement. When the anti-Maastricht list headed by de Villiers won 2,389,565 votes in the June 1994 European elections, compared to 2,038,843 for the Front, Le Pen complained that de Villiers's program was "lifted from the National Front. ... His votes and our votes should be added together."[102] During a nationally televised interview the following November, Le Pen said of de Villiers, "I don't know who he is working for, but he is certainly giving his voters a working over."[103] When de Villiers announced in early 1995 that he would run in the April presidential election, the Socialists accused him of being a "Le Penist Trojan Horse" who was "expanding the scope of the hard-line right," while Bruno Mégret for the NF said that de Villiers's candidacy was a "political maneuver."[104]

Despite Le Pen's claim that de Villiers's policies are lifted from those of the Front, or accusations from the left that de Villiers is a carbon copy of Le Pen, there are differences between the two. Although de Villiers takes a hard-line position on immigration, for example, he has never resorted to the coded language, the thinly veiled racism, or the anti-Semitism that is Le Pen's trademark and that pervades the National Front. Although de Villiers has called on the government to treat the "problem" of immigration with "the greatest firmness," he has also asked that "individual cases be treated with the greatest humanity."[105] According to one study of de Villiers: "If Jean-Marie Le Pen shares certain views with de Villiers, the reverse isn't the case. One never finds de Villiers talking about 'France for the French,' ... nor the xenophobia which reigns in the Front ... nor its anti-Semitism."[106]

It is not just style that separates de Villiers from Le Pen; the centerpieces of their programs are different. Le Pen and the Front link immigrants to almost every economic and social problem in France and propose to solve these problems by sharply restricting the rights of immigrants within France or by deporting them. De Villiers, by contrast, focuses on the European Union (EU), emphasizing that the EU, Maastricht, and particularly the proposed single European currency threaten French sovereignty. Like Le Pen, de Villiers sees the family as the basic unit of society, tradition and values as its cement, and the nation as the natural framework for social and economic life. And both see in globalization and the European Union political currents that are economically unviable, contrary to human nature, and hostile to the societal traditions that bind nations together. But when it comes to specific proposals, the two differ.

De Villiers wants to end immigration, but he has not followed Le Pen's suggestions about deporting millions of immigrants or implementing policies that would discriminate against immigrants in social welfare, housing, and employment. Rather, de Villiers argues that massive tax reductions and privatization of government-owned firms such as Air France or Électricité de France would reduce unemployment.[107] While Le Pen hammers home a law-and-order message, focusing particularly on "ethnic gangs," de Villiers prefers to focus on the fight against political corruption and drugs. And while Le Pen has called for restoration of the death penalty, de Villiers has kept his own counsel on the issue. Finally, throughout Le Pen's career, and in the history of the Front, one can always find disparaging remarks about French democracy and praise for dictators the world over. In 1995 Le Pen started to talk about the "Sixth Republic," promising that if he became president, he would include in the constitution the policy of national preference, giving priority to French citizens in economic and social life. Always in the Front's discourse there are hints that once in power a National Front president or government would make radical changes in the French constitution and parliamentary practices. By contrast, there is nothing of this kind to be found in de Villiers's program—although he clearly wishes to renegotiate France's relationship with Europe.

In terms of their respective electorates, there are also major differences between de Villiers and Le Pen. De Villiers gets most of his votes from rural areas in departments in the west around Vendée that traditionally support the conservative right and in some departments in the Champagne-Ardennes area east of Paris. By contrast, the National Front draws most of its support from the far south, from urban areas around Marseilles and nearby cities, from within Paris, and, increasingly, from the northern industrial areas. The sociology of the two electorates is also different. De Villiers's voters are older than those who support the Front, and he draws much more support from farmers, artisans, and the self-employed than the Front does. Whereas more than half of de Villiers vote (54 percent) in the June 1994 European election came from retired people, the Front list derived 42 percent of its support from retirees. And while de Villiers drew 45 percent of his vote from practicing Catholics, Le Pen received only 22 percent from this group and 59 percent from non-practicing Catholics. But the most striking correlation is not between sociological variables and vote but between political self-identification and vote. Whereas 62 percent of those who placed themselves on the extreme right voted for the Le Pen list in 1994, only 23 percent on the extreme right voted for the de Villiers list. And while 54 percent of those who placed themselves on the right voted for de Villiers, only 5 percent on the right voted for Le Pen. Clearly, de Villiers appeals to voters who are on the right but not on the extreme right.

Where does all this put de Villiers? According to analyst Jean-Louis Schlegel, de Villiers's ideas resemble the "conservative right which recruits amongst the urban bourgeoisie and amongst ordinary people in rural areas."[108] According to de Villiers himself, he represents "neo-conservatism," or a "'rooted' [*enraciné*] conservatism." Wherever one places him, the question is whether de Villiers is in direct competition with Le Pen and the Front. From one angle, one might argue that, details aside, the substance of his policies on Europe, immigration, and taxation are not radically different from those of Le Pen and the Front. From another angle, the methods he intends to use to achieve his goals and his political style are distinctly different from those of the Front. Finally, he is not anti-Semitic, racist, or antidemocratic. Certainly, the voters distinguish between Le Pen and de Villiers since only a minority of extreme right voters support de Villiers, while the vast majority of Front voters put themselves on the extreme right. For these reasons, it might be argued that de Villiers represents the extreme of the mainstream right rather than the extreme right.

The Front and Local Politics

The presidential and municipal elections of 1995 were major landmarks for the National Front. Le Pen's 15 percent score on the first round of the presidential election reaffirmed the fact that the National Front is a major force in French politics. The Front's near-victories and victories in the municipal elections were equally significant in helping the Front sink roots in local politics as well as giving three newly elected Front mayors their first opportunity actually to implement Front policies. The following figures show that both the presidential and municipal elections represented a major breakthrough for the Front. Especially important were the 1,075 seats the Front won on local councils throughout France.

1992 cantonal elections, 12.18 percent, 1 elected
1994 cantonal elections, 9.76 percent, 1 elected
1992 regional elections, 13.90 percent, 239 elected
1993 legislative elections, 12.52 percent, 0 elected
1994 European elections, 10.51 percent, 11 elected
1995 presidential election, 15.00 percent, 0 elected
1995 municipal elections, 6.7 percent, 1,075 elected

Every six years the French vote to choose more than 500,000 municipal councillors and mayors for more than 36,000 communes in France. Most of these communes are tiny villages or towns, but 225 have populations of more than 30,000, and 35 have populations of more than 100,000. In the largest cities there is no direct election for mayor; rather, each party submits lists with as many names as there are council seats, and the list is headed by the person who will become mayor if the party wins enough seats to elect him or her. Voters choose a list, not individuals from the list, and the council seats are divided on the basis of a complicated system that combines proportional representation and choice by majority. The voting takes place in two rounds, one week apart. If a list obtains an absolute majority of the votes on the first ballot, the candidates on that list are elected, and no further election in held; if no list obtains an absolute majority, it must win a minimum of 10 percent of the vote to proceed to the second ballot.

Obviously, the complexities of this two-ballot system mean that a party's success or failure at the polls is influenced by the complicated tactical game that takes place between the two rounds of the election. After the first round of the municipal elections on June 11, 1995, for example, enough

Front candidates had won more than the 10 percent threshold of votes to run for city councillor seats in 150 cities with populations of more than 20,000. With Communist, Socialist, mainstream right, and a variety of ecological lists also in contention, almost all parties from the Communists to the mainstream right agreed that a top priority should be to defeat the Front on the second ballot.

Led by the newly elected President Chirac, the mainstream right reiterated its long-standing principle that it would not enter into any kind of election alliance with the National Front. The Socialists stated that in those cities where the Front and the mainstream right lists were running neck and neck, and where the NF list had a serious chance of topping the polls, rather than split the anti-Front vote, the Socialists would withdraw their candidates before the second round of the election and ask their supporters to vote for the mainstream right. Where these promises were kept, the tactics worked, for one week later the Front list came in first in only three cities of any size: Toulon, Marignane, and Orange. In Toulon, the ninth biggest city in France, with a population of more than 170,000, National Front candidate Jean-Marie Le Chevallier won with 26,879 votes because the mainstream right list, with 25,279 votes, and the Socialists, who refused to withdraw from the election after the first round, received 20,446 votes, thus splitting the remaining votes.[109] In the small city of Marignane (population, 32,000), two right-wing lists split the vote on the second round, allowing the Front candidate, Daniel Simonpieri, to win with 37 percent of the vote. In Orange, Jacques Bompard was elected when the NF list won by only 87 votes over the Socialists.[110]

One very important victory for the extreme right, although not literally for the National Front, came with ex-NF member Jacques Peyrat's election to the mayoralty of Nice, the seventh largest city in France, with a population of 342,000. Although Peyrat quit the NF in 1994, it was generally agreed that his departure had more to do with election tactics than with a difference of principle. Peyrat assumed, probably rightly, that his chances for election would be improved if he disencumbered himself of the NF label.[111]

By contrast, sixty miles west of Paris in the city of Dreux, where Jean-Pierre Stirbois first established a Front beachhead in 1983 by winning election to the municipal council, the Socialist candidate withdrew after the first round. This allowed the mainstream right candidate to beat the NF list headed by ex-deputy Marie-France Stirbois in a two-way fight: 6,177 to 3,998. After her defeat, Stirbois bitterly commented that the successful candidate had "solicited [*racolé*] the '*beurs*.'"[112]

Another Front defeat occurred just west of Marseilles in Vitrolles, where NF mayoralty candidate Bruno Mégret, whose list had won 43.05 percent of the vote on the first ballot, lost to the Socialists on the second round.

Between the rounds the Communists and ecologists withdrew their candidates from the race and united behind the Socialists. The united left then campaigned vigorously to bring first-round abstentionists to the polls on the second round (the election law allows voters who abstained on the first round to vote on the second round). As a result, the Socialists won 45.02 percent of the vote as against Mégret's 42.89 percent and the mainstream right's 12.07 percent.

Thus, despite the fact that the Front's overall percentage of the vote in the municipal elections was down from Le Pen's 15 percent score in the presidential elections seven weeks before, the Front had accomplished two important objectives. It had extended its voting base outside the Marseilles area, heavily populated by immigrants and former *pieds-noirs* French settlers from Algeria, to working-class areas around Paris and to the industrial departments in the north. Polls confirmed that the Front was beginning to benefit from the support of working-class voters. Of equal and, in the long run, perhaps more importance was the election of 1,075 National Front representatives to municipal councils throughout France.[113] Whereas the 1983 election of Jean-Pierre Stirbois to the Dreux municipal council had made national headlines and inspired a soul-searching debate about the reappearance of the extreme right, the fact that 7 National Front councillors were elected to the city of Tourcoing (population 93,765), or 3 to the city of Lille (population 172,142), or 4 to the city of Lyon (population 415,487), inspired much less comment. It is true that the 1,075 Front councillors made up a tiny percentage of the more than 500,000 local politicians who serve at any one time in France, but by tripling the number from the previous election in 1989, the Front had obtained a firm foothold in local politics. Moreover, in France participation in local politics has a direct effect on the party's fortunes in national politics.

France is unusual in permitting politicians to hold multiple offices. Quite often deputies, or even cabinet ministers, simultaneously serve as mayors or municipal, regional, or cantonal councillors. Even the prime minister can hold local office: Soon after being chosen as prime minister in 1995, Alain Juppé ran for and won election as mayor of Bordeaux, France's fifth largest city, with a population of 700,000. Eleven members of his government also won mayoralty seats in 1995, and eight others were elected as municipal councillors.

This *cumul des mandats* (overlapping mandates) has many advantages. It means that deputies can use their position in Paris to ensure that the central administration in Paris takes account of the needs of the local community they represent.[114] In addition, mayors in France play a big role in the legislative election campaigns that take place within 577 election districts, one for each of the deputies in the National Assembly. Mayors can lend their prestige to a candidate or provide services in the form of funds, office space, or other perquisites to a campaign. And, of course, being a mayor helps when the mayor campaigns for national office. Local politics in France is highly personalized, with voters often more interested in the ability of the mayor to successfully obtain funds or services from departmental, regional, or national authorities than in questions of political ideology. For this reason, mayors often retain their posts even when there is a change of party and government at the national level. This means that parties with roots in local politics remain in the public eye and continue to exercise local power even when the tide of opinion turns against these parties at the national level.

For all these reasons, National Front gains in the June 1995 municipal elections were a milestone in the Front's history. The Front's electoral base had expanded into hitherto closed areas, the NF was now deeply implanted in local politics across France, it could use the prestige and levers of local office to help in future elections for national office, and as an active participant in politics it had a chance to implement its program.

Notes

1. See the October 28, 1987, interview with Olivier d'Ormesson and the April 16, 1988, interview with Le Pen in *Le Monde*. Pasqua was once again to become minister of the interior after the mainstream right victory in the March 1993 legislative election. He was not appointed to a cabinet post in the 1995 Juppé government.

2. Olivier d'Ormesson, in *Le Monde*, October 28, 1987.

3. Yann Piat, *Seule tout en haut à droite* (Paris: Fixot, 1991), pp. 164–165.

4. Jean Lecanuet, a centrist senator, proposed that "national discipline" characterize the electoral relations between the center and the National Front, i.e., that the mainstream right enter into election alliances with the Front. *Le Monde*, May 19, 1987.

5. Ibid.

6. Christophe Hameau, *Le campagne de Jean-Marie Le Pen pour l'élection présidentielle de 1988* (Paris: Travaux et Recherches de l'Université Panthéon-Assas [Paris II], n.d.), pp. 89–90.

7. Ibid.

8. *Le Monde*, March 12, 1988.

9. Ibid.

10. *Le Monde*, March 12, 1988. Appointed minister of the interior in March 1993 by RPR prime minister Édouard Balladur, Pasqua eventually pushed through an immigration law that sharply restricted access to French nationality for new immigrants, required immigrant children to positively declare for French nationality rather than automatically receiving it as under the previous law, and restored to the police draconian powers of stopping and searching suspected illegal immigrants.

11. Quoted in Hameau, *Le campagne*, p. 90.

12. Quoted in ibid.

13. Jacques Toubon, in *Le Monde*, May 12, 1987; Michel Noir, in *Le Monde*, May 15, 1987.

14. Quoted in Hameau, *Le campagne*, p. 90.

15. *Le Monde*, January 16, 1986.

16. Hameau, *Le campagne*, p. 88.

17. Quoted in *Le Monde*, May 4, 1988.

18. Quoted in Hameau, *Le campagne*, p. 67.

19. Quoted in Piat, *Seule*, p. 186.

20. Ibid., pp. 186–187.

21. *L'Année politique* (1988):57.

22. Piat, *Seule*, p. 189.

23. SOFRES, *L'état de l'opinion* (Paris: Seuil, 1989), p. 81.

24. Yann Piat spoke of "panic" in the NF leadership when it learned of Mitterrand's decision. Piat, *Seule*, p. 192. In November 1986 Le Pen accused Théo Klein of the Conseil Représentatif des Institutions Juives de France (Representative Council of Jewish Organizations in France, or CRIF) of "soliciting from the RPR an electoral promise that would eliminate the National Front." When asked by a reporter whether there were other lobby groups involved, Le Pen said that, although CRIF was the "main" one, SOS-Racisme was also involved. *Le Monde*, November 30, 1986.

25. The UDF was a federation of center-right parties that included Giscard's Republican Party, the Centre des Démocrates Sociaux (Center of Social Democrats), and representatives from some smaller parties.

26. *Le Monde*, May 19, 1988.

27. *Le Monde*, June 9, 1988.

28. While the Socialists and Communists sharply criticized the RPR, right-wing commentators supported the election deal. According to former Minister Alain Peyrefitte, "Which is the greatest danger for liberals—two or three National Front deputies or a majority for a socialist-communist coalition?" *Le Figaro*, June 8, 1988.

29. Before the second ballot, a polling organization had predicted that Le Pen would be defeated. Le Pen bet the president of the organization Fr 100,000 that he would win. Although he won 43.57 percent of the vote on the second ballot, Le Pen lost to the Socialist candidate—and paid off his bet.

30. *Le Monde*, June 14, 1988.

31. *Le Monde*, December 13, 1989. After the rhyme incident, Le Pen was shocked to be given his own medicine. Cardiologist Salem Kacet, attending a television debate between Le Pen and Socialist deputy Bernard Tapie, referred to "M. Le Punk." Le Pen corrected him: "Le Pen." Kacet replied: "Sorry, but I know you like jibes and since my children call you M. Le Punk . . . ." Quoted in Philippe Reinhard, *Bernard Tapie* (Paris: Éditions France-Empire, 1991), p. 205.

32. Piat, *Seule*, p. 205. Yann Piat reported that in summer 1988 ex-NF deputy François Bachelot predicted, "The National Front is looking to get some attention through some sort of provocation."

33. The incident is recounted in ibid., p. 206.

34. Guy Birenbaum argued that Arrighi, Bachelot, and Piat were already at odds with party general secretary Jean-Pierre Stirbois and that Le Pen's anti-Semitic re-

marks were an excuse, but not the grounds, for their resignations from the NF. Guy Birenbaum, *Le Front national en politique* (Paris: Balland, 1992), pp. 146ff. Yann Piat was murdered in February 1994, apparently because of her hard-line stance against drugs.

35. *Le Figaro-Magazine*, December 9, 1989. Pauwel cited no evidence showing that giving immigrants the right to vote had any relationship to ghettoization.

36. Quoted in Françoise Gaspard, *A Small City in France* (Cambridge, Mass.: Harvard University Press, 1995), p. 219.

37. Ibid., p. 237.

38. Ibid., p. 198.

39. *Le Monde*, December 5, 1989. According to *Le Monde*, "The National Front conducted openly racist campaigns [in addition to the legislative by-election, cantonal elections had also been held at this time]."

40. *Le Monde*, April 3, 1990.

41. This revision in the law was enacted by the Balladur government in 1995.

42. *Le Monde*, April 1, 1990.

43. Quoted in *Le Monde*, June 21, 1991.

44. *Le Figaro-Magazine*, September 21, 1991.

45. Although many people were shocked by Giscard's hard-line proposals on immigration, they were well in line with proposals he had put forward during his presidency to forcibly repatriate five hundred thousand Algerians and to impose quotas on the number of immigrants who might renew their residence and work permits. Robert Schneider, "Giscard: Les secrets d'une dérive," *Le Nouvel Observateur,* September 25, 1991.

46. *Le Monde*, April 19, 1988.

47. *Le Monde*, November 28, 1988.

48. *Le Monde*, April 19, 1988.

49. *Le Monde*, August 31, 1989. In May 1990 a French court found Le Gallou guilty of racial slander because of comments he had made in an article in the far right journal *Présent*, which he edited. *Le Monde*, May 4, 1990.

50. According to Yann Piat, Le Pen refused to shift his focus from immigration. When after the 1988 presidential elections a member of the party's political bureau asked if the "moment has not come to diversify and make our message more flexible," Le Pen responded: "The French who didn't vote for me, will only do so if we look like the only ones, beside the softies in the RPR and UDF, who are in touch on the immigration question. With the return of the left to power, we'll see a rush of Maghrebians to our cities. Tensions will increase. With this Arab invasion, we can tap an inexhaustible reservoir of discontented voters. We're going to focus even more on a tougher Le Pen and on immigration." Piat, *Seule*, p. 191.

51. *Le Figaro-Magazine*, December 6, 1989.

52. Four years earlier, in June 1985, NF general secretary Jean-Pierre Stirbois said that "people who are today naturalized French, perhaps will not be so after the arrival of the right in power because they will not satisfy the demands that we will retroactively put into effect." Quoted in *Le Monde*, October 18, 1985.

53. *Le Monde*, November 19, 1991.

54. Bruno Mégret, quoted in Marc Ferro, "Le Pen contre la France," *Le Nouvel Observateur,* November 28, 1991. According to Mégret: "Ecology is above all fi-

delity to the laws of nature, that is, to refuse mixtures and loss of identity. Why fight for the preservation of animal species and accept at the same time the disappearance of human races by general cross-breeding?"

55. Ibid.

56. Robert Solé, in *Le Monde*, November 19, 1991.

57. *Le Monde*, July 12, 1991.

58. *Le Monde*, November 23, 1991.

59. *Le Monde*, December 18, 1991.

60. Paul Yonnet, "La machine Carpentras: Histoire et sociologie d'un syndrome d'un épuration," *Le Débat* 61 (September-October 1990):18–34.

61. *Le Monde*, May 10, 1990. According to Paul Yonnet, the incident deeply shocked the French, many of whom believe that the existence of the mortal remains is a guarantee of eternal life for the soul. Ibid., p. 277.

62. Maurice Barrès, quoted in J. S. McClelland, *The French Right (from DeMaistre to Maurras)* (London: Jonathan Cape, 1970), p. 192. Barrès (1862–1923) was an anti-Semitic nationalist who influenced, among others, Charles Maurras.

63. *Le Monde*, May 18, 1990.

64. *Le Monde*, November 8, 1995.

65. Pierre Birnbaum described the evolution of anti-Semitic perspectives on Palestine and Israel in *La France aux Français* (Paris: Seuil, 1993), Chap. 9.

66. Ibid., p. 239.

67. Ibid., pp. 272–273.

68. Quoted in ibid., p. 280.

69. *Le Monde*, October 16, 1990.

70. Quoted in Birenbaum, *Le Front national*, p. 185.

71. Le Pen on FR3, August 15, 1990, quoted in ibid., p. 184.

72. René Monzat, *Enquêtes sur la droite extrême* (Paris: Le Monde Éditions, 1992), p. 301.

73. Front National, *300 mesures pour la renaissance de la France* (Paris: Éditions Nationales, 1993), p. 331.

74. Cited in Birenbaum, *Le Front national*, p. 182.

75. Quoted in ibid., p. 183.

76. Quoted in ibid., p. 187.

77. *Le Monde*, October 3, 1990.

78. Le Pen's support for Iraq and his endorsement of Saddam Hussein provoked opposition within the NF. One of the most popular of NF leaders, Pierre Sergent, a former member of the OAS who described himself as pro-Israel, stated that he did not want his name connected to Saddam Hussein.

79. *Le Monde*, October 3, 1990.

80. *Le Monde*, October 22, 1985.

81. Ibid.

82. *Le Monde*, October 26, 1985.

83. *Le Monde*, January 12, 1988.

84. *Le Monde*, September 29, 1993.

85. *Le Monde*, May 20, 1994.

86. *Le Monde*, April 1, 1990.

87. Quoted by Olivier Biffaud in *Le Monde,* November 8–9, 1992.

88. *Le Monde,* November 10, 1992.

89. Quoted by Olivier Biffaud, in *Le Monde,* November 13, 1992.

90. The author was present at this meeting, held March 7, 1993.

91. *Présent,* March 19, 1993.

92. *National Hebdo,* March 11–17, 1993.

93. *Le Monde,* September 26, 1995.

94. *Le Monde,* February 2, 1994.

95. *Le Monde,* June 11, 1993. A Socialist deputy asked how one could establish whether a foreigner and a French national married for love or for French citizenship, "unless one verified it at their bedside?" *Le Monde,* June 16, 1993.

96. *Présent,* May 4, 1993.

97. Ibid.

98. *Le Monde,* September 26–27, 1993.

99. Denis Jeambar and Jean-Marc Lech, *Le self-service électoral* (Paris: Flammarion, 1992), p. 28.

100. Ibid.

101. Pascal Perrineau, "Vers une recomposition du politique?" in *L'état de la France* (Paris: La Découverte, 1994), pp. 32–34; and interview in *Le Monde,* April 25, 1995.

102. Quoted in *Le Monde,* June 14, 1994.

103. Quoted in *Le Monde,* November 13–14, 1994.

104. *Le Monde,* January 10, 1995.

105. *Le Monde,* February 11, 1995.

106. Jean-Louis Schlegel, "Philippe de Villiers, ou les valeurs de l'enracinement," *Ésprit* 209 (February 1995):62.

107. *Le Monde,* February 11, 1995.

108. Schlegel, "Philippe de Villers," p. 55.

109. Jean-Marie Le Chevallier was a member of Giscard d'Estaing's Republican Party in the mid-1970s but became friendly with Le Pen in the late 1970s. Le Chevallier joined the National Front in 1983 and became Le Pen's executive assistant, a member of the front's political bureau, a municipal and regional councillor, and, since 1984, a member of the European Parliament.

110. Bompard, a dentist, was a member in the 1960s of the violent, racist, and anti-Semitic Ordre Nouveau. He was a founding member of the Front in 1972 and is a member of its political bureau. He was a deputy from 1986 to 1988 and has been active in regional and local politics as a municipal and regional councillor.

111. Peyrat was educated in Nice, practiced there as a lawyer, and served on the municipal council in the 1960s and in the 1980s and 1990s. He was a supporter of former mayor Jacques Médecin, who fled to South America after being indicted for fraud. Peyrat was a National Front deputy from 1986 to 1988.

112. Quoted in *Le Monde,* June 20, 1995.

113. The exact number elected is difficult to calculate because some NF councillors concealed their party allegiance during the election. The Ministry of the Interior estimated that the NF elected 992 NF municipal councillors; *Le Monde* put the number at 1,075. *Le Monde,* June 21, 1995.

114. The NF's 1985 program proposed that politicians not be allowed to simultaneously hold more than one national and one local office and that civil servants no longer be allowed to retain their posts while serving in regional or national elected positions. Jean-Marie Le Pen, *Pour la France* (Paris: Albatros, 1985), p. 42. This proposition was not repeated in the Front's major 1993 policy statement, *300 mesures*. Of the eleven Front candidates elected to the European Parliament in 1994, four simultaneously held more than one national and one local elected post.

PART 2

Analysis

———

6

Anti-Semitism

The aim of the National Front is to bring about the revival of racism and anti-semitism.

—François Bachelot, *in* Le Monde, *September 8, 1988*

For me, an antisemite is someone who persecutes Jews because they are Jewish. It's clear. I am not one.

—Jean-Marie Le Pen, *in* Le Monde, *December 17, 1987*

François Mitterrand is a master of the Kabbalah. He is scattering around the French capital geometric shapes whose basis we know about. . . . Today the religion of the golden calf is replacing Christianity.

—Jean-Marie Le Pen, *quoted in Pierre Birnbaum,* La France aux Français

Anti-Semitism has been one of the main features of the French extreme right since the end of the nineteenth century.[1] It has taken the form of violent diatribes by anti-Semitic authors such as Édouard Drumont, Drieu la Rochelle, and Charles Maurras; anti-Jewish mass rallies or riots like those that occurred during the Dreyfus Affair in the 1880s or in Paris during the 1930s; and genocidal policies such as the deadly roundup and transportation to concentration camps of Jews by French police during the Vichy period in the 1940s. However, the Nazi defeat, the disclosures about the Holocaust, and the marginalization of the extreme right after 1945 led to the adoption of laws severely punishing blatantly racist or anti-Semitic statements and to an attenuation of anti-Semitism. However, attitudes began to change in 1967 when de Gaulle reacted against Israel after the 1967 Arab-Israeli War. In a November 11, 1967, press conference, President de Gaulle referred to the Jews as "an elite people, sure of itself and dominating."[2] In 1968 philosopher Raymond Aron complained that de Gaulle's remarks had made anti-Semitism acceptable in the best circles.[3] By the 1970s anti-Zionism had begun to merge imperceptibly with anti-Semitism. Traditional views of the Jews as the "other" were inadvertently revealed in October 1980 after a bomb exploded at the rue Copernic synagogue in Paris, killing four people. Prime Minister Raymond Barre commented that the bomb was intended to "kill Jews, but wound up killing innocent Frenchmen."[4] This distinction between Jews and Frenchmen provoked widespread public criticism.

Nonetheless, because anti-Semitism still had not reached prewar levels, when the National Front was established in 1972, the leadership decided that open expressions of anti-Semitism were politically unwise as well as too risky in the existing legal climate. The Front therefore wrapped its anti-Semitism in a fog of codewords and coded phrases that allowed it to react with disingenuous innocence when accused of anti-Semitism but that at the same time conveyed the essential message.

For the French extreme right, Jews have always stood for everything that is anti-French. Traditionally, the figure of the Wandering Jew featured prominently in extreme right propaganda, symbolizing the rootless cosmopolitan doomed to wander the earth for having disavowed Christ. For extreme right nationalists, the Jew stood for modernity as opposed to tradition, the Republic as opposed to monarchy, equality as opposed to hierarchy, cosmopolitanism as opposed to rootedness, parliamentary democracy as opposed to authoritarianism, and capitalism as opposed to corporatism. Carrying on from a medieval tradition that portrayed the Jew as physically repulsive and as the source of a myriad of sexual perversions, the anti-Semitic caricature of the French Jew took shape: Jews do not drink wine, they do not fight during wartime, they do not work the land and so feel no attachment to the soil, they are deeply hostile to Christianity, and their only loyalty is to their co-religionists. Although Front leaders today avoid these canards in speeches and publications aimed at the wider public, the pro-Front press and many Front leaders express blatantly anti-Semitic sentiments within the party itself.

The fact that Jews constitute only 1.3 percent of the total French population of 58 million is irrelevant. For the Front, Jewish influence flows from the key roles that Jews are supposed to play in education, the media, and government—the major instruments in the production of ideas.[5] In contrast to North Africans and Muslims, who threaten to undermine French national values and culture by sheer weight of numbers, the threat from the forces of cosmopolitanism and *mondialisme* is more insidious. Thus, even though the Front is obsessed with the statistics on the actual numbers of Muslims and North Africans in France, it is more interested in identifying Jews in the media and business. Each discovery of a Jewish presence (even one individual) in a position of power supports the presumption of a Jewish conspiracy and confirms the Front as self-appointed guardian of the French nation and culture.[6] According to one critic, in the Front's lexicon, "to be French is . . . to be non-Jewish."[7]

The most virulent anti-Semitism is preached by journalists of the pro–National Front press such as François Brigneau, formerly with *Présent* and more recently with *National Hebdo*.[8] Although he is not a party member, Brigneau is an undeviating supporter of the National Front and in his column "Le Journal d'un Homme Libre" he explains almost all political events in terms of the machinations of Jews and of Jewish organizations such as B'nai B'rith.[9] Like many anti-Semites, Brigneau favors a heavily sarcastic, ad hominem style, interweaving personal insults with allegations concerning a Jewish conspiracy. In 1984 he described Socialist minister of justice Robert Badinter as a "wandering furrier . . . [whose] mouth was twisted with black blood. . . . By heredity, he is for nomads against sedentary people, for the cosmopolitans against those who are indigenous, for the chicken thief against the farmer."[10]

In 1984 Socialist leader Laurent Fabius was depicted as a monkey with clawed feet.[11] In 1992, at a time when Fabius was under investigation for the role that he played as prime minister in connection with the distribution by French hospitals of AIDS-contaminated blood, the anti-Semitic weekly *Minute–La France* published a cartoon under the title "La Fin de Fabius" (The End of Fabius) and written in red letters. Fabius was depicted with a large, hooked nose, rapacious face, and hands tinted yellow and with red blood dripping from vampirelike fingers.[12] When asked about the cartoon, Le Pen replied in the same way as he had in 1958 when questioned about his description of Mendès-France: "Caricatures consist of exaggerating the features of the people one sketches. True, it's difficult to see Mr. Fabius passing for a Viking."[13]

Divided Loyalties

One recurring anti-Semitic accusation before World War II was that Jews could not be accepted as fully French because they put loyalty to their co-religionists above France; after 1948 anti-Semites accused Jews of putting the interests of Israel above those of France. Le Pen alluded to this in a December 5, 1989, television discussion when he asked Lionel Stoleru, the Socialist secretary of state for planning, if he held dual nationality. When Stoleru replied that he was French, Le Pen said that he was "glad" because "I would have been a little disturbed if . . . you had another nationality. You are a French Minister. One has a right to know who you are." In case this exchange left some viewers confused, the moderator noted: "Mr. Stoleru, you are Jewish? Because Mr. Le Pen without doubt is alluding to the fact that you could have dual Israeli and French nationality?" "To be Jewish," Stoleru answered, "is not a nationality. . . . Until now, it is a religion."[14] In 1987 André Figueras, an anti-Semitic author close to the Front, drew the logical conclusion from the Front's accusation that Jewish loyalties lay outside France when he told Jews that if they were really Jewish, they should emigrate to Israel.[15]

Doubting the Holocaust

Another anti-Semitic tactic that features prominently in Front propaganda is to question the number of Jews killed during the Holocaust, to minimize its impact, or to deny that it even occurred. Le Pen expressed his views on the Holocaust during a September 1987 television interview when he was asked to comment on the "revisionist" or negationist historians who deny that the Holocaust occurred. "I don't say that the gas chambers didn't exist," he replied. "I wasn't able to see them myself. I haven't especially studied the question. But I believe that it [the question of the gas chambers] is a point of detail in the history of the Second World War."[16]

Le Pen's September 1988 "Durafour-*crématoire*" remark was greeted with outrage, and the European Parliament lifted Le Pen's parliamentary immunity, making him eligible for a libel suit.[17] Le Pen, undaunted, referred to a "methodic organization, methodically directed, of cosmopolitan subversion trying through collective mechanisms to get the Jewish community to oppose the National Front and the idea of the nation."[18] In an April 1995 campaign speech, Le Pen used the phrase *la verité qui nous rendra libre* (the truth that will make us free), which, a *Le Monde* journalist observed, was the French translation of *Wahrheit macht frei*, the watchword of German neo-Nazi negationists (who deny that the Holocaust occurred).[19]

In September 1989, after questioning the existence of the Holocaust, Front MEP (member of the European Parliament) Claude Autant-Lara stated, "When people talk to me about genocide, I say, in any case, they missed 'Mother' Veil."[20] Autant-Lara was here referring to Simone Veil, one of the most popular politicians in France, a member of the European Parliament, and a Jewish survivor of a World War II concentration camp. When this remark provoked widespread condemnation, journalist François Brigneau wrote in the pro-Front *National Hebdo*: "If there was extermination—which has been contested by an entire school of serious historians . . . Mrs. Veil happily escaped. What is injurious or condemnable in stating that?"[21] When asked to comment on Autant-Lara's remarks, Le Pen responded in a typical, "on the one hand, on the other hand," fashion:

"Implicating Mrs. Veil is quite open to criticism. . . . [Although] it doesn't merit such media and political attention while there are much more important problems in France."[22] To draw attention to the fact that Veil is not a "French" name, Le Pen tends to pronounce her name by emphasizing the final "l"—this is not usually done in French.[23]

The Jewish Conspiracy

According to the Front, the key to understanding French politics can be found in the notion of a Jewish conspiracy aimed at destroying France and ruling it, and ultimately the world, in the interests of a "cosmopolitan oligarchy." The prototype for this idea is, of course, the *Protocols of the Elders of Zion*, a nineteenth-century forgery concocted by the czarist secret police that purported to be the minutes of a meeting of an international Jewish conspiracy. Front leaders argue that Jewish organizations such as Conseil Représentatif des Institutions Juives en France (CRIF) or B'nai B'rith, which is a Jewish fraternal and charitable organization, are at the heart of this sinister conspiracy. In 1977 Le Pen remarked to an extreme right journalist: "Everybody has a right to a country, and each people must have a nation, but that doesn't imply the takeover of French politics by lobbies. Israel must exist, not the Jewish lobby. The large number of Jews in the areas of information or politics implies a certain pressure of a cosmopolitan tendency. Thus, contrary to national interests, these people always oppose nationalism and the idea of the nation. Their large number and their common attitude explain many things. It's up to the law to reduce and eliminate these abnormal oligarchies."[24]

One Front leader who is particularly infatuated with the international conspiracy idea is Bernard Antony (alias Roman Marie). Antony is the founder of the extreme right Christianity-Solidarity organization and co-founder of the pro-Front newspaper *Présent*.[25] Although a supporter of extreme right bishop Marcel Lefebvre, Antony remained within the Catholic Church after Lefebvre was suspended from his duties in 1976. Antony is also an NF member of the European Parliament and a member of the Front's political bureau, and he was part of the eight-man team that drafted the Front's 1993 election program. According to Antony, there is an international Jewish conspiracy working behind the scenes to rule the world. In 1979 he described "the tendency that Jews have to occupy all the key posts in Western nations. . . . The modern world is characterized by a new intrusion of the Jewish phenomenon. . . . Marx and Rothschild are a little like two faces on the same coin."[26] In a 1991 debate in the European Parliament on the Gulf War, Antony observed: "So there is to be a new world order, but who is going to be in charge? A select band of citizens from various parts of the world, the same who are more equal than others, meeting in secret societies for which they have to swear oaths, like members of the B'nai B'rith with which the National Front will never be forming any associations."[27] At a October 3, 1991, meeting organized by Antony and NF MEP Jean-Claude Martinez under the theme "Let's get out of Europe!" the twelve-star European flag was replaced by one bearing a Socialist rose, a Communist hammer and sickle, an American dollar, a Masonic compass, a Muslim crescent, and a Jewish star of David.[28]

In the anti-Semitic tradition, Jews as well as Freemasons are vilified for opposing the core values of French society. Among fundamentalist circles in the Front, the problem with Jews is that they are not Catholic and as such cannot be truly French.[29] In 1989 a Front publication said: "The cosmopolitan ideology is a war machine. Under the cover of The Rights of Man, it is a weapon against the ideas of 'rootedness' [*enracinement*], of tradition, of heritage and of heredity; it is even a weapon against European civilization itself."[30] Above all, Jews and their allies are seen as "antinational."[31] In an August 12, 1989, interview published in *Présent*, Le Pen declared that the "Freemasons, the Trilateral Commission and the great internationals like the Jewish International play a not unimportant role in the creation of an antinational spirit," although he qualified this assertion, remarking that "not all Jewish organizations or Jews" were involved in antinational maneuvers.[32]

An expanded version of this thesis appeared in the Front's 1993 election program, *300 mesures pour la renaissance de France* (300 steps toward the rebirth of France).[33] In a two-page preface, Le Pen stated that the political establishment has, "in a servile fashion, aligned itself with external foreign powers and internal lobbies, and, with the complicity of a media power under orders, systematically gagged those who tried to speak the truth."[34] It is left to the reader's imagination to determine the identity of the lobbies or those who give orders to the media.

Over the past few years the Front has added a new word, *mondial* or *mondialiste*, to the conspiracy theory vocabulary. In the eight-page introduction to the program, the words *mondial* and *mondialiste* occur fourteen times, six times as part of the phrase *idéologie mondialiste* and once as *doctrine mondialiste*. The term *oligarchie* appears five times, once as *oligarchie mondialiste*, once as *oligarchie*, once as *oligarchie tout-puissante* (all-powerful), once as *dangereuse oligarchie*, and once as *régime oligarchique*. The term *mondialiste* often appears in conjunction with the traditional codeword for Jews, *cosmopolitan*, although *mondialiste* has a slightly different meaning. Whereas the term *cosmopolitan* is associated with rootlessness and lack of commitment to any country or organization, *mondial* refers to individuals and organizations committed to international organizations such as the United Nations or to transnational organizations such as the

European Community. Because Jews are assumed to favor anything that will weaken the nation-state (except, of course, Israel), they inevitably support *mondialiste* causes.[35]

According to the NF, a *mondialiste* doctrine has arisen to take the place of Marxism. It is "usually dressed up as the rights of man, preaches the destruction of nations, the abolition of frontiers, mixing of races, cultures and peoples. Formerly the Marxists looked to eliminate inequalities in their search for a classless society. Today, the *mondialistes* attack what they call "exclusion" and instead stand for the establishment of a society without differences. The myth of Paradise has given way to a utopia of a *café au lait* Paradise. Now that the dictatorship of the proletariat is no longer popular, the idea of the melting-pot has become de rigeur."[36]

The result is that the nation is considered as "old hat and bad. . . . Patriotism is seen as a kind of racism."[37] French identity is threatened by "massive immigration coming from other continents and other civilizations which might submerge it."[38] This, along with the construction of the European Community, is the first step toward world government. In February 1990 Georges-Paul Wagner, a member of the Front's political bureau, noted in *Présent:* "France did not have to await Hitler and his lash to discover the perils of *mondialisme* and cosmopolitanism, which under the pretext of lowering frontiers raises other barriers between people and prepares civil war."[39] Wagner was here referring to the accusation that Jews favor lowering barriers to immigration, which increases internal tension, saps the nation's morale, and leads ultimately to the decline of France itself.

In August 1992 Le Pen accused "those who demand secure and recognized frontiers for Israel" of wanting to "destroy those of France." Le Pen went on to claim that the Maastricht Treaty (which extended the scope of the European Community) was "one of the keys of a true *mondialiste* and internationalist plot. . . . The promoters of Maastricht make no mystery of the hatred that they bear toward the nation, to the national fact, to national values. And one of them, the most illustrious, said, 'It only remains to surmount the final obstacle, the nation.'" According to *Le Monde,* Le Pen was referring to the purported remarks of Baron de Rothschild quoted in *Présent.*[40]

At the same time, however, Front ideologists have not abandoned the idea that a specifically national Jewish conspiracy is working to undermine France. According to the Front, all the political parties have combined into a "dangerous" oligarchy that holds *mondialiste* views and is attempting to impose them on the French nation. The result is that France is no longer a democracy and what the majority of the French want is subsumed to a "new official ideology, the *mondialiste* ideology."[41] France is living under an oligarchy "comparable, making due allowances, to that of the ex-soviet system." Before the 1993 legislative elections, Yvan Blot, a member of the NF's political bureau and a founding member of the Club de l'Horloge (Clock Club), speculated in *Présent* on why the mainstream right had refused to form an election alliance with the Front: "In reality, the essential choices and strategy are worked out by secret committees consisting of men who carefully avoid presenting themselves in elections."[42] According to Blot, these "little-known" men are "F. Heilbronner, Jacques Friedmann, Jérôme Monod and Denis Baudoin." Lest the reader miss the point, Blot noted that "the connections of these high civil servants with the Masons, B'nai B'rith or CRIF are crucial in fixing the ideological and strategic choices of the party concerned. . . . The façade of democracy hides the true power of secret committees, with all the defects of this kind of oligarchy."[43]

Although on the face of it, this seems little more than another variation of anti-Semitic conspiracy theories, there is more to Blot's remarks than meets the eye. In his 1985 book *Les racines de la liberté* (The roots of liberty), Blot accused the Socialists of establishing a series of little feudal kingdoms within the French state, specifically in the civil service. This *nomenklatura* then uses its position of power to further the interests of socialism by giving economic and political advantages to socialist supporters or by using state-controlled organs of propaganda to spread the socialist message. For Blot, those who represent "authentic democracy" must bypass these "feudalities" and return power to the majority of the people.[44] From this perspective, Jews constitute one of the feudalities that compose the oligarchy working for socialism and against the people. Or, as Blot likes to put it, the Socialists have used the state to attack the nation. The job of the Front, therefore, is to abolish the fiefdoms, destroy the oligarchy, and, through mechanisms such as popular referenda, build a political system that will bring the people into direct contact with government.

A cruder variation on this theme comes from François Brigneau of *National Hebdo,* who in 1993 accused B'nai B'rith of forcing the "parliamentary opposition" to a "servile obedience to [its] orders."[45] The notorious anti-Semite and ardent NF supporter Jean Madiran (also known as Jean Arfel), cofounder and political director of *Présent,* also sees the hand of B'nai B'rith behind anything inimical to the National Front. In March 1990 he accused President François Mitterrand of "responding to the demands of the B'nai B'rith and to a cosmo-*mondialiste* ideology" in the struggle against racism and anti-Semitism.[46]

Anti-Semitism and Divisions in the Front

Front leaders, including Le Pen, strongly reject accusations of anti-Semitism, accusing the Jewish community of being overly sensitive or of trading on the memory of the Holocaust to escape legitimate criticism. At one point, Yann Piat, NF deputy from 1986 to 1988, argued that Le Pen's infamous "detail" remark was merely a slip of the tongue and not an expression of anti-Semitic convictions. "It is doubtful that Le Pen knowingly wanted to insult the memory of the victims of the holocaust. I think that he meant that the means utilized to exterminate the deportees (whether it was gas or some other technique for bringing about death) was a detail which did not modify at all the barbarism of genocide."[47]

Along these lines, Le Pen was reported to have commented to his chief of staff, Jean-Marie Le Chevallier, "In forty years of political life, it is the most unfortunate word that ever left my mouth"; to another colleague he observed, "What stupidity."[48] And Piat quoted Le Pen's wife, Pierrette, as saying that he was "very discouraged and furious at himself."[49] Some NF officials asked Le Pen to apologize for the detail remark, and one extreme right newspaper in Marseilles asked if Le Pen had committed an "irreversible error."[50] Yann Piat criticized Le Pen's remark as a "dormitory joke."[51] At one point Le Pen seemed to retreat from the implications of the detail remark, reading a statement to the press that said, "I would like to say to French Jews that France has the same love for all its children, whatever their race or religion."[52] But this cryptic remark was as close as Le Pen ever got to apologizing to the French Jewish community, although it managed to enrage NF secretary general Jean-Paul Stirbois, who complained that the "international Jewish conspiracy" had extended its influence to the Front. "One should throw out of the party all those who don't have a [party] card," he fulminated. "Le Pen has around him a group paid by the international Jewish bank. That's too much!"[53]

Despite Le Pen's denial, there is overwhelming evidence that Le Pen is steeped in anti-Semitism. All his life he has associated with some of France's most notorious anti-Semites; he has never disavowed their anti-Semitic remarks, and many of these individuals are top members of the National Front. Two of his closest friends, who also happened to be his personal physicians, Jean-Maurice Demarquet and François Bachelot, accused him of anti-Semitism.[54] His ex-wife, Pierrette, quoted him as saying: "Hitler was a jerk with his gas chambers. He fouled up. For the Jews, I would have used giant crushers: it would have been quicker and final."[55] On numerous occasions French courts have fined Le Pen or other Front spokespersons for making racist or anti-Semitic remarks. Front literature is filled with anti-Semitic allusions, and the pro-Front press, especially *Présent* and *National Hebdo,* often publishes anti-Semitic articles, cartoons, and quotations. Moreover, Le Pen's repeated anti-Semitic slurs leave no room for doubt about his own sentiments.[56]

Yet not every member of the Front is anti-Semitic, and Le Pen's anti-Semitism has occasionally provoked resignations. Le Pen's detail remark led to the resignation of several local party officials as well as to the resignation of MEP Olivier d'Ormesson, a leading party moderate and president of Le Pen's presidential nomination committee.[57] D'Ormesson was replaced as committee head by Bruno Mégret, a member of the Club de l'Horloge, formerly a member of the RPR, and a hard-line member of the Front. NF deputy Pascal Arrighi also criticized Le Pen's slighting of the Holocaust, and he resigned a year later after Le Pen's "rhyme" remark. According to François Bachelot:

> The play on words was the last straw. On the "detail' story I thought that Le Pen had been trapped like a student. But I then understood that there were no taboo subjects in the party, and that the "revisionist" thesis was a permanent subject of discussion. This was finally confirmed to me when I was convoked before a discipline meeting. ... Jean-Marie Le Pen recalled to me that the National Front was there to revenge itself against the anti-France, the Jews and the Freemasons. ... In reality, Le Pen and his friends wanted to make the Jews pay for [the extreme right] being cast off the French political stage since 1945.[58]

By this time Le Pen's anti-Semitism had driven a deep wedge between the committed anti-Semites and a minority in the Front who were not personally anti-Semitic or who thought it politically unwise for Le Pen to harp on the anti-Semitic theme. After the 1988 presidential and legislative elections, NF deputy Yann Piat joined François Bachelot for a drink. Bachelot commented: "Our president is the victim of a fixed idea, colored with paranoia. It can be treated." According to Piat: "Bachelot tried to explain to Le Pen that the NF must modify its strategy and its message, under penalty of losing popular support. The chief got irritated. In his opinion, the movement must, on the contrary, toughen its positions and accentuate its reputation for intransigence. 'With the president, all political analysis is impossible,' Bachelot said. 'He [Le Pen] ended the conversation by saying to me[,] ... "There are 30 percent of the French who are against immigration and against the Jews: these 30 percent will sooner or later vote for the National Front."'"[59]

Anti-Semitism and Party Tactics

In view of the widespread outrage that greets Le Pen every time he makes an anti-Semitic remark, and the fact that the majority of French citizens do not hold anti-Semitic views, why does the Front cling so tenaciously to anti-Semitism?[60] One reason is that anti-Semitism is part of a century-old tradition on the extreme right and is a major element holding together the various factions that compose the Front. Whatever differences may exist among

NF Catholic fundamentalists, neopagans, royalists, anti-Americans, pro-Americans, neofascists, and moderates, almost all share in the Front's pervasive anti-Semitism.[61] This point was made after the detail remark to Le Pen himself by Jacques Dominati, an old friend and a member of Giscard's Republican Party, when he met Le Pen in the National Assembly. Le Pen accused the press of trapping him.

> Dominati: It's your fault.
> Le Pen: Why? You can see what they do to crush me. At all costs, the Jews want me to be against them.
> Dominati: Jean-Marie, I know nothing of the kind, for a simple reason. When you were asked the question about the "detail," I was listening and I saw how you beat about the bush. Why? Because you didn't want to upset your friends who deny genocide. They're anti-Semites. And little by little, you are becoming one.[62]

Dominati's remark was very acute. In fact, the NF's political bureau reads like a Who's Who of anti-Semitism in France: Bernard Antony, Yvon Blot, Roland Gaucher, Bruno Mégret, Jean-Pierre Stirbois, and Georges-Paul Wagner have all expressed anti-Semitic sentiments in speeches or in the pro-Front press or have been associated with anti-Semitic organizations. The constant references in the Front's 1993 election program to a cosmopolitan, *mondialiste* plot can leave no doubt about the central role that anti-Semitism plays in the Front's doctrine.

A second reason for the pervasive anti-Semitism is that the idea of a Jewish conspiracy can be used to explain practically any political event. For example, between the rounds of the 1988 presidential election, the NF was torn between two equally distasteful choices: throwing its support to Mitterrand in order to defeat Chirac, who was deeply loathed by the party for refusing to make election alliances with the Front, or supporting Chirac against the socialist Mitterrand. According to Yann Piat, when Le Pen came to the regular Monday morning meeting of the Front's political bureau on May 2, before the second round of the election, he was "furious." There was a long silence. Eventually someone had the courage to ask Le Pen if the Front would support Chirac on the second ballot. Le Pen replied: "Never! And you know why? ... Because I have a copy of a letter that Théo Klein, the President of CRIF addressed to Jacques Toubon [the secretary general of the RPR]. And you know what he asked him! ... The boss of the CRIF clearly stated that the RPR would not benefit from any support from the Jews if it did not erect a complete roadblock against the National Front."[63]

Later at a press conference Le Pen observed: "In any case, the RPR and UDF are only obeying orders." Question: "Who gives these orders?" Le Pen: "The lobbies. ... If you had read the letter that Mr. Klein sent to [the secretary general] of the RPR! Even I wouldn't have spoken to my servants that way."[64] Le Pen thus avoided taking a clear-cut position on the presidential election, accused the RPR of caving in to Jewish influence, and clearly implied that the Front was the only party that would resist pressure from the Jewish community. The fact is, however, that Le Pen's antics at the St. Cloud breakfast and his remarks at the subsequent press conference were a charade, for Le Pen certainly knew that the CRIF's letter was an entirely legitimate means for trying to influence the RPR's policies and that it in no way demonstrated that the Jewish community exercised some kind of mysterious influence over Chirac.[65]

Indeed, Yann Piat referred to the Klein letter, the detail incident, and the Front's election maneuvers as "a fairy tale," and she concluded, "In fact, neither the one [Le Pen], nor the other [Chirac] had any intention of agreeing: the positions taken were just a façade determined by the situation."[66] Thus, Le Pen's anger at the CRIF was feigned: He knew full well that with or without pressure from a Jewish organization, Chirac would not enter into negotiations with the National Front. By dragging in a putative Jewish conspiracy, however, Le Pen neatly finessed the political problem posed to the Front by the second ballot of the presidential election.[67]

Despite Le Pen's maneuvers, Chirac decided to publicly disavow any possibility of cooperation with the National Front at either the national or local level. The RPR stipulated that any politician who concluded such an alliance would be excluded from the RPR and that the party would welcome ex–National Front members as long as they unequivocally "condemned the curse of racism and anti-Semitism."[68] The RPR declaration referred specifically to Le Pen's "recent statements," thus leaving no doubt that Le Pen's continued anti-Semitism constituted a major obstacle to cooperation between the two parties.[69] The importance of this step by the RPR should not be underestimated, for it laid the groundwork for the agreement between the RPR and the UDR to nominate joint candidates for the first round of the 1993 legislative elections, thus effectively nullifying any possibility that the National Front could hold the balance of power between the two rounds of the election and thereby induce any of the mainstream parties into an election alliance.

The Centrality of Anti-Semitism

In the early 1990s some members of the French right tried to convince Le Pen that abandoning anti-Semitism might clear the way for a broad-based coalition composed of the mainstream right and the National Front. In an attempt to shock Le Pen into action, Louis Pauwels, editor of the conservative Le Figaro–Magazine, accused Le Pen of serving the cause of

Mitterrand's Socialist government by splitting the forces of the right.[70] At a round-table discussion in 1990, Pauwels pressed Le Pen to abandon anti-Semitism for the sake of right-wing unity. Le Pen flatly refused. Pauwels pointed out that the mainstream right took positions that hardly differed from those of the National Front on the economy or immigration. "What is it, then, that separates you?" Pauwels asked. Le Pen answered that the right was not willing to take the "courageous measures which will be necessary" with regard to immigration. Le Pen added that the National Front did not intend to become a diluted version of either the RPR or the UDF and that the mainstream right would have to break with policies that stood in the way of a "renaissance." "There must be other reasons," Pauwels said, "why it is impossible for the right to live with you?"[71] Clearly, Pauwels was referring to anti-Semitism and pleading with Le Pen to reconsider his position for the sake of unity. But Le Pen replied, as he had in the past, that he was not anti-Semitic and that "every time that one brings to bear on the Jews an appreciation which does not consist exclusively of praise, one is suspected of being an anti-Semite."[72]

But Pauwels and Le Pen were talking past each other. For Pauwels, Le Pen's anti-Semitism was an unfortunate deviation from the existing political consensus and a personal prejudice that could be abandoned to clear the way for a grand coalition of the right. For Le Pen and the extreme right, anti-Semitism was a central tenet of a doctrine that held that the hand of the Jewish conspiracy could be detected behind the great events of French history, from the revolution, to the Dreyfus Affair, the rise of Socialism, World War II, and the European Community. For the extreme right, Jews were the essence of everything anti-French and anti-France. In what Pierre Birnbaum referred to as the "Franco-French war" between those who support the Republic, universalism, secularism, and the values of parliamentary democracy and those who support counterrevolution, authoritarianism, fundamentalist Catholicism, and nationalism, the Jew is the archsymbol of the hated Republic.

The tenacious anti-Semitism of the extreme right also reflects nostalgia for Vichy and resentment at the way Vichy has been discussed by intellectuals since 1945. According to historian Henry Rousso, French politics since the Liberation has been marked by competition between left and right over whose definition of, and explanation for, the Vichy years will dominate. Three elements compose what Rousso called the "Vichy syndrome": a traditional, counterrevolutionary Catholic element devoted to rehabilitating the memory of Marshal Pétain, an extreme right element nostalgic for the values of the Vichy era as summed up in its *"Travail-Famille-Patrie"* slogan, and anti-Semitism.[73] Le Pen and the National Front certainly fit this definition of the Vichy syndrome. This was made explicit in September 1989 when, after having been excluded from the NF for criticizing Le Pen's

"Durafour-*crématoire*" rhyme, François Bachelot stated that "the new line is founded openly on racism and anti-Semitism. . . . Le Pen has only one fixed idea: to finally see the Catholic population get the upper hand over the lobbies, what he calls anti-France, that is to say the press lobby, the Masonic lobby, and the Jewish lobby."[74] According to Bachelot, Le Pen's anti-Semitic remarks were far from being a slip of the tongue. They were instead part of a grand strategy to convince the public that the "lobbies" were anti-French.

Thus, the NF's anti-Semitism is at one and the same time a reflection of Le Pen's personal and political history, an attempt to rehabilitate Vichy, a tactical response to the problem of differentiating the NF from the mainstream parties of the right, a theme around which the feuding factions of the extreme right can unite, and an important weapon in the NF's unceasing struggle to alter the nature and language of political discourse and ideology in France. As Carl Lang, secretary general of the National Front, put it in August 1989, "The National Front demands the right to freedom of expression and refuses to submit to the dominant ideology and to conformity with those in power who oppose popular sovereignty and the nation."

This perspective on party doctrine throws light on the question of why Le Pen and the NF cling to anti-Semitism when to abandon it might actually improve the party's electoral fortunes. If the object of the NF were to win elections or to form election alliances with the mainstream right, then the anti-Semitism would have disappeared long ago. But the insistence of many in the Front that to be French is to be Catholic, or at least to have belonged to the Christian nations of Western Europe, means that Jews cannot be considered full members of the French political community. To accept them as such would open to the door to claims for membership from Muslims, North Africans, and others from "alien" cultures and religions. Doubtless there are those in the Front who would argue that some Jews (those who have "proven' their "Frenchness" by, say, serving in the armed forces or even supporting the Front) should be accepted as part of the French nation—and even Le Pen has on occasion alluded to this possibility—but given the heavily anti-Semitic bias of the pro-Front press and the weight of anti-Semitism among Front leaders and cadres, it is highly unlikely that this opinion has much support.

Notes

1. Political leaders on all sides of the political spectrum have occasionally expressed anti-Semitic sentiments. When in the 1950s Premier Pierre Mendès-France refused to count Communist votes in parliament as part of his majority, Communist leader Jacques Duclos said: "He's a coward, a little, timid Jew who prattles but

doesn't dare act. He's a shit except without the silk stockings." Quoted in Pierre Birnbaum, *Un mythe politique: "La République juive"* (Paris: Fayard, 1988), p. 112.

2. *Le Monde*, November 12, 1967.

3. The word Aron used was *"salonfähig."* Quoted in Henry H. Weinberg, *The Myth of the Jew in France, 1967–1982* (Oakville, Ontario: Mosaic Press, 1987) , p. 22.

4. Quoted in ibid., p. 78.

5. In a 1990 poll of 1,002 cadres attending the Front's eighth national congress, 62 percent agreed that "the Jews have too much power in France." *Le Monde*, April 8–9, 1990.

6. The Janus face of anti-Semitism is that, although anti-Semites want to rid the world of Jews and the Jewish conspiracy, at the same time they need Jews to confirm the existence of a conspiracy. Thus, the anti-Semite delights in revealing the "Jewish names" of eminent figures who have "non-Jewish names." Of course, in the absence of Jews, the focus shifts to the international arena, where anti-Semites can hunt for the Jews behind the "international Jewish conspiracy."

7. Michel Winock, *Nationalisme, antisémitisme et fascisme en France* (Paris: Seuil, 1982), p. 81. In the nineteenth century anti-Semites characterized the Jew as the embodiment of everything that was not French, thereby creating a symbol whose negative traits, when reversed, defined what it was to be truly French.

8. Brigneau was a Vichy supporter during World War II and a member of the infamous Milice, which specialized in hunting and torturing members of the Resistance. After the Liberation, Brigneau floated from one extreme right group to another. In December 1969 he was a founder of Ordre Nouveau, a violent extreme right organization. François Borella, *Les partis politiques dans la France d'aujour-d'hui* (Paris: Seuil, 1990), p. 205.

9. The accusation that B'nai B'rith is part of an international Jewish conspiracy has a long history. In 1942 it was said of Léon Blum that he was "under the orders of international Jewish finance, which decided to make war on Hitler, while he was simply a docile instrument in the hands of the international lodge of the B'nai B'rith." Hector Ghilini, quoted in Birnbaum, *La France aux Français* (Paris: Seuil, 1993), p. 110.

10. *Le Monde*, February 14, 1984. A nomad has no roots, and his emotions will never vibrate in tune with the patriotism and nationalism of "real" Frenchmen. "Deprived of his country and dispossessed of any national territory, the Jew is, essentially, a voyager and a nomad. He never stays, he is only passing through. . . . He has, therefore, no serious reason to take care of his home." Édouard Drumont, quoted in Michel Winock, *Édouard Drumont et Cie* (Paris: Seuil, 1982), p. 9.

11. Birnbaum, *Un mythe politique*, p. 203.

12. *Le Monde*, November 6, 1992.

13. *Le Monde*, November 10, 1992.

14. *Le Monde*, December 7, 1989.

15. André Figueras, *L'adieux aux juifs* (Paris: Publications André Figueras, 1987), pp. 42ff.

16. *Le Monde*, September 15, 1987.

17. In *Le Choc du Mois*, a pro-Front weekly, Jean Bourdier defended Le Pen by arguing that "in using the word 'crematorium' Le Pen was ignorant of the fact that he was entering onto private property. Crematorium ovens exist in all the large cities in France and the world, and function profitably, but it is apparently forbidden to name them under penalty of offending Jewish sensibilities—or, let's be frank, offending the pseudo-sensibilities of over-possessive Jews. The others, beginning with those whose parents really died during deportation, don't kick up such a fuss." *National Hebdo* was more to the point, denouncing "this anti-goy racism." Quoted in *Le Monde*, November 10, 1988. After this incident, NF deputies Pascal Arrighi, François Bachelot, and Yann Piat resigned from the party. In March 1991 Le Pen was fined Fr 10,000 for "publicly insulting a [government] Minister." *Le Monde*, June 6, 1991.

18. *Le Monde*, September 20, 1988.

19. *Le Monde*, April 22, 1995. Over the entrance to the Auschwitz concentration camp was a sign that said, "*Arbeit macht frei.*"

20. *Le Monde*, September 8, 1989.

21. *Le Monde*, September 16, 1989. Bruno Mégret characterized Autant-Lara as "a cultured man," "a great French director," a "creative man." Bruno Mégret, *La flamme* (Paris: Robert Laffont, 1990), p. 50.

22. *Le Monde*, September 11, 1989.

23. This is noted by John Frears, *Parties and Voters in France* (New York: St. Martin's Press, 1991), p. 115.

24. Quoted in Gregory Pons, *Les rats noirs* (N.p.: Jean-Claude Simeon, 1977), p. 51.

25. He is also the leader of the Alliance Générale Contre le Racisme et pour le Respect de l'Identité Française et Chrétienne (General Alliance Against Racism and for Respect for French and Christian Identity).

26. Quoted in *Le Monde*, February 14, 1984.

27. European Parliament, *Debates*, April 17, 1991, p. 133.

28. *Le Monde*, May 10, 1991.

29. Pierre Birnbaum emphasized the extent to which French nationalism at different times has found its identity in Catholicism. Pierre Birnbaum, *La France aux Français* (Paris: Seuil, 1993), pp. 288ff.

30. Quoted in *Le Monde*, June 26, 1991.

31. Mégret, *La flamme*, p. 153.

32. *Présent*, August 12, 1989. In the 1993 election program the Front stated that the law on abortion (the "Veil law") was based, "word for word" on a text drafted in "Masonic lodges." Front National, *300 mesures pour la renaissance de la France* (Paris: Éditions Nationales, 1993), p. 392.

33. Ibid. The editorial committee was headed by Bruno Mégret and consisted of Bernard Antony, Yvan Blot, Bruno Gollnisch, Jean-Yves Le Gallou, Jean-Claude Martinez, Thierry Martin, and Pierre Milloz.

34. Ibid.

35. On August 12, 1989, Le Pen was asked by Jean Madiran, the editor of *Présent*: "Many times you have spoken about the '*mondialiste* lobby.' What does one know about the people or the groups which compose it and the goals which it pursues?" Le Pen replied: "I don't need to tell people of your political background about the forces that are aiming to establish an egalitarian, leveling and *mondialiste*

ideology. I am thinking about the the completely false, misleading and mistaken use that is made of the rights of man by the Freemasons. I believe that the Trilateral [Commission] plays a role. The great internationals like the Jewish international play a not negligible role in the creation of this anti-national spirit. I will say that it is almost natural that that these forces, which are structurally, fundamentally internationalist, collide with national interests. But it is necessary to be careful when one says that the Freemasons and the Jewish international play a role. That doesn't mean all the Freemasons nor all Jewish organizations, nor all Jews, that is clear. But there are people who speak in the name of these others and act in this fashion." *Présent*, August 12, 1989.

36. Front National, *300 mesures*, p. 16.

37. Ibid.

38. Ibid.

39. *Présent*, February 21, 1990.

40. Quoted in *Le Monde*, August 25, 1992.

41. Front National, *300 mesures*, p. 18.

42. *Présent*, March 18, 1993.

43. According to a 1986 edition of *Présent*, Le Pen stated that "certain lobbies have obtained specific commitments from the RPR to vote an election law eliminating the National Front." For the extreme right, the codeword *lobbies* refers inter alia to B'nai B'rith. Quoted in René Monzat, *Enquêtes sur la droite extrême* (Paris: Le Monde Éditions, 1992), p. 154, fn. 21.

44. Yvan Blot, *Les racines de la liberté* (Paris: Albin Michel, 1985), pp. 32–33, 236.

45. *National Hebdo*, March 11–17, 1993. Brigneau's intellectual tool kit consists mainly of the all-purpose explanation that behind every political event lies a Jewish conspiracy. For example, Brigneau explained that the Los Angeles riot following the Rodney King affair was orchestrated by Jewish interests to punish the U.S. Congress for its failure to pass a loan guarantee bill for Israel. In an obsessive search for the hand of the Jewish conspiracy, anti-Semites often draw bizarre connections between apparently unrelated events. In January 1910, when the river Seine overflowed its banks and the waters lapped at the carpets in his Paris apartment, Édouard Drumont argued that deforestation undertaken by companies owned by cousins of the Rothschilds had caused the flooding. Winock, *Édouard Drumont*, p. 7.

46. *Présent*, March 4, 1990.

47. Yann Piat, *Seule, tout en haut à droite* (Paris: Fixot, 1991), p. 161.

48. Ibid.

49. Ibid., p. 162.

50. *Le Monde*, September 18, 1987.

51. *Le Monde*, September 6, 1988.

52. Quoted in Piat, *Seule*, p. 167.

53. *Le Monde*, October 1, 1987. In *Le Monde*, Daniel Carton saw Stirbois's outburst as part of a struggle between the "dangerous and vigilant guardians of the temple of the extreme right and the new prophets of a populist right, grand priests of respectability and openness."

54. See the interview with Jean-Maurice Demarquet in *Le Monde*, October 16, 1985. For the statements of François Bachelot, see *Le Monde*, September 8, 1988,

October 8, 1988, and February 7, 1992. French courts have ruled on many occasions that Le Pen has made anti-Semitic remarks. In 1992 a court of appeal in Chambéry noted that "Mr. Le Pen does not hide his resentment toward Jews. . . . He never hesitates to speak of a Judeo-Masonic plot, inciting therefore to anti-Semitism." *Le Monde*, November 29–30, 1992. Le Pen was also condemned for anti-Semitism on March 11, 1986.

55. *Globe* (April 1988), cited in Guy Birenbaum, *Le Front national en politique* (Paris: Balland, 1992), p. 32. Former NF MEP, Olivier d'Ormesson, claimed that Le Pen denied the existence of the gas chambers. Gilles Bresson and Christian Lionet, *Le Pen* (Paris: Seuil, 1994), p. 456.

56. According to Gilles Bresson and Christian Lionet, just before Le Pen's detail remark, plans had been finalized for Le Pen to fly to Israel, where he was to be met by General Ariel Sharon. Bresson and Lionet also reported that in February 1987 Le Pen gave a speech to the leaders of twenty-four Jewish organizations, among them Edgar Bronfman, the head of the World Jewish Congress, in which Le Pen argued for closing the Palestine Liberation Organization office in Paris, stated that Israel was a "pillar of the free world," and called Kurt Waldheim "a Soviet agent." Ibid., p. 455.

57. According to Le Pen's ex-wife, Pierrette, French aircraft manufacturer Dassault had contributed a substantial sum of money to the NF to ensure that d'Ormesson was placed near the top of the NF list for the European election. Blandine Hennion, *Le Front national l'argent et l'establishment* (Paris: La Découverte, 1993), pp. 190–191.

58. *Le Monde*, February 7, 1992.

59. Piat, *Seule*, p. 202. By Le Pen's "fixed idea," Bachelot meant Le Pen's anti-Semitism.

60. In 1990 a poll was conducted of Front cadres attending the party's eighth congress. Sixty-two percent were in "complete agreement" with the statement "The Jews have too much power in France," and 26 percent were "rather in agreement." *Le Monde*, March 8–9, 1990. By comparison, when asked to respond to the statement "Today the Jews have too much power in France," 3 percent of a sample of French public opinion were in "complete agreement," and 14 percent were "rather in agreement." *Le Monde*, May 18, 1990.

61. On factions in the Front, see Jean-Yves Camus, "Political Cultures Within the Front National: The Emergence of a Counter-Ideology on the French Far-Right," *Patterns of Prejudice* 26, 1–2 (1992):5–16.

62. Quoted in Bresson and Lionet, *Le Pen*, p. 458.

63. Quoted in Piat, *Seule*, p. 159.

64. Quoted in *Le Monde*, May 19, 1988.

65. When questioned about this letter, Théo Klein answered: "I think it was in 1985 or 1986 at a time when we were protesting against the change in the electoral system [to proportional representation]. It's true that we wrote to the democratic parties in order to alert them to the dangers posed by the National Front and on the necessity to marginalize it. But I didn't know that I had such powers of persuasion!" Ibid.

66. Piat, *Seule*, p. 166.

67. Weeks after the presidential election, Le Pen was still furious at having come in fourth. At the Front's Blue-White-Red festival, he told a crowd of supporters: "Despite the rigging, despite the fraud, the national candidate [Le Pen] was almost able to equal the score of his competitors on the right. . . . I maintain that if the consultation had been fair, and democratic, I would have come in on top in the presidential election, before Messrs. Chirac and Barre and that I would have been the flag-carrier of the national French against François Mitterrand on the second turn." *Le Monde*, September 20, 1988.

68. *Le Monde*, September 10, 1988.

69. Ibid.

70. Louis Pauwels, in *Le Figaro-Magazine*, January 27, 1990.

71. *Le Figaro-Magazine*, February 17, 1990.

72. Ibid.

73. Henry Rousso, *The Vichy Syndrome: History and Memory in France Since 1944* (Cambridge, Mass.: Harvard University Press, 1991), p. 300.

74. *Le Monde*, September 9, 1988. The claim that the National Front is the victim of a "cosmopolite plot," or an "oligarchy," lays the groundwork for a further argument, which admittedly the Front has not yet made, that the party has the right to attack these organizations in the name of self-defense. This would mirror the anti-Semitic line that Hitler's persecution of the Jews was provoked by the hostility of international Jewish organizations in the 1930s.

7

Immigration and Racism

Imagine that a Mr. Smith decides to construct for himself a system of general cultural, ethical, rational values, in which the highest values will be those of Mr. Smith. The size of his skull, the color of his skin and of his hair become the ideal size and the ideal color. His specific characteristics become virtues, and to the degree that his neighbors differ from him, they are inferior. If he wants to praise something, he says that it is "Smithian." The most severe condemnation is when something is not "Smithian." He accepts without question everything nasty the newspapers or mere rumor report about his neighbors. Anyone who asks for evidence is guilty of high treason. If they take up arms, it is to attack him; if he bears arms, it is only to defend public order and the most sacred possessions of humanity. He makes a Smith flag whose colors he considers the most beautiful in the world. On his belt buckle there is an inscription: "Gott mit Smith!" On every occasion he sings: "Smith über alles," or if he sees his destiny is on the oceans or the land, he sings "Rule Smith, rule the waves!" or "Aux armes, Smith, qu'un sang impur abreuve nos sillons!" At best one would find this Smith ridiculous, or at worst, lock him up. But if a few million people do what for Smith is only a personal pleasure, only those living far away will see this behavior as ridiculous, or those who, living in the middle of these Smiths, find some way to escape from Smith's contagious psychosis.
—*Henri de Man, quoted in Pierre-André Taguieff,*
"Le national-populism en question"

La France aux Français
—*Édouard Drumont, cited in Michel Winock, Édouard Drumont et Cie*

In 1995 Bruno Mégret estimated the "number of people of foreign origin" in France at 10 million, and he proposed repatriating 3 million over seven years.[1] However, the government's High Council on Integration states that on the basis of the 1990 census, there were in 1993 approximately 4.1 immigrants in France, of whom 1.29 million had French nationality.[2] Moreover, official publications distinguish between an *étranger,* one who does not have French nationality, regardless of place of birth, and an *immigré*, someone born abroad as a foreigner but who lives in France and might have acquired French nationality.[3] That Mégret did not distinguish between those foreigners who hold and those foreigners who do not hold French nationality, that he drastically overstated the actual number of foreigners on French soil, and that he made no distinctions between foreigners and immigrants were not accidental. This was a typical attempt by a Front leader to mislead people into thinking that there were vastly more non-French nationals on French soil than is actually the case.[4]

Whereas Le Pen uttered hardly a word about immigrants in his 1974 election campaign, by the 1990s anti-immigrant sentiments were being expressed by a large majority of NF voters and supporters and had become the central feature of the NF's propaganda.[5] When the Front elected three big-city mayors in the June 1995 elections, all spoke of the threat to security posed by immigrants and the desirability of discriminating against immigrants in providing housing and welfare service. In August 1995 the Chirac administration proposed that fifteen thousand "illegal" immigrants be deported by charter flight at the end of 1996 and that thirty thousand be deported in 1997. Once again, the Front's anti-immigrant message had set the agenda for the mainstream right.

Despite the fact that attacking immigration and repatriating immigrants (in the Front's vocabulary, the term *immigrants* always refers to immigrants from North Africa and Africa) have become the gravamen of the Front's program, immigration policy has not always been at the center of the Front's concerns, nor was it a major issue for French political parties until the early 1980s.[6] At that time media attention began to shift away from sympathetic descriptions of the poor living conditions and socioeconomic problems of immigrants in French society and toward a focus on the "problems" immigrants posed for the French. Soon *delinquency, tension,* and *threshold of tolerance* became key words in articles on immigrants.[7] Thus, growing hostility to immigrants and the emergence of immigration as a major political issue are historically contingent; they have not always been a feature of French politics and can be understood only against the background of 145 years of immigration policy.[8]

Immigration in Perspective

Throughout European history people have migrated from one area to another or, when national states were formed, from one country to another. These movements were inspired by a variety of factors: peasants looking for new land to farm, workers seeking jobs, refugees escaping from political or religious persecution, or victims of war seeking refuge and safety. In 1861 one French scholar thought that foreigners immigrated to France because of the agreeable climate, the opportunity to finish their studies, curiosity, or a passion for travel.[9] In 1851, the first year in which the census counted immigrants, 380,000 foreigners were identified, making up 1 percent of the French population. By 1921 the total had reached 1.5 million, or 3.95 percent, of the population. The majority of these were Italians (29.5 percent), followed by Belgians (22.8 percent) and Spanish (16.7 percent). The census counted immigrants from sixty different countries, including 1 immigrant from Finland, 1 from "Siam," 1 from "Persia," and 3 from Malta.[10] Four years later the largest group consisted of 807,659 Italians, followed by 460,352 Belgians, 310,265 Poles, and 146,273 Swiss. The only non-European, non-American (both North and South American) immigrants mentioned were 20,108 "Ottomans," who, one presumes, came from the Ottoman Empire. During the 1920s the influx continued; by 1930 France had the highest rate of immigrants of any country in the world, with 515 per 100,000, compared to 492 for the United States.[11] At this time there were 2.7 million foreigners in France, constituting 6.59 percent of the French population.[12]

The historical statistics on the number of immigrants in France are not always reliable because terms such as *foreigner, immigrant,* and *alien* do not have the same unvarying meaning from one generation to another. In the early nineteenth century, for example, there was some confusion over the difference between immigrants, people who came from outside France, and internal migrants, people from one region of France who moved to another in search of jobs. According to police records in the southern department of Bouches-du-Rhône, the category of "foreigner" referred not only to people born outside France but also to French citizens from other departments.[13]

Until 1889 French immigration policy consisted of a myriad of confusing and often contradictory rules and regulations. A comprehensive law on immigration and naturalization was passed in 1889 and then substantially revised in 1927 in an attempt to direct immigration policy toward specific economic and social objectives. Nevertheless, immigrants were subjected to a variety of discriminatory measures. For example, although naturalized citizens had the right to permanent residence on French soil, they could not vote, run for public office, or hold jobs in the civil service.

Attitudes Toward Immigrants

The problem with trying to generalize about popular reactions to foreigners over long periods of time is that humdrum coexistence between populations or ethnic groups does not make news. Because dramatic incidents of conflict and violence are more likely to catch the attention of popular chroniclers and historians than those periods when foreigners and natives lived together peacefully, conflict is sometimes overdramatized in contrast to consensus. Most likely, neither xenophobia nor tolerance is an instinctive reaction to foreigners, and the actual reception they are accorded varies with time and place. At the end of the nineteenth century, when French workers in the north were questioned about the extent to which Belgian immigrants contributed to economic crisis in the area, the respondents either omitted mentioning the Belgians or were quite moderate in their remarks.[14] For most of the nineteenth century, it seems that the presence of foreigners in France was of such little consequence that jurists complained it was impossible to find a clear legal definition of a foreigner.[15]

At other times, however, reactions to foreigners living and working in northern France were intensely hostile. In 1848 there were daily demonstrations against Belgians and occasional attacks on the Flemish in the north of France. In 1892 French miners forced Belgian miners to flee the Pas-de-Calais area.[16] From August 16 to 19, 1893, there were pitched battles between Italian immigrants and French citizens in the southern town of Aigues-Mortes during which at least seven Italians were killed and hundreds were injured.[17] One newspaper described the Italians as "arriving like grasshoppers from the Piedmont, Lombardy, Venice, Rome or Naples, even Sicily. They are dirty, sad, ragged; entire tribes emigrating toward the North. . . . Then they settle down among their own . . . remaining strangers to the people who receive them, working for low wages, playing the accordion or with their knives."[18]

Anti-immigrant feeling was not exclusively the preserve of the right; the left was occasionally hostile to immigrants. In 1886 Socialist leader Jules Guesde denounced "these 800,000 foreigners who work for low wages, outrageously low salaries or take away work from our workers expelled from factories."[19] During the period between the wars, interethnic violence tapered off, but in the north in 1923 there were brawls between striking French miners and immigrant nonstrikers, and in 1931 there were battles between French strikers and Belgian nonstrikers.[20]

Identification and Numbers

Even though the number of immigrants continued to increase during the nineteenth century, the government was barely able to identify and keep track of them. It was not until the end of the century that the development of statistics and of new methods of identification based on fingerprints, facial characteristics, and bone structure provided the police and other authorities with a "scientific" and effective method of identification and classification.[21] Thanks to the work of Alphonse Bertillon, foreigners (as well as criminals, the mentally retarded, and the mentally ill) could be identified by the shape of the nose, mouth, eyes, and ears as well as by bone structure. New ideas on classification and differentiation of races percolated through public and private bureaucracies and into the public at large. Soon the average citizen became conscious of the notion that foreigners looked "different" from the French and was more easily able to identify them.[22] In 1889 legislation was passed distinguishing between foreigners and nationals and laying down the ground rules for obtaining French nationality.

At the beginning of the twentieth century, immigration continued apace as the government tried to compensate for World War I losses (estimated at 1.39 million, the highest percentage of any combatant nation), which had led to a decline in the French population from 41.4 million in 1913 to 39.1 million in 1920.[23] Faced with a declining birthrate and fearful of the growing populations of Germany and Italy, French authorities saw no alternative to opening the gates to large-scale immigration. However, the French felt ambivalent about the new immigrants. According to Albert Thomas, director of the International Labour Office, people resented foreigners, who, they claimed, fought with French workers for vacant places in cheap housing, took up hospital beds, and committed crimes. Thomas also complained that, compared to other European countries or to the United States, France had no immigration policy at all. Thomas proposed admitting races "which have the most affinity with ours: Italians, Belgians, Spanish, Polish, etc. It is necessary to keep out undesirables. In view of the depopulation of our countryside, it is necessary above all to look for agricultural workers."[24] Thomas was echoing the conventional wisdom that immigration policy should exclude foreigners who did not share French values or easily integrate into French society. According to Marcel Paon, an expert on immigration, it had been necessary to "renounce" using "Asiatics" as soldiers during World War I because they could not adapt to French conditions; "the results with North Africans weren't much better, so it was very wise to take measures to do everything possible to prevent their departure from North Africa, where the active population is insufficient."[25] Nevertheless, the need for immigrants was so great that the government made policy on an ad hoc basis, solving problems as they arose and leaving day-to-day policy matters in the hands of administrators.[26]

Immigration and Policy

Under the 1889 law children born in France to foreigners who were born abroad became French at the age of majority, unless they declined to accept

French citizenship. Children born to foreigners who were themselves born in France were automatically French. At this time nationality was conveyed by the father, not the mother. This law was based on the principle of *jus solis*, which meant that being born on French soil carried with it the acquisition of French nationality. This contrasts with the law of *jus sanguinis*, whereby rights accrue only to those born of parents who are French nationals. The first law facilitates naturalization because birth on French soil is sufficient to confer citizenship. The second is more restrictive because generations of people born on French soil might not become French because their parents did not hold French citizenship. From 1804 to 1851 nationality was governed by the law of *jus sanguinis*. Unsurprisingly, the National Front endorses citizenship laws based on *jus sanguinis*.[27]

The 1889 legislation was based on *jus solis* because the government wanted a continuing supply of cheap labor and because at the end of the nineteenth century, with war looming on the horizon, the government wanted to ensure that foreigners were not exempted from military service.[28] During the debates over the 1889 law, the question of race was hardly raised. Immigrants may have been criticized for being unwilling to abide by French law, for trying to avoid military service, for taking jobs from French workers, or for displaying laziness or criminality, but immigrants' behavior was not explained in terms of biologically determined racial factors, nor, on the whole, were invidious comparisons made between the races. Even in 1927, when a new citizenship law was under discussion, racialism played a minor role in the debate.[29] Léon Barety proposed in the National Assembly that in view of the large number of crimes committed by "Orientals and Levantines," naturalization be rescinded in the event a crime was committed within five years of a person's naturalization. But the debate was devoted mainly to questions of a technical nature, and in the end the new law passed on a voice vote.

However, the 1927 law did stipulate that naturalized French citizens could not hold elective office until ten years had elapsed or until a male citizen had completed his military service. This provision arose because citizenship had to be withdrawn from some mayors of German origin who "remained faithful to the Emperor" during World War I.[30] Moreover, since the French Revolution army service had been considered both a sign and an obligation of citizenship, the ultimate expression of solidarity with the French nation, and a symbol of assimilation to its culture. The 1927 law also reflected social and economic goals—namely, to maintain the level of the French population compared to Germany and Italy, to keep France economically competitive by stemming the depopulation of the countryside and supplying labor for industry, and to provide a continuing pool of manpower for the army.

The Extreme Right and Immigration

Not everyone agreed with the policy of encouraging immigration so as to achieve economic or demographic objectives. Before World War II the extreme right argued that "the invasion of immigrants, that's what it must be called, is directed and organized from above. It seems to result from a concerted plan."[31] According to the extreme right, the conspiracy to hand France over to foreigners was the work of international communism, Freemasons, Germans, Jews, and "American-Germano-Judeo finance."[32] As racism and anti-Semitism spread during the 1920s and 1930s, immigration policy was no longer discussed in terms of utility but in terms of the preservation of French culture and traditions, national character, race, and the ability of immigrants to assimilate into French culture and society. It became important for new immigrants to affirm that they had become truly French by demonstrating fluency in the language and by rigidly conforming to French customs and law. Whereas immigrants and foreigners used to circulate freely throughout the country and participate in society almost without restriction, by the late nineteenth century foreigners and naturalized French were increasingly subjected to a myriad of bureaucratic restrictions on travel and work.

In 1934 the government passed a law forbidding naturalized citizens from holding positions remunerated by the state. In 1938 antiforeigner sentiment was reflected in tougher laws on naturalization, which, the government complained, had become too "automatic." The new law reaffirmed the barring of naturalized citizens for ten years from holding public office or an elected position and forbade naturalized citizens from voting for five years. "The new Frenchman ought to further his education as a citizen of the Republic," the law said, "before exercising its sovereign right." In addition to these restrictions, naturalized citizens could be stripped of nationality for "having committed an act contrary to public order; or for having in France or abroad committed a crime involving at least one year's imprisonment." In this case the naturalized citizen could lose his or her citizenship for up to ten years after naturalization. These provisions did not apply to native-born French citizens. "It is important that the responsible authorities have at their disposal prompt and effective means for withdrawing our nationality from naturalized citizens who show themselves unworthy of the title of French citizen."[33] Naturalized citizens had to pass a language test.[34]

According to historians Michael Marrus and Robert Paxton, the increased animus toward foreigners was due to a number of factors: the Great Depression led to increased unemployment and declining productivity, unstable government and political scandals increased public disillusion with the political system and led to a sense of crisis, and there had been a rapid increase in the number of refugees, from only a relatively small number in 1931 to 180,000 in 1938. Approximately 55,000 of these refugees were Jews fleeing economic and political instability and anti-Semitism in central Europe and in Germany. These foreigners arrived at a time when the right and the extreme right were vigorously promoting xenophobia, anti-Semitism, and racialism and when the Communist Party had begun to oppose immigration.[35] Although it is true that even in this climate Léon Blum became the first Jewish premier of France in 1936, his selection as premier and the anti-Semitism he evoked illustrate the deep divisions in French politics and society in the 1930s.

With the fall of France and the advent of Vichy, anti-Semitism culminated in the infamous *statut des juifs,* followed by police roundups of Jews and their subsequent deportation to extermination camps.[36] Without waiting for German prompting, the deeply anti-Semitic Vichy government passed laws in 1940 barring Jews from holding all public or elective offices but allowing them to continue in the professions, subject to a quota. Exceptions were allowed for Jewish veterans of World War I or of the 1939–1940 "campaign." Jews were also barred from working in education, in the press, or on the radio. Both the exceptions granted to war veterans and the absolute bar from working in any area that impinged on culture implied a view of the Jew as an alien whose only route to admission to French nationality was through a willingness to sacrifice himself for the nation. Even then, to be Jewish was to belong to a race that could never be fully French, however much individual Jews might try to assimilate. For the Vichy authorities, Jews constituted a permanent and mortal threat to French culture, which had to be protected, whatever the cost. One Vichy "expert," George Mauco, characterized Jews as "intelligent slaves" who, "as a result of centuries of persecution, had developed a mimetic ability but who lacked the robust and virile characteristics of the French. The . . . aptitude for compiling knowledge and money allows them to flood into the managerial areas of the nation. . . . The Jews . . . head toward the nerve centers of the country and act on its directive activities."[37] According to Patrick Weil, before 1940 French immigration policy included a right to asylum. Between 1940 and 1945, however, under Vichy there was a "deep break in policy: a logic based on an ethnic hierarchy imposed itself." The republican tradition, which was based on tolerance of ethnicity and race, would not be reestablished until the Liberation.[38]

Immigration After 1945

With the restoration of democracy in 1945, immigration policy was influenced by the continued low birthrate and consequent shortage of labor power. The revival of French agriculture and industry was seen to depend on increasing the number of immigrant workers, which had declined from 2.7 million in 1936 to 1.7 million in 1946 (4.12 percent of the population). Over the years the ethnic composition of this population had altered only slightly: Italians remained the largest group, with 26 percent of the total; Spanish made up 17.3 percent; and Poles followed with 15.2 percent. Immigrants from the Maghreb, namely, Algerians, Moroccans, and Tunisians, constituted only 3.1 percent of the total. In 1946 there was unanimous agreement that France desperately needed immigrants, with some experts estimating that an additional 5.3 million inhabitants were required to compensate for the decline in population resulting from the losses of World War I, high mortality, and continuing low natality and to provide the labor power needed to revitalize the French economy.[39] In a 1945 speech General de Gaulle had said: "In order to bring to life the 12 million beautiful babies that France needs in ten years, to reduce our absurd rate of mortality and infant and juvenile morbidity, to introduce in the course of the following years, with method and intelligence, good elements from immigration into the French collective, an important plan is sketched . . . to obtain this vital and sacred result at any price."[40] Toward that end, the government established the Ministry of Population and an immigration office responsible for establishing and staffing immigration offices abroad.[41] In contrast to the immediate prewar and Vichy experiences, immigration policy after 1945 reflected the generous ideals of the French Republic as an asylum for refugees and as receptive to immigrants from all nations.

For nearly three decades following the 1945 Liberation, the question of immigration hardly entered the public realm, with policy worked out largely between experts and politicians. During this time, the major problems were to determine how many immigrants to admit, to establish criteria for admission, and to elaborate methods for controlling the movements of immigrants and integrating them into the economy. A 1947 law had granted Muslim Algerians French citizenship, thus permitting them to enter and leave France at will. As a result, some Algerians immigrated to France and became permanent residents; others worked for a time and then returned home. Naturalization was facilitated by 1945 and 1961 laws granting French nationality in five years to those resident in France for that time or in two years to those born in France or married to a Frenchwoman, possessing advanced degrees, or having made an important contribution to French technical, literary, or artistic life. No residence period was required for other classes of foreigners, and a child born in France of foreign parents could assume French nationality at the age of majority. But restrictions on naturalized citizens holding electoral office remained. These were gradually relaxed until finally, in 1983, nationality laws passed under the Socialists removed restrictions on the rights of naturalized citizens.

Turning off the Tap

After Algerian independence in 1962, French immigration policy was governed by two contradictory motives: On the one hand, French authorities feared the economic and social consequences of the large number of Algerians who wished to enter France; on the other, business leaders wanted to ensure a continued supply of cheap, docile labor. According to President Pompidou in 1963, "Immigration is a way to create a certain freeing up of the labor market and of resisting social pressure." Under the 1962 Evian Accord, Algerians were allowed to freely circulate between Algeria and France. With a demographic explosion in Algeria, and an economy ruined by eight years of brutal warfare, the number of Algerians arriving in France continued to increase, with seventy thousand arriving each week during October 1962.[42] In 1964 the French and Algerian governments agreed on a quota system for immigrants, although for the remainder of the decade the French tried to limit immigration from Algeria, while the Algerian authorities pressed the French to open the gates wider.[43]

By the 1960s the proportion of immigrants from the Maghreb had begun to increase. Whereas immigrants from Africa, including the Maghreb, made up 13 percent of the total number of immigrants in 1954, by 1968, 24.8 percent, or one out of every four immigrants, came from the Maghreb or the rest of Africa. By far the largest number of immigrants from the Maghreb consisted of Algerians, who constituted 18.1 percent of the total. However, Algerians were still in third place behind Spanish and Italians, who made up 23.2 and 21.8 percent, respectively, of the total number of immigrants. By 1968 there were in all 2.62 million immigrants in France, or 6.28 percent of the population. The percentage of immigrants in the French population had increased by 50 percent since 1946.

At this time North African immigrants were employed mainly in the building and construction trades or in industry and production. A very small number worked in agriculture or domestic employment. In contrast, immigrants from the rest of Africa were often employed in the lowest-paid menial jobs, working as street cleaners or as domestics. One reason for the difference between the two groups was that North Africans, including Algerians and Moroccans, spoke French, whereas those from the rest of Africa did not. Often, too, Algerians had a higher level of education than other Africans.[44] Because Algerians tended to work in industry or in industry-related trades, they were concentrated in the region around Paris, in the very far north in the industrial and mining departments of Nord and Pas-de-Calais, around the Lyon area, and in the far south near Marseilles. Many of the immigrants, particularly the new ones, lived in *bidonvilles,* or shantytowns, on the outskirts of urban areas.[45]

In 1966 Francette Vidal painted a somber picture of one such *bidonville,* La Campa, located in an industrial suburb of Paris. Most of the fifteen hundred Spanish, Portuguese, Algerians, French, and Gypsies lived in sheds piled one against the other, with only a single water tap for the area. The largest group consisted of single Algerian men, many of them in bad health and without jobs, who spent their time in nearby cafés, often brawling and creating a general climate of insecurity for their neighbors.[46] However, Vidal noted with approval the work of social service agencies in the *bidonvilles* and the slow but steady increase in subsidized housing: "In the end, one must seek the beginnings of a solution to all these problems at the individual level. Expatriate foreigners need above all human warmth: they need a quiet and disinterested welcome. If their route is dotted with friends willing to facilitate their adaptation, their difficulties will appear less insurmountable."[47]

Against Immigration

These were generous sentiments, and doubtless many people shared them. But anti-immigrant sentiment mounted during the brutal Algerian War. In 1959, referring to Algerian accusations of torture and abuse at the hands of French authorities, Prime Minister Michel Debré said disparagingly that he did not believe that "Algerians, even students, are capable of holding a pen in order to write about what they have been subjected to."[48] In turn, Algerians resident in France accused French police of consistent brutality in their relations with the North African community.[49]

The worst incident took place in 1961 at a time when de Gaulle appeared ready to negotiate Algerian independence and when both the Algerian Front de Libération Nationale and the French extreme right Organisation de l'Armée Secrète had embarked on terrorist campaigns in mainland France. With the police and the Algerian community at loggerheads, on October 5, 1961, the police warned Algerians not to go out at night, not to form groups, and to close their shops and cafés at 7:00 in the evening. But the FLN called on Algerians to protest these restrictive measures, and on October 17 thirty thousand Algerians tried to march through the center of Paris. The police reacted with enormous violence, beating to death or drowning hundreds of marchers and herding thousands of others into parks and stadiums. The following day corpses were found floating in the Seine, while others hung from trees or were found in rubbish dumps.[50]

For years after Algeria gained its independence in 1962, there were continuing incidents of extreme right violence against Algerians. By 1973 attacks against Algerians and other immigrants had reached a new level. In

August a Molotov cocktail was thrown into an apartment in Marseilles housing North African immigrants. According to estimates by an Algerian organization, eleven Algerians were killed between August 29 and September 19, 1973. At the same time, criticisms of "uncontrolled immigration" led the minister of the interior to declare that he would expel any foreigner "troubling public order" and that he would increase border controls.[51] Finally, in September 1973 the government of Algeria announced that in view of the racial attacks on Algerians, it was cutting off all further Algerian emigration. In an interview with *Le Monde*, Algerian president Houari Boumediene said: "Frankly, if the French government doesn't want our workers, let it say so. We will take them back. . . . If, on the other hand, France needs our workers, its government has the duty of protecting them."[52] Three months later four people were killed and twenty-two wounded in an attack on the Algerian consulate in Marseilles. The extreme right Charles-Martel organization claimed responsibility for the attack.

According to Pierre Weil, by cutting off all immigration to France in 1973, the Algerian government was responding partially to growing anti-immigrant attacks in France but even more to domestic pressures. The order to end emigration came just when a conference of the Non-Aligned Countries was being held in Algiers. According to Weil, "Algeria wanted to publicly demonstrate, at a time when it was assuming the presidency of the Conference, that henceforth it had the means to impose certain constraints on its former colonial master and force it to accord a more respectful treatment to its residents, as well as to demonstrate that, in the now favorable economic climate, it did not need emigration."[53]

During the late 1960s, French and Algerian authorities negotiated agreements giving Algeria more control over potential emigrants and France more control over Algerian immigrants in France. At the same time, the French tried to reduce the large number of Algerians entering France but favored immigration from other countries in North Africa and from Yugoslavia and Portugal. The authorities paid little attention to the social and economic conditions under which the immigrants lived, assuming that most of them were temporary residents who would ultimately return home. By the early 1970s, however, with anti-immigrant incidents on the increase, and the press and the public objecting to the *bidonvilles*, the Pompidou government passed some measures against racism (a July 1, 1972, law made racism a crime) and took minimal steps to provide better social welfare for immigrants.

In 1974 Valéry Giscard d'Estaing narrowly defeated François Mitterrand on the second ballot of the presidential election. By the time Giscard assumed office, the circumstances surrounding immigration had changed. The effects of the rise in oil prices occasioned by Arab oil boycott after the

October 1973 Yom Kippur War had forced sharp rises in energy prices in France. The growing size of immigrant slums and the potential social costs of dealing with large numbers of poor, and increasingly unemployed, immigrant workers also affected policy. Although some business leaders opposed any restriction on immigration, Giscard adopted a two-pronged policy. On the economic front, Giscard raised taxes and reduced social expenditures to discourage immigration. To coordinate immigration policy, Giscard created the post of secretary of state for immigration, and in July 1974 the French government decided to suspend all immigration of non-Europeans, except in cases of family reunification. Business organizations and most trade unions supported the measure.[54] At this time estimates of the number of immigrants varied from the 1975 census figure of 3.4 million to the minister of the interior's estimate of 4 million.[55]

As unemployment grew and public opinion became increasingly hostile toward immigrants, Giscard decided to embark on a policy of forced repatriation of five hundred thousand foreigners over five years. Algerians were the main targets. Because Algerians constituted the largest number of immigrants from the Maghreb, were the most demanding immigrants from the former colonies, and were active in the trade union movement, they had become an obstacle to the freedom of government to regulate immigration from Algeria.[56] According to Patrick Weil, for symbolic and historical reasons, Algerians evoked the most passionate reactions from those opposed to the presence of foreigners in France.[57]

Because many immigrants had residence permits that were about to run out, the government merely had to refuse to renew the permits and force the immigrants to return home. But there was mounting opposition to this plan from trade unions, the Gaullist RPR, and the left. Not only were many people repelled by the idea of forced repatriation. There also were technical problems: Many Algerian immigrants enjoyed a special status under the 1962 Evian Accord, and repatriation would breach that agreement; immigrant children born in France and considered French by virtue of nationality laws would be forced out of their own country; and the proposal violated the European Social Charter.[58] After a long battle in the legislature and the country, the proposal was withdrawn, although the government continued its policy of voluntary repatriation, offering rewards of up to Fr 10,000 to immigrants willing to return to their home countries. Although the intended targets were North African, mainly Algerian, immigrants, Portuguese and Spanish workers took advantage of the repatriation offer.[59]

Nevertheless, the government continued its crackdown on illegal immigrants, authorizing the police to make on-the-spot identification checks of those suspected of breaking the law. Inevitably, Muslims and Africans were most often subjected to police questioning; a policy of controlling immigrants had been substituted for a policy of controlling immigration. In 1980 Giscard's minister of the interior, Christian Bonnet, introduced legislation permitting the government to take away work permits from immigrants sentenced to jail for minor infractions of the law, which meant they could then be forcibly expelled from French soil. But the Constitutional Council struck down a provision of the law that denied immigrants access to a lawyer.[60]

The mood in the legislature, however, was negative. Legislative discussions in 1979–1980 over immigration laws tended to focus attention on questions of nationality or ethnicity, thus emphasizing differences, rather than similarities, between immigrants and the rest of the population.[61] Immigrants were increasingly blamed for unemployment. In a television broadcast before the 1981 presidential election, President Giscard linked the problem of 1.8 million unemployed French workers with the presence of 1.8 million immigrants from the Maghreb on French soil.[62]

Although during the 1960s the Communist Party and its trade union, the Confédération Générale du Travail, had opposed restrictions on immigration, mounting unemployment and growing racism within the party led to a reversal of policy. On November 4, 1980, the Communist Party demanded an end to immigration. Six weeks later the Communist mayor of Vitry-sur-Seine, claiming that his municipality was being unfairly asked to house a disproportionate number of immigrants, led a bulldozer attack on a building where workers from Mali were to be housed. The mayor was supported by the Communist Party and the Communist newspaper *L'Humanité,* which asked that there be a more equitable distribution of immigrant families in the country.[63] The Socialists and the noncommunist trade unions condemned the attack.[64]

While governments wrestled with the problem of finding a legislative response to the thorny questions of regulating entry into France, integrating into French society those immigrants on French soil who were unlikely to return to their countries of origin, and dealing with the growing numbers of illegal and clandestine immigrants, a major change began to occur in the terms of the debate. A study of press coverage of the immigration issue during the period from 1974 to 1984 found that the extreme right press always gave a negative slant to its coverage of immigrants and immigration. In reporting on a 1974 bomb explosion at the Algerian consulate in Marseilles, the extreme right newspaper *Minute* presented the incident in terms of a conflict between immigrant groups, whereas the left-wing *Le Nouvel Observateur* explained it as a racist attack on Algerians. When mainly immigrant rapid transit workers struck in 1980, *Minute* published a picture that obscured the faces of the immigrants and there implied that nonimmigrant workers constituted the bulk of the strikers.

The extreme right press often gave dramatic coverage to murders or rapes, which put immigrants in a negative light, whereas the left-wing press often ignored these incidents or interpreted them differently.[65] The extreme right consistently took an anti-immigrant stand, presenting itself as the sole defender of France against a foreign invasion. Simone Bonnafous showed that one of the major differences between the extreme right press and the center and left-wing press was the unremitting use made by the extreme right of "we," "us," and "our." In this way the extreme right press drew a sharp distinction between itself as the embodiment and defender of the French national community and the immigrant as "other." By contrast, the left-wing press tended toward a "non-definition of national reference groups, effacing of collective, clearly enunciated identification marks, confused use of terms such as 'foreigner' and 'immigrant,' absence of a direct argument concerning migration, all of which pointed toward a lack of identity, toward lost attachments."[66] Thus, the purely negative campaign of the extreme right shaped the terms and grounds of the argument about immigration. Bonnafous concluded:

> From 1974 to 1984 our study shows that the lexical evolution in [press] articles reflects a general thematic change from the conditions of life and the work of the "immigrants" to the difficulties of cohabiting with the French, and from that to the problems of "assimilation" and of "integration." ... [Entry] cards and frontiers, these symbols of separation between "us" and "them" are newly rendered visible for all citizens, and with them, the extraneousness of "immigrants." The way is thus opened for an interrogation on the capacities of "absorption" of the "French nation."[67]

By the 1980s, therefore, growing hostility to immigrants was the result not just of pressure from the extreme right but also of a secular change in policy and attitude that had begun during the Algerian War and that all political parties, with the brief exception of the Socialist government of 1981, did little to stem. The National Front did not create a climate of hostility to immigrants. Rather, the NF hopped onto a bandwagon that was already under way.

The Socialists and Immigration

The Socialist victories in the legislative and presidential elections of 1981 seemed to mark a clear break with the immigration policy of the Giscard administration. The Bonnet law was abrogated, as was the program of providing financial rewards to immigrants willing to return home.

Prior to the 1981 presidential election, François Mitterrand had published his 110 "proposals for France," which included ending discrimination against immigrant workers, giving immigrant workers the same social rights as French nationals, granting immigrant workers the right to vote in local elections after five years' residence on French soil, democratizing the National Immigration Office, and, at the same time, imposing tougher controls on clandestine workers. Given the clear antipathy of public opinion toward immigrants, this was a courageous move and was in line with Socialist ideas on expanding the boundaries of social and political democracy.[68] Initially, the new Socialist government tried to implement as many as possible of the 110 propositions, including regularizing the situation of clandestine immigrants already in the country and ensuring that no more illegal immigrants entered.[69] To achieve the first goal, the Socialists gave amnesty to 130,000 illegal immigrants and granted them permits to stay in France for ten years, with an automatic right of renewal. During a trip to Algeria in 1981, Minister of Foreign Affairs Claude Cheysson mentioned a proposal to give immigrants the right to vote in the 1983 municipal elections—although his statement was quickly disavowed by a government spokesman. While regularizing the situation of immigrants on French soil and implementing measures for their integration in French society, the Socialists tried as best they could to discourage an influx of illegal immigrants from North Africa. But actions to impose tough border controls inevitably spilled over to internal controls so that by the mid-1980s the police were again stopping and questioning "suspicious-looking" people, thereby recreating the same climate of mutual suspicion and hostility that had existed between the immigrant community and the authorities ten years earlier. At the same time, young, mainly North African, immigrants had been radicalized by what they saw as police oppression and a lack of jobs. The summers of 1981 and 1982 were marked by violent clashes between police and youngsters in suburbs around Lyon, characterized by the press as the "Minguettes rodeos."[70]

By December 1982 the Socialist government had rounded up and deported sixteen thousand illegal immigrants. Officials at airports and ports were so energetic in refusing entry to immigrants lacking proper papers that Algerian groups protested that the policy was applied "without any reason and without any distinction."[71] In 1984 the Socialist government established a program whereby businesses could contract with the state to provide up to Fr 70,000 to an immigrant wishing to return home, but only if the immigrant could demonstrate the he or she was returning to establish a business or take a job.[72] But these policies did nothing to mitigate the storm of controversy around the proposal to grant immigrants the right to vote in local elections.[73]

The National Front and Immigration

During the 1973 legislative election campaign, immigration was mentioned only once in the National Front's thirty-one-page program: "The NF demands an end to the ridiculous policies which tolerate uncontrolled immigration in conditions both materially and morally disastrous for those concerned."[74] In April 1973, when the Front met to plan strategy for the 1974 presidential elections, Le Pen rejected the suggestion that "uncontrolled" immigration be one of its themes, preferring to emphasize traditional right-wing themes. When Ordre Nouveau (at that time still part of the NF) held a June 1973 meeting under the slogan "End uncontrolled immigration," Le Pen shied away from the immigration theme, fearing it might hurt the Front's image. Immigration policy played very little role in Le Pen's campaign for the presidency. On April 29, 1974, he condemned the situation "created by strong pressure from immigrants," but that was all. Immigration was not mentioned in his platform.[75]

By the 1980s, however, Front arguments against immigration were beginning to meet with a positive response. Opinion polls in the mid-1980s repeatedly found majorities of 60 percent and above opposed to giving immigrants the right to vote in local elections.[76] The Front attacked the government's immigration policy by dramatizing and exaggerating the number of illegal immigrants in France, linking them to every conceivable social problem, and arguing that immigrants from North Africa, most of whom were Muslim, could not and would never be able to fully assimilate into French culture and traditions. In an October 1985 issue of the center-right newspaper *Le Figaro*, the cover depicted Marianne, the symbol of the French Republic, wearing a chador under the heading "Will we still be French in twenty years?" The article then extrapolated from the birthrate among North African immigrants and predicted that by the year 2015 there would be a decline of 5.2 million French and an equal increase in the number of immigrants. During a televised debate in autumn 1985, both Socialist prime minister Laurent Fabius and RPR leader Jacques Chirac said that there was not "strong disagreement" between them on the problem of immigration.[77]

By the 1990s the National Front's anti-immigration message had become immensely popular and was contributing to the party's success in elections.[78] An October 1991 poll showed that 32 percent of those questioned agreed with Le Pen's ideas, while 38 percent approved of his position on immigration.[79] Polls consistently showed that immigration and security ranked at the top or among the top three issues of greatest concern to Front voters, and the fact that increased expenditure on police and discrimination against immigrants were the top two priorities of the three National Front mayors elected in 1995 confirms this linkage. Every new NF attack on im-migrants or immigration and every new NF policy proposal was given wide prominence in the press and on television. Moreover, as the mainstream right and the Socialists began to echo the National Front's line on cracking down on illegal immigrants, the Front moved to the right in order to out-flank the opposition.

The Social Costs of Immigration

In 1984 Le Pen wrote, "Civil war is at our gates," and he warned that "the influx of immigrant families—traditionally prolific—in the guise of reunit-ing families, means the demographic submersion of France and the substi-tution of a Third World population. . . . Let's not fool ourselves: the very existence of the French people is at stake. . . . Insecurity has been consider-ably aggravated by immigration. This is normal, taking into account that immigrants are socially uprooted in the large, modern megalopolis."[80]

The NF is severely critical of the social costs of North African and black African immigrants, arguing that they are major contributors to unemploy-ment, delinquency, and crime and that they impose an economic burden on the French economy.[81] According to the Front, North African and black African immigrants pose a major threat to the law itself, the very founda-tion of society. The Front contends that immigrants make up a dispropor-tionate number of delinquents and criminals. Pro-Front newspapers such as *Présent* and *National Hebdo* give dramatic play to incidents involving im-migrants in trouble with the law.[82] The first chapter of the Front's program *300 mesures pour la renaissance de la France* (1993), which to this point is the most complete exposition of the Front's policies and program, is de-voted to immigration and is packed with figures and charts designed to show the social costs of immigration. It is because immigrants are "deraci-nated, cut off from their traditions," that they are "a major source of inse-curity."[83] At the same time, the Front hammers home the putative link be-tween unemployment and immigration. Front election posters almost always contain an equation that links unemployment and immigration: "4 million immigrants = 4 million unemployed," for example. The Front pro-gram offers simple arguments: France has the highest percentage of immi-grants in the active population (available for work) and the highest unem-ployment rate among industrialized countries; Japan, which has "no immigration," has the lowest unemployment rate. Ergo, immigration causes unemployment. According to Pierre Milloz, Front expert on immigration, the total cost to France of immigration is Fr 210 billion, a figure equal to all the taxes the French pay on their salaries each year.

On National Identity and Racism

The Front links utilitarian arguments about the social cost of immigration to an ideology of "difference," namely, that immigrants from North Africa and black Africa cannot and will not assimilate into French culture and that their culture poses a mortal threat to the preservation of French culture and traditions. According to Jean-Yves Le Gallou, an individual's most basic need is for a personal identity that enables a distinction between self and other and a national identity that confirms the individual as part of a "social reality." Both of these rights are primordial. Thus, "the right to be oneself is the first of the rights of man."[84] But since the individual must live in social groupings of some kind, and since the modern form of social groups is the nation, to "be oneself," one must be part of a nation and have some sense of national identity. Therefore, both the right to be oneself and the right to a national identity are the most basic rights of all. But, Le Gallou claimed, national identity has been under constant threat from such ideologies as communism and socialism, which try to subordinate the individual to an all-powerful, collectivist state, or, more recently from Islam, which tries to subsume individuals and entire nations to an all-encompassing religion.[85]

Front ideologists claim that the true racists today are those who wish to get rid of national differences and to subsume national identity under some universalistic or *mondialiste* philosophy. According to Jean-Yves Le Gallou, it is insulting to accuse of racism those who merely wish to defend the unique qualities of French national identity from the threat posed by those holding different values and beliefs. After all, Front ideologists protest, the Front does not say that French values and French culture are better than others, only that French national identity differs from, say, Algerian, Tunisian, or Moroccan national identity.[86] Do not the French have the right to defend the integrity of their national identity, just as do Algerians, Tunisians, and Moroccans?

Of course, this argument begs the question of why, if the values that compose French national identity (however defined) are no better than, but merely different from, those of other nations or cultures, they should be defended at all. In any case the Front claims that each nation has a "right to be different" and that this right must be defended. Thus, it is imperative to defend French national identity against the threat posed by immigrants from the Maghreb and Africa who have radically different beliefs and values.[87]

How do these immigrants threaten French national identity? According to Bruno Mégret, the essence of French national identity does not derive from the fact that the Declaration of the Rights of Man, a separation between church and state, and democratic pluralism can be found in France.

Such a definition of French national identity would "reduce France to an ensemble of juridical norms, defined only by the text of its constitutional principles."[88] For Mégret, to be French is to share a heritage of myths, values, language, ethnicity, and (Christian) religion.[89] Thus, French national identity derives from shared, nonrational, metaphysical values. Mégret defines the nation as "the dream of a people which wants to endure in history. It is composed of the dead, the living and of those who are going to be born in the heart of the community. It is not reduced to an agglomeration of individuals."[90]

Arguing that "Frenchness" does not reside in political phenomena such as the Declaration of the Rights of Man or parliamentary democracy allows Mégret to deny that a recent immigrant is as "French" as, say, a Breton whose family has lived in France for centuries. Only those people are French who, through their origins and their family, share the long history of the French nation. Mégret contends that "the nation is constituted of a soil, a people and a culture, and it can't exist without the work of time. It becomes a nation only after many generations have passed. . . . To claim, as do those who support cosmopolitanism, that this entire structure can be modified and reconstructed along new lines so as to integrate Islam and the populations of Africa and Asia is absurd."[91]

As party spokesperson, Le Pen often conveys the anti-immigrant message in a crude, sometimes overly racist fashion, using the same techniques as when he expresses anti-Semitism—through insulting remarks, calculated slips of the tongue, or racist jokes. In one notorious remark he said, "Tomorrow the immigrants will move in with you, eat your soup and they will sleep with your wife, your daughter or your son."[92] In 1987 he referred to "Maghrebian women in rut [*en rut*] . . . pardon, in struggle [*en lutte*]."[93] In May 1991 Le Pen referred to the Socialist secretary of state for integration, Kofi Yamgnane, as "miam-miam [yum-yum]."[94] Although the Front takes the position that no race is superior to another, Le Pen once remarked that "since I can't state that Switzerland is as large as the United States, I also can't say that Bantus have the same ethnological aptitudes as Californians, because that is simply contrary to reality. . . . Citizens are equal in rights, not men. . . . Even if men have a right to be equally respected, it is evident that hierarchies exist."[95]

Le Pen also emphasizes the ineffable nature of French national identity: "The homeland [*la Patrie*] is the land of our fathers . . . a country fashioned by its countryside, its cities, its language, history and enriched by their efforts, fertilized by their sweat and blood. . . . All living things are assigned by nature to those areas conforming to their dispositions or affinities. It is the same thing for men and peoples. . . . The best, that is the most capable, survive and prosper. . . . We are proud that France has succeeded for more than a thousand years."[96]

Beyond utilitarian arguments, therefore, the notion of national identity imposes additional, almost insuperable barriers to immigrants wishing to integrate into the French nation: "Foreigners can enter into a nation by an artificial act: naturalization. They can only be integrated into the homeland by a sacrificial act: the spilling of their blood. . . . It is when the body become dust mingles with French soil, and only then, that one's sons and daughters will have their homeland here."[97]

Le Pen often refers to his origins as part of a Celtic tradition dating to the megaliths, "the proof of man's intelligence for thousands of years."[98] Le Pen admits that in the past France was a country of immigration, but apparently only the Europeans who belong to the historic groups that amalgamated in the tenth century to compose the French race can possibly join the nation today. According to Le Pen, "From the tenth to the twentieth century, the composition of the French population has not changed."[99]

The Front and "Anti-French Racism"

The Front often charges its opponents with "anti-French racism." The Front agrees with biologists that it is difficult to find a scientific definition of race and that there are neither superior nor inferior races. It also agrees that no particular value judgments should be drawn from the obvious fact that peoples and nations differ from each other in terms of culture, values, religion, and other characteristics. But, the Front claims, the simple human fact is that groups or cultures or nations wish to preserve their distinctive characteristics—or differences—and feel threatened when large numbers of people with quite different beliefs and characteristics appear on the scene. This is as true of the French as it is of the Germans, Americans, Algerians, or Moroccans. Thus, the Front says it is justly defending the particular characteristics of the French nation against a threatened tidal wave of immigration from nations with radically different cultural and religious traditions. It follows, therefore, that those who attack the Front and defend immigrants are anti-French racists since their policies would lead to the ultimate destruction of the French nation.

According to Pierre-André Taguieff, the Front's views are not racist but rather "neoracist."[100] Neoracism is based on an "'absolutization' of difference," that is, a defining of differences between groups in such a way that a merging of the two will lead to the disappearance of the unique qualities that distinguish between them. For the Front, such merging or mixing of races inevitably means an end to those things that are uniquely French. According to the Front, "A people that loses its identity, that no longer knows who it is or where it comes from, or what values it embodies, is a people condemned to death. . . . No people can assimilate and integrate a large number of foreigners belonging to civilizations totally different from its own."[101] Clearly, the Front's model of French national identity based on shared ties of blood, soil, and religion excludes from the charmed circle immigrants from the Maghreb and Africa whose history runs along different lines from that of the French.

Notes

1. *National Hebdo,* February 16–22, 1995.

2. Haut Conseil à l'Intégration, *L'Intégration à la Française* (Paris: Union Générale d'Éditions, 1993), p. 32.

3. Ibid., p. 257. The Haut Conseil (High Council) also uses a third term, *immigrant,* which refers to foreigners authorized to reside in France for a year or less.

4. For a critique of the Front's arguments, see Pierre-André Taguieff, ed., *Face au racisme* (Paris: La Découverte, 1991), vols. 1, 2.

5. A 1990 survey of delegates to a National Front conference found that 50 percent agreed with the proposition that "there are inferior and superior people," 88 percent with the proposition that "immigrants cause criminality," 87 percent with the proposition that immigrants should not receive social security, and 94 percent with the proposition that clandestine immigrants should be shipped back home. Piero Ignazi and Colette Ysmal, "New and Old Extreme Right Parties: The French National Front and the Italian Movimento Sociale," *European Journal of Political Research* 22, 1 (July 1992):111.

6. "Beginning in the 1980s, immigration occupied an important place in political debate in France." Agnès Hochet, "L'immigration dans le débat politique français de 1981 à 1988," *Pouvoirs* 47 (1988):5.

7. Simone Bonnafous, *L'immigration prise aux mots* (Paris: Kimé, 1991), p. 226.

8. The terms *immigrant* and *foreigner* are sometimes used interchangeably, particularly by the National Front. Strictly speaking, a foreigner is someone residing in France who does not have French nationality. Under current French law, however, children of non-French immigrants who have not yet reached the age of majority are also considered foreigners. An immigrant is one who has French nationality through naturalization. Maxim Silverman, *Deconstructing the Nation: Immigration, Racism, and Citizenship in Modern France* (New York: Routledge, 1992), p. 3.

9. Cited in Gérard Noiriel, *Le creuset Français* (Paris: Seuil, 1988), p. 73.

10. Marcel Paon, *L'immigration en France* (Paris: Payot, 1926), p. 209.

11. Noiriel, *Le creuset,* p. 21.

12. Alain Bockel, *L'immigration au pays des droits de l'homme* (Paris: Publisud, 1991), p. 17.

13. Noiriel, *Le creuset,* p. 76.

14. Ibid., p. 282.

15. Ibid., p. 73.

16. Ibid., pp. 258–259.

17. Marianne Amar and Pierre Milza, *L'immigration en France au XXe siècle* (Paris: Armand Colin, 1990), pp. 29–32. By contrast, in 1920 Italian immigrants to

the Paris industrial suburb of Puteaux were received by a marching band. Yves Lequin, ed., *La mosaïque France* (Paris: Larousse, 1988), p. 360.

18. Quoted in Amar and Milza, *L'immigration*, p. 34.

19. Quoted in Françoise Gaspard, "Les immigrés comme enjeu politique," *Revue politique et parlementaire*, 916–917 (May-June 1985):175.

20. Noiriel, *Le creuset*, p. 261.

21. Ibid., pp. 79–82.

22. Dark skin and a foreign accent became "scientific" indications that a person was foreign. Ibid., pp. 95–107.

23. See Édouard Catalogne, *La Politique de l'immigration en France depuis la guerre de 1914* (Paris: Imprimerie André Tournon, 1925), pp. 20ff.

24. Quoted in Paon, *L'immigration*, p. 8.

25. Ibid., p. 203.

26. Bockel, *L'immigration*, p. 27.

27. This is the basis of nationality law in Germany.

28. Military service was made compulsory in July 1872.

29. See Journal Officiel, *Annales de la Chambre des Deputés, Débats Parlementaires*, March 31, 1927, p. 876. Pierre Guillaume claimed that racism was expressed with "virulence" during the debates. A close reading of these debates discloses only a few remarks that might be characterized as racist. Pierre Guillaume, "L'Accession à la nationalité: Le grand débat (1882–1932)," in Dominique Colas et al., *Citoyenneté et nationalité* (Paris: Presses Universitaires de France, 1991), p. 145.

30. Jules Valéry, *La nationalité française* (Paris: Librairie Générale de Droit et de Jurisprudence, 1927), p. 59.

31. Charles d'Heristal, quoted in Ralph Schor, *L'Opinion française et les étrangers, 1919–1939* (Paris: Publications de la Sorbonne, 1985), p. 206.

32. Ibid., p. 207.

33. Journal Officiel, *Lois et décrets*, November 13, 1938, p. 12921. See also Michael Marrus and Robert O. Paxton, *Vichy France and the Jews* (New York: Basic Books, 1981), p. 56.

34. Noiriel, *Le creuset*, p. 94.

35. Ibid., pp. 34–37.

36. The Law on Foreign Residents of the Jewish Race of October 4, 1940, stipulated that non-French Jews were to be interned in "special camps." It was from these French camps that Jews were shipped to the death camps. Journal Officiel, *Lois et décrets*, October 18, 1940, p. 5324.

37. Georges Mauco, in the March 1942 edition of *L'Ethnie française*, cited in Patrick Weil, *La France et ses étrangers* (Paris: Calmann-Lévy, 1991), p. 51. After the war Mauco was appointed to head the High Committee on Population and the Family, a post he held until 1970.

38. Ibid., p. 53.

39. See M. T. Pouillet and J. M. Bouttier, "L'accueil officiel," *Ésprit* 348 (April 1966):585.

40. Quoted in Weil, *La France*, p. 55.

41. Menie Gregoire, "Politique de l'immigration," *Ésprit* 348 (April 1966):575.

42. Weil, *La France*, pp. 66–70.

43. Association France-Algérie, *Compte-rendu des trauvaux du colloque sur la migration algérienne en France, 13–15 October 1966* (Paris: Association France-Algérie, 1966), p. 30.

44. Michele Guibert, "Présentation des étrangers," *Ésprit* 348 (April 1966):565–566.

45. A *bidon* is a can used for carrying oil or water.

46. Francette Vidal, "La Campa," *Ésprit* 348 (April 1966):651–661.

47. Ibid., p. 661.

48. Quoted in Olivier Milza, *Les français devant l'immigration* (Brussels: Complexe, 1988), p. 119.

49. Paul H. Maucorps, Albert Memmi, and Jean-Francis Held, *Les français et le racisme* (Paris: Payot, 1965), p. 41.

50. See *L'Année politique* (1961), which published without comment the police figure of two deaths. For a more accurate account see Milza, *Les français*, pp. 119–121.

51. *L'Année politique* (1973):166.

52. Quoted in Weil, *La France*, p. 78.

53. Ibid. Weil suggested that the Algerian government's decision to terminate emigration was part of the jockeying for position among groups claiming to represent the interests of Algerians in France because the Algerian government feared that an Algerian interest group established in France to represent immigrants would become a center of opposition to the government.

54. Ibid., pp. 73–85.

55. Bockel, *L'immigration*, p. 68.

56. Weil, *La France*, p. 111.

57. Patrick Weil, "La politique française d'immigration," *Pouvoirs* 47 (1988):57.

58. Weil, *La France*, pp. 111ff.

59. Patrick Weil, "Les politiques de l'immigration en France depuis la Seconde Guerre mondiale," in Taguieff, *Face au racisme*, vol. 2, p. 141.

60. *L'Année politique* (1980):25.

61. Bonnafous, *L'immigration*, p. 263.

62. Bockel, *L'immigration*, p. 76.

63. *L'Année politique* (1980):129.

64. Socialist leader Pierre Bérégovoy condemned "the undignified attitude of a party which claims to be on the left but which behaves like a small extreme right group." Quoted in Gaspard, "Les immigrés," p. 176.

65. Bonnafous, *L'immigration*, pp. 107ff.

66. Ibid., p. 107.

67. Ibid., pp. 252–269.

68. In 1978 the Socialist group in the National Assembly proposed granting to "all workers, independent of their nationality, the same rights." The only restriction was that family allowances would have been paid only to those residing in France and voting rights restricted to local elections. Gaspard, "Les immigrés," p. 176.

69. Weil, *La France*, pp. 140–141.

70. These clashes were named "Minguettes" after a suburb of Lyon with a large concentration of immigrants.

71. *L'Année politique* (1982):396.

72. Bockel, *L'immigration*, p. 110.

73. Weil, *La France*, p. 159.

74. Quoted in Gilles Bresson and Christian Lionet, *Le Pen* (Paris: Seuil, 1994), p. 364.

75. Weil, *La France*, p. 81.

76. Christopher Husbands, "The Politics of Immigration in France," *Ethnic and Racial Studies* 14, 2 (April 1991):184–185.

77. Hochet, *L'immigration*, pp. 26–27.

78. Anne Tristan reported that the ordinary militants she encountered in Marseilles constantly discussed Arabs. "Of all the subjects, that was the one they preferred. Arabs were the cause of everything wrong, they covered them with insults and complaints. The broken bus shelters, defective telephone booths, blocked bus doors ... all this was the fault of the Arabs." Anne Tristan, *Au Front* (Paris: Gallimard, 1987), p. 49.

79. See the polls published in *Le Monde*, September 21 and October 25, 1991.

80. Jean-Marie Le Pen, *Les Français d'abord* (Paris: Carrère/Laffon, 1984), pp. 75–76, 103–105, 121.

81. The French use the term *black Africans* for Africans who come from outside the Maghreb.

82. Pierre-André Taguieff, "Les Métamorphoses Idéologiques du Racisme et la Crise de l'Antiracisme," in Taguieff, *Face au racisme*, vol. 2, pp. 51ff.

83. Front National, *300 mesures pour la renaissance de la France* (Paris: Éditions Nationales, 1993), p. 33.

84. Jean-Yves Le Gallou, "Identité nationale et préférence nationale," in Club de l'Horloge, *L'Identité de la France* (Paris: Albin Michel, 1985), p. 14.

85. "Islam is not only something spiritual, it is also a social and legal bloc which is barely compatible with a laic conception of the state (because everything comes from God), with the civil code and rights of man: the Koran stipulates notably that as a witness a man is worth two women, while the 'charia' grants different rights to the master and the slave, to the Muslim and the non-Muslim." Ibid., p. 246.

86. "The French must defend their identity, that is to say, their morals, their customs, their language, their culture, their religious traditions, their conception of the relation between men." Ibid., p. 254.

87. At the April 1985 Club de l'Horloge conference on national identity, Henri de la Bastide, professor of the civilization of the Maghreb at the National Institute of Languages and Oriental Civilizations in Paris, argued that the real problems in France came from the Algerians because they were used to living in communities within which they subsumed their individual differences. "When out of work ... they form gangs because they only know how to exist in communities." Professor de la Bastide characterized civilizations as follows: "the Arab civilization or 'the civilization of the word'; Indian civilization, or 'the civilization of the gesture'; Chinese civilization, or 'the civilization of the sign'; and African civilization, or 'the civilization of rhythm.'" Henri de la Bastide, "Le problème des immigrés maghrébins," in Club de l'Horloge, *L'Identité*, pp. 220–221.

88. Bruno Mégret, *La flamme* (Paris: Robert Laffont, 1990), p. 192.

89. "Viewed from a global perspective, Europeans are part of the same family. They share the same ethnic origins, the same Christian religion, the same history, the same customs, the same morals." Ibid., p. 207.

90. Henry de Lesquen, quoted in ibid., p. 203. The same sentiments can be found in the works of Charles Maurras.

91. Ibid., p. 202.

92. Le Pen, *Les Français*, p. 227.

93. Quoted in Christophe Hameau, *La campagne de Jean-Marie Le Pen pour l'élection présidentielle de 1988* (Paris: Travaux et Recherches de l'Université Panthéon-Assas [Paris II], n.d.) p. 77.

94. Quoted in *Le Monde*, May 28, 1991.

95. Quoted in Alain Rollat, *L'Effet Le Pen* (Paris: La Découverte, 1984), p. 129.

96. Le Pen, *Les Français*, p. 75.

97. Ibid.

98. Quoted in Hameau, *La campagne*, p. 73.

99. Quoted in ibid., p. 74.

100. Taguieff, *Face au racisme*, vol. 2, p. 43.

101. Front National, *300 mesures*, pp. 36–37.

8

Electorate

*The Gulf war will come to an end. . . . The soldiers will then come home.
. . . And then time will go by. They will revert to being paras, skinheads, and
then perhaps* Front National *voters.*

—Jean-Claude Martinez, Debates of the European Parliament, *January 23, 1991*

If Jean-Marie Le Pen is a bastard, his voters are bastards.

—Bernard Tapie, quoted in Emmanual Faux et al., La main droite de Dieu

Who are the millions of French voters who support a man and a party that
are anti-Semitic and racist? Why do these people vote for the Front? Are extreme right voters different from those who vote for the traditional parties
of the right? Are they racists and anti-Semites? And does the vote for the
Front represent a new current in French politics, or is it part of a long tradition of extreme right voting in France?

These troubling questions are difficult to answer given the relatively brief
political history of the Front, the lack of serious long-term studies of the extreme right electorate in France, and the problems involved in the very definition of extreme right. Is it fair, for example, to label as extreme right
those voters who supported Pierre Poujade in 1956, Jean-Louis Tixier-
Vignancour in the 1965 presidential election, and Le Pen and the National
Front in the 1980s and 1990s? Or were the men, parties, and issues in these
widely spaced elections so different from one another that each should be
analyzed separately and no general conclusions drawn about the nature of
the extreme right? Further complicating the issue is that, with the exception
of the Poujadist legislative campaign of 1956 and Jean-Louis Tixier-
Vignancour's 1965 presidential campaign, French voters after World War II
never had an opportunity to support a national party of the extreme right

until the National Front emerged as a major political force in the middle 1980s. Thus, voters who placed themselves on the extreme right of the spectrum were forced to choose among candidates who would not have been their first choice if an extreme right candidate had been present. And even when candidates such as Poujade or Tixier-Vignancour, whom the press or scholars labeled as extreme right, did run in elections, many self-described extreme right voters did not vote for them. And because the term *extreme right* has negative connotations in France, even those parties and candidates that the public thinks of as being on the extreme right often reject the label. In 1967, when voters and candidates were asked to arrange parties along a left-right spectrum, the majority placed Jean-Louis Tixier-Vignancour's Alliance Républicaine (Republican Alliance) on the extreme right of French politics; yet in his election campaign fifteen months before, Tixier-Vignancour had rejected the notion that he was on the extreme right and after the first round of the election called on his voters to support Mitterrand against de Gaulle.[1] Even today the National Front angrily rejects the extreme right label. Finally, until recently French election studies paid scant attention to the extreme right, and when they did, their results had to be taken with a grain of salt: In a study of the 1965 presidential election sponsored by the National Political Science Foundation, generalizations about Tixier-Vignancour's electorate were based on responses from forty-three voters, hardly a representative sample of the 1.25 million voters who supported him on the first round of the election.

The Extreme Right and Poujadism

The extreme right never really counted in postwar politics until the Poujadists appeared on the scene in 1956. It quickly became clear that the Poujadists drew the bulk of their votes from what one French analyst called "static France"—from those southern and western areas of France devoted to agriculture or wine and from artisans and small businesspeople, exactly those groups that Poujade's movement was supposed to defend.[2] According to French historians Serge Bernstein and Pierre Milza, "Doubtless not all those who applauded Poujade's slogans supported the extreme right, which tried to use a movement whose concerns it barely shared."[3] Unlike the extreme right, whose objective was to create a new man in a new, nondemocratic authoritarian society, Poujadism was backward looking, defensive of the interests of its rural supporters, somewhat anarchistic, and, its greatest sin in the eyes of the extreme right, not hostile enough to the Republic.[4] Nonetheless, many elements of the extreme right, including Jean-Marie Le Pen, gave Poujade their grudging support.

After the collapse of Poujadism, the next opportunity voters had to support the extreme right came in 1965 when Jean-Louis Tixier-Vignancour ran for the presidency against de Gaulle. Here, too, any discussion of the nature of the extreme right vote based on contemporaneous polls is difficult because 80 percent of those who placed themselves on the extreme right intended to vote for de Gaulle in the 1965 election.[5] Generalizations about the Tixier-Vignancour "electorate," therefore, were based on forty-three of his voters, whose opinions were solicited in the 1965 election study, and a larger sample of approximately two hundred extreme right voters who were polled from 1964 to 1966 by Emeric Deutsch, Denis Lindon, and Pierre Weil in their study of French "political families."

Nonetheless, polls did show that most of Tixier-Vignancour's voters as well as those who placed themselves on the extreme right were male.[6] This male gender bias has been typical of the extreme right since polls began, although it mitigated in polls taken of Front voters in the mid–1990s. One reason for the male bias, it is argued, is that women do not like war or political conflict, and the extreme right has usually been associated with both.[7] The fact that 63 percent of Tixier-Vignancour's electorate was male, while 54 percent of de Gaulle's electorate was female, larger than that of Mitterrand or Lecanuet, was probably due to de Gaulle's antiparty stance and to the fact that he eased the transition to the Fifth Republic, ended the Algerian War, and calmed domestic strife. Another reason for women's lack of support for the extreme right in the 1960s might have been that they were less interested in politics than men: Only 53 percent of women in the Boulogne-Billancourt study expressed any interest at all in politics in 1965, compared to 64 percent of men.

However, studies showed that Poujadist voters were only a sample of the extreme right electorate, with Poujade drawing his support disproportionately from farmers, artisans, and small-town businesspeople. There also seems to have been little overlap between the Poujadist electorate and those who voted for Tixier-Vignancour: Only 16 percent of those social groups that supported Poujade in 1956 voted for Tixier-Vignancour in 1965. According to François Goguel, there was no "relation between the geographic distribution of the extreme right in 1965 and past elections. It is clear that the principal factor in favor of Mr. Tixier-Vignancour is the presence of a considerable number of repatriates from Algeria."[8] On most survey questions, those who voted for Tixier-Vignancour hardly differed in their responses from those who voted for the moderate right or the center— except when it came to questions on colonization and de Gaulle. While 76 percent of extreme right voters agreed that "it is too bad that France lost all its colonies," only 54 percent of those who supported the moderate right agreed with this proposition. The animosity of Tixier-Vignancour voters toward de Gaulle was so great in the 1965 election that 70 percent followed Tixier-Vignancour's plea to vote for Mitterrand on the second ballot.

The 1965 study asked only a few questions concerning issues. On some there were clear differences between those who voted for Tixier-Vignancour and those who voted for the other candidates. For example, only 16 percent of Tixier-Vignancour voters thought that defending secular schools was an important issue, compared to 66 percent of Mitterrand voters and 36 percent of de Gaulle voters. There is a historical division in France between the left, which supports secular education and generally has been hostile to state support for Catholic schools, and the right, which sees the state school system as a breeding ground for socialist and antireligious values. This question clearly tapped that sentiment. Tixier-Vignancour voters also scored lowest when asked if improving the condition of women, instituting an equitable division of income, or defending workers (from economic hardship) was important.

None of these results are surprising since one expects extreme right voters to support traditional conceptions of the family and of the roles of men and women and to oppose economic equality as infringing on freedom. However, one surprising finding was that 84 percent of Tixier-Vignancour voters supported the "diffusion" of birth control devices, ranking second only to the 89 percent of Mitterrand voters who also favored birth control. Another was that only 2 percent of Tixier-Vignancour voters supported maintaining a French nuclear strike force (*force de frappe*), with 47 percent in favor of putting French weapons at the disposal of a European alliance and another 47 percent in favor of scrapping the strike force altogether. It is difficult to generalize on the basis of these findings because the sample size was small and because no real attempt was made, through multiple regression analysis, for example, to determine which were the important and which the unimportant variables influencing the Tixier-Vignancour vote.

Front Voters: Extreme Right or on the Extreme of the Right?

In a 1966 study of French voters, Emeric Deutsch and his colleagues distinguished among six "political families": from the extreme left, the moderate left, the center, the moderate right, and the extreme right to a group of nonparticipants whom Deutsch called the *marais*, or the "swamp." The swamp consisted of those voters who were uninterested in politics, had no opinions on most issues of the day, and could not say whom they would vote for in the next election. Interestingly, in the 1965 presidential election fewer than 6 percent of the swamp voted for Tixier-Vignancour on the first ballot, while 55 percent supported de Gaulle. Part of the reason must have been that because the swamp is uninterested in politics, members of this group would probably have been unaware of a marginal candidate like Tixier-Vignancour. However, voters who placed themselves on the extreme right were very interested in politics: Only 12 percent answered "don't know" to most of the questions asked, compared to 18 percent of voters on the moderate right.[9]

The 1966 study also found that, except for a preponderance of men and an underrepresentation of white-collar workers, the sociological character-istics of extreme right supporters in 1966 resembled those of the electorate as a whole. Even their opinions did not sharply differentiate the extreme right from the moderate right, which led Deutsch, Lindon, and Weil to com-ment, "One might argue that moderate right and extreme right voters are only separated by nuances, and that the right wing electorate as a whole constitutes a homogeneous block in view of its opinions and sentiments."[10] There were, however, some marginal differences between the moderate and the extreme right. When respondents were asked if they agreed with the statement "It is necessary to maintain the authority of government," 62 percent of extreme right supporters agreed, followed by 54 percent of the moderate right. When asked whether they agreed that France should have a "powerful army," the extreme right was more in agreement (66 percent) than the moderate right (54 percent). On whether France should construct its own nuclear deterrent, the extreme right again slightly outdistanced the moderate right, with 55 percent in agreement, compared to 45 percent of moderate right respondents.[11]

On one question the extreme right did stand out from all other French political parties. When respondents were asked their sentiments on the statement "It's too bad that France lost all its colonies," 76 percent on the extreme right agreed, followed by only 54 percent of the moderate right. Here, too, the finding is to be expected not only because Tixier-Vignancour praised France's colonial mission in an attempt to woo *pieds-noirs* voters in the south, but because the extreme right exalts nationalism, and colonial-ism is often understood as an expression of nationalism. The 1966 survey asked no questions tapping anti-Semitic or racist attitudes. However, judg-ing from the tone of extreme right newspapers and reviews, many extreme right supporters of Tixier-Vignancour, and probably of de Gaulle, too, shared the anti-Semitic, racist sentiments of journals such as *Rivarol* or re-views such as *Europe-Action*.

When Tixier-Vignancour vanished from the scene in 1965, the extreme right disappeared as an electoral force until the 1980s. In 1969 Pierre Sidos, an extreme right leader, could not get the minimum 100 notables to sign his presidential nomination papers. In the 1974 presidential election, Le Pen received only 74 percent of the vote. In 1981 he failed to get 500 political notables to sign his presidential nomination papers.

After the Dreux breakthrough and the NF's 11.2 percent score in the 1984 European elections, questions arose about the nature of the NF's electorate. At first it appeared that the Front drew support from Pierre Poujade's old constituency—shopkeepers, farmers in areas of rural decline, and members of the lower middle class—and it was argued that Le Pen's blend of chauvinism, anti-Semitism, economic liberalism, and xenophobia had struck an echo among ex-Poujadist voters.[12] But if the NF drew some support from ex-Poujadists, it could not account for most of its vote. As Michael Lewis-Beck put it: "*The Poujadist hypothesis can account for some Le Pen support, but not much.*"[13] Studies showed that, even though the extreme right electorate remained preponderately male, the voters were evenly distributed across sociological categories and geographically across French territory. This immediately differentiated them from Poujadist supporters, who had been mainly farmers, artisans, or small businesspeople and whose base of support was mainly in the rural southwest.

In the early 1980s it was suspected that the Front was benefiting from the support of disillusioned Communist or Socialist voters. When it appeared that about 20 percent of those who voted for the Front in the early 1980s had voted for François Mitterrand in the 1981 presidential election, there was some speculation that Socialist, and even Communist, voters has shifted to the NF. But it turned out that very few Socialists or Communists had voted for the Front.[14] Jérôme Jaffré's 1984 poll indicated that only 2 percent of NF supporters placed themselves on the extreme left of the political spectrum and only 3 percent on the left. A 1985 synthesis of different poll results confirmed this finding: Only a tiny percentage of NF voters placed themselves on the left side of the political spectrum. Two percent of those who voted for Georges Marchais, the Communist candidate in the 1981 presidential election, claimed to be NF supporters.[15]

By the late 1980s the Front was drawing support from across the sociological spectrum so that the Front electorate more nearly resembled the French population as a whole than did the electorate of any other French political party. Religion, which, according to French political scientist André Siegfried, was "the dominant dividing line of all our politics," was no help at all in predicting the Front vote, and there even seemed to be an inverse correlation between (Catholic) religiosity and a vote for the Front.[16] The exception was among the minority of Front voters who support the "integrist," or right-wing fundamentalist, faction in French Catholicism and who heavily favored the Front.[17]

In a 1984 study Jérôme Jaffré noted that the differences between NF supporters and mainstream right supporters were "often of degree rather than nature," and he suggested that the NF's electorate should be characterized as "right extreme" rather than extreme right: It was "tougher, more resolved than the other components of the opposition."[18] Three years later Jaffré contended that mainstream right leaders such as Jacques Chirac and Raymond Barre were wrong to assume that the NF electorate consisted largely of "stray sheep" who had temporarily wandered from the fold and could be wooed back to the mainstream right by appealing to them over the head of Le Pen. The NF electorate should not be viewed as on the extreme end of the right, Jaffré further contended, but rather as having hardened into a voting bloc separate from the mainstream right. "It has progressively separated itself from the classic right, it no longer consists of stray sheep, but of a young, populist electorate that is not very politicized. It will be difficult for the RPR and the UDF to win its support since its electorate is very different from theirs."[19]

Analyzing the Front Vote

As scholars wrestled with the problem of trying to understand the Front vote, a consensus slowly emerged. The Front vote could not be fully explained by socioeconomic variables. Voters were not so much "pushed" or predisposed to vote for political parties because of occupation, social condition, or age. Rather, they were "pulled" or attracted to parties because of their stand on crucial issues of the day. In other words, one had to take account of both political "supply" and "demand": The availability of a party and of party candidates and the attractions of its program were as important as the presence of voters of a certain age, class, gender, or occupation.

When in the late 1980s Jacqueline Blondel, Bernard Lacroix, and their students conducted in-depth interviews with NF voters, they found that the reasons behind the Front vote were complex and that there was little relation between the "standard variables" and the way in which people voted. One thirty-two-year-old auditor apparently supported the Front because he regretted the disappearance of an idealized past. A career military officer voted for the Front because of his attachment to traditional values and his opposition to the "softness" of the mainstream right. A businessman dealing in tomatoes liked Le Pen because he "spoke simply about the truth." A sixty-year-old retired woman observed: "I am not versed in politics. I don't know about political programs; it's more a question of intuition, something like that." Another voter liked the fact that after National Front meetings everyone stood around chatting and gossiping, "like after Mass." Other voters chose the National Front in order to protest against the other parties. A thirty-two-year-old auditor observed: "Le Pen is a negative choice: I think mainly that he will force the others to react, especially after the election! In this way, Communism will become less and less dangerous."[20] In the Department of Nord a large number of voters supported the National Front in protest against a joint list of the two mainstream right parties headed by centrist (and Jewish) cabinet minister Simone Veil.[21]

As Nonna Mayer and Pascal Perrineau put it in 1992, "The so-called 'sociological variables' do not predict the Lepenist vote."[22] Numerous voting studies confirmed that the Front vote could not be explained by disproportionate support from any one sociological category, such as class, age group, occupation, religious commitment, or educational background. Even the preponderance of male voters, which traditionally characterized the extreme right electorate, shrank to a difference of 1 percent (14 percent male to 13 percent female) in the 1993 legislative elections.[23] English psephologist Christopher Husbands reached the same conclusion: "The . . . significant point about FN voting . . . is the degree to which it has come to be based upon genuine partisan attachment. It is no longer a flash movement . . . but a party with a bedrock of support from a consistent and relatively stable section of the French electorate."[24]

Evidence shows that National Front voters are the most loyal of all party supporters. Two key indicators of party loyalty and party identification tell the story: 73 percent of those who voted for the Front in the 1993 legislative elections voted for the Front in 1994, and 46 percent of those who voted for the Front in 1994 identified themselves as on the extreme right. Only the Communists, who in 1994 attracted 67 percent of their 1993 vote, came close to the National Front.

Exit polls conducted during the 1995 presidential election confirmed the loyalty of Front voters: 80 percent of those who felt themselves "close" to the Front voted for Le Pen, followed by 78 percent of Socialists supporting Lionel Jospin and 72 percent of Communists supporting Robert Hue. Moreover, 77 percent of Le Pen voters placed themselves "very far to the right" on the political spectrum, signifying that the vast majority of extreme right voters saw Le Pen as best representing their views.

Just before the 1995 presidential election, the pro-Front weekly *National Hebdo* boasted that "the national vote is not a sociological vote, it is a political vote."[25] The Front electorate, wrote *National Hebdo,* consists of "an entire people without the artificial divisions that politicians want to impose on it." Bruno Mégret contended that "voters decide on the basis of ideas, not because of their professional category."[26]

Certainly, one cannot understand or explain voting behavior solely in terms of a mechanical relationship between underlying sociological variables and vote, and one surely must take into account the way in which voters perceive and react to the nature, appeal, program, and propaganda of political parties. These concerns are not mutually exclusive: When there is a high correlation between vote and a particular sociological characteristic in the electorate, then this marks the beginning, not the end, of inquiry. A striking example occurred in the 1995 presidential election when Le Pen won more support from workers (27 percent) than any other candidate in the election (Lionel Jospin won 21 percent of the vote from workers). Le Pen also won disproportionate support from those voters who said they were "disadvantaged" when asked to describe their place on the social ladder: 34 percent compared to the 17 percent who supported Jospin. Without further analysis, it is difficult to know how much overlap there was between the workers and the "disadvantaged" or, for that matter, among any of the categories in the 1995 election report.[27] Clearly, however, Le Pen's vote was encroaching on the working class, a group traditionally considered the preserve of the Communist and Socialist Parties.

Front Voters, Immigration, and Security

Unquestionably, the Front's anti-immigrant stance is one of its main attractions.[28] Whereas in the 1970s Le Pen and the Front paid little attention to the immigration issue, by the 1980s the Front had made it the centerpiece of the party program. In 1985 NF voters were three times as likely as other voters to have been motivated by concerns over insecurity and delinquency and five times as likely to vote NF because of concerns about immigrants.

National Front voters are much more hostile to immigrants than those who vote for parties of the left and right. In 1988 Mayer and Perrineau found that 75 percent of those who voted for Le Pen thought that there were too many immigrants in France, compared to 35 percent for the French population as a whole. Fifty-five percent of Le Pen voters did not think Muslims should be allowed to build mosques in France, as opposed to 24 percent of the population. Yet the anti-immigrant sentiments of Front voters were not motivated by their living in close proximity to immigrants: Studies in Grenoble and Paris showed there was no apparent correlation between people living with or near immigrants and voting for the National Front.[29] A survey of the traditionally Socialist industrial and textile Department of Nord found only a weak correlation between a person living in locality with a large number of immigrants and voting for the National Front. Pascal Perrineau argued that there was no link between NF vote and the presence of immigrants in individual cities, towns, and neighborhoods.[30] The anti-immigrant sentiment of Front supporters and voters is explained in terms of a "halo effect," that is, the negative reaction of voters who live near but not in areas with foreign populations.[31] In other words, fear of immigrants, rather than actual proximity, seemed to correlate with support for the Front. However, the evidence for this conclusion is mixed.

One illuminating insight into the anti-immigrant sentiments of Front voters comes from a study of 126 Front voters conducted between 1986 and 1988 in Paris and Bordeaux. What emerges is a bewildering variety of reasons, emotions, and objectives that lay behind their views. Among workers in the building trades, the researchers found respondents linking their experiences at work or with unemployment and their fears about the future to immigrants. One construction worker complained that his immigrant fellow workers did not speak French, which meant they "could make rude insults in their language. In France one speaks French! They know how to speak it when they want dough!"[32] Although working together with immigrants on the same building site, this French worker perceived these immigrants as potential freeloaders and justified his hostility in terms of the threat immigrants posed to his own sense of identity.

Certainly public opinion polls showed that National Front voters were disproportionately in favor of returning immigrant workers to their homeland (67 percent of National Front voters as contrasted to 20 percent of all voters), that 59 percent voted for Le Pen because of the immigrant issue (compared to 22 percent of the electorate), and that 55 percent voted for Le Pen because of violence and lack of security, as compared to 31 percent of the electorate. The complex nature of people's reactions to immigrants in their neighborhood was illustrated in 1992 by *Le Monde* journalists Edwy Plenel and Alain Rollat. They described the anguish of the residents of the Department of Seine-Saint-Denis, a former Communist working-class stronghold on the periphery of Paris, confronted with a changing community:

> Seine-Saint-Denis is overflowing with repressed hatred, anguish, real pain, with a store of rancor toward Paris, so close and so indifferent—a mosaic of a thousand complaints: "When Paris kicks out the drug dealers, that's terrific," said a deputy, "but where do you think they come to? Here! . . . In Bosquets there were three bakeries. All three are closed today. The grocery stores which remain sell fruits, vegetables and exotic jams. More and more the school canteens, to avoid problems, no longer serve ham or pork. . . . When the prefect came to visit a local hospital he found photos of Khomeini in many rooms."[33]

A representative of SOS-Racisme, the influential antiracist pressure group founded by Harlem Désir, told a *Le Monde* journalist: "I don't know how to tell you this, but it's true that there are a lot of foreigners. Sometimes I try to put myself in the shoes of a native-born French person whose twenty-year-old sons are unemployed, who on Saturdays come to the Saint-Denis market [largely given over to immigrant Arab and North African shops and stalls] and who hear Le Pen on TV tell them that this isn't their own country. Don't you think that flips them out?"[34]

Some residents were angry at the Communist Party, which they accused of ignoring their problems and favoring immigrants. Learning that the RPR had appointed a government commission to investigate the situation of immigrants in France, a group of unemployed workers demanded of a young RPR deputy: "And us? Is there no report on us?"[35] Clearly, in this situation of economic and social tension many voters felt betrayed by the traditional parties of left and right and looked to the National Front for a solution to their problems.[36] Three years later the National Front increased its vote during the 1995 municipal elections in Seine-Saint-Denis by between 20 and 25 percent. Although it failed to elect a mayor in the area, the NF list ran second or third in the area behind the left or the mainstream right.

Above all, Front voters are more pessimistic about the future, more concerned about law-and-order issues, and more skeptical about democracy than are voters of any other political party. When asked in 1988 if they wanted the opposition to act illegally against the left, 27 percent of extreme right supporters said that it should, compared to 8 percent of Gaullists and 10 percent of Giscardians. On issues such as political alienation, respect for the authority of the state, and capital punishment, extreme right supporters were more authoritarian than the mainstream right. In 1988 Mayer and Perrineau ranked voters on a "pessimism scale" that asked voters whether they thought democracy was working, whether life was better than before, and whether the money they took home from work allowed them to live decently. More Le Pen voters (62 percent) answered negatively to these questions than those who had voted for the other presidential candidates— Mitterrand supporters (51 percent) were the next highest on this scale. In a 1994 poll during the European election, Front voters evidenced a higher degree of disaffection for democracy and sense of pessimism than did voters from any other party. Seventy percent of Front voters thought that "democracy is working badly," a figure that far outdistanced the shared opinion of 59 percent of those voting for the fringe rural party, "Hunting-Fishing-Nature-Tradition." An astounding 82 percent of Front voters were "anxious" when they thought about their personal and professional future. Only 77 percent of Communist voters even came close to Front voters in expressing this anxiety.[37]

These sentiments were echoed during the 1995 presidential election. This time 76 percent of Le Pen's supporters felt anxious about their personal and professional future, and 69 percent felt that democracy was working badly.[38] Only Communist voters were equally anxious about the future, followed by supporters of Philippe de Villiers.

Local Factors

In the 1990s the Front draws most of its voting support from the southern part of France in the area around Marseilles, from urban areas around Paris, from northern departments hit by a recession in the steel and textile industries, and from the Alsace area in the east. In a study of the Seine-Saint-Denis department, François Platone and Henri Rey claimed that high levels of Front support in certain cities could be explained by a radical increase in population, including numbers of "problem families"; a large proportion of foreigners; and a poor municipal infrastructure. But even within the department, NF support varied from city to city. Where the Communist Party was able to maintain a network of political and community organizations, support for the NF was low. But in those quarters that Platone and Rey described, in English, as "no man's land," areas without industry or equipment and crisscrossed with roads and highways, "where nothing has come to create a new industrial dynamic, the extreme right has made some headway."[39]

Since the 1980s the NF has scored well in the Department of Nord, formerly a textile center but now suffering from recession. Here, too, it is difficult to generalize about the NF vote. In the past the Departments of Nord and Pas-de-Calais were dominated by the Socialist Party, closely followed by the Communists. In the 1983 municipal elections, however, an anti-immigrant list, "Roubaix for the Roubasians," won 9.58 percent of the vote and elected two municipal councillors to office in the city of Roubaix. The National Front then began to present candidates in the area, winning respectable scores of 10–20 percent in local, parliamentary, and European elections. Yet studies show there was no direct correlation between the NF vote and the presence of foreigners; once again the halo effect was operating. It was not so much the actual presence of foreigners in a particular district as a fear of immigrants that correlated with the NF vote.[40] In addition, the NF seems to have benefited from the presence in its ranks of local notables from the Nord. In France mayors or municipal councillors win a loyal following through long years of service to the community and through their connections at the departmental and national levels. Local allegiances often cut across party lines, and many mayors survive their party's election defeat at the national level. Serge Etchebarne showed how the NF vote increased in certain localities in the Nord when a favored notable joined the party, but then dropped when he left it.[41] The sinking of roots in local politics is vital for the survival of a political party, and it provides a jumping-off point for success at the national level. Although the Front had met with some limited success in municipal elections during the 1989 municipal elections, in 1995 the Front increased its score in the north, winning 32 percent of the vote in Tourcoing (population: 93,765), and 24 percent in Roubaix (population: 97,746).

In Alsace, on the German and Swiss border, Le Pen won 22 percent of the 1988 presidential vote, more than either Jacques Chirac or Raymond Barre. In the 1995 presidential election, Le Pen did even better, winning 25.4 percent of the vote, more than any other presidential candidate. Yet Le Pen's success in prosperous and stable Alsace challenges the assumption that Front voters mainly come from urban areas subjected to economic or social stress.

One 1988 study tried to explain Le Pen's score in Alsace in terms of a damaging split in the mainstream right that worked to Le Pen's advantage and as a reaction by many of the forty thousand Alsatian workers to the difference between the economic conditions they witnessed as immigrant day-workers in Germany and Switzerland and the economic situation in Alsace. Although in 1988 economic conditions in Alsace were relatively good compared to the rest of France, with the percentage of immigrants at the national average and the rate of unemployment below the French average, the local economy had been undergoing radical change. The number of farmers had declined by one-third from 1962 to 1982, and big manufacturing enterprises were giving way to smaller organizations, some of which were under foreign control. Apparently, many workers were drawing invidious comparisons between the economic prosperity of neighboring Germany and Switzerland and the situation in Alsace and were voting for the Front in protest.

When, seven years later Le Pen again topped the 1995 presidential poll in Alsace, another explanation was put forward. Le Pen voters were expressing not only their frustration at the comparative prosperity of Germany and Switzerland but also nostalgia for a time when Alsace had been proud of its own culture, regional accent, and identity. According to an Alsatian journalist, "A good part of the Alsatian voters who support the ultra-nationalist Jean-Marie Le Pen want in their own way to say 'No' to France, to being citizens of France and to affirm a neo-autonomist kind of spirit."[42] Whatever the reasons for the Le Pen vote, in the municipal elections two months later the NF came in a poor third in most Alsatian cities and in some cases was out of the running altogether.

The Nature of the National Front Vote

Mayer and Perrineau contended that a majority of those who vote for the National Front want to protest against the mainstream political parties. They found that a vast majority (72 percent) of those who intended to vote for Le Pen in the 1988 presidential elections did not wish to see him elected president, that more than 40 percent who agreed with him on immigration did not think he had a solution to the problem, and that only 36 percent of those who "feel close to the National Front" thought it was "'capable of governing France.'" When asked the direct question "Do you think that people who vote for a candidate or a list of the National Front do so rather to protest against today's political system?" 52 percent of those who described themselves as "very close to the National Front" agreed. Based on these findings, Mayer and Perrineau concluded that, except for an estimated 15 percent of hard-core extreme right voters, the majority of Front supporters were not deeply committed to its ideology or policies and supported it mainly out of protest. The NF vote, they said, is "more expressive of resentment, than instrumental."[43]

However, in view of the 1995 presidential and municipal elections, one should be skeptical of claims that the NF vote is merely a protest vote. Ironically, even if a majority of NF voters do not want to see the NF in government, a vote is a vote, and if enough people support the National Front, even out of protest, the result is to elect Frontists to office. Moreover, the 1995 elections indicated that large numbers of voters actually wished to see Le Pen elected president of France and Front candidates elected to city halls and as mayors. In 1995, 86 percent of those who supported Le Pen said that the candidate's plan counted most for them in determining their vote. The scores for Chirac were 51 percent and Balladur, 52 percent; the remaining candidates scored in the 80 percent range. On the basis of this evidence, one might hypothesize that the vast majority of those who voted for Le Pen saw him as their first choice and genuinely wanted to see him elected to office. By contrast, it appears that those who voted for Balladur and Chirac did so reluctantly to protest against the other major candidates—Jospin and Le Pen.

When asked to rank the candidates' advantages, only 5 percent of Le Pen's voters said that most of all "he inspires confidence." Indeed, Le Pen's score on this question was the lowest of all the candidates. Rather, 37 percent of the voters said Le Pen's greatest asset was that he "incarnated change." By comparison, only 10 percent of the electorate said that Jospin's greatest advantage was that he incarnated change. This was an odd situation: Voters were attracted to the candidates of the extreme right (and of the extreme left) because they incarnated change, while voters were attracted to the Socialist candidate because of his program and because he appeared "close" to their concerns. Moreover, fewer Le Pen voters (20 percent) decided to support their candidate in the last days or at the last moment of the campaign than was the case for the other candidates.

The picture that emerges of the Le Pen electorate in the 1995 presidential election, and of the National Front electorate in the municipal election two months later, is different from the stereotype. Rather than voting for Le Pen in protest against the shortcomings of the other parties, the Front electorate seems to be aware of, attracted to, and interested in the implementation of the Front's program. Front voters are more committed to and more loyal to Le Pen and the Front than are the voters of any other political party. Only 15 percent of Le Pen supporters in 1995 said they were not close to any political party; this was fewer than Chirac (19 percent) or Balladur (23 percent). Front voters are also consistent. They, more than the voters of any other party, feel anxious about the future, disadvantaged in society, and skeptical about democracy. They are afraid of immigrants, crime, and social breakdown. They are hostile to the European Community and what it implies for France. One would assume, therefore, that these voters would look for a candidate whose views were close to their own and who was committed to change. Apparently, Le Pen and the National Front meet these concerns. Unlike the Poujadists, who drew their support from mainly rural areas of France and from small-town businesspeople, artisans, and farmers, the Front draws support from across France and from across all sociological categories. It has sunk roots in town and city halls across France, and it has elected three city mayors. There is some truth to Bruno Mégret's statement on the 1995 presidential election that "those who talk about a protest vote don't understand anything. This has been a vote against what exists, and of support for a current, a politician and a political party which has proposals and is ready to govern."[44]

Notes

1. Philip E. Converse and Roy Pierce, *Political Representation in France* (Cambridge, Mass.: Harvard University Press, 1986), pp. 115–116. For Tixier-Vignancour's refusal of the extreme right label, see Roland Cayrol and Jean-Luc Parodi, "Relais," in *L'élection présidentielle de décembre 1965* (Paris: Armand Colin, 1970), p. 137.

2. François Goguel, *Géographie des élections françaises sous la troisième et la quatrième république* (Paris: Armand Colin, 1970), p. 142.

3. Serge Bernstein and Pierre Milza, *Histoire de la France au XXe siècle* (Brussels: Complexe, 1991), p. 262.

4. Pierre Milza, *Fascisme français: Passé et présent* (Paris: Flammarion, 1987), pp. 307ff.

5. Emeric Deutsch, Denis Lindon, and Pierre Weil, *Les familles politiques aujourd'hui en France* (Paris: Minuit, 1966), p. 63.

6. Guy Michelat, "Attitudes et comportements politiques dans une agglomération de la région parisienne," in *L'élection présidentielle*, p. 380.

7. Michelat's 1965 study of voters in the Boulogne-Billancourt area of Paris found that 61 percent of women expressed hostility to political parties, compared to 56 percent of men. Michelat, "Attitudes," p. 355.

8. François Goguel, "Analyse des résultats," in *L'élection présidentielle*, p. 402.

9. Deutsch et al., *Les familles*, p. 31.

10. Ibid., p. 33.

11. This is in direct contradiction to the 1965 study and is probably due to sampling errors in 1965.

12. Christopher Husbands, "The Support for the *Front National:* Analyses and Findings," *Ethnic and Racial Studies* 14, 3 (July 1991):Table 3.

13. Michael Lewis-Beck and Glenn E. Mitchell, II, "French Electoral Theory: The National Front Test," *Electoral Studies* 12, 2 (1993):117.

14. Jérôme Jaffré, *Le Monde*, February 14, 1984.

15. Husbands, "The Support," p. 408.

16. Quoted in Colette Ysmal, "The History of Electoral Studies in France," *European Journal of Political Research* 25 (1994):374.

17. Husbands, "The Support," p. 405.

18. Jaffré, in *Le Monde*.

19. Jérôme Jaffre, in *Le Monde*, May 26, 1987.

20. Jacqueline Blondel and Bernard Lacroix, "Pourquoi votent-ils FN?" in Nonna Mayer and Pascal Perrineau, *Le Front national à découvert* (Paris: Presses de la Fondation Nationale des Sciences Politiques, 1989), pp. 159, 158. A 1989 poll in Dreux found that only 44 percent of those who voted for the National Front in the legislative election wanted it to win a majority in the next election. Pierre Bréchon and Subrata Kumar Mitra, "The National Front in France: The Emergence of an Extreme Right Protest Movement," *Comparative Politics* 25, 1 (October 1992):77.

21. Serge Etchebarne, "FN dans le Nord," in Mayer and Perrineau, *Le Front national*, p. 293.

22. Nonna Mayer and Pascal Perrineau, "Why Do They Vote for Le Pen?" *European Journal of Political Research* 22, 1 (July 1992):129.

23. However, the BVA polling agency estimated that the gap remained as wide as ever in 1993, with 15 percent of men and 10 percent of women voting for Front candidates in the 1993 legislative elections. Janine Mossuz-Lavau, "Le vote des femmes en France (1945–1993)," *Revue française de science politique* 43, 4 (August 1994):681.

24. Husbands, "The Support," p. 409. Christopher Husbands has rightly criticized French voting studies for their lack of statistical sophistication. There is still heavy reliance on ecological correlations and little use of multiple regression analysis, which at least might help determine the relationship between different variables. Thus, it is assumed that the correlation between the NF vote and the presence of *pieds-noirs*, French Algerians who came to France after 1962, in a particular constituency explains the NF vote—without determining whether in fact individual *pieds-noirs* did vote for Le Pen or what the interplay might be between other variables, such as age, class, and sex.

25. *National Hebdo*, February 16–22, 1995.

26. *Le Monde*, April 27, 1995.

27. *Le Monde*, April 25, 1995.

28. "Between 1972 and 1977 the FN devoted only one front page of the 26 issues of its paper to immigration." Peter Fysh and Jim Wolfreys, "Le Pen, the

National Front, and the Extreme Right in France," *Parliamentary Affairs* 45, 3 (July 1992):319.

29. Mayer and Perrineau, "Why Do They Vote?" p. 132.

30. Pascal Perrineau, "Front national: L'écho politique de l'anomie urbaine," *Ésprit* 3–4 (March-April 1988):29.

31. Etchebarne, "FN dans le Nord," p. 292.

32. Quoted in Blondel and Lacroix, "Pourquoi votent-ils FN?" p. 154.

33. Quoted in Edwy Plenel and Alain Rollat, *La République menacée* (Paris: Le Monde Éditions, 1992), p. 125.

34. Quoted in ibid.

35. Ibid., p. 127.

36. François Platone and Henri Rey, "FN en terre communiste," in Mayer and Perrineau, *Le Front national*, pp. 279ff.

37. Cited in *Le Monde*, June 14, 1994.

38. *Le Monde*, April 25, 1995.

39. Platone and Rey, "FN en terre communiste," p. 281.

40. Etchebarne, "FN dans le Nord," pp. 291ff.

41. Ibid., pp. 300–301.

42. Bernard Reumaux, in *Le Monde*, April 29, 1995.

43. Mayer and Perrineau, "Why Do They Vote?" p. 134.

44. Quoted in *Le Monde*, April 27, 1995.

9

Party Organization

The National Front has become the Planet of the Apes.
—*Jean-Maurice Demarquet, in* Le Monde, *October 16, 1985*

If you disagree with the political party which got you elected, either shut your trap or resign your post.
—*Jean-Marie Le Chevallier, in* Le Monde, *November 1, 1993*

In the 1970s the NF was a heterogeneous coalition of extreme right groups. By the 1990s, however, the National Front had become a party-army: a highly disciplined, efficient, and authoritarian organization with ninety-five departmental federations and approximately fifty thousand members. The NF was also completely under the thumb of Le Pen and his handpicked group of party leaders.[1] Following the examples of the Communist and Socialist Parties, the National Front has tried, with some success, to create a countersociety or counterculture of the extreme right, consisting of affiliated organizations, pressure groups, clubs, and newspapers aimed at reinforcing the bonds of solidarity among party militants and socializing new recruits into the Front's political culture.

The impressive efficiency of the Front's party machine owes a great deal to the skill and energy of Jean-Pierre Stirbois, the party's secretary general after 1980. Both Le Pen and Stirbois had vast funds of experience in the politics of the extreme right and knew what to avoid. Le Pen's stint as a Poujadist deputy had taught him that a successful party leader must lead, and not sit, literally, as was the case with Poujade, on the sidelines. Years later when organizing the National Front, Le Pen and his associates did everything possible to get away from the incessant doctrinal quarrels and internecine squabbling that plagued the extreme right. As Ordre Nouveau, the founding organization of the NF, put it, the new party needed "total discipline. . . . Every political party must have a true core of steel, a unified and effective center for direction. . . . It is necessary to repeat that the Nationalist Revolution is not a game. . . . It is total, an absolute commitment."[2]

In a 1988 interview in *National Hebdo,* Le Pen referred to the need for unity: "There is no reason whatever among us to create currents which, necessarily, would end in confrontation and would bear the seeds of splits. There is on the left . . . a cement which . . . does not exist among us. . . . Besides, the 'nationals' come from such different horizons that it is more useful to emphasize what keeps them together rather than the differences between them."[3]

Clearly, the NF's organization was to be forged out of steel, totally dedicated to the task of winning respectability for the extreme right, taking power, and bringing about a radical change in French society. Because the NF sees its mission as bringing about a national "renaissance" in the face of "foreign powers and domestic lobbies," it developed an organization that is disciplined and highly centralized.

The Front is headed by a president, who is elected by the 1,600 delegates to the party congress, which met nine times from 1972 to 1994. The delegates also elect a 100-member central committee, to which the president can add 20 members chosen by him personally. In turn, the party president submits to the central committee a list of 40 nominees for the political bureau, but the central committee has to accept or reject the entire list. In 1994 all but two members of the political bureau were men.

The president is assisted by an executive office consisting of a vice president, a delegate general, and a secretary general. Like the Communist Party, appointment to office in the NF is done on the basis of cooptation, with officials at higher levels appointing those at lower levels. The secretary general (Stirbois and, after 1988, Carl Lang) appoints the departmental (federation) secretary, who, in turn, appoints the departmental political bureau. The departmental secretary appoints local section secretaries.

Realizing that the verbal and physical violence of the 1950s and 1960s had cut the party off from the political mainstream, the Front stipulates strict rules of behavior and dress for party militants.[4] "Always remain courteous," militants are warned. "Never reply to insults. Do not lower yourself to that level nor waste your time in discussions with fervent adversaries. Evade incidents or provocations which unfailingly will be exploited by our adversaries. Some people will refuse to take a pamphlet or tear it up. That is their right. Your priority is to concern yourself with those you want to convince."[5] Party militants are admonished to dress neatly and to avoid the skinhead look of the 1950s and 1960s.

Party secretary general Jean-Pierre Stirbois was the very model of an NF militant. His whole life had been spent working with the most violent extreme right groups of the 1960s and 1970s: Mouvement Jeune Révolution (Young Revolution Movement), Mouvement Solidariste (Solidarist Movement), and Groupe Action Jeunesse (Youth Action Group).[6] Stirbois also supported the fundamentalist, or "integrist," stream in French Catholicism, a movement that is highly authoritarian and pessimistic and that rejects both democracy and ideas of progress.

Stirbois joined the NF in 1977, and in November 1980 he became a member of the NF's political bureau and secretary general. As such, he was responsible for the day-to-day running of the party. Within three years Stirbois had boosted the number of party federations from thirty to ninety-five, one in each French department, and he claimed the NF had a total membership of seventy thousand.[7] By the early 1980s he was the second most powerful man in the party after Le Pen, the master of the party organization, and the leader of the party's hard-line faction. By all accounts he was a ruthless manager who disregarded rules of office or seniority and appointed to top party posts militants who supported his hard-line position and who were personally loyal to him.[8] Since party statutes placed absolute power in the hands of the leader and the party oligarchy, and since Stirbois enjoyed Le Pen's support, his position was unshakable. While he was secretary general, Stirbois ensured that there was absolutely no discussion of, or dissent from, the party line. According to the late Yann Piat, former National Front deputy and member of the party's political bureau, Stirbois's ruthless manner and his austere, secretive personality inspired both fear and suspicion.[9] He was the "Stasi [the East German secret police] of the National Front: everyone was on file, everything was known about the candidate. . . . There were . . . rumors that Stirbois had files or tape recordings of the majority of us."[10] In 1987 some party members even feared Stirbois might resort to physical intimidation to achieve his ends.[11]

Party discipline extends to the local level, where section secretaries perform mainly administrative and recruitment tasks.[12] An obsession with discipline and hierarchy led the Front to forbid local sections from entering into contact with each other except through the executive organs at the top. In many ways the Front models itself along the lines of underground organizations in enemy territory or the old-style Communist Party, where fear of penetration by government agents led the party to organize itself into a series of independent, watertight local sections communicating with each other only through party officials at the next higher level of the hierarchy. Doubtless as well, the Front's obsession with maintaining secrecy and repressing dissent is prompted by the desire to avoid the quarreling and splitting that weakened the extreme right in the past. Article 11 of the party statutes states, "Internal criticism should in no case be spread across party organizational lines, there is an *obligation* not to bandy about differences which might exist between National Front members."[13] Even the selection of candidates for political office is tightly controlled from the center. Unlike traditional political parties, where years of devoted service as a militant is usually the first step on the ladder to elected office, by the early 1980s Stirbois and Le Pen had decided that the sine qua non for a candidate was the ability to speak in public, to express the party ideology in a convincing and articulate fashion, and, above all, to attract potential voters. If this meant discouraging or even alienating some militants who hoped to crown their party career with office, then this was a price that had to be paid to maintain discipline. The ultimate objective was victory at the polls, not reward of militants for their years of service to the party.[14]

On numerous occasions this policy has led local party militants to complain about high-profile candidates being parachuted into their areas by the national party. In January 1986, for example, four members of the NF departmental bureau in Isère resigned after Bruno Mégret was designated as the head of the NF list in their department; they denounced the NF leadership as "authoritarian" and criticized the "racist statements," "the unhealthy climate of corruption," and the behavior of "fascist elements" in the party.[15] Internal friction is not confined to disputes between the party leadership in Paris and local party organizations: In 1989 when political bureau member Jean-Claude Martinez failed to get elected to the European Parliament, he complained about the "pendulum club" (a sarcastic references to the Club de l'Horloge) and about efforts to install an "aristocratic and Parisian caste" in positions of power.[16]

Power at the Top

Unquestionably, Le Pen rules the National Front with an iron hand. According to Roger Holeindre, a veteran of the extreme right and a member of the NF's political bureau: "In the National Front, you keep your mouth shut. There is a chief and you follow him!"[17] Describing a 1986 meeting of the party's political bureau, Yann Piat noted:

> Around the table there ought to have been an exchange of ideas, some liberty of expression and opinion which would have allowed the movement to progress. In fact, apart from the precise and cold exposé of Stirbois, no one dared discuss, let alone criticize. When Le Pen speaks, everyone keeps quiet; when Le Pen decides, no one dares whisper the least contradiction. In the Front, during this period, the political bureau was the court of King Jean-

Marie I. Around him, courtiers, friends and the faithful listened. No one confronted the King under penalty of triggering a frightening rage, pierced with such contempt that the target only wanted to disappear under his chair, while all around was a deathly silence as everyone held his breath.[18]

The NF's disciplined, centralized, undemocratic organization has both benefits and costs. On the plus side, National Front militants are famous for their energy, efficiency, and discipline. On the negative side, the cost of maintaining an authoritarian party organization is a constant turnover of disappointed or recalcitrant members. In 1990 one ex-Front member claimed that 35 percent of the regional councillors elected in 1986, 30 percent of the members of the central committee, and 15 percent of the municipal councillors elected in 1989 had resigned from the party.[19] In September 1988 NF deputy François Bachelot stated, "There is no political discussion in the political bureau."[20] One local NF politician resigned in 1988, complaining that the party was "monolithic" and "totalitarian."[21] In June 1989 almost the entire Bouches-du-Rhône federation was reorganized because of differences between the party's central organization and the federation over party finances.[22] The following August there was a wave of resignations from the Bas-Rhin and Haut-Rhin federations, amid criticism of the "courtesans" who surrounded Le Pen and calls for more party democracy.[23] In 1990 dissidents from Bouches-du-Rhône, critical of what they saw as Le Pen's overwillingness to compromise party principles for an alliance with the mainstream right, suggested that Marie-France Stirbois, the widow of Jean-Pierre Stirbois and at that time the NF's only deputy, be appointed secretary general of the movement. Criticism continued into June 1993, when three regional councillors resigned from the National Front, rejecting orders from the party executive to abstain from participating in the work of the regional council and in all external organizations.[24]

Associated Organizations

The National Front, to broaden its appeal, has created a series of associated organizations that generally support the Front line but do not demand membership in the Front as a condition for admission. In 1985, for example, the Front created the Entreprise Moderne et Liberté (Modern and Free Enterprise, or EML), with the aim of "allowing all the officials of private enterprise in France, whether or not they own their company, to participate effectively, if not directly, in the reestablishment of free enterprise in our country."[25] The EML, in turn, created a number of "circles" aimed at eliciting support for the Front from specific socio-professional groups. For example, the Cercle National Santé (National Health Circle) includes doctors, pharmacists, and dentists, while the Cercle National Droit et Liberté (National Law and Liberty Circle) includes lawyers, notaries, and some judges.[26]

In 1974 the NF established the Front National de la Jeunesse (Youth National Front, or FNJ) under the authority of national director Martial Bild. Open to young people from sixteen to twenty-four years of age, the FNJ claims to have fifteen thousand members, although estimates put the figure at around five thousand. The FNJ is active in Paris university student circles, publishes a large number of reviews and bulletins, and sponsors lectures and courses for its members. Adhering to the line that neither the NF nor its associated organizations have anything to do with the traditionally violent groups of the extreme right, the FNJ has denied any links with Groupe Union et Défense (GUD), an extremely violent student organization that since the 1960s had been based in the Faculty of Law in Paris but was finally ejected in 1995. However, the FNJ continues to maintain relations with the GUD and with similar extreme right student organizations in Paris and in the provinces.[27]

There are also organizations and groups that are not affiliated with the National Front but that can be counted as staunch supporters. These include fundamentalist religious organizations such as Christian-Solidarity, led by Bernard Antony; the Comité National des Juifs Français (National Committee of French Jews), presided over by Jean-Charles Bloch; the Cercle National des Femmes d'Europe (National Circle of European Women), led by Martine Lehideux, an NF member of the European Parliament;[28] the Mouvement de la Jeunesse d'Europe (Movement of European Youth), founded by Carl Lang, who succeeded Jean-Pierre Stirbois as secretary general of the Front in 1988; organizations of police and army veterans; and the Friends of Le Pen Center in Washington, D.C.[29]

Ideological questions play a much larger role in the internal life of the National Front than in the mainstream parties of the right. This is in keeping with the prewar tradition of the French extreme right, where intellectuals such as Charles Maurras, Robert Brassilach, and Maurice Bardèche set the political agenda on the extreme right and provoked both fierce loyalties and violent hostility. The genius of Le Pen and the party leadership has been to contain this ideological effervescence within the Front and use it to benefit the party. In the case of Horlogers such as Mégret, Yvan Blot, and Jean-Yves Le Gallou, this containment has been achieved by giving them prominent positions at the top of the party hierarchy. In other cases the Front has created associated organizations aimed at providing pro-Front intellectuals, academics, and civil servants with an opportunity to discuss and refine doctrine, provide the Front with position and policy papers, and, of course, boost the party's prestige before the public. Among these organizations are the Cercle Montherlant (Montherlant Circle), a direct creation of the Front but without formal links to it; the Conseil Scientifique (Scientific Council), which includes mainly academics; the Union Nationale Interuniversitaire (Interuniversity National Union), a student organization; and most important, the Club de l'Horloge, the National Front's powerhouse of ideas but with no formal links to the NF.[30]

Party Finance

As is the case with most political parties, it is difficult to determine the amount and source of NF funds. However, the NF obtains funds in the same way as most political parties: from contributions by members and individuals, from business and other organizations, from the sale of party literature and trinkets, and, particular to the Front, from a tithe put on the salaries of elected officials, and from fees charged to members wishing to run for public office. According to French journalist Blandine Hennion, some members of the business community relate to the NF through the myriad of associated organizations established specifically to provide links between the party organization and outside interest groups or individuals.[31] Others are linked to the NF through friendship, family ties, or common political sympathies, especially toward Vichy or the cause of French Algeria. There is little evidence of widespread overt support for the Front among the top ranks of French business and industry. According to one prominent businessman: "If the business is open to the international market, it is protected against retrograde nationalist tendencies. But there are some sectors such as the real estate business, the building trades or local retailers which are open to Front ideas."[32]

Banking, communications, and advertising also seem impervious to the charms of Le Pen and to the influence of the Front. However, some prominent French businesspeople make no secret of their sympathy for the Front and contribute generously to party coffers. Such is the case with press baron Robert Hersant, owner of the newspaper *Le Figaro,* or Baroness Laurence Bich, the widow of Marcel Bich of the Bic pen and cigarette lighter empire. She ran as an NF candidate in the 1986 legislative elections.

Organizations associated with the National Front also act as conduits for funds: André Dufraisse, secretary general of the EML and a member of the Front's political bureau, stated that the EML contributed Fr 300,000 to Le Pen's 1988 presidential campaign. A month later he raised that figure to Fr 600,000.[33] There is also some evidence that Le Pen and the Front have received funds from the Unification Church of South Korean reverend Sun Myung Moon—the Moonies.[34] Ex-NF deputy Yann Piat noted that Pierre Ceyrac, a member of the Front's political bureau, was the French director of the Confederation of Associations for the Unity of the Societies of

America (CAUSA), the violently anticommunist political arm of the Unification Church. According to Piat: "In the entourage of Jean-Marie, it was whispered that he [Ceyrac] was one of the chosen because he was supposed to be the representative of the Moon sect in France, generous supplier of funds to the Front. It was also reported that it was because of this financial aid from the Moonies that Le Pen embellished almost all his speeches with invocations of God."[35]

Ex-deputy Pascal Arrighi stated that "the Moon story is strictly about money."[36] The president of the Centre National des Indépendants and former NF member Yvon Briant referred to Le Pen's relations with Moon as taking place on a "financial high wire."[37] Another NF ex-deputy, Michel de Rostolan, was a regular participant in meetings of the World Anti-Communist League and was also associated with CAUSA.[38] According to Daniel Carton of *Le Monde,* the first contacts between the Unification Church and Le Pen took place just before the 1984 European elections when South Korean colonel Cho Hi Pak, Moon's associate, attended a National Front meeting and was so impressed by the anticommunism of the Front that he volunteered his support to the party.

To curry favor with the Reverend Moon, Le Pen included on the NF's 1984 European election list the mysterious Gustav Pordea, a Rumanian who had been associated with the Unification Church for the previous six years.[39] According to Jean Marcilly, Le Pen's biographer, and a publicist for the Unification Church, Pordea was placed on the NF list after the Unification Church contributed Fr 4 million to Le Pen.[40] Le Pen's ex-wife, Pierrette, told *Libération* journalists Gilles Bresson and Christian Lionet that the Fr 4 million was to be handed over at 7 A.M. one Sunday, but that Le Pen, a late sleeper, told Pierrette to take delivery of a first installment. "He said to me: it's Pordea's money." After receiving half the funds, however, Le Pen told her two weeks later that the other half had been deposited in their Swiss bank account.[41] Although Pierre Ceyrac of CAUSA confirmed that Pordea had been a member of the Unification Church since the early 1970s, Ceyrac claimed to know nothing of any negotiations between the church and Le Pen.[42]

Just before the 1988 French presidential election, Le Pen traveled to the United States and to South Korea, where he apparently met with representatives of the Unification Church and with Moon himself.[43] During Le Pen's 1988 presidential campaign, François Bachelot recalled, "every time I needed money, I went to Saint-Cloud [Le Pen's residence]. Le Pen took his checkbook out of a drawer, and I left with what I needed."[44] Another Front member, Bruno Chauvierre, recalled that in 1986 the "big question among National Front militants in the Nord Department was to know how much we could get from Moon's dowry. At the time it was said in the party that the sect had poured Fr 20–30 million into the legislative and regional elections. All I know is that putting Pierre Ceyrac third on the list was worth Fr 1 million."[45] Another Moonie, Roger Johnstone, was twelfth on the NF's list for the European election, but when he failed to be elected, he was appointed assistant secretary general of the European right parliamentary group in Brussels and Strasbourg.

The Front also seems to have benefited from the Moonies in a different way. In 1988 almost two hundred "missionaries" from the Unification Church were sent to help with Le Pen's presidential campaign. One member of the Front recalled: "The orders were never to let them make contact with our militants. They were lodged in a house in Strasbourg. They worked like crazy, distributing millions of tracts and putting up hundreds of posters. They returned at the end of the day with bloody feet and passed the night praying."[46] Pascal Arrighi noted: "They sent 20 of them to Marseilles. I agreed to dine with them and I immediately asked that they be sent somewhere else. If the people of Marseilles had known that they had been sent Germans and Japanese, we would have looked like idiots."[47]

Not only were the Front's coffers swelled by contributions from the Unification Church. Le Pen himself also became a rich man in 1976 after inheriting a chateau in the exclusive Paris suburb of St. Cloud and Fr 6 million from wealthy French businessman Hubert Lambert. Before Lambert died at the age of forty-two, he made Le Pen his heir; but Lambert's cousin Philippe contested the will, arguing that he was the victim of a "fraud." There then ensued a complicated legal duel, which ended in 1977 with an agreement between Le Pen and Lambert a few weeks before the case was brought to court. Le Pen inherited Fr 20 million, the Lambert manor, and a surrounding park. However, eight years later, in a dramatic 1985 interview, Jean-Maurice Demarquet, Le Pen's close friend and personal physician to both Le Pen and Lambert, leveled a number of serious charges against Le Pen. According to Demarquet, when Le Pen learned in early 1985 that Lambert's death was to be the subject of a newspaper investigation, he implored Demarquet to state that Lambert had been healthy when he drew up his will in Le Pen's favor. But Demarquet refused, claiming that professional reasons prevented him from revealing his opinion of Lambert's health at the time of his death. To *Le Monde*, however, Demarquet claimed that at the time of his final illness Lambert "was in a lamentable state. . . . He was completely manipulated by Le Pen."[48] Demarquet went on to recount how Le Pen had been opposed to Demarquet bringing another physician in for consultation:

I showed Hubert Lambert to a professor [of neurology] so that no one could later accuse me of having been Le Pen's accomplice in this affair. . . . The last time I saw Hubert Lambert [was] the evening of his death. I had been alerted by Pierrette Le Pen, who found him very bad. Why was I warned that evening? Because he didn't want to hear any more talk of Le Pen. I immediately made an appointment for the following afternoon with the same Professor of neurology. But Lambert died in the night. Bizarre![49]

In reply, Le Pen accused Demarquet of being psychotic, mad, and politically unstable.[50] Le Pen also accused the RPR of putting Demarquet up to the accusations. Given that Demarquet waited eight years before making his accusations, and that just before Demarquet's revelations Le Pen had brusquely informed his former close friend and companion-in-arms that he was not on the NF list for the 1986 legislative election, there is reason to doubt Demarquet's story.[51] The affair eventually vanished from the headlines, with no one the wiser about the actual circumstances of the inheritance. Nine years after Lambert's death, Le Pen again inherited a chateau from an NF sympathizer, Pierre Briffaut. However, after losing Fr 10 million on the stock market, Le Pen had to sell the chateau to pay off his debts. Clearly, Le Pen treated his inheritances as personal income rather than as contributions to the National Front. Moreover, in late 1987 Pierrette Le Pen stated that "Le Pen deposited a total of Fr 40 million inherited from Lambert and from other sources in a Swiss bank in order to avoid taxes."[52] In a biography of Le Pen, French journalists Gilles Bresson and Christian Lionet note that in a 1994 interview a Swiss banker confirmed that Le Pen had deposited a total of Fr 45 million in a joint account for himself and his wife.[53]

The Front insists that NF candidates and elected politicians contribute to party expenses. After the Front won ten seats in the European Parliament in 1984, Le Pen began to charge would-be candidates for the privilege of being placed on Front election lists, with premium fees being charged for the top spots. MEP Jean-Claude Martinez, a member of the Front's political bureau, stated that he had to pay Fr 500,000 to be placed tenth on the Front's list for the 1989 European elections.[54] Party members running for political office routinely are asked to contribute to the party's coffers: In 1992 candidates were asked to contribute between Fr 30,000 and 40,000.[55] In February 1993 Germaine Burgaz, a former NF vice president and a member of the party's central committee, announced that she would not concede to the party's "racket methods" when it demanded that she sign over Fr 180,000 to the party's coffers to become the NF candidate in the regional elections. According to Burgaz, the Front received as much as Fr 60 million from regional councillors as their contribution to the election campaigns. "Since 1984–1986, the National Front has concealed badly its totalitarian ideology, and the coercive methods that it uses are like the Communist Party: pressure, intimidation, threats, blackmail and lies. . . . God save us from the arrival in power of the current leaders of the National Front."[56]

The Front also forces any candidate for regional councillor to sign a promissory note for Fr 252,000. Not only does this defray the cost of election expenses; it also deters members from resigning their posts (and losing their salaries). Candidates for local elections are asked to sign statements agreeing to turn over 50 percent of their pay to the NF if they are elected, and the Front does not hesitate to pursue in the courts politicians who refuse to honor the agreement to reimburse the party for part of their campaign expenses.[57]

Unlike other political parties, the National Front accepts gifts paid by check but does not provide contributors with receipts.[58] In 1990 party dissidents accused Le Pen, without giving details, of "financing his activities according to the same procedures as the 'gang of four' [Le Pen's term for the leaders of the four major French political parties]."[59] Although Le Pen regularly lambastes the gang of four or the "establishment" for corruption, the NF has never hesitated to exploit the generous funding made available to MEPs. In 1991 it was estimated that the 14 members of the right-wing group in the European Parliament spent Fr 1.5 million on meetings outside Strasbourg, compared to less than Fr 1 million for the 189-member Socialist group. Much of the time ostensibly spent on meetings was devoted to tourism.[60]

The Pro-Front Press

In addition to the internal bulletin *La Lettre de Jean-Marie Le Pen* (The Jean-Marie Le Pen Newsletter), which mainly reports on Le Pen's activities, there are a variety of Front publications aimed at party militants and supporters. The Front also benefits from the support of a number of nonparty newspapers, principally *Présent* (which claims a circulation of forty thousand but probably has about twenty thousand readers), *National Hebdo* (which in 1991 had a circulation of about fifteen thousand), *Le Choc du Mois* (circulation about ten thousand), *Minute* (circulation forty to forty-five thousand), and *Rivarol* (circulation about eighteen thousand). Founded in 1951 by ex-Vichyites, *Rivarol* is anti-Semitic and provides a forum for negationist historians such as Robert Faurisson.[61]

The editorial boards of *Présent* and *National Hebdo*, the two press organs closest to the NF, compose a Who's Who of ex-Vichyites and of the extreme right. Jean Madiran (pseudonym for Jean Arfel), editor in chief of *Présent*, was a member of Action Française during World War II. After the war he taught philosophy and became one of the leading critics of progressivism in the Catholic Church. Madiran argued that both the Socialist Party and the mainstream right are manipulated by B'nai B'rith. The codirector of *Présent*, Pierre Durand, is a member of the NF's political bureau. The editorial board of *Présent* used to include anti-Semites Henri Coston and François Brigneau but both moved to *National Hebdo*. Although both newspapers support the Front, *Présent* opposes, and *National Hebdo* supports, the breakaway Catholic sect established by Monseigneur Lefebvre, who opposed Vatican II. The editor in chief of *National Hebdo*, Roland Gaucher (pseudonym for Roland Goguillot), belonged to a collaborationist political party during World War II and is the author of anti-Semitic tracts. He is also director of the extreme right journal *Le Crapouillet*, a former NF deputy, and a former member of the NF's political bureau.[62] *Le Choc du Mois* (claimed circulation of fifteen thousand) is a glossy monthly whose editor is Catherine Barnay. She is a former member of Ordre Nouveau and the Parti des Forces Nouvelles.[63]

In late 1992 *Minute, Le Choc du Mois,* and a number of other extreme right publications were taken over by Gérald Penciolelli. Jean-Claude Valla, appointed editorial director of *Minute* (Jean-Pierre Cohen is editor in chief), had belonged for a brief time to GRECE, but there was some suspicion among the other extreme right publications that the so-called neopagans of GRECE were about to make a comeback in the Penciolelli publications in order to exercise their influence over the National Front.[64]

Factions in the Front

Unlike the Socialist Party, which permits the establishment of organized factions or tendencies, the National Front forbids factions and frowns on public expressions of disagreement. However, like all political parties, personal quarrels and ideological differences swirl through the party, sometimes breaking out into the open and into the press.[65] These factions are not hard and fast, although different terms have been applied to them: *ancients, moderns, hard-liners, moderates, solidarists, technocrats, Horlogers, traditionalists, new right,* and *royalists.*[66] This bewildering variety of labels reflects the shifting nature of the issues and quarrels that divide the Front and attests to the fact that some individuals may belong to two or more groups at the same time. In the mid-1990s there were, roughly speaking, four ideological groupings: the solidarists, integrists (fundamentalists), Horlogers, and moderates.

Solidarists

The solidarists were represented by, above all, Jean-Pierre Stirbois until his death in 1988. This group is corporatist, favors finding a "third way" between the West and the former Soviet bloc, and opposes any compromise with the mainstream parties of the right, arguing that a National Front that is *pur et dur* (pure and tough) will eventually be seen by the electorate as the only viable opposition to the left. Stirbois wanted to build the NF into an ideologically coherent, militant party negotiating with the mainstream right only on the Front's terms. His political style was marked by invective and inflammatory language. In this he mirrored Le Pen's tendency toward insult, exaggeration, and vulgarity. The result was to reinforce the image of the National Front as an extremist party with which no compromise was possible.

When Le Pen's anti-Semitic remarks provoked general criticism, Stirbois urged him to ride out the storm and make no apology for the remarks. In May 1988 Stirbois observed that defeating Jacques Chirac (whom he had called an "imbecile") in the presidential election would "reinforce the National Front as the only political force dedicated to breaking with socialism."[67] The solidarists assumed that a Socialist government would so exacerbate societal divisions that the Front would emerge as a major alternative to the existing parties of both left and right.[68] The solidarists also believed that splitting the right-wing vote would help defeat the RPR and UDF and demonstrate that without the support of the Front, the mainstream right was doomed to defeat. Refusing to compromise with the mainstream right would avenge the NF for being snubbed in every legislative and presidential election. This argument was strongly put by *National Hebdo* columnist François Brigneau (although not an FN member, Brigneau staunchly supported Stirbois's position), who explained that voting for RPR leader Jacques Chirac on the second ballot of the 1988 presidential election would "help push the car of someone who has punctured your tires. Moreover, it would encourage Chirac to continue in an ostracism that is not justified."[69] Another argument for maintaining NF candidates on the second round of elections was to hold up before the public the image of a political party that, unlike the others, refused to compromise its principles for the sake of office. Finally, splitting the right-wing vote would demonstrate to the public that the Front was a party in its own right and not an opportunistic organization open to deals with whatever party came along.

Integrists (Fundamentalists)

The integrists, of whom the most egregious is Bernard Antony (Romain Marie), are part of an authoritarian tradition within the Catholic Church that goes back at least to the late nineteenth century and the theories of Charles Maurras. The founder of Action Française, Maurras had argued that the rights of individuals take second place to the coherence of the nation. There can be society without justice, Maurras stated, but no justice without society. During the Dreyfus Affair, Maurras argued that it was better to allow the captain to suffer an injustice than sap the morale and prestige of the army because the latter would ultimately undermine the basis of national unity. Although Action Française was condemned by the church in 1926 (the condemnation was lifted in 1939), there still exists on the periphery of French Catholicism a current that opposes the Republic, rejects humanism and democracy, and adheres closely to what it sees as traditional

Catholic values. Today's fundamentalists oppose the progressivism of the Catholic Church, Vatican II, and, especially, the decision to abandon the Latin mass in favor of the vernacular.

By the 1970s the fundamentalists had split over the attitude to take toward Monseigneur Marcel Lefebvre, who refused to implement the reforms of Vatican II, defended anti-Semitic and racist positions, and refused to accede to the authority of Rome. When Lefebvre was excommunicated in 1988, some NF supporters associated with *National Hebdo* followed Lefebvre into opposition and joined the Sacerdotal Fraternity of Saint Pius X, which since Lefebvre's death continues to ordain its own priests and to attack the Vatican. Others, such as Bernard Antony, remained within the church but oppose it on almost every issue. Those who followed Lefebvre tended toward monarchism and opposed not only socialism but also democracy and the Republic. "The religion of fundamentalism is basically authoritarian and pessimistic; it emphasizes the disciplinary, hierarchical and dogmatic aspects of Catholicism and especially the absoluteness of a truth which cannot be opposed by the rights of man. This religion looks to the theology of original sin for reasons to reject modern ideas of democracy and progress."[70]

Out of this murky swamp of fundamentalism Bernard Antony created the Comités d'Action Politique et Sociale (Political and Social Action Committee, or CAPS) grouped around *Présent,* which become a daily newspaper in 1975. At the inception of CAPS, the organization claimed that it aimed to take political power at the same time as it "rejected suicidal democracy" and fought for "Christianity."[71]

Within the National Front, the fortunes of the fundamentalists were boosted when Jean-Pierre Stirbois joined the party in 1977. Stirbois had spent his entire political life on the extreme right of French political and religious movements. He had been a member, along with Bernard Antony, of Mouvement Jeune Revolution, and as NF secretary general Stirbois ensured that fundamentalists held key positions within the Front. Some factions within the fundamentalist movement were active during the 1960s in the OAS. Those grouped around the so-called Cité Catholique (Catholic City) included military officers who cited Saint Thomas Aquinas to justify the use of torture.[72] Both *Présent* and *National Hebdo* take fundamentalists positions, and Jean Madiran, director of *Présent,* in 1983 called for a law punishing "blasphemy against holy things; the French nation or the Catholic faith." He also argued that if racism was punishable by law, then communism, "which is much worse and much more dangerous than racism," should be a crime.[73] According to a study of 1,002 delegates to the 1990 National Front congress, 30.8 percent belonged to organizations associated with the fundamentalist movement.[74]

In *La France est de retour,* Le Pen noted that, although he had been raised and educated as a Catholic, like "90 percent" of the French, he did not often go to church on Sunday—"mainly because of the 'desacralization' of the liturgy."[75] The abandonment of "the common language for the vernacular" had alienated him from the religion of his ancestors.[76] He felt, he wrote, a particular "tenderness" for the Virgin Mary and for Joan of Arc, "symbol of patriotism, virtue and courage."[77] Le Pen insists that the church should stay out of politics. "I invite the bishops to stick to the difficult job of leading the French church and its faithful. ... It's not a good idea to mix fields. I don't give the religious authorities advice about questions of faith."[78] Yet after meeting with Pope John Paul II in 1985, Le Pen remarked that the pope "was very firm against abortion, moral decadence and terrorism, and he reaffirmed the necessity for Europe to redefine its roots, to defend its identity—in a certain way he called for a European preference, as I have in France called on us to return to a national preference [granting preference to French nationals over North African immigrants in social welfare and housing]."[79]

Horlogers

The Horlogers, members of the Club de l'Horloge, consist of many high civil servants and refugees from the mainstream right. The group is prominently represented by the NF's second in command, Bruno Mégret. By the early 1990s the Horlogers had moved into important positions within the party. Mégret headed the eight-man editorial committee that drafted the NF's 1993 election program and whose membership included Yvan Blot and Jean-Yves Le Gallou, both cofounders of the Club de l'Horloge. The contribution of the Horlogers to the Front has been immense: They have raised ideological discussions within the Front to a high level of sophistication; they have realized the immense importance of language, or political discourse, in politics and have made artful use of their talents in Front propaganda; they have helped elaborate an economic policy that, although not a direct reflection of Vichyite corporatism, nonetheless subsumes market capitalism under the control of the state; and they have tried to divest the party of its associations with Vichy and neofascism while still maintaining the core elements of extreme right doctrine. According to journalist Edwy Plenel, "The results reveal a coherent strategy linking the internal life of the National Front where the key words are extreme centralization and faultless cohesion, and an external propaganda that is more respectable and characterized by the desire to present the party as the single 'assembly of the French people.'"[80]

Moderates

Although it may seem ironic to call moderate any member of an extreme right party, moderates favor making doctrinal and/or tactical concessions in order to establish electoral alliances with the mainstream right; abandoning the Front's, and especially Le Pen's, provocative and extreme language; and mitigating or even abandoning anti-Semitism. Among those who have been counted as moderate are Jean-Marie Le Chevallier (currently mayor of Toulon), Pascal Arrighi, Édouard Frédéric-Dupont, Pierre Ceyrac, and Bruno Mégret (who is moderate on political tactics but hard-line on anti-Semitism and racism). During the 1986 legislative campaign, for example, Mégret had established links between the NF, which ran under the label Rassemblement National, and various pressure groups.[81]

Unlike the solidarists, the moderates wanted the NF to support the right-wing candidate, Jacques Chirac, on the second ballot of the 1988 presidential election and to demonstrate to the mainstream right that the NF was both responsible and respectable. Once this had been accomplished, and the NF was able to elect a sufficient number of deputies to the National Assembly, then the NF might become a rallying point for those disillusioned with the mainstream right. But Le Pen resisted this strategy. As ex-deputy François Bachelot commented in September 1988, while the French were "concerned with problems other than insecurity and immigration, . . . Le Pen has based his career uniquely on 'political shocks.'"[82]

After Stirbois's death in 1988, thirty-one-year-old Carl Lang was appointed secretary general. Unlike Stirbois, who had floated from one extreme right group to another during his youth, Lang was, according to *National Hebdo* director Roland Gaucher, a "pure product of the party."[83] Too young to have had any direct experience of the Algerian War, Lang was twenty when he joined the NF and had been an active member of the party's youth movement.[84] Lang also differed from Stirbois in that he had no ideological ax to grind and focused his efforts exclusively on the party organization. By the 1990s Lang had "decentralized [and] multiplied [the number of] local sections, and placed a new level between the section secretary and the departmental secretary." "The organization of the movement did not exist before," Lang said, "because we were uniquely an election machine and not a deeply rooted political movement." For Lang, the NF is to be shaped into an instrument at the disposal of its leader, Jean-Marie Le Pen. "It is necessary," he said in 1990, "to give Le Pen a tool which is as effective as possible."[85] Thus far, that tool has been very effective indeed.

Notes

1. According to the NF secretary general, "The National Front is the 1805 army [the Napoleonic army] which has spent two years training." *Le Monde*, January 24, 1990. The NF claimed to have ten thousand members in September 1983, twenty-five thousand in June 1984, sixty thousand in June 1985, and eighty thousand in February 1994. But these figures were probably inflated.

2. Quoted in Alain Rollat, *Les hommes de l'extrême droite* (Paris: Calmann-Lévy, 1985), pp. 53, 54, 55.

3. Quoted in Christophe Hameau, *La campagne de Jean-Marie Le Pen pour l'élection présidentielle de 1988* (Paris: Travaux et Recherches de l'Universite Pantheon-Assas [Paris II], n.d.), p. 68.

4. In Paris a party official noted that his organization had been inspired to imitate the methods of the Communist Party, its "discipline, organization in cells, implantation in businesses and cities." Ibid., p. 25.

5. From *Passeport pour la victoire*, a party pamphlet of 1987, quoted in ibid., pp. 24–25.

6. The Group Action Jeunesse was founded in 1973 and specialized in violent commando attacks on rival student groups. Soon after joining the Front, Stirbois entered into conflict with François Duprat, another member of the extreme right, who was killed by a car bomb in 1978.

7. Hameau, *La campagne*, p. 22.

8. "There was no doubt that, since he became national secretary, Jean-Pierre [Stirbois] resolved to purge the federations and to place at their head officials he had selected." Yann Piat, *Seule tout en haut à bas* (Paris: Fixot, 1991), p. 122. See also Hameau, *La campagne*, p. 21. In the Bouches-du-Rhône federation, Stirbois outmaneuvered NF deputy Pascal Arrighi (who was later to resign after the "rhyme" incident), replacing him as the NF leader with Stirbois's friend Ronald Perdomo. *Le Monde*, October 1, 1987.

9. Stirbois's personality provoked an NF militant to say, "It's curious that Stirbois is in the National Front, he looks normal." *Le Monde*, October 8, 1987.

10. Piat, *Seule*, p. 171.

11. Stirbois was said to have threatened physical violence against a NF regional councillor unless he resigned his post after breaking with the NF over Le Pen's detail remark. *Le Monde*, October 8, 1987.

12. Guy Birenbaum, *Le Front national en politique* (Paris: Balland, 1992), p. 58.

13. Edwy Plenel, in *Le Monde*, March 30, 1990.

14. Birenbaum, *Le Front national*, pp. 60ff.

15. *Le Monde*, January 8, 1986.

16. *Le Monde*, July 14, 1989.

17. Quoted in Birenbaum, *Le Front national*, p. 53.

18. Piat, *Seule*, p. 129.

19. Michel Schneider, a former associate of Jean-Pierre Stirbois, cited in Birenbaum, *Le Front national*, pp. 197–198.

20. Quoted in *Le Monde*, September 7, 1988.

21. Eric Pellegrini, in *Le Monde*, September 11–12, 1988.

22. *Le Monde*, June 6, 1989.

23. *Le Monde*, August 22, 1989.

24. *Le Monde*, June 9, 1993.

25. Quoted in Hameau, *La campagne*, p. 26. The general secretary of EML was André Dufraisse, a member of the NF's political bureau and central committee. During World War II, Durfraisse was a member of the pro-Nazi Parti Populaire Français and a volunteer in the Légion des Volontaires Français Contre le Bolchevisme, which fought alongside the Nazis against the Russians.

26. There were additional circles aimed at people working in the banking sector, public service, transport (particularly airplane pilots and navigators) as well as stew-

ards and stewardesses, railroads, and the Paris mass transit system. Hameau, *La campagne*, pp. 27–28.

27. See the report on the first national convention of the FNJ in November 1992 in *Le Monde*, November 28–29, 1993.

28. According to Hameau, the Cercle National includes a "few hundred" women. Hameau, *La campagne*, p. 31.

29. Ibid., p. 32. On June 20–21, 1993, *Le Monde* reported that the Fédération Professionelle Indépendante de la Police (Independent Professional Police Federation, or FPIP), an organization close to the National Front, obtained 16.2 percent of the vote among police officers and 18.7 percent of the vote among commissioners and cadres in internal administrative elections in Paris and the metropolitan area. In 1986 the FPIP stated that the democratic system could not deal with terrorism and that "only a strong regime, founded on the concepts of order and nation and ignoring all these decadent humanitarian theories will be our salvation." *Le Monde*, September 19, 1986.

30. Hameau, *La campagne*, p. 32.

31. Blandine Hennion, *Le Front national l'argent et l'establishment*. (Paris: La Découverte, 1993).

32. Jean Frydman, quoted in ibid., p. 96.

33. Hameau, *La campagne*, p. 27.

34. Although Le Pen denied receiving funds from the Moonies, in March 1988 when he was questioned about the Moonies, he replied: "When I receive money I always say to the person who is giving it to me that I assume it was given in support of my ideas, but that in any case, it doesn't mean that I am in any way committed to them." Ibid., p. 46.

35. Piat, *Seule*, p. 143. Ceyrac was one of the thirty-five National Front deputies elected in 1986.

36. Quoted in *Le Monde*, February 8, 1992.

37. Ibid.

38. When Mitterrand dissolved the National Assembly and called for new elections in 1988, Le Pen decided to contest a seat in Marseilles. The Unification Church sent a group of its members to help with the campaigning, but they were kept away from ordinary party militants. Piat, *Seule*, p. 194.

39. According to Jean-François Boyer, Pordea joined the Moonies in 1978 at the age of sixty-eight and was used by the church to gain entry into the National Front. There were rumors that he was an agent of the Rumanian intelligence services, but in any case he played a very minor role in the National Front. Jean-François Boyer, *L'Empire Moon* (Paris: La Découverte, 1986), pp. 363–366. See also *Le Monde*, February 3–4, 1985.

40. Marcilly broke with Le Pen and eventually married Pierrette, Le Pen's ex-wife.

41. Gilles Bresson and Christian Lionet, *Le Pen* (Paris: Seuil, 1994), pp. 413–414. However, Dominique Chaboche of the NF characterized Pierrette Le Pen's account as "fiction."

42. *Le Monde*, February 8, 1992.

43. Le Pen also met with representatives of the Moonies during a visit to Japan in November 1986. *Le Monde*, November 10, 1986.

44. Quoted in *Le Monde*, February 8, 1992.

45. Quoted in ibid.

46. Quoted in ibid.

47. Quoted in ibid.

48. Quoted in *Le Monde*, October 16, 1985.

49. Quoted in ibid.

50. *Le Monde*, October 18, 1985.

51. The entire affair is described in Bresson and Lionet, *Le Pen*, pp. 315–331.

52. Quoted in *Le Monde*, December 15, 1987.

53. Bresson and Lionet, *Le Pen*, pp. 334–336.

54. *Le Monde*, July 14, 1989. Martinez was bumped to eleventh place on the list shortly before the election when Le Pen inserted filmmaker Claude Autant-Lara in ninth place. As a result, Martinez lost his seat when the first ten candidates on the Front list won seats in the European Parliament, but he regained it when Autant-Lara resigned in late 1989.

55. *Le Monde*, February 8, 1992.

56. Quoted in *Le Monde*, February 2, 1993.

57. *Le Monde*, November 1, 1993.

58. According to the party's *Candidate's Guide*, "It is difficult to prevent a candidate from filling a secret cashbox with cash coming from gifts, collections, etc. if he takes the precaution of not providing a receipt which could be used by the donor to obtain a tax deduction." *Le Monde*, February 8, 1992.

59. *Le Monde*, July 7, 1990.

60. Sociologist Alain Bihr, quoted in Bresson and Lionet, *Le Pen*, p. 418. See also *The Guardian*, June 17, 1993, which noted that European taxpayers paid for a trip to Corfu by right-wing MEPs, led by Le Pen, which involved four hours of discussion during a four-day "conference."

61. Hennion, *Le Front national*, p. 200.

62. *Le Monde*, January 23, 1993.

63. The PFN was founded in 1974 by Pascal Gauchon and for a while competed with the NF for the support of the extreme right. It accepted the antiegalitarian positions of GRECE, and, unlike the National Front, it entered into local electoral alliances with the mainstream right, especially the Giscardians. Jean-Yves Camus and René Monzat, *Les droites nationales et radicales en France* (Lyon: Presses Universitaires de Lyon, 1992), pp. 56–58.

64. Olivier Biffaud, in *Le Monde*, March 6, 1993.

65. In *Le Monde*, October 1, 1987, Daniel Carton spoke of a struggle between "the dangerous and vigilant guardians of the temple of the extreme right, and the new prophets of a populist right, the grand priests of openness and respectability."

66. *Le Monde*, October 28, 1987, May 23, 1989; Birenbaum, *Le Front national*, p. 179; and Jean-Yves Camus, "Political Cultures Within the Front National: The Emergence of a Counter-Ideology on the French Far-Right," *Patterns of Prejudice* 26, 1–2 (1992):8–10.

67. *Le Monde*, February 16, 1988; and quoted in Hameau, *La campagne*, p. 67.

68. This analysis was only partially right: Although the voters were clearly exasperated by five years of Socialist government, in 1993 they turned not to the National Front but to the mainstream right to form a new government.

69. Quoted in Birenbaum, *Le Front national*, p. 137.

70. Étienne Borne, quoted in Michel Winock, ed., *Histoire de l'extrême droite en France* (Paris: Seuil, 1993), p. 47.

71. Gregory Pons, *Les rats noirs* (N.p.: Jean-Claude Simeon, 1977), pp. 154ff.

72. Ibid., pp. 116ff.

73. Jean Madiran, quoted in Pierre-André Taguieff, "Les métamorphoses idéologiques du racisme et la crise de la antiracisme," in Pierre-André Taguieff, ed., *Face au racisme* (Paris: La Découverte, 1990), vol. 2, p. 57.

74. Of this number, 8.5 percent belonged to Christian-Solidarity Committees and 22.3 percent to the Alliance Générale Contre le Racisme et pour le Respect de l'Identité Française et Chrétienne. Birenbaum, *Le Front national*, p. 252.

75. Jean-Marie Le Pen, *La France est de retour* (Paris: Carrère/Laffon, 1985), p. 45.

76. Ibid., p. 145. Le Pen's hostility to the church was hardly prompted by theological concerns. During his entire student career from high school through university, Le Pen constantly criticized the clergy, sang bawdy songs about the church, and on at least one occasion, while in a drunken rage, violently abused a Catholic priest. Bresson and Lionet, *Le Pen*, p. 70.

77. Le Pen, *La France*, p. 146.

78. Quoted in Birenbaum, *Le Front national*, p. 132.

79. Quoted in Serge Dumont, Joseph Lorien, and Karl Criton, *Le système Le Pen* (Anvers, Belgium: Éditions EPO, 1985), p. 246.

80. *Le Monde*, March 30, 1990.

81. *Le Monde*, October 1, 1987. Ceyrac quit the NF in February 1994 because of opposition to its anti-Semitism and racism. *Le Monde*, February 17, 1994.

82. *Le Monde*, September 7, 1988.

83. Quoted in Birenbaum, *Le Front national*, p. 160.

84. *Présent*, March 7, 1990.

85. Carl Lang, quoted in *Le Monde*, January 24, 1990. In October 1995 Lang was replaced as secretary general by Bruno Gollnisch, professor of international law, vice president of the NF, MEP, and regional councillor in Rhône-Alpes. Gollnisch purportedly belongs to the Catholic traditionalist side of the NF and seems to have been chosen to offset the growing influence of Bruno Mégret. *Le Monde*, October 11, 1995.

10

The New Political Discourse
of the Extreme Right

GRECE has revealed that the right, a certain right, does not correspond to the usual definition[;] [it] can be "open," curious, supple, inventive and at the same time careful enough to become acceptable.

—*Maurice Bardèche, quoted in Anne-Marie Duranton-Crabol,*
Visages de la nouvelle droite

For decades the semantic superiority of the left has been put at the service of its cultural, and then its political influence. . . . The National Front has decided to counter-attack and to disseminate through public debate its own expressions, which carry its own vision of the world.

—*Bruno Mégret,* **La flamme**

No word is innocent.

—*NF pamphlet, quoted in* **Le Monde**, *May 10, 1990*

In the course of a television debate in February 1984, Jean-Marie Le Pen was asked whether his remark "Tomorrow the immigrants will move in with you, eat your soup and they will sleep with your wife, your daughter or your son" was racist. He replied that it was not racist because he considered "all French without distinction of color, race and religion to be brothers within the nation. . . . To be specific, I am not xenophobic, nor does the fact that I like the French and France best mean that I hate foreigners or hate other countries."[1] Elsewhere, Le Pen has stated that he supports the "right to be different"—that is, the right of every country to maintain the integrity of its culture and traditions by ensuring, for example, that immigrants share the country's culture and that those who do not be kept out or encouraged to emigrate. In the case of France, the latter means immigrants of North African cultures. According to Le Pen, this view is hardly racism since racism implies the belief that some races are better than others, whereas he merely accepts the self-evident fact that races and cultures differ from each other. When critics persist in calling him a racist, Le Pen responds by saying that those who support policies that will result in the destruction of the French nation and culture are themselves anti-French racists.

What is one to make of this argument? Most French political commentators agree that this style of discourse makes it very difficult to fit Le Pen and the National Front into traditional political categories, such as fascism or Poujadism. This is not accidental, for since the late 1960s the ideology of the extreme right has been subjected to a process of revision and reform deliberately calculated to dissociate it from traditional doctrines of wartime fascism or extremism and to adjust it to mainstream political discourse.

The process first began in the late 1960s and early 1970s with the establishment of a series of extreme right political clubs and think-tanks. These mirrored the establishment by left intellectuals, civil servants, and politicians in the 1960s of left-wing clubs such as the Club Jean Moulin, devoted to modernizing socialist doctrine. The extreme right was motivated by the same factors as the left: disillusionment with the existing political parties, disaffection from political elites, and a desire to break out of the political ghetto in which it had languished since 1945.

Two clubs played key roles in renovating right-wing doctrine and in establishing links with the National Front and with the mainstream right: GRECE and the Club de l'Horloge.[2] From the early 1970s to the early 1980s, the doctrines of GRECE had a major impact on the ideology of the entire right. In recent years the club has declined, and its leaders have gone their separate ways. But the NF was particularly influenced by GRECE's ideas on race and immigration, although the club's idiosyncratic ideas on religion (it vehemently attacked the Judeo-Christian heritage of the West and supported neopaganism) led the NF as well as the mainstream right to keep its distance.[3] By contrast, the Club de l'Horloge, an offshoot of GRECE established in 1974 by ex-members of GRECE, continues to play an extremely important part in the National Front and, to a certain extent, in Giscard d'Estaing's Republican Party. Although the Club de l'Horloge follows the same line as GRECE on race, immigration, and equality, its more orthodox views on religion and its pro-American attitude helped it assume a role similar to that played by American or British think-tanks as a testing ground for unusual or new ideas, an intellectual powerhouse, and an elite pressure group within the right.[4]

GRECE

GRECE was formally established in the southern city of Nice in January 1968.[5] Nice provided a particularly receptive setting because of the presence there of large numbers of French ex-colonists from Algeria and because of the sympathetic views of its longtime mayor, Jacques Médicin. The intellectual roots of GRECE can be traced back to the racist and anti-Semitic Europe-Action group, whose journal, *Europe-Action*, first appeared in January 1963.[6] Europe-Action realized that to have a discernible influence, the extreme right would have to abandon the violence, infighting, and sterile doctrinal quarrels characteristic of the extreme right during the 1940s and 1950s. Above all, some way had to be found to make extreme right ideas more acceptable to French public opinion. This was to be accomplished by Europe-Action theorists providing a "scientific foundation" for racism; dumping the outmoded *Führer-prinzip*, or emphasis on the importance of a charismatic leader; and giving conditional support to parliamentary democracy.[7] It was from Europe-Action that GRECE adopted its controversial anti-Christian, elitist, and racial doctrines.

Two traumatic events played a major role in shaping the thinking of those around GRECE—the Algerian War and the 1968 student revolution. Although the young intellectuals who established GRECE were ardent supporters of French Algeria, and in some cases members of the OAS, by the late 1960s they were beginning to have second thoughts about die-hard support for French Algeria and about resistance to decolonization. Alain de Benoist of GRECE wrote: "The OAS enterprise revealed itself to be enormously sterile. . . . The independence of the Third World produced neither the miracles the left hoped for, nor the catastrophes the right predicted."[8] De Benoist saw in the rise of the Third World proof of the unique and enduring differences between cultures as well as the possibility of erecting a bulwark against American imperialism.

Deeply impressed by the sophistication of Marxist theories and moved by the idealism of the 1968 student revolutionaries, these mainly Parisian-based intellectuals sought to adapt Marxism, and particularly the work of Antonio Gramsci, to the project of renewing right-wing ideology. They accepted Gramsci's argument that the route to political power did not lie in winning elections or in fighting in the streets (that favorite activity of the extreme and fascist right), but rather in changing people's ideas. Gramsci observed that state power depended less on structures such as the army, the police, or the government and more on the state's ability to determine people's concepts, ideas, and even the kind of language they used. The true instruments of power were the media (press, television, radio, and other instruments of communication) and education. Those who were able to shape the social consensus, to achieve ideological hegemony, possessed more power than all the politicians, soldiers, policemen, and judges combined. The ability to determine the "taken for granted" beliefs of the ordinary citizen was the ability to control society itself.

Much like the English Fabian Society at the turn of the century, GRECE adopted the tactic of permeation—that is, of spreading new ideas and a new political vocabulary throughout the political elite on the extreme right and, through it, GRECE hoped, to the entire French political spectrum.[9] By the late 1970s Alain de Benoist was writing a weekly column in the middle-class newspaper *Figaro*, while Louis Pauwels, director of *Figaro*, described himself as a member of the "new right, which has nothing to do with the bourgeois, conservative and reactionary right."[10]

However, GRECE knew that its attacks on the Judeo-Christian heritage and its support for polytheism might alienate potential supporters. In the late 1970s, therefore, it tried to distance itself from its review *Nouvelle Ecole* by establishing an independent committee of sponsors. At the same time, in confidential bulletins "to be destroyed after reading" the organization suggested that GRECE members write letters protesting any articles critical of GRECE.[11]

The intellectual doyen of GRECE has been Alain de Benoist (who has used the pseudonyms Robert de Herte or Fabrice Laroche), a former member of Europe-Action.[12] Born in 1943, Alain de Benoist was a member of the Fédération des Étudiants Nationalistes (Federation of Nationalist Students), then joined Europe-Action to become the editor in chief in 1964 of its weekly publication, *Europe-Action Hebdomadaire*. He later became a member of the national council of the Rassemblement Européen pour la Liberté (European Assembly for Liberty) and worked with the fascist Maurice Bardèche on *Défense de l'Occident*.[13] In 1979 Alain de Benoist wrote in the introduction to his *Vu de droite* (Seen from the right): "Without a precise theory, there is no effective action. . . . All the great revolutions of history have only *transposed into facts* an evolution that had already occurred in spirit. One can't have a Lenin before having had Marx. . . . The French right is Leninist without having read Lenin. It hasn't realized the importance of Gramsci. It hasn't seen that *cultural* power threatens the apparatus of the state."[14]

For de Benoist, it was clear that political power flowed not from the barrel of a gun but from the tip of a pen. Altering the terms of French political discourse by gaining acceptability for a new vocabulary of the extreme right became GRECE's primary objective. In the beginning GRECE was supposed to maintain a nonpartisan stance, steering clear of any of the orthodox parties, groups, or movements of the right or extreme right. GRECE's purpose was to form a "community of work and thought" and to establish "an ideological corpus as coherent as possible" for the right.[15] But for many extreme right intellectuals, it was clear that scholarship and journalism were not sufficient to influence the terms of French political debate and that active participation in politics had to be envisaged. In 1974, therefore, GRECE endorsed Valéry Giscard d'Estaing for president. But GRECE then withdrew its support when the Republican Party began to pick and choose from among GRECE's ideas, adopting the ideas of antiegalitarianism to support selectivity and choice in the school and university system but rejecting GRECE's ideas on culture.

With the establishment of the Club de l'Horloge as an offshoot of GRECE, the National Front began to profit from the influx of intellectuals and civil servants associated with both groups. Although the Front, and Jean-Marie Le Pen himself, disagreed with GRECE on its paganism, Le Pen very quickly realized the importance of using—and adapting—ideas as weapons in the struggle to unify the extreme right behind the NF banner and to change the terms of political debate in France. But not everyone from GRECE was an ardent supporter of the National Front. Writing of the Front, de Benoist maintained:

> We are not on the same level, we don't address the same public, and the NF's ideas are completely foreign to ours. . . . We disagree with the anti-immigrant campaign. The criticism of immigration is legitimate to the degree where it is a form of forced uprooting. But one must side with immigrants who are its first victims and who in the end are confronted with the same problems as us: how to conserve a cultural identity in a world which is increasingly submitted to an homogenizing logic.[16]

According to Alain Rollat, the sources for GRECE's ideology can be found in the German "conservative revolution" of the period between 1918 to 1933. "Through their historical references," Rollat said, "the animators of the new right current of thought have used arguments which justify the fears of those who oppose fascism about the unpredictable consequences of its resurgence."[17] However, there are some on the left who admit to being confused about GRECE and its implications for political theory. Jean-Marie Domenach, former editor of the left Christian journal *Ésprit*, argued, "Here is a right which is not for colonization, not for the nation nor for the West—for Europe, no doubt, but a Europe which looks to its origins, which do not lie in Asia where Christianity came from, but to the North from whence poured forth the poetic and hierarchical barbarians: Celts, Vikings and Germans."[18]

Doctrine

The real difference between the NF and GRECE lies in the anti-Christianism and paganism of GRECE. One of the principal villains in the history of the world, according to GRECE, is the Hebrew prophet Abraham: "Totalitarianism was born the day when the idea of monotheism appeared, which implied the submission of human beings to the will of a single, omniscient, all-powerful, and eternal God. Everything began with Abraham. It is not unimportant that the followers of the three monotheistic religions, Judaism, Christianity and Islam, call themselves children of Abraham."[19]

Monotheism created a Manichean view of life that militated against variety and heterogeneity. One was either good or bad, saved or damned, a believer or an atheist. In the modern world, according to GRECE, this view led to totalitarianism, a system that judged each individual in terms of only one dimension—conformity to the regime. For GRECE, therefore, true liberty, today, can only be found outside Judeo-Christian monotheism in a pantheistic, and therefore tolerant, system.[20]

For GRECE, egalitarianism is the source of almost all societal problems. According to Jean-Claude Valla, one of the founders of GRECE: "To me, the enemy is not *the left* or *communism* or even *subversion,* but above all this egalitarian ideology whose secular or religious formulations, metaphysical or so-called *scientific,* have never stopped flourishing for two thousand years, and of which *the ideas of 1789* were only one step."[21] The Judeo-Christian tradition mistakenly argued that differences between people in intelligence, appearance, or social position were superficial and that what really mattered was a shared, essential human nature, which made everyone equal in the eyes of God. By contrast, to support "the right to difference," GRECE adduces ethology and sociobiology, which claim that inequality and hierarchy arise from essential biological facts. GRECE lays claims to an "intelligent racism . . . positive xenophobia" based on IQ differences between races and on eugenic arguments.[22] This belief necessarily implies a root-and-branch attack on democracy, individualism, universalism, and equality.

Rather than attack head-on the core values of Western society and become a target for accusations of neofascism, GRECE jettisoned the vocabulary of anti-Semitism, antiparliamentarianism, and racism of the neofascist right and formulated a new, apparently neutral, apolitical, and "scholarly" discourse that referred to "peoples," "cultures," "identities," and "right to difference." According to Pierre-André Taguieff, GRECE's objective was nothing more or less than "to destroy the humanism which is the basis of the democratic consensus," which is why "the rights of man" was subjected to unremitting attack by GRECE and continues to be a major target of the National Front.[23]

Following the approach laid down by Europe-Action, GRECE initially discussed race in hierarchical terms, with the hierarchy based on "scientific" findings on IQ or ethology. A January 1971 editorial in a GRECE review referred to "biological scum" and "biological dregs."[24] But the doyen of GRECE, Alain de Benoist, soon realized that this kind of scientific racism led to a dead end: It involved interminable and arcane debates over statistics and science, and it was too abstract a concept to use in public debate. A happier alternative was to ground racism in the notion of cultural difference. As Maurice Bardèche put it: "This substitution of the idea of culture for the idea of heredity is a pivot on which swings the renewal of the right that GRECE proposes. Through this means one can henceforth recognize, even affirm, the diversity of races which one calls ethnic preference. . . . The right, thus transfigured by the discovery of culture, can now call itself antiracist."[25]

GRECE therefore denies that one race is superior to another because all races have qualities and defects. What is indisputable is that races are different. GRECE stands for the right to be different and at the same time heaps scorn on those that it accuses of love of race—"racialphilia."[26] In this way GRECE has adopted the language and terms of the left and of antiracists for use by the extreme right. Thus, de Benoist condemns the colonial powers for trying to impose their culture on Third World countries and in the process destroying indigenous cultures. "Of all the forms of destruction and depersonalization of peoples, from exterminist racism to the attempts to break up old identities and build a new culture, one of the most perverse has probably been assimilationism."[27] By the same token, since it is possible to be colonized "economically, culturally, ideologically, religiously or spiritually," then nations have the right to protect themselves against colonialism of whatever kind. For example, France has the right to defend itself against American culture as well as against capitalism, which "breaks apart organic structures [and] depersonalizes people. Capitalism creates happy robots: it air-conditions Hell, it kills souls."[28] On occasion the plea to defend French culture against American influences is couched in coded anti-Semitic language. For example, in 1995 Pierre Vial, former secretary general of GRECE and a member of the Front's central committee, argued in *National Hebdo* in favor of a "cultural war" to protect France against the threat of a "cosmopolite civilization which includes Americanism, and American cultural imperialism."[29] Only in this way could one resist being passed through the "New York mill." The use of the term *cosmopolite* and the reference to New York hint at Jewish influences. And Vial praised Claude Autant-Lara (who had questioned the existence of the

Holocaust and slurred concentration camp survivor Simone Veil in a September 1989 speech to the European Parliament) as "a great voice preaching in the desert of the European Parliament."[30]

From this perspective, cultures or "peoples" constitute historically closed vessels that distinguish between "us" and "them" and between "our" culture and traditions and "their culture and traditions."[31] This is a "recycling" of racist language so that terms such as *culture and European identity* really mean *biology and race* and terms such as *Indo-European heritage* mean the *white race*.[32] This substitution of acceptable for unacceptable vocabulary was pioneered by GRECE and quickly adopted by Le Pen and the National Front. In the course of a debate with Pierre-André Taguieff, Alain de Benoist attacked the ideas of "universalism, which claims that in suppressing differences one facilitates integration."[33] For GRECE, it is impossible, and therefore dangerous, to try suppressing differences between races and cultures. "Frontiers allow collective identities to be built. I am completely hostile to assimilation, which is a mutilation. I am for a France where the communities conserve the right to express their particularities and their specific heritage. I am ready to defend my difference and, with an equal ardor, that of immigrants."[34] But Taguieff responded that, although GRECE seemed to have abandoned the sociobiological arguments of the 1970s for a cultural argument, this new argument "has been intelligently exploited by NF propaganda. In September 1982, Le Pen declared: 'We have the duty of defending our national personality and our right to difference.' The true question is whether racism disappears just because one speaks of 'cultures' in place of 'races.'"[35]

Although GRECE claimed to represent a new approach to the study of capitalism and democracy, in fact its doctrine is a recapitulation and a rewording of traditional criticisms of the economistic nature of capitalism and the mediocre culture of a bourgeois society whose nadir has been reached in the United States.[36] GRECE argues that historically the economic system was subsumed by the political system and that only recently have economic values become the sole criterion for all values. This shift has enabled the bourgeoisie to emerge as the dominant force in society, carrying everything, including religion and politics, before it. Even religion has been pressed into the service of capitalist values.[37] By contrast, GRECE argues, the only just society is one in which economics is subsumed to politics and people are not treated as mere commodities.

Another way to view GRECE's doctrine is to treat it as an early manifestation of conservative postmodernism—that is, as a radical rejection of all received ideologies, including fascism, liberalism, socialism, and the Judeo-Christian heritage; an attack on the materialist values of welfare capitalism and modernity; a sophisticated awareness of the role that language and culture play in politics; and a yearning for a new societal consensus built on a common language, culture, religion, and heritage. The one crucial difference between postmodernism and the doctrines of both GRECE and the National Front, however, is the attitude toward social science and history. Whereas postmodernism is skeptical about "objective" social science and history, preferring the terms *narratives* and *metanarratives* (with all their implications of relativism), the intellectuals of the French extreme right insist that they are offering a different but nonetheless factual reading of history from that put forward by mainstream intellectuals and scholars.

Club de l'Horloge

The Club de l'Horloge defines itself above all as anti-Socialist and declares its goal as "preparing for the period after socialism by contributing to a renewal of the political ideas of the opposition."[38] Unlike GRECE, which concentrates on abstract issues of doctrine and ideology, the Club de l'Horloge has focused its attention both on doctrine and on practical policy issues.[39] Over the past two decades it has published or sponsored books on decentralization, religion, French identity, and socialism and equality.[40] It was founded in 1974, principally by young members of the elite National Administration School (whose members are popularly known as "enarchs"), many of whom had been members of GRECE. Both Yvan Blot (Michel Norey), who became its president, and Jean-Yves Gallou were leading members of GRECE, and both became prominent members of the National Front in the 1990s.[41] The Club de l'Horloge adopted a pro-American, procapitalist, and pro-Catholic line quite out of keeping with the views of GRECE. Moreover, unlike GRECE, which insisted that its members could not join other organizations, members of the Club de l'Horloge had close links with the Giscardians and the Chiracians. Club de l'Horloge president Yvan Blot was a member of the central committee of the RPR, and secretary general Jean-Yves Gallou was a member of the Giscardian Republican Party.[42]

Blot's career is typical of a number of high civil servants who worked in the mainstream right and then decided to throw in their lot with the National Front. He began his administrative career in the Ministry of the Interior, worked for the Planning Commission, and then from 1978 to 1983 was a high official in Chirac's RPR. From 1984 to 1986 Blot worked for Charles Pasqua, the hard-line minister of the interior in the 1986 Chirac government.[43] Blot has lectured and written widely about the new right and in the 1980s, through his contacts with the American Heritage Foundation, popularized Reaganite ideas in France.[44] Along with Bruno Mégret, both Blot and Le Gallou are now members of the NF's political bureau.

Political Discourse

One of the most remarkable features of the National Front has been its spon-gelike ability to absorb and integrate into its doctrine new ideas emanating from modern social movements. In its 1993 election program, *300 mesures pour la renaissance de la France,* the Front announced that it "believes strongly in the values of ecology and in this sense it defines itself as ecologist."[45] Of course, the Front's conception of ecology is different from what the mainstream ecology movement has in mind: For the Front, defending the environment means defending national identity. The Front proposes to establish within cities "a relatively homogeneous community of inhabitants" by giving preference in jobs, housing, social welfare, and education to French citizens.[46] The Front argues that a necessary prerequisite to ensuring a harmonious relationship between people and environment is to ensure comity within society itself; this means protecting national identity against disruptive forces such as immigration. Jean-Claude Bardet, NF municipal councillor and editor in chief of the new right review *Identité,* asked, "Is not defending ecology and the laws of nature the same as rejecting immigration and cosmopolitanism, which calls into question the cultural identity of the French and the unity of the nation?"[47]

Not only has the Front demonstrated enormous ingenuity in redefining new ideas to serve its own ideological ends. The Front is also highly skilled in taking away terms from opposition groups and using them in the Front's lexical armory. In *La flamme* (The flame), Bruno Mégret claimed that the militant antiracism of the establishment is, in reality, "an authentic anti-French racism. . . . The object of 'antiracism' is to break the legitimate and natural resistance of the French to the increase in immigration and cosmopolitanism, and the best means for achieving that is to devalue the French in their own eyes and to make them ashamed of themselves."[48]

"Anti-racism," according to Jean Madiran, "wants the exclusion of the French and of Catholics, defenders of the spiritual, religious and moral order."[49] When Sébastien Deyzieu, an extreme right militant fleeing the police, fell to his death in May 1994, the Front youth organization laid a wreath calling for a "Halt to anti-national repression. After Malik, Sébastien." The reference was to Malik Oussékine, a youth of North African descent killed by the police during a 1986 student demonstration. The point was to claim that Front student activists were as vulnerable to police repression as other "minorities" and at the same time to draw an invidious comparison between the protests and demonstrations that followed Malik's killing and the general indifference, outside extreme right circles, that met Deyzieu's death.

Examples of this tactic of appropriating the language of one's enemies abound on the extreme right. During the trial of collaborationist Paul Touvier, accused of having tortured and executed Jews and Resistance members during World War II, his defense lawyer, Jacques Trèmolet de Villers, said, "In fact, Touvier is Schindler."[50] In recent years the tactic has spread to all sides of the political spectrum. Antiabortionists in the United States, and increasingly in France, refer to abortion as a "holocaust." Alleged Oklahoma City bomber Timothy McVeigh was linked to the Michigan militia, which uses the Warsaw Ghetto as an example of how unarmed civilians were massacred by a despotic government. And in Great Britain Tony Blair, leader of the Labour Party, has appropriated the phrase *law and order*, previously identified with the conservative right, and now claims that the Labour Party, not the Conservative Party, is the party of law and order.

The Vocabulary Battle

These rhetorical techniques are an essential part of what Bruno Mégret calls the "vocabulary battle." This battle was first joined in the 1960s when extreme right intellectuals began to argue that the road to political power would be permanently blocked as long as the left defined the terms of political discourse. These intellectuals claimed that the left had induced the public to endorse ideas such as egalitarianism, consumerism, internationalism, and statism through its influence over the media, schools, universities, and other avenues of information and propaganda. As a result, the alternative ideas of the extreme right were easily painted by their opponents as being out of tune with the times or as reflecting nostalgia for Vichy or fascism.[51] According to Bruno Mégret: "The semantic superiority of the left helped its culture and then political influence. Language is a form of subtle code. In choosing a word, one's thoughts are inscribed, sometimes even without wishing it, within a pre-established ideological schema. To speak of 'social classes,' of 'workers,' of the 'proletariat,' is not innocent. To utilize these words is to push forward marxist doctrine."[52]

In the past the left was highly skilled in using ideas as weapons in the political battle and in forcing the right on the defensive—at least as regards ideology. The left understood the importance of Gramsci's perception that before winning political power, one had to achieve ideological hegemony. Mégret cited Jacques Attali, a former close adviser to President Mitterrand, as saying, "The stake in society is not an economic or a political one, but fundamentally a cultural one."[53] In these circumstances how could the extreme right contest political power when even terms such as *the right* evoked images of fascism, Vichy, and collaboration? With the route to political power strewn with linguistic minefields, no wonder the extreme right had been marginalized.

The stake in the vocabulary battle was to insert the Front's language and terms into political debate so that the NF's ideas and vision of the world would be conveyed to the public and come to be taken for granted. According to a 1990 publication of the Front's National Training Institute, two kinds of words were to be avoided: those belonging to Marxist ideology and those belonging to the ideology of the rights of man.[54] By 1990 Bruno Mégret was claiming that the Front had succeeded in substituting many of its own words and its own meanings for those of the opposition.

> Today, the force of words has changed sides: now one hears the man in the street, politicians, and journalists situate themselves, in spite of themselves, in the problematic of the national movement in talking about "identity," "Lebanonization," "politico-media class," and more and more of the "establishment," of "cosmopolitanism," of the "people," and of "hidden totalitarianism." Passing into current language, these words . . . progressively reveal the reality of the National Front's analysis and allow the French to become more quickly conscious of the true political stakes.[55]

The first task was to obtain a clear understanding of how language is used in everyday politics and what had to be done to change the vocabulary and alter the meaning of the terms of political discourse. According to journalist Anne Tristan, who posed as a secretary and joined a local branch of the National Front in Marseilles, officials charged with party propaganda were given a Front circular that told them how to employ

> double language . . . to take account of the pre-existing mental "substratum" of people they were talking to, and, to try and amalgamate them with the main ideas of the Front. . . . Out of 10 memberships, only two or three are the result of a considered decision, the others result from an emotional shock when the member hears one of our ideas. Despite their diverse origins, it's necessary that every militant defend without reservation all our ideas. . . . In the end, when faced with this or that event, the cadres should react together at the same time, with the same arguments, through a simple conditioned reflex.[56]

For example, instead of using the phrase *liberation movement,* Front members should substitute the phrase *terrorist movements;* for the term *neutrality,* Front members should say *Finlandization;* and for the word *boss,* Front members should substitute the word *employer.*[57]

The Front therefore uses coded language in an absolutely self-conscious fashion. There can be no question here of inadvertence in using words that have multiple meanings. Yvan Blot of the Club de l'Horloge made this clear in 1985 when he noted that "the same word can have a different significance according to the semantic field where it appears. The word 'liberty' will not have the same meaning in the mouth of a communist party leader as it does in that of a republican political leader."[58] By the same token, the words *cos-*

mopolitan and *oligarchy* will have quite different meanings when used by a member of the French Socialist Party or a member of the National Front.

In the course of political debate, people understand words and terms in two ways: first, in a literal sense, according to the dictionary definitions, and second, in a connotative sense, according to the accretions of meaning these terms have taken on in specific historical contexts. During any political speech or discussion, therefore, different people hear different things. Those unaware of the historical background to a particular word or phrase will interpret it according to its commonly accepted meanings in everyday speech. Others will interpret the speech differently when, for them, the same word or phrase has additional meanings. For example, hearing the word *cosmopolitan* in the course of a speech, one person will think of someone who has traveled around a lot or easily adjusts to the mores and manners of any society in which he or she happens to live. Another person, however, will add to the term the unexpressed term *Jew* and will hear the phrase *cosmopolitan Jew*. As the former editor of the extreme right newspaper *Minute* put it in a 1993 speech, "There is something foreign here, or to be perfectly clear, cosmopolitan . . . that's clear, it's the word Jew."[59]

These different levels of interpretation give rise to ambiguities that, in the hands of a skilled orator, can be used to convey multiple layers of meaning within the same speech. Among the most skilled in the art of using double, or coded, language is Jean-Marie Le Pen. In public speeches, on radio, or on television, through insinuations, hints, or jokes, Le Pen conveys anti-Semitic messages, which inevitably provoke a storm of criticism and, typically, a reaction of offended innocence from Le Pen. Speaking before party members and militants, however, Front spokespersons are more explicit, accusing B'nai B'rith or "the Jewish International" of controlling French politics from behind the scenes and mounting an attack on French national identity. The ambiguities that arise in the use of coded language provide a convenient line of defense when implicit messages of anti-Semitism or racism provoke criticism, for the critics are accused of reading prejudice into words or terms that, taken literally, are neutral. Thus, the tables are turned, and the critics are criticized for unjustly smearing the Front.

When Le Pen referred to "the Jewish International" playing a "not unimportant role in the creation of an antinational spirit,"[60] he defended himself against criticisms of anti-Semitism by replying that international Jewish organizations existed and that, by nature, international organizations promote internationalism. Taken absolutely literally, this is, of course, true. But the singling out of the so-called Jewish International echoes anti-Semitic claims that there is a Jewish conspiracy to rule the world.[61] Another example of this technique of turning the tables comes from Mégret's *La flamme*. According to Mégret, after Le Pen's remark about the Jewish International, "immediately, there was an explosion. Nonetheless, nothing he said was defamatory. There exist Jewish internationals, no one denies it, even Israelite institutions: chapter six of the very official *Guide to French Judaism* is completely dedicated to this subject under the heading: 'International Jewish Organizations.' With regard to saying that these movements favor the diffusion of an anti-national feeling, this is only an opinion, which, besides, is neither insulting nor defamatory."[62]

Mégret's comments bear closer examination. First, Mégret deliberately changes the sense of Le Pen's remark. Le Pen referred to *the* Jewish international, whereas Mégret refers to the plural "Jewish internationals." Second, by linking Jewish organizations to an "antinational" attitude, Mégret implies that Jews are not truly French. Third, Mégret links Jewish international organizations to a conspiracy to silence the NF. Thus, by claiming that Jews and Jewish organizations are opposed to the French nation, and try to limit the Front's freedom of speech, Mégret implies that it is not anti-Semitism but moral outrage that provokes Le Pen's and the NF's criticisms of the Jewish community. "If there is a refusal to debate with the representatives of the National Front and if one proceeds through anathemas, it is because of a logic which has nothing to do with politics. France is in effect dominated by a cosmopolite power of an inquisitorial and theocratic nature, and the National Front, the champion of the values of identity is its enemy and, therefore, the incarnation of Evil."[63]

Le Pen took the same approach when defending his remark that the Nazi gas chambers were a "detail" of World War II. According to Le Pen, he literally meant that the gas chambers were just one detail among all the others that composed that event called World War II. Details, he said, were obviously part of the whole. Taken literally, he was right. But to call the Holocaust a detail is to reduce it to the level of banality.

When he was asked during a television program why he questioned government minister Lionel Stoleru about his citizenship, Le Pen replied that the audience had the right to know about the nationality of a government minister. But why ask that particular question in the middle of a televised debate unless Le Pen wanted to cast suspicion on Stoleru's patriotism since as a Jew Stoleru could conceivably claim Israeli citizenship? And, of course, Le Pen's coded remark was meant to evoke anti-Semitic claims that Jews owe their primary allegiance to their "race" or religion rather than to the country in which they live. In turn, this remark links with the suggestion that Jews are "cosmopolitans."

Thus, the vocabulary battle depends heavily on the utilization of four techniques:

1. The revitalization of words or terms that (outside the narrow confines of the extreme right) had taken on purely negative connotations

2. The reintroduction of terms such as *cosmopolitan* or *complot* (plot) that had in the past referred almost exclusively to Jews and the broadening of their (negative) meaning to include additional Front targets such as the media, civil liberties organizations, B'nai B'rith, the Freemasons, and the Trilateral Commission

3. The redefinition and recruitment into the service of the extreme right of words, such as antiracism, that had previously served its opponents

4. The coining of neologisms such as *xénomania* (mania for foreigners), *sidaïque* (crazy from AIDS), and *Euroefédéraste* (a play on "Eurofederation" and "pederast") or the redefinition of neutral terms such as *mondialiste* for use as weapons against critics

These techniques have been put to work in the construction of a conspiracy theory of French politics that asserts that behind the scenes a cosmopolitan, or *mondialiste*, oligarchy is hard at work undermining the French nation.

Cosmopolitanism

The first use of the term *cosmopolitanism* in *La flamme* occurs on page 20: "An increasingly vigorous cosmopolitanism, is trying to deprive our fellow citizens of their ethnic and cultural references." Mégret then defines cosmopolitanism as "the desire to get rid of differences and identities and to glorify mixing, cross-breeding [*métissage*], the melting pot [in English], and cultural and ethnic deracination."[64] Mégret uses the term in a number of ways. Sometimes his usage is literal, as in the dictionary definition of a cosmopolitan as "one who lives sometimes in one country, sometimes in another, and who easily adopts the morals and the usages of the country that he inhabits."[65] More frequently, Mégret evokes the anti-Semitic overtones that the term acquired during the heyday of anti-Semitism in France in the late nineteenth century and from the 1930s to 1945. Mégret talks about the "assault" on France committed by cosmopolitanism. He claims that officials and the media have taken over the language of cosmopolitanism, and as evidence in his attacks on the media he refers exclusively to Jewish journalists.[66] He also claims that national education prepares students for their "cosmopolite future."[67] The reassertion of the traditional link between Jews and cosmopolitanism could not be more clear. But in line with the Front's tactic of broadening traditional terms of opprobrium to encompass new targets, Mégret includes within the rubric of cosmopolitan the "immigration lobby," which in turn encompasses every left-wing political party or antiracist organization in France.[68]

From a term whose literal meaning is neutral and could imply an attitude of accommodation to different cultures and nations, Mégret has redefined cosmopolitanism as a disease that threatens French values and identity. He has reaffirmed the traditional anti-Semitic link between Jews and cosmopolitanism, but he has also broadened the term so as to include within it a variety of political parties, groups, and institutions in French society that support immigration and therefore are antinational. Loaded with historical significance, subject to a wide range of interpretations, and enormously ambiguous, cosmopolitanism was a perfect weapon in the Front's vocabulary battle. But by 1993 the term was being replaced by a new and even more effective one, *mondialisme.*

Mondialisme

In 1989 Le Pen was asked by Jean Madiran, the editor of *Présent:* "Many times you have spoken about the '*mondialiste* lobby.' What does one know about the people or the groups which compose it and the goals which it pursues?" Len Pen replied:

> I don't need to tell people of your political background about the forces that are aiming to establish an egalitarian, leveling [*réductrice*] and *mondialiste* ideology. I am thinking about the completely false, misleading and mistaken use that is made of the rights of man by the Freemasons. I believe that the Trilateral [Commission] plays a role. The great internationals, like the Jewish international, play a not negligible role in the creation of this anti-national spirit. I will say that it is almost natural that these forces, which are structurally, fundamentally internationalist, collide with national interests. But it is necessary to be careful when one says that the Freemasons and the Jewish international play a role. That doesn't mean all the Freemasons nor all Jewish organizations, nor all Jews, that is clear. But there are people who speak in the name of these others and act in this fashion.[69]

A year later in *La flamme,* Mégret wrote: "This *mondialiste* structure, which exercises an orienting power over the international community, favors the uniformization of national communities . . . . Think of the press empire of Mr. Maxwell which is spreading over a number of countries and whose agencies and newspapers contribute to the advancement of cosmopolite ideas across the world."[70] Here Mégret associates the Jewish press baron Robert Maxwell with *mondialiste* and cosmopolitan ideas.

By 1993 *mondial, mondialiste,* and *mondialisme* had begun to replace *cosmopolitanism* in the Front's political discourse. The first chapter of *300 mesures* begins, "The most serious threat weighing on the future of France today is that of *mondialisme.*"[71] In the Introduction, the terms *mondial, mondialiste,* and *mondialisme* are used fifteen times in nine pages. On six occasions the reference is to *mondialiste* ideology, on three occasions to *mondialistes*, on two occasions to *mondialisme*, and one each to *mondialiste* doctrine, *mondialiste* government, and *mondial* conflict.[72] The term *cosmopolitan* is not used in any form.

Apparently, cosmopolitanism was too overtly anti-Semitic and therefore too inflexible to serve in the vocabulary battle.[73] This did not mean that the Front was about to abandon anti-Semitism, but the advantage of *mondial* in all its versions was that it lacked historical baggage. For the general public, the word had the appearance of neutrality and might catch on as part of the general vocabulary. For the extreme right, the word's anti-Semitic and racist connotations could easily be encoded through the pro-Front press. In 1992 Mégret defined *mondialisme* as

the utopia which sees happiness in the human world in superseding all differences and all identities. It is looking to create a world government by the destruction of nations, by the mixing of races, by superseding frontiers and by a mixing of cultures. From the marxist utopia which wanted to get rid of classes, reduce inequalities and construct a Red paradise, we have moved to a *mondialiste* utopia which wants to suppress differences and to create a multicolored paradise.[74]

Although the terms *mondial, mondialiste*, and *mondialisme* often appear at the beginning of *300 mesures*, they cannot be found in the index. Aside from Le Pen's 1989 definition and Mégret's 1990 reference, the *mondialistes* are so vaguely defined that it allows the Front to include any real or imagined enemies within the term's scope.

Racism and Antiracism

When the National Front is accused of racism, the NF responds by accusing critics of being anti-French racists because they want to drown the French nation in a sea of immigrants. When critics accuse the NF of being xenophobic, the NF argues that the immigration lobby, which aims to destroy French national identity, consists of, to use Bruno Mégret's term, *xenophiles*, that is, people who love foreigners. An interesting example of the Front's turning the language and symbols of criticism against the critics occurred in the mid-1980s. At this time the antiracist pressure group SOS-Racisme had attracted enormous support in France, and its badge, a yellow hand palm upward with the slogan "*Touche pas à mon pote*" (Hands off my pal) was worn by hundreds of thousands of young people. In 1985 after a series of attacks on the headquarters of *Minute*, the National Front distributed a yellow badge that bore the inscription "*Touche pas à Minute.*"[75]

The Front is well aware that merely putting forward an alternative vocabulary to that used by its opponents is not sufficient. Ideas may be weapons in the political battle, but ideas alone are insufficient to win it. According to Yvan Blot, "A language can be effective in communication and action only if it is 'rooted.'"[76] By this Blot means that in addition to an attractive or striking use of language, the Front must put forward a coherent and relevant ideology that will attract supporters. That is why the Front always attempts to "demystify" its opponents' language and to show the "real" implications that lay behind it. In January 1988 the NF published a "Blue Book" that consisted of 130 definitions of various political terms. Racism was defined as "a doctrine denying the right of people to be themselves. The French are today the principal victims of it in their own country."[77] The following year Le Pen defined racism as an "incitation to hate and violence based on differences of religion, race or nation."[78] In *La flamme*, Mégret explained that "the object of 'anti-racism' is to break the legitimate and natural resistance of the French to the rise in immigration and cosmopolitanism. . . . In this enterprise, Mr. Bernard-Henri Lévy holds a privileged place."[79]

AIDS

Another illustration of how Le Pen and the Front manipulate language occurred with the storm of criticism that greeted Le Pen's 1987 remarks that AIDS could be transmitted through "sweat, tears and saliva," and his references to AIDS victims as "*Sidaïques*" (in French, AIDS is translated as *Sida*; by using the word *Sidaïque*, Le Pen deliberately aimed to evoke terms such as *maniaque* [maniac]) and to the necessity of creating *Sidatoriums* to incarcerate AIDS victims.[80] Roundly attacked by the scientific community both for the inaccuracy of his statements and the inefficacy of his proposed measures, Le Pen counterattacked by accusing his critics of being afflicted with "mental AIDS."[81] Le Pen and Bruno Mégret use the term *AIDS* in four ways: (1) as a literal reference to the disease; (2) as an insult—implying that the Front's critics have AIDS; (3) as a criticism of specific policies (e.g., analogizing the Maastricht Treaty to a case of AIDS);[82] and (4) as a way of distinguishing between those who fit the National Front's image of true French citizens and those who do not. AIDS, the Front claimed, "came from abroad." Even tuberculosis was "imported" into France.[83] For the Front, AIDS became a metaphor for all things foreign, from immigrants to ideas such as cosmopolitanism and *mondialisme*. An illustration of AIDS as metaphor can be found in *La flamme*, where Mégret observed that "by establishing a true cult of the 'other,' in accepting without reservation as a systematic benefit for the system everything that comes from abroad, [cosmopolitanism] acts on the nation in the same way as AIDS on the human body: it destroys the immune defenses, those which actually allow the organism to protect itself against noxious and undesirable foreign bodies."[84] The double meaning of the term *foreign bodies* is, in this context, not accidental.

As Michael Hastings has pointed out, "To purify is to purge."[85] To purge France of AIDS, the Front proposed testing for the disease people crossing the frontier into France, couples about to marry, pregnant women, armed forces personnel, people in institutions, prostitutes, "and all those with collective responsibilities."[86] Those found to have AIDS were to be placed in special hospitals. Just as AIDS posed a danger to the human body, so, too, immigrants, in the Front's view, posed a metaphorical threat to the French body politic—and were to be dealt with in the same way. Illegal immigrants, like the AIDS virus, would be identified and the body politic purged by returning these foreign elements to their country of origin. Unless the body politic cleansed itself of AIDS (foreign ideas, foreign bodies), it would die. "An organism which does not react against sickness," said Le Pen, "is condemned to death. It is necessary to react against aggressions, against things which imperil our integrity, our life, our future. One can only progress in reacting. The words reactionary or conservative don't frighten me."[87]

The Front's Conspiracy Theory

Illustrations of this conspiracy theory can be found in *La flamme* (1990), in the Front's comprehensive 1993 election program, and in the pro-Front press. All the ingredients for a conspiracy theory of politics are there: (1) the claim that the apparent realities of politics are merely an illusion that conceals mysterious forces working behind the scenes; (2) the accusation that these forces deliberately obscure reality while conspiring together to achieve a secret objective; (3) the assertion that this objective is against the national interest; and (4) the announcement that it is therefore the obligation of the "national" party to reveal the nature of the conspiracy.

According to the Front, behind the realities of French politics lurks a dangerous and mysterious "oligarchy."

This oligarchy is "all-powerful," omnipotent, and "dangerous."[88] Exactly who or what composes the oligarchy is never made completely clear. At various points in *La flamme*, Mégret said it consists of "unions, the bureaucracy, and especially the media and the lobbies," but he never attempted a specific answer to this important question.[89] The work of the "establishment," or oligarchy, is carried out by a series of "lobbies," the most important of which, in the Front's view, is the immigration lobby, which includes "parties of the left as well as trade unions namely, the Socialist Party, the FEN [Fédération de l'Éducation Nationale, or National Education Federation], the CFDT [Confédération Française Démocratique du Travail, or French Democratic Labor Confederation], the MRAP [Mouvement Contre le Racisme et pour l'Amitié Entre les Peuples, or Movement Against Racism and for Friendship Between Peoples], LICRA and the League for the Rights of Man."[90] Working with this lobby are the "politico-media establishment," the "cosmopolitan establishment," and other lobbies.[91]

The identity of the conspirators at the heart of the oligarchy is left to the readers' imagination in *La flamme* and *300 mesures,* but it is more clearly defined in the pro-Front press. A February 1990 editorial in *Présent* stated that its readers "know that the right is a prisoner of a pledge taken by its chief officials before the dignitaries of the B'nai B'rith not to ally themselves in any case with the National Front."[92] Another issue contained a cartoon showing a line of people with black faces and thick lips. At the end of the line a black man with thick lips says, "But I don't want to vote," while behind him a man with a long nose and thick lips says, "You'll do what I tell you to do."[93]

One of the most hallucinatory conspiracy theorists on the extreme right is François Brigneau, an ardent supporter of the NF. Brigneau manages to explain the 1968 French student revolution, the 1992 Los Angeles riots, and the policies of the RPR in terms of a Jewish conspiracy. His argument is that a few months after President de Gaulle's famous statement about the Jews being a people "sure of themselves," the 1968 student revolution broke out. Similarly, after Washington refused to back a $10 billion loan guarantee for Israel and U.S. secretary of state James Baker was quoted as making an anti-Semitic remark, riots broke out in the black areas of Los Angeles. According to Brigneau, "All this demands reflection and it seems that Jacques Chirac, Édouard Balladur and François Léotard reflected on it."[94] Le Pen puts things more subtly, but the point is the same: "The establishment aligns itself in an increasingly servile fashion with foreign powers on the outside, and with lobbies inside France, and, with the complicity of a media power, which is under orders. . . . It abases the State in France."[95]

Because conspiracy theories demand some statement of how the wishes of the majority of the population are being subverted by forces beyond its control, *300 mesures* stated: "The system in which we live is no longer really one of liberty and democracy. The legitimacy of decisions is no longer based on the sovereignty of the people. For the members of the oligarchy, what is legitimate is no longer what is wanted by the majority of the French, it is what is recognized as conforming to the new official ideology, the *mondialiste* ideology which is presented under the guise of the Rights of Man."[96] In the same vein, Bruno Mégret claimed: "There has constituted itself an authentic oligarchy which is concentrating in its hands the quintessence of power in France, exercising it through channels other than those laid down by the Constitution, and utilizing it above all for its own survival. It has confiscated democracy: France has become its property."[97]

However, the Front's conspiracy theory runs into the problem of explaining how an oligarchy (rule by the few) can include Socialists, who were in power until 1993; the mainstream right, which was out of power; and an array of pressure groups of varying size and influence. How can an oligarchy composed of such contrary elements agree on policy? This difficulty is dealt with in a number of ways. The simplest, and crudest, response is to argue that there are different levels of power within the oligarchy but that at the very peak, one or two conspirators hold absolute power. Thus, differences within the oligarchy may crop up over minor issues, but on the main issues—French identity or the preservation of the French nation—the dominant faction within the oligarchy enforces its rule. Yvon Blot, a member of the NF's political bureau, writing in *Présent* in 1993, explained how the majority of French citizens are manipulated by "secret committees," which he linked to a Jewish conspiracy:

> The RPR . . . is theoretically governed by its president Jacques Chirac and its secretary general Alain Juppé, with the support of . . . Bernard Pons and Charles Pasqua. All these men present themselves regularly at elections and are known to the French. Good. But in reality, the essential options and strategies are elaborated by secret committees on which sit men who are careful not to submit themselves to universal suffrage. The majority are high civil servants imbued with what they consider to be their intellectual and moral superiority over the vulgar crowd. Their names are little known: François Heilbrenner, Jacques Friedmann, Jérôme Monod, Denis Baudoin. . . . The connections of these high civil servants with the Grand Orient [Freemasons] of France, B'nai B'rith or the CRIF of Jean Kahn determine the fixing of the ideological and strategic choices of the party concerned. The facade of democracy hides the true power of secret committees, with all the defects of this kind of oligarchy.[98]

A variation on this theme appeared in the pro-Front, anti-Semitic newspaper *Rivarol,* where Jean Denipierre wrote:

> The little left-right ballet is only a procedure which permits changing teams exhausted by power, for another team which appears new. Doubtless, there are a few small differences: a little more or a little less of the State, a little more or less of dirigisme or of liberalism, but, on essentials, policy remains the same, a policy whose object is the destruction and the installation of a world order directed by the masters of finance. Everything else is only a trifle.[99]

Along the same lines, *300 mesures* recapitulated Blot's argument about the behind-the-scenes power of high civil servants and then observed: "The technical reality of power is held by a small number of men who, without any mandate or control by the people, take decisions under the influence of lobbies of all kinds. Did not Senator Caillavet state that the law relative to abortions, called the Veil law, repeated, word for word, the text elaborated on the question in Masonic workshops?"[100]

For the Front, the oligarchy is dominated by the traditional enemies of the extreme right—Jews and Freemasons. In *La flamme*, Mégret attempted a more subtle solution to the problem of how an oligarchy composed of Socialists and the mainstream right can conspire to undermine France. He argued that the mainstream right has somehow been manipulated, or "hypnotized," by the Socialists into accepting their "New Socialist Ideology," that is, "social-liberalism in economic matters and cosmopolitanism on societal questions."[101] Exactly how this is achieved is not made clear, but Mégret accused the mainstream right of being unable to develop an ideology that would distinguish it from that of the left. As a result, the right has been coopted into the prevailing oligarchy. In the end the reader is given the impression that there is a powerful motive force in French politics called cosmopolitanism ("France is undergoing the attacks of cosmopolitanism") but that the exact structure behind that force remains mysterious.[102]

The Extreme Right

Although Le Pen apparently has no trouble with words such as *reactionary* and *conservative*, there is one term that the Front has been unable to manipulate to its own advantage and that it never loses an opportunity to attack: *extreme right*. Like cosmopolitanism, extreme right is laden with historical connotations—but in this case, with the wrong ones. "The Front is termed a party of the extreme right. That's false!"[103] According to the Front, the extreme right was associated with the monarchy, rejected the secular state and elections, and was "openly racist and anti-Semitic."[104] It "preached the coming of an omnipotent State, conceived as the incarnation of the nation and charged with a totalitarian mission toward society."[105] Although some people might think that, except for supporting the monarchy, this is a pretty fair description of the National Front, Bruno Mégret disagreed. The Front has always played the election game, he said, and no "position of an anti-Semitic or racist character" has ever figured in the writings or proposals of the leaders of the National Front."[106] Mégret pointed out that the sociology of NF voters and supporters differs from that of the historical extreme right. "Contrary to a widespread opinion, the national movement is not an extreme right current. Nothing links it to the extreme right: neither its doctrine, its strategy or its sociology."[107]

The NF has been working for years to convince the public that the NF is a party of the right and not of the extreme right. In the 1980s the Club de l'Horloge put forward the thesis that both communism and socialism derived from and were different forms of fascism. As such, they were antidemocratic and antirepublican. According to this reasoning, the right stood for the Republic against the Marxists; the opposition was between the Marxists on one side and the Republicans on the other. Because Marxism is a dying philosophy, while nationalism and "rootedness" are gaining ground, the Marxists are the reactionaries, and rightists are those who stand for progress. Arguments of this kind were put forward by the extreme right to steal away from the left words such as *republic* and *progress,* which have a positive connotation, and to pin on the left negative words such as *reactionary* and *fascist.*[108] According to *300 mesures,* the Front is "not a construction inherited from the past. . . . It is a new and original political expression whose roots, to be sure, extend deeply into the subsoil of our history . . . but which [is] authentically current as a political response to the political crisis of our country."[109]

There are a number of reasons that the Front wishes to present itself as a new force on the French political scene. First, as the Front itself admits, the extreme right is associated with all the lost battles of French history: opposition to the Republic, secularism, democracy, and toleration. Second, the Front claims to offer a new and alternative choice to voters. Even Jean-Marie Le Pen, the ex-Poujadist deputy, is presented by Mégret as "not a political man like the others. He doesn't come from the mold of the [elite] schools of the establishment and from political machines. His value and his force come rather, like Churchill, from his anticonformism."[110] According to the Front, the Socialists, Communists, the RPR, and the UDF are "brother enemies" and are all part of the political establishment. They are "old political warhorses."[111] Third, the Front's tactic is to present itself as the only real opposition to the left. It contrasts the "little alternation" between a government of the left and a government of the mainstream right with the "big political alternation" (*grande alternance politique*) between the National Front and all the other parties. To pose as a new and major alternative to the other political parties, the Front must divest itself of an image that links it both to the margins of French politics and to a tradition that was discredited during the prewar and Vichy periods.

Why, then, does the press continue to refer to the National Front as an extreme right party? According to Bruno Mégret, it is the cosmopolitan oligarchy that labels the Front as extreme right because "it threatens the privileges of the political class and contests the dominant ideas."[112] Thus, unlike the prewar extreme right, which was racist and anti-Semitic, it is the Front that is persecuted.[113] Indeed, the "persecution" of the Front is compared to the persecution of the Jews.[114] According to the director of *Présent*, the "national movement" has nothing to do with Nazism or the extreme right. "Besides, nazism is a philosophy of the left, of the extreme left, and even less extreme than Communism."[115]

Has the Front won or lost the vocabulary battle? The evidence is mixed. On the one hand, there is no sign that words such as *mondialiste* and *cosmopolitan*, or *anti-French racism*, have entered the vocabulary in the way that the Front wishes. Nor is there any sign in France that the Front is viewed with less suspicion than in the past. On the contrary, an opinion poll in February 1994 showed that record numbers rejected the Front's ideas and thought that the Front was dangerous for democracy. On the other hand, there can be no question that the way in which the Front defines immigration policy and characterizes immigrants has had an impact on French immigration policy. In summer and fall 1993 the French National Assembly adopted a series of measures that might have come directly from the Front's *300 mesures:* giving mayors the right to delay marriages between immigrants and French nationals, giving the police wider powers to conduct identification checks, and requiring children of non-French nationals to positively affirm their desire to become French citizens. Negative and denigrating references to immigrants from politicians such as François Mitterrand, Laurent Fabius, Jacques Chirac, Valéry Giscard d'Estaing, and Raymond Barre all reflect the ability of the Front to disseminate its anti-immigrant propaganda to the general public.

A dramatic illustration of the Front's success in banalizing its language appeared in a June 24, 1994, headline in *Le Monde* that read, in large black letters, "*LE DROIT À LA DIFFÉRENCE* [The Right to Be Different]." On first glance, the reader thinks that the National Front has taken a full-page advertisement in *Le Monde;* but in fact the ad is an appeal to the central government by the department of Seine-et-Marne to change discriminatory tax policies, which, it is claimed, reduces business investment. The advertisement was a deliberate attempt to capitalize on the notoriety of the phrase, associated as it is with the anti-immigration policies of the Front, and attract the reader's attention. But the use of the phrase as an advertising slogan inevitably reduces its shock value and "normalizes" it. This is exactly what the Front has in mind.

Notes

1. Jean-Marie Le Pen, *Les Français d'abord* (Paris: Carrère/Laffon, 1984), p. 228.

2. Founded by graduates of the elite École Nationale d'Administration and the École Polytechnique, the name was chosen because the group used to meet in a room at the École Nationale adorned with an ornate clock. Douglas Johnson, "The

New Right in France," in Luciano Cheles, Ronnie Ferguson, and Michalina Vaughan, eds., *Neo-Fascism in Europe* (Essex: Longman, 1991), p. 235. According to Pierre-André Taguieff, "A majority of the intellectuals in the National Front come from GRECE and the Club de l'Horloge." *Le Nouvel Observateur,* November 28–December 4, 1991.

3. Members of GRECE take very seriously their commitment to paganism. During the "Indo-European" marriage of two members of GRECE in the presence of Alain de Benoist, the couple exchanged a dagger (a martial symbol) for a key (symbol of the household). Some members of GRECE have celebrated the winter solstice, and in summer 1979 Pierre Vial, a leading member of GRECE, reported that thirty of its members had met in Greece for a "pilgrimage to the sources." There Vial gave a speech beginning: "We Hellenes, Italians, Belgians, French, assembled under the sign of Apollo and speaking in the name of our European brothers swear to work with all our energy and will for the renaissance of European culture. . . . By the lyre of Apollo whose songs accompany our steps, we swear it." Quoted in Anne-Marie Duranton-Crabol, *Visages de la nouvelle droite: Le grece et son histoire* (Paris: Presses Universitaires de France, 1988), pp. 50–53.

4. The Club de l'Horloge has received assistance from the right-wing American Heritage Foundation, a think-tank closely associated with the Reagan and Bush administrations. Club de l'Horloge, *L'Identité de la France* (Paris: Albin Michel, 1985), p. 9. According to Pierre-André Taguieff, without the club's help in forging a new doctrine of cultural identity and the theme of the "right to difference," the National Front would have been stuck with an outmoded philosophy and would have remained a fringe organization. *Le Nouvel Observateur,* November 28–December 4, 1991.

5. GRECE was formally registered at the prefecture of the Alpes-Maritimes Department on January 17, 1969. Duranton-Crabol, *Visages,* p. 30. Jacques Peyrat, an ex-member of the National Front, was elected mayor of Nice in 1995.

6. Pierre Milza, *Fascisme français: Passée et présent* (Paris: Flammarion, 1987), p. 328. The journal disappeared in 1966.

7. Ibid., p. 329. Europe-Action had links with the Italian extreme-right wing Ordine Nouvo as well as with similar groups in Belgium, Germany, Portugal, South Africa, and Spain.

8. Alain de Benoist, *Vu de droite* (Paris: Copernic, 1979), p. 71.

9. The GRECE journal *Nouvelle Ecole* described its objective as putting in place, or attaching itself to, "influential men with positions in decision-making circles today and tomorrow." Quoted by Thierry Pfister, in *Le Monde,* June 22, 1979. Like the Fabians, GRECE opted for quality of its membership rather than quantity. In 1969 it had about one hundred members, and new recruits were asked to complete questionnaires concerning their education, intellectual and research interests. The new recruit was also asked to state which magazines and journals he or she read. In 1978 GRECE had between one thousand and two thousand members. Duranton-Crabol, *Visages,* p. 42.

10. *Le Monde,* June 22, 1979.

11. Thierry Pfister, "La nouvelle droite s'installe," *Le Monde,* June 22 ,1979.

12. Pierre-André Taguieff, "Alain de Benoist philosophe," *Temps Modernes* 451 (February 1984):1464–1470.

13. Taguieff has argued that de Benoist "is one of the most typical representatives of those publicists with encyclopedic pretensions using the scissors rather than the pen." In other words, de Benoist is not an original thinker. Pierre-André Taguieff, "La stratégie culturelle de la 'nouvelle droite' en France (1968–1983)," in Robert Badinter, ed., *Vous avez dit fascisme* (Paris: Montalba, 1984), p. 79.

14. De Benoist, *Vu de droite*, p. 19.

15. Quoted in Ariane Chebel d'Appolonia, *L'extrême droite en France: De Maurras à Le Pen* (Brussels: Complexe, 1987), p. 320.

16. Quoted in Alain Rollat, *Les hommes de l'extrême droite* (Paris: Calmann-Lévy, 1985), p. 146.

17. Ibid., p. 157.

18. Quoted in Duranton-Crabol, *Visages*, p. 101.

19. Pierre Vial, quoted in Rollat, *Les hommes*, p. 148.

20. Unlike the National Front and the fundamentalist (integrist) Catholics, GRECE does not oppose abortion and is much less puritan in its views on sexual mores. However, GRECE defended abortion on eugenic grounds rather than in terms of women's right to choose.

21. Jean-Claude Valla, quoted in Taguieff, "La stratégie culturelle," p. 103.

22. Rollat, *Les hommes*, p. 152.

23. Taguieff, "La stratégie culturelle," p. 21. The NF's 1993 election program, *300 mesures pour la renaissance de la France* (Paris: Éditions Nationales, 1993), is filled with attacks on "the rights of man."

24. Quoted in Duranton-Crabol, *Visages*, p. 38.

25. Quoted in ibid., p. 58.

26. Ibid., p. 74.

27. De Benoist, *Vu de droite*, p. 219.

28. Ibid.

29. *National Hebdo*, April 13–19, 1995.

30. Ibid.

31. Alain de Benoist and GRECE proposed that the Third World, Europe, and Japan ally themselves against the two (then) superpowers—the United States and the Soviet Union. The goal was to prevent the spread of Western liberalism and Eastern Marxism. De Benoist said that just as left intellectuals turned toward the Third World to "hasten the decline of European culture," so too, "we turn toward it today to maintain alive all cultures, to attempt to preserve the diversity of the world and to restore to the world political game its necessary plurality." De Benoist, *Vu de droite*, p. 222.

32. Duranton-Crabol, *Visages*, p. 64.

33. "Vous avez dit difference?" debate between Alain de Benoist and Pierre-André Taguieff, in *Le Nouvel Observateur*, September 25, 1987.

34. Alain de Benoist, *Europe, tiers monde, même combat* (Paris: Robert Laffont, 1986), p. 212. This put de Benoist in the position of defending the right of communities within France to maintain cultural differences, as when he defended the right of Muslim girls to wear the chador to school during the scarves affair. However, de Benoist has argued for the opposite position when writing about ancient Athens, the "paradigm of 'genuine' democracy." "The proper functioning of both Greek and Icelandic democracy was the result of cultural cohesion and a clear sense of shared heritage. The closer the members of a community are to each other the more they

are likely to hold common sentiments, values and ways of looking at the world and the easier it is for them to make collective decisions in regard to the common good without the help of mediators." For de Benoist, smoothly functioning democracies require a homogeneous population. Alain de Benoist, "Democracy Revisited," *Telos* 95 (Spring 1993):75.

35. Quoted in *Le Nouvel Observateur,* September 25, 1987.

36. Pierre Vial, ed., *Pour une renaissance culturel: La Grece prends la parole* (Paris: Copernic, 1979), pp. 9ff.

37. "The bourgeoisie . . . has drowned the most heavenly ecstasies of religious fervour, of chivalrous enthusiasm, of philistine sentimentalism, in the icy water of egotistical calculation." These are similar sentiments to those of GRECE, but expressed one hundred years earlier and in *The Communist Manifesto.* Karl Marx and Frederick Engels, *Selected Works* (Moscow: Foreign Languages Publishing House, 1958), vol. 1, p. 36.

38. "Qu'est-ce que le Club de l'Horloge?" in Club de l'Horloge, *L'Identité de la France* (Paris: Albin Michel, 1985), p. 351.

39. Julien Brunn implied that GRECE created the Club de l'Horloge as a means of "entryism," that is, to infiltrate some of GRECE's ideas into political parties that were alienated by its neopaganism. Julien Brunn, *La nouvelle droite* (Paris: Nouvelles Éditions Oswald, 1979), pp. 385–386.

40. Club de l'Horloge, *La décentralisation locale* (Paris: Éditions Paris, 1990); Club de l'Horloge, *Socialisme et religion*; Club de l'Horloge, *L'Identité de la France*; and Philippe Baccou and the Club de l'Horloge, *Le grand tabou* (Paris: Albin Michel, 1981).

41. Brunn, *La nouvelle droite*, p. 385.

42. The Club de l'Horloge had overlapping membership with GRECE (Yvan Blot was active in GRECE) and a shared interest in eugenic, sociobiological, and etho-logical theories. Rollat, *Les hommes,* pp. 157–158.

43. Pasqua was appointed minister of the interior once again in 1993 by Édouard Balladur, prime minister in the new RPR government, but after supporting Balladur's presidential bid in 1995, Pasqua was dropped from the cabinet when Chirac won the presidential election and appointed Alain Juppé prime minister.

44. Peter Fysh, "Gaullism Today," *Parliamentary Affairs* 46, 3 (July 1993):402.

45. Front National, *300 mesures*, p. 111.

46. Ibid., p. 117.

47. *Le Monde*, March 3, 1990.

48. Bruno Mégret, *La flamme* (Paris: Robert Laffont, 1990), p. 61.

49. *Présent*, March 18, 1993.

50. *Le Monde*, April 19, 1994.

51. Mégret, *La flamme*, p. 166.

52. Ibid., p. 166.

53. Quoted in ibid., p. 124.

54. *Le Monde*, May 10, 1990.

55. Mégret, *La flamme*, pp. 165–166.

56. Anne Tristan, *Au front* (Paris: Gallimard, 1987), p. 245.

57. See Guy Birenbaum, *Le Front national en politique* (Paris: Éditions Balland, 1992), pp. 311–312; and *Le Monde*, May 10, 1990.

58. Yvan Blot, *Les racines de la liberté* (Paris: Albin Michel, 1985), p. 23. Blot, like many NF intellectuals, was deeply impressed by the success of the French Communist Party in appealing to a broad public. "Very simple, and accessible to the public . . . the communist language results from strategic analyses and doctrinal refinements. Words take their meaning from their relation to a system of references which itself is built around a project" (p. 24).

59. Serge de Beketch speaking before the young royalists of Action Française. Quoted in *Le Monde*, May 11, 1993.

60. *Présent*, August 12, 1989.

61. During his trial for defamation, Le Pen was asked if there was such a thing as the "Catholic International": "Yes, of course," he replied. *Le Monde*, April 24, 1991.

62. Mégret, *La flamme*, p. 153.

63. Ibid., pp. 151–153.

64. Ibid., p. 36.

65. Paul Robert, *Dictionnaire alphabétique et analytique de la langue Française* (Paris: Presses Universitaires de France, 1953).

66. Mégret referred to Bernard-Henri Lévy and Georges-Marc Banamou, founders of *Globe;* to Robert Maxwell, the late English newspaper mogul; and to various media journalists, all of them Jewish. Mégret, *La flamme*, pp. 44ff.

67. Ibid.

68. Ibid., p. 66. According to Eric Delcroix, defense counsel for negationist Robert Faurisson, MRAP, LICRA, the Ligue des Droits de l'Homme (League of Human Rights), SOS-Racisme, and the CRIF are "the visible section of the 'Alien Party' or the 'Pro-Immigration Lobby.'" *Le Monde*, May 27, 1990.

69. Interview in *Présent*, August 11, 1989, conducted by Jean Madiran, director of *Présent*.

70. Mégret, *La flamme*, p. 47.

71. Front National, *300 mesures*, p. 23.

72. Ibid., pp. 12–21.

73. In 1990 Mégret did not feel the need to differentiate between the two terms. In the index to *La flamme*, under "*Mondialisme*," the reader is referred to "*Cosmopolitanisme*."

74. Mégret, quoted in *Le Monde*, September 17, 1992.

75. Jean-Marie Le Pen, *La France est de retour* (Paris: Carrère/Laffon, 1985), plate 7.

76. Blot, *Les racines*, p. 41.

77. ·*Le Monde*, January 11, 1988.

78. *Le Monde*, August 29, 1989.

79. Mégret, *La flamme*, p. 61.

80. *Le Monde*, April 16, 1987, May 8, 1987, and May 27, 1987. At a January 1988 NF election meeting, Le Pen stated: "The common factor during these fourteen years of decadence in France is socialism and socialism is a kind of political AIDS, mental AIDS. . . . In this illness, there is a final stage close to agony, that of the 'socialiques' and that of the 'socialo-positives' who are the RPR and UDF, both having the same illness." Quoted in Birenbaum, *Le Front national*, p. 116.

81. Le Pen also argued that AIDS was a disease that almost exclusively affected homosexuals, thus implying that his critics were homosexual.

82. Referring to the Maastricht Treaty, Le Pen said: "It's like AIDS; we are in a blood positive zone. We are in the phase where we're not even aware of the illness." *Le Monde*, August 29, 1992.

83. Front National, *300 mesures*, p. 272.

84. Mégret, *La flamme*, p. 43. The organic image of the body politic recurs in Front writings and derives from an organic model of politics common on the European right. See Pierre-André Taguieff, "La Metaphysique de Jean-Marie Le Pen," in Nonna Mayer and Pascal Perrineau, *Le front national à découvert* (Paris: Presses de la Fondation Nationale des Sciences Politiques, 1989), pp. 174–175.

85. Michael Hastings, "La Rhétorique hygiéniste de Jean-Marie Le Pen," *Revue politique et parlementaire* 933 (January-February 1988):57.

86. Front National, *300 mesures*, p. 271.

87. Jean-Marie Le Pen, in Jean-Pierre Apparu, *La Droite aujourd'hui* (Paris: Albin Michel, 1979), p. 180.

88. Front National, *300 mesures*, pp. 13, 17; Mégret, *La flamme*, p. 118.

89. Mégret, *La flamme*, p. 23.

90. Ibid., p. 66.

91. Ibid., p. 43.

92. *Présent*, February 17, 1990.

93. *Présent*, January 11, 1990.

94. *Présent*, May 1–12, 1992. Brigneau now writes for *National Hebdo*. The beauty of conspiracy theory is that it can be used to explain everything and its opposite. For example, the dean of French anti-Semites, Henri Coston, noted that "one knows that the B'nai B'rith have been the quartermasters of communism. . . . After the collapse of communism one would like to know if they will play the role of depositaries of the permanent interests of the revolution momentarily put under sequestration . . . waiting for better days." *National Hebdo*, February 1–7, 1990. According to this line of reasoning, both the rise and the fall of communism are due to an international Jewish conspiracy.

95. Front National, *300 mesures*, p. 9.

96. Ibid., pp. 17–18.

97. Mégret, *La flamme*, p. 102.

98. *Présent*, March 18, 1993.

99. *Rivarol*, March 12, 1993. The infinitely flexible nature of conspiracy theory was again illustrated when a group of European skinheads appeared at a National Front parade. *Présent* asked: "Who has the material means to organize such a provocation at an international level? Who would manipulate the 'skinhead international'? . . . This means an international organization, at the least, on a European scale, perhaps supporting itself on the infrastructure of a state. Which one?" For anti-Semites, the right answer would be: "The Jewish International." *Présent*, March 4, 1993.

100. Front National, *300 mesures*, pp. 391–392.

101. Mégret, *La flamme*, pp. 125, 171.

102. Ibid., p. 42.

103. Ibid., p. 145.

104. Ibid., pp. 146–147.

105. Ibid., p. 146.

106. Ibid., p. 147. See, however, the Annex to Pierre-André Taguieff, ed., *Face au racisme* (Paris: La Découverte, 1991), vol. 1, pp. 235–241, which lists six condemnations (up to 1987) by French courts of Le Pen for "justifying war crimes," racism, anti-Semitism, and incitation to hatred.

107. Mégret, *La flamme*, p. 148.

108. On this strategy, see Blot, *Les racines*, p. 16.

109. Front National, *300 mesures*, p. 12.

110. Mégret, *La flamme*, p. 151.

111. Front National, *300 mesures*, pp. 8–9.

112. Mégret, *La flamme*, p. 151.

113. *Présent*, March 18, 1993.

114. *Le Monde*, September 20, 1988.

115. *Présent*, March 18, 1993.

11

Metaphors of War: Women and the National Front

While every year there lack 150,000 French to ensure the renewal of our country, the state finances death. It does this in two ways: by reimbursement for abortions, and then by providing considerable financial assistance to Malthusian organizations like "Family Planning."

— Jean-Marie Le Pen, Pour la France

In an advanced democratic country like France, an extreme right political party like the National Front is caught on the horns of a dilemma. If it clings to the traditional image of woman as wife and mother and rails against abortion and pornography, it risks the unpopularity that goes with swimming against the tide. But if it accommodates itself too much to contemporary ideas on women's role in society, it risks losing support from traditionalist members.

To escape this dilemma, the Front's strategy is to radically redefine the social situation, to present French society as locked in mortal combat with both external and internal enemies, and to offer natalist policies as a solution. According to the Front, waves of illegal Muslim and African immigrants threaten French society because of the weight of their numbers and because their religious and cultural beliefs force them into contradiction with French culture and traditions. Once inside France, the Front claims, these immigrants ally themselves with Jews, *métèques*, "lobbies," and the so-called *mondialists* already working to undermine French values and culture. The Front thus presents French politics as a struggle between the forces of "anti-France" and the last-ditch defenders of true French values and culture.

237

Recasting what is at stake in politics allows the Front to present women's role in society in terms different from what is generally accepted today. After all, if France is at war with an internal enemy, if politics is a life-and-death struggle over the soul of France, it is pointless and self-defeating to argue over the proper allocation of social roles or over arcane questions of masculine versus feminine nature. In wartime what counts is social cohesion and morale; a crisis situation is no time for experiments or radical change, and morale is best maintained by reliance on traditional values and practices. In all-out war the home front must be organized along rigidly hierarchical lines. Social roles are rigidly prescribed, and there is a clear sexual division of labor. Loyalty, obedience, and self-sacrifice are the primary virtues.

In this conflict, which takes place not on a foreign battlefield but within France itself, women play a vitally important role. By refusing abortion and choosing instead to bear children, "Frenchwomen" defend France against the tidal wave of immigrants that threatens to swamp the "French" population. By staying at home and educating children in the traditional values of French society, mothers keep at bay the cosmopolitan, leveling influences of the "media-oligarchy" dominated by Jews and *mondialistes*. And by subsuming personal needs to those of husbands and family, mothers reaffirm the complementarity of roles that nature has set for the two sexes. In this way the Front has tried to tap historical French concerns about low natality and use them in its campaign against immigrants and the "occult" forces that threaten France from within.

Joan of Arc: Virgin and Warrior

On May 1 every year since 1987, the National Front has held a parade that is both a commemoration of Joan of Arc and an attempt to appropriate the rich symbolism of Joan's legend for the exclusive use of the extreme right. According to Jean-Marie Le Pen, Saint Joan, "a victorious general at eighteen years of age," represents "an ideal model of feminine and human qualities."[1] She is the "supreme expression of the love of country, of the people and of liberty . . . a universal model of whom we are proud to be the compatriots."[2]

Ironically, for, after all, Joan was a virgin (*la Pucelle*), Front parades are led by a phalanx of pregnant women symbolizing the Front's view that Frenchwomen must have more babies as a defense against growing numbers of immigrants from the Middle East and Africa. Behind the pregnant women follows a second group of women pushing empty baby carriages representing the decline in the French birthrate. According to former NF deputy Marie-France Stirbois, Frenchwomen should "make French babies with Frenchmen."[3]

The parading mothers-to-be and mothers manqué conjoin the image of Joan the warrior, Joan *la Pucelle,* and the ultimate symbol of motherhood—the Virgin Mary—in a celebration of marriage and procreation. Le Pen affirmed this link between virgin and mother in 1985 when he referred to "our devotion to the national heroine, Saint Joan of Arc and the fundamental role that we recognize in mothers of families."[4]

> I have a great affection for Joan of Arc. I must say that the cult of the Virgin Mary has been part of the formation of Christian humanism, and particularly French humanism, where the presence of Our Lady is constant, especially in the creation of French knighthood, which was the image of . . . our society. The French knight is filled with respect for his Lady by a kind of reflection from the Lady of Ladies, that is, Our Lady, the mother of Jesus who combines the myth of Virgin and mother. . . .
>
> The most moving image is that of the mother crucified in her heart by the death of the most beautiful love possible, that of the mother for her son.[5]

The mothers heading the May 1 parade evoke not only the linked images of Joan the virgin and Mary the mother but also the image of Joan as warrior. Because France lacks the "120,000 French births" needed each year to maintain the current level of the "French" population (the Front discounts the birthrate among immigrants when calculating the "French" birthrate), France is in imminent danger of being swamped by a tidal wave of immigrants and immigrant births.[6] According to the Front, France has entered into a decisive phase of the struggle to preserve its national identity against non-European immigrants.[7]

Bruno Mégret put the problem dramatically: "Natality is not only a personal question, it is also the business of the entire community, and it is criminal to ignore the evil that threatens us. . . . A major natalist policy is vital and urgent."[8] In the battle of the birthrate, Frenchwomen are asked to emulate Joan of Arc in the campaign to evict foreigners from French soil. Unlike Joan, of course, contemporary women are not expected to don armor and wield swords; their uniform consists of the maternity dress, their armor is the baby carriage, and their sword is the infant they bear. This is why, in the Front's discourse, childbirth and motherhood are discussed in language more suitable to the battlefield than the nursery. "Let us break the curtain of silence which masks the dangers of the decrease in the birthrate," said Mégret, "in order to win what Jean-Marie Le Chevallier calls, 'the battle of the interior.'" Raising children is an "essential mission" that "works toward the survival of our people."[9] Le Pen compares an underpopulated France to a house that, left vacant by its owners, risks break-ins or occupation by squatters. Unless women bear more children, France will be "condemned to become the property of foreigners, the victim of all kinds of pillage and all kinds of oppressions."[10] According to one woman, "The wife of a militant ought to be both mother and quartermaster-general: thanks to her, the home front holds the line."[11]

Women Defending the Home Front

In the past French natality policies were driven by the specter of Germany, with its enormous advantage in population, threatening invasion from without. Today, however, the enemy is already within the gates, which explains the Front's obsession with crime and security. In a situation of total war where one cannot distinguish between the home front and the battlefield, a soldier's greatest fear, after concern for his own safety, is that his wife may be raped or murdered or his children taken away or killed by the enemy. These fears are heightened when the struggle takes on tribalistic overtones, when the battle is not only about keeping territory but also about preserving the "purity" of the race against the "other." "I am," Le Pen said, "a redskin chief who does not want to see his people submerged and liquidated by a tide of immigrants."[12] To lose territory would be a defeat; to lose the race through rape or intermarriage would mean total disaster. In an often-quoted remark, Le Pen warned on television in 1984, "Tomorrow the immigrants will move in with you, eat your soup and they will sleep with your wife, your daughter or your son."

The image of the wife-mother violated by the immigrant enemy is a favorite theme of the pro-Front press. In a September 1985 article in *National Hebdo* discussing a series of rapes that had taken place in Paris, NF Eurodeputy Martine Lehideux referred to "three women. Three Frenchwomen." Thus, it was not just women who had been attacked; it was France itself that had been sullied. The rapes were attributed to women's new style of living and to immigration.[13] During a 1989 demonstration protesting an attack on a woman in Avignon, Le Pen spoke of the victim as having "fallen before the Occupier." The crime was "a veritable taking symbolic possession of our earth and our people."[14]

The fear of racial mixing is endemic on the extreme right and was expressed most forcefully in November 1989 by the fundamentalist Monseigneur Lefebvre (excommunicated by the Catholic Church in June 1988) when he remarked: "The Muslims cannot be Catholics, they cannot even be truly French. They should not be allowed to organize either on the political or religious level.... It is your wives, your daughters, your children who will be kidnapped and brought to reserved areas like those that exist in Casablanca."[15]

According to the Front, morale on the home front is undermined by forces that attack the family and refuse to implement the natalist policies that are so essential in the struggle against immigrants. Particularly pernicious is the so-called feminist lobby, which is "remarkably" well positioned in the media and in political organizations. The feminist lobby has "inspired a whole series of laws which have encouraged the development of feminine wage-earners and imposed a devalued image of mothers of families." In addition, "socialists and social-democrats," obsessed by their egalitarian "vision" and their "contempt for the family," have worked to dissolve the family and "organic and natural communities" in order to isolate individuals within a "false and inorganic unity in a collectivist state."[16]

Women and Biology

In a situation of total war the individual must subsume her particular interest to the common cause. War is by its very nature anti-individualist; armies are, after all, the ultimate in corporatist institutions. In this context the Front's traditionalist views on women and the family fit neatly within the martial paradigm. For the Front, the fundamental institution in society is the family, whose rights and obligations are determined by the degree to which they contribute to the national interest. "One cannot conceive of man outside the family," wrote Yvan Blot, one of the Front's main theorists. "Neither can one conceive of him outside society or the framework of civilization."[17] From this perspective, the necessary precondition for the existence of society is the family. Moreover, societies can exist only if there are order and discipline. "A society lacking order," according to Yvan Blot, "is unthinkable, not only from the collective point of view but also because of the deepest part of human nature."[18] Individual obligations follow from the absolute necessity of maintaining societal order and stability; and societal order in turn depends on maintaining the integrity of the different groups that compose the whole, especially the family. Within the family "biological and cultural reality" determines that men and women must play different roles.[19] "Woman is by constitution, as Molière would say, predestined to assure the long life of the family and of the family line, and the physical, moral and affective education of her child."[20] Thus, women's "fundamental mission" is to give birth and educate children.[21] Of course, this is straightforward naturalism, the view that the political and social order must reflect an underlying natural order—or risk moral decay and political anarchy. In this the Front reflects not only traditional French conservative values but also the influence of Catholic fundamentalists in the Front for whom procreation is the "destiny," and "finality" of women; it is their "mission," their "original vocation." An article in the *Bulletin* of the Centre National des Femmes d'Europe (National Center of European Women), an ancillary organization of the Front, speaks of women "accomplishing their biological destiny in the transmission of life and their social destiny in the education of their children."[22] According to one Front member: "For me, women's role is above all the transmission of life. Because without giving life there is death. The day when we cease transmitting life people will die; civilization will die."[23] From this perspective, women possess rights and privileges only insofar as they are in accordance with the "facts" of biology, culture, or history and do not conflict with the higher interests of the French nation. Obviously, this view nicely combines biological teleology with the imperatives of war.

Women and the Family

Within the Front's organic, anti-individualist, antiegalitarian view of society, women are expected to subsume their own interests to those of the nation as a whole. Thus, the mothers who lead the Front's May Day parade celebrate not only Joan-Mary as virgin-mother and Joan as warrior but also Joan's willingness to sacrifice herself for the nation, the ultimate virtue of the soldier. Subordination of self for the larger good is a constant theme in the works of extreme right ideologues such as Charles Maurras. According to Maurras, the nation is

> the largest of the communitarian circles which are, in the temporal world, solid and complete. . . . It is necessary to defend the nation, whatever it may cost. . . . In a word, the nation occupies the summit of the hierarchy of political ideas. . . . Subsuming all the other great common interests and holding them dependent, it is perfectly clear that in the event of conflict all interests ought to cede to it. . . . The nation is superior to all the groups [that compose] the nation.[24]

Among these "circles," the Front gives pride of place to the family as "one of the principal foundations of society."[25] This is consistent with Maurras, for whom "the family founds the State. . . . Society begins with the family, its first unit. It continues in the commune, the professional and religious association, the infinite variety of groups, bodies, companies and communities, lacking which human life would perish."[26]

It is to the family that the individual owes her first obligation, which is why the family plays such a large role in the Front's political discourse. In the chapter devoted to "Family" in *300 mesures,* the word *family* appears fifty-two times; the word *mother,* nine times; the phrase *pregnant mother,* once; and the word *woman,* four times. For the Front, the primacy of the family follows from the facts of human nature. In the words of Le Pen's trademark refrain: "I like my daughters more than my cousins, my cousins more than my neighbors, my neighbors better than those I don't know and those I don't know better than my enemies. Consequently I like the French better. . . . I like the Europeans next, and then I like westerners, and then I like those countries in the world which are allies and those which like France."[27]

An ideology that sees the family as the primary unit of society must naturally oppose a philosophy that takes the individual as the basic unit of society. Thus, the Front attacks the Declaration of the Rights of Man as a Socialist propaganda "tool, a 'quasi-religion' which has passed out of the political domain and entered into the moral order of good and evil. . . . It puts the accent on the individual and passes over in silence all reference to communities which are nonetheless indispensable for the development of man, like the family and the country."[28] It is the individualism of the Declaration of the Rights of Man that "denies the general principle of authority" and that does not recognize the "rights of the family, of the nation and of the rights linked to the survival and continued existence of the line."[29] Society cannot survive as a conglomeration of "narcissistic individuals" without roots in the community and in the groups that compose it. It is individualism that has led to the declining birthrate and to the threat to France's national identity. According to Bruno Mégret, the "turning inward to oneself [and] lack of interest in the homeland [la patrie] lead to a refusal to give birth."[30] The nation can survive only if individuals look beyond their private interests to the larger interests of the family and of the nation. Since the family is the basic building block of the nation, both can survive only if women bear children. Women perform an invaluable role, which is, according to Le Pen, "to transmit and conserve life" and to "defend the values of the household, education and upbringing."[31]

One can see the opposition between women's rights and group rights expressed in a negative way by Bruno Mégret, who stated that "the socialist version of 'women's rights,' is opposed to the right of families."[32] Because individual rights and privileges must be subsumed to the higher interests of corporate groups or bodies, women's access to abortion ("anti-French genocide," according to Bernard Antony) must give way to the higher interests of the family and the nation.[33] Most Front leaders, especially those from the fundamentalist right, oppose abortion on natural law grounds, but in public discourse the Front stresses how abortion undermines the battle of the birthrate.[34] According to the Front, "The demographic survival of the nation is a major point which justifies every sacrifice."[35] Women who refuse to become mothers, or who reject the maternal ideal, strike at the very heart of society. In 1978 Le Pen said: "It isn't easy to say to a woman, in order to save society and our future, that women must have children, that they must accept the fact that these children will eventually serve [in the army] and perhaps die to defend the freedom of the country, that there must be an authority and we think that men are the best qualified authority in the household."[36]

Women, Equality, and the Natural Order

In 1992 *Présent* attacked a 1991 decision of the European Court of Justice enjoining France to allow women to work at night. According to *Présent*, the French law banning night work for women was "protective inequality, the fruit of centuries of Christian civilization . . . one of whose flowers remains courtesy and the chivalric spirit. Obsessed by the egalitarian myth . . . the complementarity of the sexes has become for the government an unknown notion."[37]

The organic view of society prescribes that the sexes have different and complementary roles to play. Moreover, the process of natural selection has governed the rate and direction of human progress and the different roles that men and women play in society. Nature itself suggests that equality is impossible.

According to Le Pen: "The egalitarian movement, which consists in leveling out ages, sexes and peoples, must be criticized because it masks reality, which is fundamentally inegalitarian; that is to say, there are inequalities which are just and equalities which are unjust. We are for justice and not for equality. The theme of equality seems decadent to us."[38]

One example of a just inequality is illustrated by the Front's proposal to grant to families extra votes for each child under the age of majority.[39] Whether the mother or the father is to cast the extra votes for the children is not explained.[40] For the Front, equality falls before the fact that all civilizations are "founded on groups, communities, norms, rules and institutions and all imply difference, limits . . . a legitimate exclusion which simply constitutes the frontier between those who are part of the group and those who are not. . . . To throw down these barriers is to deny, for example, the family or the enterprise and to want to destroy the entire social structure."[41]

"All life is exclusion! The family is exclusive," proclaimed Le Pen.[42] In this view society is composed of a series of watertight vessels, each with its own role and character such that any attempt to combine them leads inevitably to their destruction. Thus, the vast majority of Muslim immigrants who have come to France from the Third World and Africa "can never be assimilated to the French people."[43] Nor can homosexuals or lesbians. If the social order ceases to reflect the natural order, then decline, decay, and, ultimately, destruction are inevitable. "Confusion of the sexes" is both a cause and a sign of "decadence." Terms such as *decline* and *decadence* are often used by the Front to characterize those aspects of French society that depart from the ideal natural order set forth in the organic model.[44]

The Front's conservative, organic ideology takes seriously the notion that individuals owe an obligation both to the past and to posterity. For the Front, to be French means that one is part of a millennia-long tradition out of which the nation and the culture have evolved. Without this inheritance, the individual would be nothing; it is therefore the obligation of each individual to preserve this tradition. But modern individualist, liberal society emphasizes private interests and selfishness over continuity and tradition. The most self-centered are the elderly, who have only a short time left on earth and who, for that reason, support short-term policies that are to their immediate benefit. Young people with children, however, are forced to look beyond their own concerns to the future of their children. This is why the Front favors a broad array of measures, including the family vote, to encourage mothers to bear children and to raise large families. However, the emphasis is on mothers, not women. Clearly, mothers whose mission is to save the nation from destruction perform a more vital role than women who work for its (and their) material benefit.

Women and Social Policy

In wartime one major goal of social policy is to preserve social cohesion. In the peculiar circumstances of the current battle revolving around the birthrate and the protection of French culture from enemies within, preservation of the family and enhancement of the role of the mother are vital weapons. The NF's social policy "consists above all of freeing the French from the exploitative State in order to help them find the protective State."[45] Although the NF wishes to sharply limit those areas of civil society in which the state plays a role, and shares New Right criticisms on the waste and inefficiency of state bureaucracies, the Front does not take a libertarian perspective that any exercise of state power is an infringement on individual liberties and is necessarily evil. Rather, the NF starts with the accusation that the French state is in the hands of the "establishment," or an "all-powerful oligarchy," and that its activities must be reoriented toward the first line of defense against immigrants and other hostile elements, namely, mothers and families.

Every policy that threatens traditional practices or structures is to be downgraded or eliminated in order to shore up threatened institutions. For example, the Front's 1985 election program stated: "One must affirm the preference for marriage: in every area the law ought to be in favor of marriage and not against it."[46] The program explicitly stated that "it can be preferable to 'de-legislate' some measures which thwart the development of the family."[47] Above all, women are encouraged to have children, and the more the better. That is why the Front proposed in 1985 to give priority to mothers with three or more children in the allocation of the "mother's income." Families would be given preferential access to a variety of collective goods, including public transport and housing. "Their [mothers'] mission, essential with regard to the community and its future, would thereby be officially recognized: a mother of a family is not 'without profession' but in charge of one of the noblest of tasks. Those who work toward the survival of our people merit at least the same treatment as women who work only toward its prosperity."[48]

The adjectives tell all. The role of a mother is "essential"; her task is "noble." Above all, the woman as warrior ensures the "survival" of the nation. No wonder the main object of the Front's social policies is to encourage women to leave the workforce, reduce their reliance on the public sector for child care and education, and spend more time with their families.

What the Front does not say, however, and what it denies, is that adoption of its policies would deprive women (including mothers) of some of the major social policy gains of the past two decades. Antinatalist measures such as state reimbursement of abortion and public funding of contraceptives and family planning clinics would be abolished. Abortion services would no longer be reimbursed by the state.[49] Le Pen and the Front also frown on unmarried people living together (mainly because they have fewer children than married couples), on "sexual dilettantism" (promiscuousness), and on divorce.[50] At the same time, those Front social policies that purport to eliminate financial disincentives for women staying at home with children would seriously undermine existing state-provided services. For example, France leads Europe in providing prekindergarten and nursery school services for working mothers. But Le Pen attacked this system when he explained that "a women who decides to raise her very young children at home will alleviate the task, and the budget as well, of the Education Ministry. There will, consequently, be a reduction in the exorbitant weight of collective institutions such as crèches whose cost to the nation is often more than the actual gain for mothers."[51]

Exactly how one calculates the difference between the "gain for women" and the cost to the nation of these services is not clear. But Le Pen's swipe at the crèche system does suggest that a Front government would discourage public provision of crèche and nursery school services. This, in turn, would force women to remain at home in order to receive government support—unless, of course, a woman had sufficient resources to make use of private day care, while those without resources would have no alternative but to remain at home with their children.

The Front's views on social policy reflect the obsession with motherhood, the birthrate, and immigrants. On retirement policy, for example, the Front explains that the decline in the number of active young people has meant a reduction in pensions, which, in turn, is due to "a systematically hostile attitude to families and birth (the active workers of tomorrow) . . . and by the encouragement of abortion."[52] In the Front women make their appearance on the social policy stage almost exclusively as wives and mothers enrolled in the battle to preserve France. Little is said about mothers with fewer than three children, widows, single women, divorced women, women who have separated from their husbands, or women living with but not married to partners—although the latter relationship is referred to disparagingly as "concubinage."

Women in the National Front

Women play an enormously important role in the symbology of the National Front. They are warriors in the battle against the immigrant-enemy, but their weapon—the bearing of children—is provided by biology. Whereas the soldier who shirks battle defaults before his duty to the country, the woman who refuses to bear children defaults before nature itself. When a soldier is wounded in battle, he evokes the horror of war. When a "Frenchwoman" is assaulted or raped by the immigrant-enemy (or voluntarily marries or lives with the immigrant-enemy), then the family, the nation, and the race itself are defiled. From this one might assume that women would play a large role in the Front's organization, but in fact they are hardly present at all in leadership positions. In the 1994 elections to the Front's executive organs, only two women, ex-deputy Marie-France Stirbois and MEP Martine Lehideux, who leads a Front women's group, were elected to the forty-member political bureau. A survey of the delegates to the NF's 1990 party congress found that 82 percent of the delegates were men and 18 percent were women.[53]

Despite the underrepresentation of women in the higher reaches of the party organization, an increasing number of women have been voting for the Front to the point where, in the March 1993 legislative elections, the percentage of women voters was nearly equal to that of male voters. This calls into question the assumption that because the Front is antifeminist, it is condemned to rely on a largely masculine electorate.[54] Unlike the Poujadists, whose leader once characterized Poujadism as having as "much intellectual content as a scream," the National Front's ideology has been developed by some of the best minds on the French extreme right. Drawing on the work of Antonio Gramsci, they have mounted a sophisticated and powerful campaign to convince the French public that metaphors of war and conflict are the best way to define the current political struggle in France. Thus far only a minority of French voters have followed their lead, but among them are a large number of women who wholeheartedly accept the martial metaphor and view the Front's conservative, organic ideology as the only possible response to the enemies within.

Notes

1. Jean-Marie Le Pen, *Le Pen 91* (Paris: Éditions de Présent, 1991), p. 64.

2. Ibid. In 1991 Leon Dégrelle, the founder of Belgian fascism, evoked Joan during the "dark days of 1944" as "guiding European warriors in the death struggle" against the "verminous" Soviet onslaught. Quoted in *Le Monde*, October 18, 1991. By contrast, Socialist leader Michel Rocard, speaking at Orleans in 1990, observed: "In Joan's time the very word 'nation' did not have its current meaning. . . . What was important in her eyes was respect for legitimate power. . . . Nothing about Joan spoke of exclusion." Quoted in *Le Monde*, May 10, 1990.

3. *Le Monde*, March 3, 1990.

4. Quoted in Claudie Lesselier, "De la Vierge Marie à Jeanne d'Arc: Images de femmes à l'extrême droite," *L'Homme et la Société* 99–100 (1991):106.

5. Jean-Marie Le Pen, *Les Français d'abord* (Paris: Carrère/Laffon, 1984), pp. 196–197, 197.

6. "It should be emphasized that official institutions underestimate the reality since they don't always distinguish between births to foreigners and births to the French." Le Pen, *Pour la France*, pp. 125–126.

7. Front National, *300 mesures pour la renaissance de la France* (Paris: Éditions Nationales, 1993), p. 53.

8. Bruno Mégret, *La flamme* (Paris: Robert Laffont, 1990), p. 257.

9. Ibid., p. 278.

10. Le Pen, *Pour la France*, p. 129.

11. Quoted in Fiametta Venner, "Le militantisme féminin d'extrême droite: Une autre manière d'etre féministe?" *French Politics and Society* 11, 2 (Spring 1993):40.

12. Quoted in *Le Monde*, February 29, 1988.

13. Le Pen, *Pour la France*, p. 129.

14. Lehideux and Le Pen, quoted in Lesselier, "De la Vierge Marie," p. 104.

15. Quoted in *Le Monde*, November 16, 1989.

16. Le Pen, *Pour la France*, p. 128.

17. Yvan Blot, *Les racines de la liberté* (Paris: Albin Michel, 1985), p. 108.

18. Ibid., p. 113.

19. "Lately, official speeches have . . . tried to devalue the role of the mother and to abolish all differences in the functions of men and women. This utopian attitude denies biological and cultural reality, which gives women a special responsibility in procreation and in the education of children." Le Pen, *Pour la France*, p. 134.

20. Quoted in Deborah R. Levy, "Women of the French National Front," *Parliamentary Affairs* 42, 1 (January 1989):107.

21. "It's not a question of imposing on women something they might think of as a new kind of servitude. It's just a question of admitting the facts; namely that women are invested with a fundamental mission both at the individual as well as the collective level—to transmit life and educate children." Jean-Marie Le Pen, *L'Espoir* (Paris: Albatros, 1989), p. 18.

22. Lesselier, "De la Vierge Marie," p. 100.

23. Catherine, a forty-two-year-old member of the Front's Cercle National des Femmes d'Europe, quoted in Fiammetta Venner, "Le militantisme féminin," p. 45.

24. Charles Maurras, *Mes idées politiques*, rpt. (Paris: Albatros, n.d.), p. 282.

25. Front National, *300 mesures*, p. 58.

26. Maurras, *Mes idées*, p. 176.

27. Le Pen repeats this remark ad nauseum in his speeches to defend the Front's anti-immigrant policies. A variation of this phrase appears in a photograph taken during the 1956 election campaign, which shows Le Pen under a banner with the slogan "I like my village more than your village; I like my province more than your province; I like France above all." Quoted in Gilles Bresson and Christian Lionet, *Le Pen* (Paris: Seuil, 1994), p. 128.

28. Mégret, *La flamme*, p. 39. According to Charles Maurras: "When our foremost political philosopher, infuriated by the constant talk of man, of his rights, of his obligations, protested that he knew Frenchmen, Englishmen, Germans and Russians, that nowhere had he encountered an abstract man, he was denouncing . . . the methodological error of those legislators who thought that the destinies of a whole people could be settled by aphorisms which did not apply to it. Politics is not morality." Quoted in J. S. McClelland, *The French Right* (London: Jonathan Cape, 1970), p. 252.

29. Jean-Marie Le Pen, *Le Monde*, August 29, 1989.

30. Mégret, *La flamme*, p. 89.

31. Quoted in *Le Monde*, November 10, 1989.

32. Mégret, *La flamme*, p. 32.

33. *Le Monde*, February 29, 1988.

34. For Le Pen and many Front leaders, abortion is murder. By contrast, however, a majority of those who vote for the Front are pro-choice.

35. Le Pen, *Pour la France*, p. 137.

36. Quoted in Jean-Pierre Apparu, *La Droite aujourd'hui*, (Paris: Albin Michel, 1978), pp. 178–179.

37. *Présent*, February 28, 1992. Charles Maurras used the term *protective inequality*. See McLelland, *The French Right*, p. 264.

38. Quoted in Apparu, *La Droite*, p. 179.

39. Under Vichy there were many proposals to give fathers the right to vote for their children. In addition, large families were encouraged by the government hiring 15 percent more civil servants who had three children and reducing by 15 percent those civil servants who had none. Jean-Pierre Azéma, "Vichy," in Michel Winock, ed., *Histoire de l'extrême droite en France* (Paris: Seuil, 1993), p. 199.

40. Front National, *300 mesures*, p. 61. The idea of a family vote had been put forward between the wars by the L'Alliance Nationale pour l'Accroissement de la Population Française (National Alliance for Increasing the French Population). Françoise Thébaud, "Maternité et famille entre les deux guerres: Idéologies et politique familiale," in Rita Thalmann, ed., *Femmes et fascismes* (Paris: Tierce, 1986), p. 89.

41. Mégret, *La flamme*, p. 35.

42. Quoted in Lesselier, "De la Vierge Marie," p. 101.

43. Ibid., p. 55.

44. When applied to the economy, the organic model takes the form of corporatism. "Our regime will make the class struggle impossible insofar as all those who cooperate in production constitute an organic whole in this regime." Internal NF document, quoted in *Le Monde*, March 6, 1992.

45. Front National, *300 mesures*, p. 221.

46. Le Pen, *Pour la France*, p. 132.

47. Ibid.

48. Mégret, *La flamme*, p. 278.

49. "The acceptance of life is one of the criteria which characterizes great civilizations and distinguishes them from periods of decadence and barbarism. While contraception is a choice made in the private sphere into which the state should not enter, it's not the same for abortion which concerns a third of infants about to be born." Front National, *300 mesures*, p. 63.

50. Ibid.; and Front National, *300 mesures*, p. 54.

51. Le Pen, *L'Espoir*, p. 19.

52. Front National, *300 mesures*, p. 219. Le Pen's personal behavior in these areas is hardly a model for Front supporters to emulate.

53. Collette Ysmal, "Les cadres du Front National: Les habits neufs de l'extrême droite," in SOFRES, ed., *L'État de l'opinion, 1991* (Paris: Seuil, 1991), pp. 181–197.

54. "The National Front promotes an image of women that is viewed by many as a regression and a threat to the rights they have won. . . . It is not difficult to see why so few women support the National Front." Levy, "Women of the French National Front," p. 102.

Conclusion

One doesn't know precisely where the extreme-right begins, but one knows very well which way it can go.
—*André Laurens, in* Le Monde, *February 28, 1965*

In our modern age, nationalism is not resurgent: it never died. Neither did racism. They are the most powerful movements in the world today.
—*Isaiah Berlin, quoted in Nathan Gardels, "Two Concepts of Nationalism"*

Exactly fifty years after the destruction of the fascist regimes, National Front leader Jean-Marie Le Pen won the support of 15 percent of the electorate in the 1995 French presidential election, thereby confirming the Front's place as the third major political force in France. Two months later in local elections, the voters sent 1,075 Frontists to city councils throughout France, while Front candidates won the mayoralty races in three French cities, including the port city of Toulon. By the mid-1990s the National Front had become the most powerful and influential extreme right political party in Europe.

What accounts for the rise of the NF? A number of factors contributed to its success. One was that by sheer virtue of intelligence, energy, combativeness, and charisma, Jean-Marie Le Pen fused together the disparate forces of the extreme right under his personal leadership. For decades after 1945 the French extreme right had wasted its energies on divisive personal and obscure doctrinal quarrels. Occasionally, one or another group would enter candidates in parliamentary elections, but on those rare occasions when a few extremists were elected to the National Assembly, they quickly abandoned their original party allegiance and switched to the mainstream parties, hoping to pursue a more secure career in politics than was offered on the fringes of the political party system.

By the mid-1960s, however, Le Pen and other extreme right leaders had begun to argue that the extreme right was doomed to marginality unless it abjured the violent street-fighting tactics of the late 1940s and 1950s and ended the infighting, personal quarrels, and ideological schisms that undercut any possibility of success at the ballot box. In 1972 Le Pen helped convince the scattered forces of the extreme right to federate under the aegis of a new political movement called the National Front. Nevertheless, it took another decade before the NF garnered enough votes to be considered a serious contender for political power. And it took twenty years before the NF first posed a serious threat to the stability of the French political system: Le Pen came in fourth in the 1988 presidential election with 14.41 percent of the vote, just behind former Prime Minister Raymond Barre with 16.55 percent. Le Pen's astounding showing led *Le Monde* to speak of a "shock wave," and it warned of the increasing dependence of the centrist parties on the extreme right.[1] Thus, the Front's success was no accident, for over the decades since 1972 Le Pen has built the NF into a formidable party machine with all the accoutrements of an orthodox political party, including a hierarchical organization, local branches throughout the country, a series of affiliated organizations, and a highly sophisticated election and propaganda apparatus.

A second factor contributing to the success of the NF was the disappearance of President de Gaulle from the French political scene in 1969. Twice in French history, during the German Occupation and then during the fall of the Fourth Republic, de Gaulle had held aloft the flame of French unity, eventually becoming an icon of France itself. De Gaulle's powerful and idiosyncratic influence on France made it impossible for either the left or the right to follow its own political compass as both floundered in his wake. As the first president of the Fifth Republic, de Gaulle had a disastrous effect on the extreme right, which never could decide whether to support him as the linchpin of French unity against the Communist menace, to oppose him as an obstacle to their own success, or, as in the case of the OAS, to kill him as the man who betrayed the cause of French Algeria. It was only after de Gaulle resigned from office in 1969 that the extreme right could oppose the government without appearing to call the Republic into question.

A third factor was the growing ideological sophistication of extreme right theorists. During the 1960s and 1970s, dynamic, young intellectuals looking for some way to save the extreme right from extinction organized small groups and political clubs, such as GRECE and the Club de l'Horloge, and subjected every aspect of their political doctrine to intense examination and criticism. Ultimately, these intellectuals stripped the extreme right doctrine of its most egregiously antidemocratic elements; tried to bring it into line with the findings of modern biology, history, and sociology; and questioned whether violence was the best way to catch the attention of the electorate and win a hearing for the party. This new breed of intellectuals tried to fashion a program that would be acceptable to the French public and organize a political party that could become a serious player in the French political game. The beneficiary was the National Front, which by the 1980s could boast a highly structured, comprehensive party organization and a doctrine that was far more sophisticated, complex, subtle—and elusive—than the doctrines of wartime or postwar fascist parties. Thanks to the efforts of intellectuals such as Alain de Benoist, civil servants such as Bruno Mégret, and, above all, Jean-Marie Le Pen, the NF developed a political vocabulary that attempted to conceal the racist and anti-Semitic elements of the Front's doctrine in a fog of rhetoric and coded language and that appealed to a broad cross-section of the French electorate threatened by social change and economic crisis.

A fourth factor contributing to the rise of the Front has to do with the inability of government to cope with the urban and political crises of the 1980s. According to Françoise Gaspard, former Socialist mayor of Dreux, where the Front won a breakthrough election in 1983, support for extremism, "like suicide, prospers in times of urban crisis and growing individualism and in the vacuum left by the disappearance of old networks of social interaction and solidarity."[2] Gaspard explained the NF's success in terms of urban decay and the fact that in France, more than most European countries, the French administrative and political apparatus "distrusted" the population. As the Socialist Party and its allied associations abandoned the cities and urban housing estates, the NF began in the early 1980s to take up the slack with its own network of organizations, which helped legitimize the NF in the eyes of residents and build a basis for electoral support.

Gaspard particularly criticized the Socialist Party for isolating itself from the social movements, trade unions, and pressure groups that form the associative life of democracy. And she cited Alain Touraine, who warned the Socialists not to mistake the party for society and who suggested that they leave the "vestibules of power" and enter into contact with the various oppressed groups of society.[3] Other analysts have suggested that the NF speaks for people who are not represented by the orthodox political parties of the left and right: the unemployed, part-time workers, workers in insecure jobs, young people without training, and white-collar workers anxious about their jobs and economic security.[4]

A fifth factor helping to explain the rise of the NF was that the major political traumas of the 1960s—the end of the Algerian War and the 1968 student revolution—removed a number of obstacles to unity on the extreme right and taught extreme right intellectuals important lessons about revising and revitalizing their outworn doctrines. De Gaulle's success in crushing the terrorist OAS, dedicated to avenging the "sellout" of French Algeria, demonstrated to extremists that terror and violence alone could not destabilize a political system or reverse a policy that enjoyed majority support. The May 1968 student revolution and the importance that new ideas, rather than any particular concatenation of socioeconomic factors, played in winning support for the students showed the way forward for an ideological renovation of the extreme right. Particularly important was the increased role that issues of culture, race, and ethnicity were playing in politics, as contrasted to the diminishing importance of class and its relation to the distribution of power.[5]

A sixth factor was the Front's ability to target Muslim and African immigrants as the source of almost every problem from AIDS to unemployment. According to Jean-Marie Le Pen, "Because of immigration, unemployment, crime, delinquency and drug abuse increase between 8–10 percent every year."[6] The solution the Front proposes is to round up and deport from France as many Muslim and African immigrants as possible. To encourage immigrants to leave "voluntarily," and to discourage any further immigration, the Front concocted the national preference policy, which means the government discriminates against immigrants by giving French nationals preference in employment, social welfare, health, and education. However, unlike overtly racist parties elsewhere, the Front does not justify its policy in terms of some putative superiority of the French over other races or nationalities. Rather, the NF rationalizes the national preference policy in the name of the right to difference. According to Bruno Mégret, "All civilizations are founded on groups and communities, norms, rules and institutions and all imply differences, limits." Mégret said that it is perfectly legitimate to want to exclude people of different cultures and religions from one's own country, and he warned that to "get rid of . . . barriers [against immigration] is to want to destroy all social structures."[7] Those who want to lower barriers against immigration are accused by the Front of being anti-French racists since their policies would lead to swamping France with hordes of unassimilable immigrants.

Although a national preference policy is contrary to French law, Mégret promised in June 1995 that if elected mayor of Vitrolles, he would implement the policy "behind the scenes," while another leading member of the Front promised that the Front would go "head to head" with the law if necessary to implement the national preference policy.[8] When three Front mayors were elected in June 1995, however, they were more cautious than Mégret, promising to implement the national preference policy within the limits of the law. Exactly how they meant to do this, given that the policy is illegal, remains to be seen.

The use of phrases such as *the right to difference* and *anti-French racism* is part of the Front's strategy of deliberately appropriating the political vocabulary of its critics to turn it against them. After all, many antiracist groups use the right to difference argument to defend their heritage and culture against incursions from the larger society, and they certainly accuse their own critics of being racists. But antiracist groups have never implied, as the Front does, that the Muslim or North African cultures are so rigid that they prevent individual Muslims or North Africans from integrating into French society and becoming fully "French." In the hands of the Front, however, the right to difference becomes the right to exclude. According to Bruno Mégret: "Today the big battalions of immigration come from the Third World and mainly Africa. They are mostly Muslims and do not assimilate to the French people." And he commented sarcastically, "It is no longer a question of the immigrants adapting themselves to French morals: it is up to us to adapt the rules of the Republic to the demands of the Koran."[9] For the Front, therefore, those who support policies of multiculturalism or integration are mortal enemies of French national identity; they are anti-French racists. French scholar Pierre-André Taguieff, a leading critic of the Front, maintained that "the cult of difference serves to make acceptable both an obsessive fear of contact [with other cultures] and a phobia about mixing races which is at the heart of racism. . . . [Racists] make cultural differences absolute."[10]

The measure of Le Pen's success in forcing immigration to the top of France's political agenda was dramatically underlined in the 1980s when France's top political leaders began to echo the Front's argument that immigration was a "problem" that had to be "solved." Former President Valéry Giscard d'Estaing expressed views very close to those of the Front when he proposed that race, rather than residence, be the basis for acquisition of French citizenship. Former Prime Minister Jacques Chirac mentioned the "noise and smell" of immigrants and talked about an "overdose" of immigration. Even Socialist president François Mitterrand spoke of a "threshold of tolerance" for immigrants.[11]

In the 1980s and 1990s the popularity of the Front's anti-immigrant message led the mainstream right to adopt some of its policies. Influenced by the Front's 1995 local election victories and public reaction to terror bombings allegedly carried out by fundamentalist Algerian groups in France, the Chirac administration stepped up its campaign against "illegal immigrants," promising to expel fifteen thousand immigrants on chartered flights in 1996 and thirty thousand in 1997. One recent book on racism in France concluded that "the rise of popular racism is worrying; the fact that it is put forward and orchestrated by the National Front is even more worrying. But most serious is that the general evolution of the political system [shows] the beginnings of an alignment of many political leaders, not with the policies of the National Front, but at least with its general themes."[12]

A seventh factor in the NF's success has been the important role that anti-Semitism plays in maintaining cohesion among party cadres. While abjuring the blatant anti-Semitism of the prewar extreme right, the Front smuggles its anti-Semitism into speeches, publications, and propaganda by resorting to codewords or coded phrases that clearly refer to Jews and Jewish organizations. Of course, the Front denies accusations of anti-

Semitism, pointing to the presence of a few Jewish members within the party as proof. Nor does the Front directly accuse Jews of being the enemies of France or call for their expulsion. The cry "*Mort aux Juifs* (Death to the Jews!)" heard at anti-Semitic rallies before the war, has never passed the lips of Front leaders—at least in public. But the Front tirelessly criticizes "cosmopolitan and *mondialiste*" lobbies, which, it claims, are "anti-France" and work to destroy French culture and traditions. Front leaders talk about "occult oligarchies" that manipulate the French political system from behind the scenes.

An eighth factor has been a major shift in the defining issues of party politics.[13] French sociologist Alain Touraine pointed out that in the past there was a loose correlation between social classes and interest groups or specific political parties, with classes, groups, and parties dividing roughly along the same lines over issues concerning the management of the economy, social welfare, or health policy. But this is no longer the case. Now questions concerning immigration, law and order, and the role of the European Community constitute new lines of division between societal groups and political parties. According to Touraine, "*The national question is replacing the social question* at the center of political life."[14] Many people fear that poor immigrants, or richer, more powerful countries, threaten French culture, language, and traditions. "It would be absurd to caricature this resistance and this defense [of French culture and society] which feels threatened by increasing and poorly directed changes. Even more absurd is to believe that this defense of national identity is characteristic only of racist extremists and fascists."[15]

Touraine's argument about the growing importance of the national question helps place the success of the National Front in the 1980s and 1990s within the context of a secular change in the nature of political ideologies. Interest politics has been replaced by value politics. As the correlation between class and party weakens, and as the centrality of questions concerning the role of the state in the economy (nationalization, worker participation in industry, union power) gives way to concern over national identity, corruption in politics, immigration, crime, and housing, a broad cross-section of the French electorate has turned to the Front for answers.

Recently, the Socialists, and now the mainstream right parties, have been rocked by scandals. The Socialists were accused while in power of funneling money into party coffers; more recently President Chirac and Prime Minister Alain Juppé were accused of providing family members with rent-subsidized apartments in the heart of Paris. Like the Italian ex-MSI or the Belgian National Front, the French National Front has taken advantage of such scandals by fiercely attacking political corruption in high places and posing as the morally pure, incorruptible alternative to the existing parties.

One of Le Pen's most popular election slogans over the past few years has been "Head held high; clean hands."

Finally, one should not ignore the contribution that old-fashioned local party organizing had made to the success of the Front. The NF can count on the devotion of thousands of party workers and militants who distribute literature, staff telephones, organize local interest groups, and attend party meetings. In 1995 *Le Monde* reported that the Front was using innovative methods to get its message across to the public: Rather than distributing pamphlets, the NF was organizing "Tupperware"-type meetings at which videocassettes from the party were played; NF activists also reportedly were trying to learn the names of people who had been victims of crime and establishing "solidarity" funds to help them.[16] The discipline and energy of ordinary Front members have begun to inspire the same respect, and fear, as Communist Party militants did during the party's heyday in the 1950s and 1960s.

The question in the 1990s is, Which way will the National Front go? Will it join the mainstream parties of the right? Will it gradually drift toward neofascism? Or will it disintegrate into a series of quarreling, doctrinaire, and violent factions, as was the case after World War II? Like other political parties, the National Front is a composite of people with different and often conflicting views and of competing factions and currents, some pulling the party toward the center, others toward outright fascism. Which direction the party will choose remains to be seen, although one indication will come from the behavior over the next few years of the more than one thousand municipal councillors and the three NF mayors who were elected in the 1995 local elections. Soon after the election, for example, the NF mayors rejected Le Pen's notion that the national preference policy should immediately be implemented. Nonetheless, the NF mayors will doubtless do everything they can to test the limits of the law while trying to curtail immigrants' access to social, welfare, and housing services. Moreover, as long as the Front continues to win elections and to hold its own in the polls, internal quarrels are unlikely to lead to serious splits in the party.

As for the future, the composition of the leadership and current party doctrine do not bode well for democracy. The National Front is led by a man, Jean-Marie Le Pen, whose anti-Semitic, racist remarks have provoked outrage and condemnation, whose commitment to democracy is uncertain, and who counts among his friends and associates ex-Nazis, Vichyites, collaborators, virulent anti-Semites, and racists. The executive organs of the National Front are staffed by some of these same people, many of whom yearn for the restoration of a Vichy-style authoritarianism or for the return of a rigidly hierarchical corporatism. In addition, polls have shown that the cadres of the National Front have only a limited commitment to democracy.

More foreboding are the views expressed by the party's second in command and Le Pen's likely successor, Bruno Mégret. Over the years he has expressed thinly veiled anti-Semitic sentiments, his immigration proposals have been racist and authoritarian, and his commitment to democratic rules of the game is in doubt. Finally, as I have shown, the coded language of the Front's program conceals a pervasive anti-Semitism, racism, and hostility to democracy. In 1996, therefore, the Front is stationed on that amorphous boundary that distinguishes legitimate, democratic parties from those that would overthrow democracy and install a dictatorial or authoritarian system. As such, it continues to pose a serious threat to French democracy.

Notes

1. *Le Monde*, April 26, 1988.

2. Françoise Gaspard, *A Small City in France* (Cambridge, Mass.: Harvard University Press, 1995), p. 161.

3. Ibid., p. 167. Other critics support the view that the National Front was more sensitive than the left or the mainstream right to the issues and concerns of various sectors of the population and social movements that began to arise in the 1980s and 1990s. See, for example, Suzanne Berger, "Politics and Antipolitics in Western Europe in the Seventies," *Daedalus* 108, 1 (Winter 1979):40 ff.

4. Michel Surya, "Editorial," *Lignes* 4 (October 1988):9.

5. On this point, see René Rémond, *Les droites en France* (Paris: Aubier Montaigne, 1982), pp. 269–270.

6. Jean-Marie Le Pen, *Le Pen 91* (Paris: Présent, 1991), p. 120.

7. Bruno Mégret, *La flamme* (Paris: Robert Laffont, 1990), p. 35.

8. In *Le Monde*, June 18–19, 1995, Mégret said that national preference could be implemented only in a *façon larvée* (concealed fashion), while Franck Timmermans spoke of a *bras de fer avec l'État* (Indian wrestling with the state).

9. Mégret, *La flamme*, pp. 55, 57.

10. Pierre-André Taguieff, "Vous avez dit différence?" *Le Nouvel Observateur*, September 25, 1987. However, some Socialists were opposed to the implications of the "right to difference." Unlike the Frontists, Chevènement's opposition to the "right to difference" was not motivated by a disguised racism but rather by fear that multiculturalism would undermine the unitary, centralized French state.

11. On October 10, 1989, President Mitterrand said: "The threshold of tolerance was reached in the 1970s when there were already 4.1 to 4.2 million residence permits. As far as possible, this figure must not be exceeded." Mitterrand subsequently regretted this remark, saying that it had been misinterpreted. According to the former Socialist mayor of Dreux, "The entire French political system, the left included, is moving to the right in adopting a vocabulary and themes imposed by what was, only ten years ago, a tiny group contained at the very edge of the Republic." Françoise Gaspard, *Une petite ville en France* (Paris: Gallimard, 1990), p. 239.

12. Michel Wieviorka, *La France raciste* (Paris: Seuil, 1992), p. 343.

13. Martin A. Schain explained the rise of the Front in terms of "the declining political confidence in the government of the left . . . the sense of economic crisis encouraged by government policy and unemployment . . . . [and] the continuing lack of confidence in the parties of the right." Martin A. Schain, "The National Front in France and the Construction of Political Legitimacy," *West European Politics* 10, 2 (April 1987):230.

14. Quoted in *Le Monde*, March 13, 1990. Two weeks after Touraine's remarks were reported in *Le Monde*, the NF's delegate general, Bruno Mégret, observed, "The major political competition . . . no longer turns on the economy or on social questions . . . but on the national question." *Le Monde,* March 31, 1990.

15. Quoted in *Le Monde*, March 13, 1990.

16. *Le Monde*, April 20, 1995.

Postscript

After the election excitement of 1995 had died away, the National Front returned in 1996 to promoting its major objectives: portraying the Front as a unique and trustworthy political force on the French political scene, ensuring that the three NF mayors elected in the June 1995 local elections forcefully implemented the national preference policy, and mobilizing public support behind the Front's anti-immigrant policies.

For almost a quarter of a century Jean-Marie Le Pen and the NF have been trying to convince the French public that the NF is different from other French political parties. Not only has the Front proposed major changes in immigration policy, but it has also developed a new political vocabulary to convey its unique message. The Front's discourse is characterized by ambiguous terms and phrases that hint at but never overtly express anti-Semitism and racism. During the 1980s and early 1990s, terms such as *oligarchie, cosmopolitanism,* and *mondialisme* or phrases such as *the right to be different, oligarchie mondialiste, national preference,* and *anti-French racism* were pressed into service in this cause. Recently, however, the NF has adopted a new slogan: The Front, it is now claimed, is "neither right nor left."

This phrase has its origins in the 1930s, when European fascist parties tried to distinguish themselves from communist and socialist parties, on the one hand, and conservative and reactionary parties, on the other. Fascists claimed that they did not support leftist arguments for state control of the economy or endorse class warfare. They did, however, oppose rightist arguments that the market economy should completely determine the fate of the nation or its citizens. In 1983 historian Zeev Sternhell called attention to this phrase in his controversial work on the history of French fascism, *Ni Droite Ni Gauche.*[1]

In 1993 Alain de Benoist of GRECE argued that the left-right dichotomy had lost its meaning in France because the "debates" over the old issues (the Republic, the church, and the economy), which used to divide left and right, were over. According to de Benoist, there was now widespread consensus that a republic was superior to a monarchy or an authoritarian dictatorship; few people believed that the Catholic church should have increased authority in the state, while almost everyone conceded that welfare state

261

capitalism was superior to both communism or an uncontrolled market system.[2] According to de Benoist: "It is not a matter of 'neither Left nor Right' but of salvaging their best features. It is a matter of developing new political configurations transcending both."[3] Of course, this still seems to boil down to "neither right nor left."

More recently, on September 1–3, 1995, the NF held its summer university in Toulon, currently headed by NF mayor Jean-Marie Le Chevallier. Speaking to eight hundred NF leaders and elected politicians, Jean-Marie Le Pen stated: "We've got to prepare an alternative to the system," which he "challenged in its entirety. We're in a position now which justifies the slogan, 'neither right nor left.'"[4]

It is this insistence that the NF is neither on the right nor on the left but that it "transcends" both that leads the Front to reject all attempts to put it on the extreme right. There are good political reasons for the Front to reject the extreme right label, which is associated with discredited prewar fascist parties and the violent neofascist or neo-Nazi groups of postwar France. That explains why, on November 19, 1995, Le Pen wrote an angry letter to *Le Monde* complaining that it "constantly called the NF a party of the extreme right."[5] According to Le Pen: "In political science, it [the term *extreme right*] has a specific definition which . . . is characterized by a rejection of democracy and elections, a call for violence and racism, and preference for a single party political system. On each of these points the NF distinguishes itself from the extreme right and even opposes it."[6] Citing a number of French scholars, Le Pen noted that "the NF is a partisan of liberal democracy; it does not want a regime that is stronger than the Fifth Republic, and it challenges anyone to find in its actions, writings or the speeches of its officials the least attempt to justify violent actions."[7] Le Pen then accused those who used the extreme right label of trying to close off debate with the NF and of using the "big lie" tactic of Nazi leader Joseph Goebbels—that is, repeating a lie often enough so that people accept it as truth. And Le Pen concluded by threatening to use an 1881 law giving him the right to a response in the press if *Le Monde* continued to characterize the Front as "extremist" or "extreme right."

Clearly Le Pen wishes to distinguish the National Front from the traditional parties of both left and right. Le Pen made this apparent shortly after the National Front mayors of Orange, Marignane, and Toulon backtracked on their commitment to implement the Front's national preference policy. In August 1995 *Le Monde* noted the moderation of the Front mayors. In Orange, Front mayor Jacques Bompard stated that his city "would not be a laboratory for Front ideas."[8] In Marignane, Front mayor Daniel Simonpierri was so innocuous that voters referred to him as "Lepenist light."[9] And the mayor of Toulon, Jean-Marie Le Chevallier, was so low key that the NF began to take on the appearance of an ordinary political party.[10]

But this was not to last. In October 1995 Le Pen ordered the three mayors to strictly adhere to Front policy by holding the line on tax increases and by giving preference in social welfare and housing to French citizens over non-European immigrants. According to Le Pen, the task of the NF was not to "manage decadence" but to "change things."[11] "These mayors," Le Pen said, "don't own their seats. They were elected as NF candidates, on the basis of the NF program, with the support of the NF and the support of its president. . . . These mayors are not like the others."[12] Front mayors were enjoined by Le Pen to check all immigrants who applied for social benefits or municipal housing to ensure that their papers were in order and, where legal, to give preference to French citizens in the allocation of benefits and housing. Front mayors were to cease subsidizing any organizations "favoring immigration," and they were to take measures to increase security, including banning begging and hiring more police.[13] In early 1996 this hard line on immigrants seemed to have borne fruit. An NF supporter in Toulon was pleased to learn that his application for public housing would be given priority over that of a Muslim immigrant. Questioned about markets in the city center, one NF municipal councillor said: "We will take care that a certain immigrant population does not install itself in the market. After all, tom-toms do not have anything to do with Provençe."[14]

While the National Front was making inroads in local politics and enjoying increased popularity, the RPR government faced an immense and highly unpopular task. Under the terms of the Maastricht Treaty, to qualify for entry into the European monetary union in 1999, government deficits had to be limited to no more than 3 percent of gross domestic product. But when Prime Minister Alain Juppé tried to meet this objective by reducing social security expenditures, he encountered a wave of strikes and demonstrations in the winter of 1995–1996.

Nor was the government's popularity boosted by continued trials of prominent government and opposition politicians on bribery and corruption charges. Moreover, the Front's anti-immigrant stance took on new luster as supporters of the Algerian Islamic Salvation Front engaged in a series of murderous bomb attacks on French railways and urban trains. At an annual meeting in November 1995, French mayors reported increased racism among their constituents and irritation at public expenditure for the *exclus,* those excluded from society. As a result, a number of mayors had begun to discriminate against immigrants in the provision of municipal services. One RPR mayor noted that "increased disenchantment with government policy is leading voters to support the National Front."[15] It was not only the mainstream right that was threatened by the Front; the left also had begun to do some soul-searching.

After election analyses showed that Le Pen had received vastly more working-class votes than any other candidate (30 percent, compared to 21 percent for Socialist Lionel Jospin), and more votes from the unemployed (25 percent) than Lionel Jospin (21 percent), the French Communist Party commissioned a poll in the Department of Rhône to explain working-class support for the NF. The Communists found that people had voted for Le Pen and the NF for a variety of motives, but most of all because they were fed up with the traditional parties, which they felt had "abandoned them." They felt that the traditional parties had been "saying the same things over and over for ten or fifteen years." And for many of these voters, the "crucial question" was unemployment.[16] Obviously, many voters had bought the NF's argument that immigrants were the source of many of France's problems, especially unemployment.

In view of the Front's growing popularity and its success in linking immigrants to every conceivable social and economic problem, the French government has resorted to dramatic gestures to convince the public that it is doing everything possible to rid France of "clandestine" immigrants. When, in 1986 RPR minister of the interior Charles Pasqua chartered a special flight to deport 101 immigrants to Mali, criticism of the "101 Malian flight" was so intense that the experience was not repeated until 1991, when a Socialist minister chartered a flight to deport illegal immigrants. However, amid general indifference, RPR minister of the interior Jean-Louis Debré announced in July 1995 that he would charter weekly flights to return the "clandestines" to their country of origin.[17] Not only would the charters demonstrate that the government would not accept clandestine immigration, the charters would also, according to the minister of the interior, "allow for the integration of those foreigners in a correct legal situation."[18]

Amid all this, in late 1995 Le Pen again raised the specter of anti-Semitism. During a demonstration at Carpentras, Le Pen attacked President Jacques Chirac, who had officially apologized in the name of the French state for Vichy's crimes against Jews during the Occupation. Le Pen accused the "Jewish lobby" of having influenced Chirac, "he who never hesitated to pay the [Jewish] 'community' for his election as President by abasing France by declaring it guilty and criminal in the face of history."[19] Le Pen also said that he could not understand how anyone could interpret as anti-Semitic his 1988 "Durafour-*crématoire*" rhyme or his remark that gas chambers were a "detail" during World War II. "The National Front is not racist, it isn't xenophobic, it is not anti-Semitic," he claimed.[20]

Once again Le Pen was engaged in the vocabulary battle. Through reiteration of ambiguous terms and phrases; through hints, allusions, rhymes, and jokes, all immediately followed by self-righteous denials of anti-Semitism, Le Pen was trying to banalize terms such as the *Jewish lobby,* and to get the public to accept jokes or disparaging remarks about the Holocaust. In other words, Le Pen was trying to legitimize a discourse intended to cast doubt on the loyalty of French Jews, to imply the existence of a national and international Jewish conspiracy to control the levers of power in France and the world, and to reduce the Holocaust to the level of a routine wartime tragedy.

Both Le Pen's anti-Semitic remarks and his pledges of allegiance to democracy reflect two major aspects of the Front's ideology. First, Le Pen both embodies and reflects the strong undercurrent of anti-Semitism that surfaces time and again in the National Front. In 1991, for example, Jacques and Marie-Claude Bompard published *Voyage Autour de la Femme*, a discussion of the situation of women throughout the world and in history. While defending a traditionalist line on the role of women, the Bompards also referred to the evils of cosmopolitanism. "Among the strands that constitute the cosmopolitan network," the Bompards noted, "are the different national Masonic lodges . . . but also international lodges of which the B'nai Brith [sic] is part."[21] It is due to the enormous influence of these clubs, or lodges, that "previously unknown people" such as Georges Pompidou (prime minister and later president of France) and Raymond Barre (former prime minister) took over the top posts in government. The "cosmopolitan lobby," it turns out, aims at world domination, and to achieve this it intends to tear nations and ethnic groups away from their roots.[22] Moreover, the Bompards claimed, the Jewish people are intent on achieving world domination, just as "their Book promises."[23] These ideas might be dismissed as the unimportant ravings of anti-Semitic conspiracy theorists, but in fact, Jacques Bompard is currently the National Front mayor of Orange.

Second, by avoiding a direct, frontal attack on democracy, Le Pen and the Front pose a highly insidious threat to the French parliamentary system. The Front's objective is to convince the majority of people that North African immigrants have a culture that is so substantially different from that of the majority that it seriously threatens the preservation of traditional French values and beliefs. At the same time, the Front insists that North African immigrants pose a danger to security and a threat to the French economy. The attack on the Jews takes a different, if familiar, form. Here the objective is to convince people that Jews have a disproportionate influence over French life and that, because of cultural or religious reasons, Jews concert to dominate the nation and even the world.

Is this racism and anti-Semitism? Yes. Is this antidemocratic? Not necessarily, for the genius of the Front's strategy is to use democratic means (free speech and a free press) to marginalize North African immigrants and Jews in order to force them into permanent minority status. In this way, the Front hopes the majority will view immigrants and Jews as having interests and goals different from and opposed to those of the majority. The ground will then have been prepared for the majority, led by the Front, to enact laws against these minorities. In these conditions, and while maintaining strict adherence to democractic rules, the majority will legally oppress the minority.

This objective or "project" helps explain why Le Pen and Front leaders maintain a drumfire of criticism against North African immigrants and Jews while at the same time ardently defending democracy. Obviously, the Front intends to use the democratic rules of the game to isolate and marginalize immigrants and Jews. For the Front, democracy is a means, not an end.

Notes

1. Zeev Sternhell, *Ni Droite Ni Gauche* (Paris: Seuil, 1983).
2. Alain de Benoist, "End of the Left-Right Dichotomy," *Telos* 102 (Winter 1993): 73–89.
3. Ibid., 89.
4. *Le Monde*, September 5, 1995.
5. *Le Monde*, November 19–20, 1995.
6. Ibid.
7. Ibid.
8. *Le Monde*, August 7, 1995.
9. *Le Monde*, September 2, 1995.
10. *Le Monde*, August 7, 1995.
11. *Le Monde*, October 31, 1995.
12. *Le Monde*, November 1, 1995.
13. Ibid.
14. *Guardian Weekly*, February 4, 1996.
15. *Le Monde*, November 12–13, 1995.
16. *Le Monde*, October 27, 1995.
17. *Le Monde*, July 12, 1995.
18. Ibid.
19. *Le Monde*, November 14, 1995.
20. Ibid.
21. Jacques and Marie-Claude Bompard, *Voyage autour de la Femme* (Avignon: A. Barthélmy, 1991), p. 129.
22. Ibid., pp. 129–130.
23. Ibid., p. 185.

APPENDIX A   The National Front at the Polls

Date	Type of Election	Percentage of Votes	Votes	Seats
1973	Legislative	0.6	147,283	–
1974	Presidential	0.8	190,921	–
1978	Legislative	0.8	213,978	–
1981	Legislative	0.3	90,422	–
1983	Municipal	0.1	27,970	175
1984	European	11.0	2,204,961	10
1985	Cantonal	8.8	1,016,398	1
1986	Legislative	9.6	2,705,336	35
1986	Regional	9.5	2,658,500	137
1988	Presidential	14.4	4,375,894	–
1988	Legislative	9.6	2,359,528	1
1988	Cantonal	5.3	476,735	1
1989	Municipal	2.1	258,401	804
1989	European	11.7	2,129,668	10
1992	Regional	13.6	3,375,079	239
1992	Cantonal	12.2	1,530,094	1
1993	Legislative	12.5	3,158,843	0
1994	European	10.5	2,049,634	11
1994	Cantonal	9.8	1,058,859	3
1995	Presidential	15.0	4,570,838	–
1995	Municipal	6.7	995,551	1,075

SOURCE: *Le Monde*, various dates

APPENDIX B   Political Bureau, February 1994

Jean Marie Le Pen (president)

Bruno Gollnisch (general secretary)
Bruno Mégret (delegate general)
Dominique Chaboche (vice president)
Jean-Yves Le Gallou
Jean-François Jalkh
Yvan Blot
Roger Holeindre
Marie-France Stirbois
Jean-Pierre Reveau (treasurer)
Jean-Claude Martinez
Fernand Le Rachinel
Damien Bariller
Pierre Vial
Georges-Paul Wagner
Michel de Rostolan
Pierre Sirgue
Pierre Descaves
Philippe Olivier
Pierre Jaboulet-Vercherre
Jean-Claude Varanne
Pierre Milloz
Jacques Lafay
Samuel Maréchal
Franck Timmermans
Christian Baeckeroot
Bernard Antony
Martial Bild
Jean-Claude Bardet
Martine Lehideux
Pierre Durand
Jacques Bompard
Jean-Marie Le Chevallier
Michel Bayvet
Alain Jamet
Jean-Pierre Schenardi
Carl Lang

Bibliography

Books

Algazy, Joseph. *La tentation néo-fasciste en France, 1944–1965*. Paris: Fayard, 1984.

_____. *L'Extrême droite en France (1965–1984)*. Paris: L'Harmattan, 1989.

Amar, Marianne, and Pierre Milza. *L'immigration en France au XXe siècle*. Paris: Armand Colin, 1990.

Apparu, Jean-Pierre. *La Droite aujourd'hui*. Paris: Albin Michel, 1979.

Aron, Raymond. *France Steadfast and Changing*. Cambridge, Mass.: Harvard University Press, 1960.

Aron, Robert. *Histoire de la Libération de France*. Paris: Fayard, 1959.

Baccou, Philippe, and the Club de l'Horloge. *Le grand tabou*. Paris: Albin Michel, 1981.

Badinter, Robert (ed.). *Vous avez dit fascisme*. Paris: Montalba, 1984.

Bardèche, Maurice. *Qu'est-ce que le fascisme?* Paris: Les Sept Couleurs, 1961.

Benoist, Alain de. *Europe, tiers monde, même combat*. Paris: Robert Laffont, 1986.

_____. *Vu de droite*. Paris: Copernic, 1979.

Bergeron, Francis, and Philippe Vilgier. *De Le Pen à Le Pen*. Bouere: Éditions Dominique Martin Morin, 1986.

Bernstein, Serge, and Pierre Milza. *Histoire de la France au XXe siècle*. Brussels: Complexe, 1991.

Birenbaum, Guy. *Le Front national en politique*. Paris: Balland, 1992.

Birnbaum, Pierre. *Un mythe politique: "La République juive."* Paris: Fayard, 1988.

_____. *La France aux Français*. Paris: Seuil, 1993.

Blot, Yvan. *Les racines de la liberté*. Paris: Albin Michel, 1985.

Bockel, Alain. *L'immigration au pays des droits de l'homme*. Paris: Publisud, 1991.

Bonnafous, Simone. *L'immigration prise aux mots*. Paris: Kimé, 1991.

Borella, François. *Les partis politiques dans la France d'aujourd'hui*. Paris: Seuil, 1990.

Boyer, Jean-François. *L'Empire Moon*. Paris: La Découverte, 1986.

Bresson, Gilles, and Christian Lionet. *Le Pen*. Paris: Seuil, 1994.

Brunn, Julien. *La Nouvelle droite*. Paris: Nouvelles Éditions Oswald, 1979.

Camus, Jean Yves, and René Monzat. *Les droites nationales et radicales en France*. Lyon: Presses Universitaires de Lyon, 1992.

Catalogne, Édouard. *La Politique de l'immigration en France depuis la guerre de 1914*. Paris: Imprimerie André Tournon, 1925.

Chatain, Jean. *Les affaires de M. Le Pen*. Paris: Éditions Messidor, 1987.

Chebel d'Appolonia, Ariane. *L'extrême-droite en France de Maurras à le Pen.* Brussels: Complexe, 1987.

Cheles, Luciano, Ronnie Ferguson, and Michalina Vaughan. *Neo-Fascism in Europe.* Essex, England: Longman Group, 1991.

Chiroux, René. *L'extrême-droite sous la Ve République.* Paris: Librairie Générale de Droit et de Jurisprudence, 1974.

Chombart de Lauwe, Marie-José. *Complots contre la démocratie: Les multiples visages du fascisme.* Paris: Fédération Nationale des Déportés et Internés Résistants et Patriotes, 1981.

Club de l'Horloge. *La décentralisation locale.* Paris: Éditions Paris: 1990.

_____. *L'Identité de la France.* Paris: Albin Michel, 1985.

_____. *Socialisme et religion.* Paris: Albatros, 1986.

Colas, Dominique et al. *Citoyenneté et nationalité.* Paris: Presses Universitaires de France, 1991.

Cole, Alistair, and Peter Campbell. *French Electoral Systems and Elections Since 1789.* Aldershot, England: Gower, 1989.

Converse, Philip E., and Roy Pierce. *Political Representation in France.* Cambridge, Mass.: Harvard University Press, 1986.

Deutsch, Emeric, Denis Lindon, and Pierre Weil. *Les familles politiques aujourd'hui en France.* Paris: Minuit, 1966.

Dumont, Serge, Joseph Lorien, and Karl Criton. *Le système Le Pen.* Anvers, Belgium: Éditions EPO, 1985.

Dupin, Eric. *Oui, non, sans opinion.* Paris: Interéditions, 1990.

Dupoirier, Elisabeth, and Gérard Grunberg. *Mars 1986: La drôle de défaite de la gauche.* Paris: Presses Universitaires de France, 1986.

Duprat, François. *Les mouvements d'extrême-droite en France depuis 1944.* Paris: Albatros, 1972.

Duranton-Crabol, Anne-Marie. *Visages de la nouvelle droite: Le grece et son histoire.* Paris: Presses Universitaires de France, 1988.

Faux, Emmanuel, Thomas Legrand, and Gilles Perez. *La main droite de Dieu.* Paris: Éditions du Seuil, 1994.

Figueras, André. *L'adieux aux juifs.* Paris: Publications André Figueras, 1987.

Flockton, Christopher, and Eleonore Kofman. *France.* London: Paul Chapman, 1989.

Fondation Nationale des Sciences Politiques. *L'Élection présidentielle des 5 et 19 décembre 1965.* Paris: Armand Colin, 1970.

Frears, John. *Parties and Voters in France.* New York: St. Martin's Press, 1991.

Front National. *300 mesures pour la renaissance de la France.* Paris: Éditions Nationales, 1993.

Gard, Roger Martin du. *Chroniques du Vichy, 1940–1944.* Paris: Flammarion, 1975.

Gaspard, Françoise. *A Small City in France.* Cambridge, Mass.: Harvard University Press, 1995 (English translation of *Une petite ville en France.* Paris: Gallimard, 1990.)

Goguel, François. *Géographie des élections françaises sous la troisième et la quatrième république.* Paris: Armand Colin, 1970.

Griffin, Roger. *The Nature of Fascism*. London: Pinter, Publishers, 1990.

Hameau, Christopher. *Le campagne de Jean-Marie Le Pen pour l'élection présidentielle de 1988*. Paris: Travaux et Recherches de l'Université Panthéon-Assas (Paris II), n.d.

Haut Conseil à l'Intégration. *L'Intégration à la Française*. Paris: Union Générale d'Éditions, 1993.

Hennion, Blandine. *Le Front national l'argent et l'establishment*. Paris: La Découverte, 1993.

Hoffmann, Stanley, ed. *Le mouvement Poujade*. Paris: André Colin, 1956.

Holmes, Stephen. *The Anatomy of Antiliberalism*. Cambridge, Mass.: Harvard University Press, 1993.

Jaeger, Hans. *The Reappearance of the Swastika*. London: Gamma Publications, January 1960, mimeograph.

Jeambar, Denis, and Jean-Marc Lech. *Le self-service électoral*. Paris: Flammarion, 1992.

Le Pen, Jean-Marie. *La France est de retour*. Paris: Carrère/Laffon, 1985.

————. *Le Pen 91*. Paris: Éditions de Présent, 1991.

————. *Les Français d'abord*. Paris: Carrère/Laffon, 1984.

————. *Pour la France: Programme du Front National*. Paris: Albatros, 1985.

Lequin, Yves (ed.). *La mosaïque France*. Paris: Larousse, 1988.

Luthy, Herbert. *The State of France*. London: Secker and Warburg, 1955.

Marrus, Michael, and Robert O. Paxton. *Vichy France and the Jews*. New York: Basic Books, 1981.

Maucorps, Paul H., Albert Memmi, and Jean-Francis Held. *Les français et le racisme*. Paris: Payot, 1965.

Mauge, Roger. *La verité sur Jean-Marie Le Pen*. Paris: Éditions, France-Empire, 1988.

Maurras, Charles. *Mes idées politiques*. Rpt. Paris: Albatros, n.d.

————. *Votre bel Aujourd'hui*. Paris: Fayard, 1953.

Mayer, Nonna, and Pascal Perrineau. *Le Front national à découvert*. Paris: Presses de la Fondation National des Sciences Politiques, 1989.

McClelland, J. S. *The French Right (from DeMaistre to Maurras)*. London: Jonathan Cape, 1970.

Mégret, Bruno. *La flamme*. Paris: Robert Laffont, 1990.

Milza, Olivier. *Les français devant l'immigration*. Brussels: Complexe, 1988.

Milza, Pierre. *Fascisme français: Passé et présent*. Paris: Flammarion, 1987.

Monzat, René. *Enquêtes sur la droite extrême*. Paris: Le Monde Éditions, 1992.

Noiriel, Gérard. *Le creuset Français*. Paris: Seuil, 1988.

Paon, Marcel. *L'immigration en France*. Paris: Payot, 1926.

Petitfils, Jean-Claude. *L'Extrême droite en France*. Paris: Presses Universitaires de France, 1983.

Piat, Yann. *Seule tout en haut à droite*. Paris: Fixot, 1991.

Plenel, Edwy, and Alain Rollat. *La République menacée*. Paris: Le Monde Éditions, 1992.

Plumyène, Jean, and Raymond Lasierra. *Les fascismes français: 1923–1963*. Paris: Seuil, 1963.

Pons, Gregory. *Les rats noirs*. N.p.: Jean-Claude Simeon, 1977.

Poujade, Pierre. *À l'heure de la colère.* Paris: Albin Michel, 1977.

_____. *J'ai choisi le combat.* Saint-Céré: Société Général des Éditions et des Publications, 1955.

Ravitch, Norman. *The Catholic Church and the French Nation, 1589–1989.* London: Routledge, 1990.

Reinhard, Philippe. *Bernard Tapie.* Paris: Éditions France-Empire, 1991.

Rémond, René. *Les droites en France.* Paris: Aubier Montaigne, 1982.

Rioux, Jean-Pierre. *The Fourth Republic, 1944–1958.* Cambridge: Cambridge University Press, 1987.

Rollat, Alain. *L'Effet Le Pen.* Paris: La Découverte, 1984.

_____. *Les hommes de l'extrême droite.* Paris: Calmann-Lévy, 1985.

Ross, George et al. *The Mitterrand Experiment.* Oxford: Basil Blackwell, 1987.

Rousso, Henry. *The Vichy Syndrome.* Cambridge, Mass.: Harvard University Press, 1991.

Schmitt, Carl. *Parlementarisme et démocratie.* Paris: Seuil, 1988.

Schor, Ralph. *L'Opinion française et les étrangers, 1919–1939.* Paris: Publications de la Sorbonne, 1985.

Silverman, Maxim. *Deconstructing the Nation: Immigration, Racism, and Citizenship in Modern France.* New York: Routledge, 1992.

Simmons, Harvey G. *French Socialists in Search of a Role.* Ithaca: Cornell University Press, 1970.

Sternhell, Zeev. *Ni Droite Ni Gauche.* Paris: Seuil, 1983.

Taguieff, Pierre-André (ed.). *Face au racisme.* Vols. 1 and 2. Paris: La Découverte, 1991.

Thalman, Rita (ed.). *Femmes et fascismes.* Paris: Tierce, 1986.

Todd, Emmanuel. *The Making of Modern France.* Oxford: Basil Blackwell, 1990.

Tristan, Anne. *Au Front.* Paris: Gallimard, 1987.

Valéry, Jules. *La nationalité française.* Paris: Librairie Générale de Droit et de Jurisprudence, 1927.

Valla, Jean-Claude. *Dix ans de combat culturel pour une renaissance.* Paris: GRECE, 1977.

Vial, Piere (ed.). *Pour une renaissance culturel: Le Grece prends la parole.* Paris: Copernic, 1979.

Weil, Patrick. *La France et ses étrangers.* Paris: Calmann-Lévy, 1991.

Weinberg, Henry H. *The Myth of the Jew in France, 1967–1982.* Oakville, Ontario: Mosaic Press, 1987.

Wieviorka, Michael. *La France raciste.* Paris: Seuil, 1992.

Williams, Philip. *Crisis and Compromise.* Hamden, Conn.: Archon Books, 1964.

Winock, Michel. *Édouard Drumont et Cie.* Paris: Seuil, 1982.

_____. *Nationalisme, antisémitisme et fascisme en France.* Paris: Seuil, 1982.

_____ (ed.). *Histoire de l'extrême droite en France.* Paris: Seuil, 1993.

Wright, Gordon. *France in Modern Times.* New York: Rand McNally, 1960.

Zuccotti, Susan. *The Holocaust, the French, and the Jews.* New York: Basic Books, 1993.

Articles

Bardèche, Maurice. "Le Poujadisme." Special edition of *Défense de l'Occident* (May 1956).

Berger, Suzanne. "Politics and Antipolitics in Western Europe in the Seventies." *Daedalus* 108, 1 (Winter 1979).

Bréchon, Pierre, and Subrata Kumar Mitra. "The National Front in France: The Emergence of an Extreme Right Protest Movement." *Comparative Politics* 25, 1 (October 1992).

Camus, Jean-Yves. "Political Cultures Within the Front National." *Patterns of Prejudice* 26, 1–2 (1992).

Collovald, Annie. "Les Poujadistes, ou l'échec en politique." *Revue d'histoire moderne et contemporaine* 36 (January-March 1989).

Fysh, Peter, and Jim Wolfreys. "Le Pen, the National Front, and the Extreme Right in France." *Parliamentary Affairs* 45, 3 (July 1992).

Gardels, Nathan. "Two Concepts of Nationalism: An Interview with Isaiah Berlin." *New York Review of Books* (November 21, 1991).

Gaspard, Nathan. "Les immigrés comme enjeu politique." *Revue politique et parlementaire* 916–917 (May-June 1985).

Goguel, François. "Conjoncture politique du néo-gaullisme." *Ésprit* 12 (1947).

Gregoire, Menie. "Politique de l'immigration." *Ésprit* 348 (April 1966).

Griffiths, Richard. "Anticapitalism and the French Extra-Parliamentary Right, 1870–1940." *Journal of Contemporary History* 13, 4 (October 1978).

Guibert, Michele. "Présentation des étrangers." *Ésprit* 348 (April 1966).

Hastings, Michael. "La Rhétorique hygiéniste de Jean-Marie Le Pen." *Revue politique et parlementaire* 933 (January-February 1988).

Hochet, Agnès. "L'immigration dans le débat politique français de 1981 à 1988." *Pouvoirs* 47 (1988).

Husbands, Christopher. "The Politics of Immigration in France." *Ethnic and Racial Studies* 14, 2 (April 1991).

Ignazi, Piero, and Colette Ysmal. "New and Old Extreme Right Parties: The French National Front and the Italian Movimento Sociale." *European Journal of Political Research* 22, 1 (July 1992).

Lancelot, Alain, and Pierre Weill. "L'évolution politique des électeurs françaises, de février à juin 1969." *Revue française de science politique* 20, 2 (April 1970).

Lesselier, Claudie. "De la Vierge Marie à Jeanne d'Arc: Images de femmes à l'extrême droite." *L'Homme et la société* 99–100 (1991).

Levy, Deborah R. "Women of the French National Front." *Parliamentary Affairs* 42, 1 (January 1989).

Lewis-Beck, Michael, and Glenn E. Mitchell, II. "French Electoral Theory: The National Front Test." *Electoral Studies* 12, 2 (1993).

Mossuz-Lavau, Janine. "Le vote des femmes en France (1945–1993). *Revue française de science politique* 43, 4 (August 1994).

Perrineau, Pascal. "Front national: L'écho politique de l'anomie urbaine." *Ésprit* 3–4 (March-April 1988).

_____. "Vers une recomposition du politique?" In *L'état de la France*. Paris: La Découverte, 1994.

Pouillet, M. T., and J. M. Bouttier. "L'accueil officiel." *Ésprit* 348 (April 1966).

Schlegel, Jean-Louis. "Philippe de Villiers, ou les valeurs de l'enracinement." *Ésprit* 2 (February 1995).

Surya, Michel. "Editorial." *Lignes* 4 (October 1988).

Taguieff, Pierre-André. "Alain de Benoist philosophe." *Temps modernes* 451 (February 1984).

_____. "De l'anti-socialisme au national-racisme: Deux aspects de la recomposition idéologique des droites en France." *Raison présente* 4 (1988).

_____. "Le national-populisme en question." *Lignes* 4 (October 1988).

Venner, Fiametta. "Le militantisme féminin d'extrême droite: Une autre manière d'être féministe?" *French Politics and Society* 11, 2 (Spring 1993).

Vidal, Francette. "La Campa." *Ésprit* 348 (April 1966).

Yonnet, Paul. "La machine Carpentras: Histoire et sociologie d'un syndrome d'un épuration." *Le Débat* 61 (September-October 1990).

Ysmal, Colette. "The History of Electoral Studies in France." *European Journal of Political Research* 25 (1994).

About the Book and Author

Over the past few decades, extreme-right political parties have won increasing support throughout Europe. The largest and most sophisticated of these is the French National Front. Led by the charismatic Jean-Marie Le Pen, the Front is now the third most important political force in France after the mainstream right and the Socialists.

This clear and comprehensive book explores the antecedents for the meteoric rise of the National Front. Beginning with a political history of the extreme right from 1945 to 1995, Harvey Simmons traces links between Le Pen and French neo-fascist and extreme-right organizations of the 1950s and 1960s and concludes with analyses of the Front's anti-Semitism, racism, organization, ideology, language, electorate, and views on women. Simmons argues that the Front is not a party like any other but a major threat to French democracy.

Harvey G. Simmons is professor and chair of the Department of Political Science at York University, Ontario, Canada.

Index

Abortion, 64, 79, 201, 238, 243, 246
Action Française (AF), 19, 28, 54, 57,
    99, 197, 199
AF. *See* Action Française
AIDS, 84, 98, 125, 221, 224–225, 254
Albertini, Georges, 14
Algazy, Joseph, 33
Algeria
    Algerian war, 14, 41–42, 253
    Algérie Française, 5, 35
    army revolt in, 41–45
    National Liberation Front (FLN), 13,
        37, 39, 44, 45, 153
    population of, 37
    torture in, 38, 39
Alliance Républicaine, 170
Alsace, 181
American Heritage Foundation, 215
Anti-French racism, 4
Antiparliamentarism, 21, 22, 29–30,
    33, 47, 78, 212
Anti-Semitism
    and Action Française, 20
    and Carpentras, 99–100
    and Charles Maurras, 19
    and cosmopolitanism, 99, 124,
        127–129, 133, 265
    and Jeune Nation, 47
    and "Jewish International," 66, 101
    and "Jewish lobby," 4, 127, 264
    and neofascism, 15, 19
    and political discourse, 219–223
    and pro-Front press, 103
    and Tixier-Vignancour, 173
    and Vichy, 150
Antony, Bernard, 101, 133, 192,
    199–200, 243

anti-Semitism of, 127
    hostility to journalists, 104
    on new world order, 127–128
Aron, Raymond, 37, 75, 124
Arrighi, Pascal, 132, 194, 202
Attali, Jacques, 217
Auriol, Vincent, 21
Autant-Lara, Claude, 126, 213

Bachelot, François, 84, 94, 131, 191,
    194, 202
    on anti-Semitism, 136
    on "detail" incident, 132
Badinter, Elisabeth, 95
Badinter, Robert, 95, 125
Baker, James, 226
Balladur, Édouard, 182–183, 226
Barbie, Klaus, 55
Bardèche, Maurice, 17, 33–34, 54, 60,
    66, 101, 192, 210
    on GRECE, 213
    on May 1968 student revolution,
        57–58
    See also Fascism; Poujadism
Baréty, Léon, 148
Barnay, Catherine, 198
Barre, Raymond, 82, 90–92, 124, 175,
    181, 265
Barrès, Maurice, 100
Baudoin, Denis, 130, 227
Benoist, Alain de, 95, 209–210,
    213–214, 253, 262–263
Berlusconi, Silvio, 108
Bernstein, Serge, 170
Bertillon, Alphonse, 147
Bich, Laurence, 193
Bich, Marcel, 193

Biffaud, Olivier, 3
Bild, Martial, 192
Binet, René, 15, 17
Birenbaum, Guy, 84
Birnbaum, Pierre, 135
Blair, Tony, 217
Bloch, Jean-Charles, 192
Blondel, Jacqueline, 175
Blot, Yvan, 84, 129–130, 133, 192, 215, 218, 224
  on conspiracy, 227
  on the family, 241
  on socialism, 130
Blum, Léon, 16, 48(n14), 86(n8), 150
B'nai B'rith, 125, 127–128, 130, 197, 219, 221, 227, 265
Bompard, Jacques, 112
Bompard, Marie-Claude, 262, 265
Bonnafous, Simone, 157
Bonnet, 156
Bordeaux, 113
Boumediene, Houari, 154
Bousquet, Pierre, 62, 67
Brasillach, Robert, 12, 16–17, 60, 192
Bresson, Gilles, 63, 194, 196
Briant, Yvon, 194
Briffaut, Pierre, 196
Brigneau, François, 61–62, 67, 125–126, 130, 197, 199, 226
Burgaz, Germaine, 196

Canard Enchainé, Le, 39
Capitalism, 18
CAPS. *See* Comités d'Action Politique et Sociale
Carton, Daniel, 194
CAUSA. *See* Confederation of Associates for the Unity of the Societies of America
Celtic cross, 17, 44, 57, 60, 62
Centre National des Femmes d'Europe, 192, 241
Centre National des Indépendants (CNI), 44–45, 194
Cercle Montherlant, 192
Cercle National Droit et Liberté, 192
Cercle National Santé, 192

Cercle du Panthéon, 56
Ceyrac, Pierre, 193–195, 202
CFDT. *See* Confédération Française Démocratique du Travail
CGT. *See* Confédération Générale du Travail
Chaban-Delmas, Jacques, 29
Charlemagne Division, 16
Charles-Martel Organization, 154
Chauvierre, Bruno, 194
Cheysson, Claude, 158
Chirac, Jacques, 71, 73–75, 83, 89, 92–93, 134, 175, 181–183, 199, 202, 226–227, 256, 264
  and immigration, 97, 159, 255
  and National Front, 82, 90, 91
Chiroux, Roger, 56, 66
Choc du Mois, Le, 197–198
Christian-Solidarity, 101, 192
Cité Catholique, 200
Club de l'Horloge, 130, 132, 190, 193, 208, 211, 215, 218, 229, 252
Club Jean Moulin, 208
CNI. *See* Centre National des Indépendants
Cohen, Jean-Pierre, 198
Cohn-Bendit, Daniel, 57
Collinot, Michel, 103
Combat pour les Valeurs, 108
Comité National des Juifs Français, 192
Comités d'Action Politique et Sociale (CAPS), 200
Communist League, 65
Communists, 4, 13, 37, 39, 46, 66, 75, 150
  and immigration, 156
  voters, 179
Confederation of Associations for the Unity of the Societies of America (CAUSA), 193–194
Confédération Française Démocratique du Travail (CFDT), 226
Confédération Générale du Travail (CGT), 17, 156
Conseil Représentatif des Institutions Juives en France (CRIF), 127, 130, 133, 134, 227

Conseil Scientifique, 193
Constitutional Council, 156
Corpo de Droit, 12
Corporatism, 14
Coston, Henri, 197
Crapouillet, Le, 198
CRIF. *See* Conseil Représentatif des
    Institutions Juives en France

Daniel, Jean, 103
Dayan, Moshe, 101
Déat, Marcel, 14
Debré, Jean-Louis, 264
Debré, Michel, 153
Défense de l'Occident, 210
Delors, Jacques, 77
Demarquet, Jean-Maurice, 31, 39,
    42–43, 131, 195–196
Denipierre, Jean, 227
Descaves, Pierre, 85
Désir, Harlem, 178
Deutsch, Emeric, 171–173
Deyzieu, Sébastien, 216
Dides, Jean, 31
Domenach, Jean-Marie, 21
Dominati, Jacques, 133
Doriot, Jacques, 28, 62
Dreux, 72–76, 78, 95–96
Dreyfus Affair, 199
Drumont, Édouard, 100, 123
Dufraisse, André, 193
Dupin, Eric, 72
Duprat, François, 15, 16, 20, 60
Durafour, Michel, 94, 126
Durand, Pierre, 46, 58, 62, 197

Eco, Umberto, ix
Eisenhower, Dwight D., 38
Elections
    1968 legislative, 58
    1969 presidential, 59
    1973 legislative, 65
    1974 presidential, 65–67
    1981 presidential, 71–72
    1984 European, 78
    1986 legislative, 80–83
    1988 legislative, 93–94

    1988 presidential, 89–93
    1995 municipal, 3, 111–114,
        180–183, 251
    1995 presidential, 181–183, 251
    proportional representation (PR), 5,
        64, 77, 79, 81, 89, 93, 111
    two-ballot system, 59, 77, 80–81,
        111
Electorate
    female, 171
    "halo effect," 177, 180
    National Front, 83–84, 110
    Poujadist, 171
    "swamp," 172–173
    Tixier-Vignancour, 83–84, 110
Elkabbach, Jean-Pierre, 103
EML. *See* Enterprise Moderne et
    Liberté
Entreprise Moderne et Liberté (EML),
    191, 193
Establishment, 4
Etchebarne, Serge, 180
Europe-Action, 47, 210, 213
Europe-Action Hebdomadaire, 210
European Community, 183
European Social Charter, 155
Evian Accord, 152, 155
Extreme right
    and capitalism, 61, 66
    and corporatism, 61
    electorate, 171
    and immigration, 149–150, 153–154
    and Jews, 124
    and Nazism, 16
    and violence, 61

Fabian Society, 210
Fabius, Laurent, 125, 159
Fabre-Luce, Alfred, 14
Faculty of Law, 11, 12, 31, 192
Fascism, 66–67, 211
    definition of, 21
    and Gaullism, 22
    international fascism, 15
    and Le Pen, 3
    and National Front, 2, 208
    neo-fascism, 19

post–World War II, 1, 14–15
and Poujadism, 32–33
theory of, 18
"Ur-fascism," ix
See also Bardèche, Maurice;
Poujadism
Faurisson, Robert, 197
Fédération de l'Éducation Nationale
(FEN), 226
Fédération des Étudiants Nationalistes,
210
FEN. *See* Fédération de l'Éducation
Nationale
Ferro, Marc, 98
Fifth Republic, 44
Figaro, Le, 85, 159
Figueras, André, 126
FLN. *See* Algeria, National Liberation
Front
FNJ. *See* Front National de la Jeunesse
Foreign Legion, 13, 41
Fourth Republic, 2, 28, 35, 42, 44
Franco, Francisco, 4, 5
Frédéric-Dupont, Édouard, 202
Freemasons, 4, 128, 130, 132, 149,
221–222, 227, 265
Friedmann, Jacques, 130, 227
Friends of Le Pen Center, 192
Front National des Combattants, 4
Front National de la Jeunesse (FNJ),
192

Galvaire, Jean-François, 61,
Gambetta, Léon, 30
Gaspard, Françoise, 74, 76, 78, 96, 253
Gaucher, Roland, 103, 105, 133, 198,
202
Gaulle, Charles de, 12, 15, 20–22, 35,
43–45, 171, 252
and Algeria, 43–45
electorate, 171
and immigration policy, 151
and Jews, 123, 226
and May 1968 student revolution,
57–58
Giscard d'Estaing, Valéry, 67, 73, 78,
97, 99, 211

on immigration, 154–156, 255
Goebbels, Joseph, 262
Goguel, François, 171
Gramsci, Antonio, 209, 217, 247
GRECE. *See* Groupement de Recherche
et d'Études pour la Civilisation
Européenne
Groupe Action Jeunesse, 189
Groupe Union et Défense (GUD), 104,
192
Groupe d'Union et de Fraternité
Française, 32
Groupement de Défense des Intérêts
Agricoles et Viticoles, 29
Groupement de Recherche et d'Études
pour la Civilisation Européenne
(GRECE), 95, 198, 208–215, 252
GUD. See Groupe Union et Défense
Guesde, Jules, 146

Hastings, Michael, 225
Heilbronner, François, 130, 227
Hennion, Blandine, 193
Hersant, Robert, 193
High Council on Integration, 143
Hitler, Adolf, 4, 14, 18–19, 46, 74, 80,
129, 131
Ho Chi Minh, 13
Hoffmann, Stanley, 33
Holeindre, Roger, 5, 56, 62, 104, 190
Holocaust, 126, 130, 132, 214, 217,
220, 264–265
Hue, Robert, 176
Husbands, Christopher, 176
Hussein, Saddam, 4, 101–102

Immigration, 2, 66, 72, 82
attitudes toward, 76, 105, 144, 146,
149–150, 159
"clandestine," 90, 99, 155, 158
and criminality, 74, 80
and law, 91, 147–149, 151, 156
policy, 75–76, 105–106, 147, 152,
155
"scarves" affair, 95
statistics, 145, 151–152
and unemployment, 79

and voting, 72, 158
Indochina, 13, 14
Iraq, 101–102
Islamic fundamentalism, 92
Islamic Salvation Front, 263
Isorni, Jacques, 12
Israel, 100–101, 123, 125–126

Jaffré, Jérôme, 174–175
Jeanbar, Denis, 107
Jeune Nation, 46–47, 60
Jeunes Indépendants de Paris, 31
Joan of Arc, 71, 201, 238–239
John Paul II, Pope, 201
Johnstone, Roger, 195
Jospin, Lionel, 176–177, 182, 264
Juppé, Alain, 74, 113, 227, 256, 263

Kahn, Jean, 227
Kahn, Jean-François, 103
Klein, Thèo, 133
Khrushchev, Nikita, 38
Kuwait, 101

Lacroix, Bernard, 175
La Lettre de Jean-Marie Le Pen, 197
Lambert, Hubert, 103, 195–196
Lang, Carl, 136, 188, 192, 202
La Rochelle, Michel, 194
Laval, Pierre, 16
League for the Rights of Man, 226
Lecanuet, Jean, 56, 93, 171
Le Chevallier, Jean-Marie, 112, 202,
    239, 262
Lefebvre, Monseigneur Marcel, 127,
    198, 200, 240
Le Gallou, Jean-Yves, 98, 161, 192,
    215
Legrand, Thomas, 77
Lehideux, Martine, 192, 240, 247
Lemonnier, Guy, 14
Lenin, Vladimir, 210
Léotard, François, 226
Le Pen, Jean-Marie
    and anti-Semitism, 79, 94, 125–127,
        131, 135–136, 264
    and army plot, 44–45

as "Churchillian democrat," 78
    and "detail" remark, 126, 131
    on de Villiers, 108
    on Hitler, 131
    on immigration, 78–79, 132, 163
    and May 1968 student revolution,
        58
    and Mitterrand, 77–78
    on *mondialisme*, 222–223
    on national identity, 162–163
    and nationalism, 101
    and national preference policy, 110
    on "the right to difference," 207–208
    and Tixier-Vignancour, 53–54
Le Pen, Pierrette, 131, 194–196
Lesourne, Jacques, 105
Levaï, Ivan, 103
Lévy, Bernard-Henri, 224
Lewis-Beck, Michael, 174
LICRA. *See* Ligue Internationale Contre
    le Rascisme et l'Antisémitisme
Ligue Internationale Contre le Racisme
    et l'Antisémitisme (LICRA), 32,
    226
Lille, 113
Lindon, Denis, 171, 173
Lionet, Christian, 63, 194, 196
Lobbies, 4, 225–226
Lyon, 113

Maastricht, 108, 129, 224, 263
McVeigh, Timothy, 217
Madiran, Jean, 99, 130, 197, 206, 216,
    222
Mainstream right, 76–78
    and 1986 legislative election, 81–82
    and 1988 legislative election, 93
    and 1988 presidential election,
        89–93
    and de Villiers, 111–112
    electorate, 83
    and immigration, 97, 106, 144, 160
    and National Front, 112
Marchais, Georges, 174
Marcilhacy, Pierre, 53
Marcilly Jean, 194
Marignane, 262

Marrus, Michael, 149
Martinez, Jean-Claude, 84, 101, 128, 190, 196
Marx, Karl, 210
Mauge, Roger, 13–14, 44–45, 58
Maurras, Charles, 3, 12, 16, 19–20, 123, 192, 199, 242
Maxwell, Robert, 222
Mayer, Nonna, 176, 179, 181–182
May 1968 student revolution, 56–58, 253–254
Médecin, Jacques, 209
Mégret, Bruno, 2–3, 84, 94, 132–133, 176, 183, 192, 202, 258
  on AIDS, 224–225
  on antiracism, 216
  and anti-Semitism, 2, 99, 228–230
  on cosmopolitanism, 221–222
  on democracy, 106
  on de Villiers, 109
  and "fifty measures," 98
  on immigration, 143–144, 255
  on Le Pen, 102
  on natality, 239–240, 243
  on national identity, 162
  and national preference policy, 87, 254
  and 1995 municipal election, 112–113
  on oligarchy, 226–227
  on parliamentary democracy, 162
  and political discourse, 217–223
Mendès-France, Pierre, 13, 28–29, 36, 54, 125
Milice, 16
Milloz, Pierre, 160
Milza, Pierre, 170
Minute, 156, 197
Mitterrand, Danielle, 95
Mitterrand, François, 31, 43, 55–56, 71, 74, 77–78, 81, 90, 92–93, 102, 130, 158, 171–172, 174, 255
Mondialisme, 4, 124, 128–129, 133, 161, 222–223
Monod, Jérôme, 130, 227
Montandon, Georges, 100
Moon, Sun Myung, 193

Moonies. *See* Unification Church
Mosley, Oswald, 14
Moulin, Jean, 55
Mounier, Emmanuel, 21
Mouvement Contre le Racisme et pour l'Amitié Entre les Peuples (MRAP), 226
Mouvement Jeune Révolution, 189, 200
Mouvement de la Jeunesse d'Europe, 192
Mouvement pour la France, 108
Mouvement Social Européen (MSE), 14, 54
Mouvement Socialiste de l'Unité Française (MSUF), 17
Mouvement Solidariste, 189
Movimento Sociale Italiano, 60–62
MRAP. *See* Mouvement Contre le Racisme et pour l'Amitié Entre les Peuples
MSE. *See* Mouvement Social Européen
MSUF. *See* Mouvement Socialiste de l'Unité Française
Multiculturalism, 82, 95
Mussolini, Benito, 4, 14, 18–19

Nasser, Gamal Abdel, 37
National Assembly, 43
National Front
  and "anti-French racism," 163
  attitude toward parliament, 84–86
  blue-white-red festival, 103–104
  conception of politics, 5
  establishment of, 62–63
  and immigration, 64–66, 78–80, 94, 144
  and Muslims, 124
  national preference policy, 3, 94, 106, 201, 230, 254, 262–263
  1993 program, 128, 160
  political discourse, 84–85, 136
  and "right to difference," 95, 161, 230, 254
  working class support for, 263–264
National Hebdo, 103, 160, 176, 197–198, 200

National Immigration Office, 158
Nazi party, 5
Nazism, 64, 90
Neoracism, 17, 163
Nice, 112
Noir, Michel, 91, 93
Nouvelle École, 210
Nouvel Observateur, 158

OAS. *See* Organisation de l'Armée
    Secrète
Occident, 54–55, 57, 59–60
Occupation, 19–20
Odessa group, 14
Oeuvre Française, 59
Orange, 112, 262, 265
Ordre Nouveau, 59–63, 65, 78, 159,
    187
Organisation de l'Armée Secrète (OAS),
    12, 45, 61, 63, 153, 209, 252
Ormesson, Marcel d', 90, 132
Oussékine, Malik, 216

Pak, Cho Hi, 194
Palestine, 100
Panfieur, Françoise de, 85
Paon, Marcel, 147
Parti des Forces Nouvelles (PFN), 67
Parti Populaire Français (PPF), 28
Pasqua, Charles, 5, 89–90, 215, 227
    and immigration policy, 105–106
    and National Front, 91, 93
Pauwels, Louis, 95, 134, 210
Paxton, Robert, 149
Penciolelli, Gérald, 198
Perez, Gilles, 77
Péron, Juan, 43
Perrineau, Pascal, 107, 176–177, 179,
    181–182
Pétain, Philippe, 12, 16, 20, 55
Peyrat, Jacques, 112
PFN. *See* Parti des Forces Nouvelles
Piat, Yann, 90, 93–94, 189–190
    on anti-Semitism, 132–134
    on "detail remark," 131
    on Unification Church, 193–194

Pieds-noirs, 46, 113, 173
Pinochet, Augusto, 4–5
Platone, François, 180
Plenel, Edwy, 178, 201
Poher, Alain, 59
Pompidou, Georges, 58–59, 65–66,
    152, 265
Pons, Bernard, 227
Popular Front government, 16
Pordea, Gustav, 194
Poujade, Pierre, 14, 22, 169–170
    Bardèche on, 33–35
    and Le Pen, 31, 35–36
Poujadism
    and Algerian War, 35
    and anti-Semitism, 29–30, 33
    and Estates-General, 27, 30–31, 35
    and fascism, 33
    and National Assembly, 30, 32–33
    and 1956 election, 29, 32, 170
    organization, 35
    and racism, 33
    support for, 29, 174
    and Tixier-Vignancour, 54
PPF. *See* Parti Populaire Français
PR. *See* Elections, proportional
    representation
Présent, 105, 160, 197–198, 200, 226,
    244
Protocols of the Elders of Zion, 127
Pujo, Pierre, 57

Rabin, Yitzhak, 101
Racism, 2, 19, 72, 85, 90, 129, 134,
    149
    and Algeria, 40
    and GRECE, 214–215
    and immigrants, 154
    and Jeune Nation, 47
Rassemblement Européen pour la
    Liberté, 210
Rassemblement National, 54
Rassemblement National (National
    Front), 84

Rassemblement pour la République (RPR), 71, 73, 75, 81, 89–90, 93, 133–134, 175, 179, 199, 215, 263
Reagan, Ronald, 76
Republican Party, 81, 108, 208, 211, 215
Resistance, 11, 16–17, 96
Rey, Henri, 180
Rivarol, 101, 197
Rivera, Primo de, 60
Rollat, Alain, 5, 62, 67, 76, 78, 103, 178, 211
Rothschild, Baron de, 129
Roubaix, 180
Rousso, Henry, 135
RPR. *See* Rassemblement pour la République

Sacerdotal Fraternity of Saint Pius X, 200
Salan, Raoul, 43
Salazar, Antonio, 4
Salo Republic, 14
Sartre, Jean-Paul, 61
Schlegel, Jean-Louis, 110
Schwartzenberg, Roger-Gérard, 59, 66–67
Sidos, Pierre, 55, 59, 173
Siegfried, André, 174
Simonpieri, Daniel, 112, 262
Skorzeny, Otto, 14, 43
Socialism 40–41
Socialists
  and "break with capitalism," 81–82
  and immigration, 157–158
  and 1986 legislative election, 80–84
Société d'Études et de Relations Publiques, 46
Solé, Robert, 98
Somoza, Anastasio, 4
SOS-Racisme, 4, 104, 178, 223
Sternhell, Zeev, 261
Stirbois, Jean-Pierre, 191, 238, 247
  character of, 189
  and integrists, 200
  on "international Jewish conspiracy," 131

in 1982 Dreux cantonal election, 74
and party organization, 187–189
and "solidarists," 198–199
Stirbois, Marie-France, 191, 238, 247
  in 1982 Dreux cantonal election, 74
  in 1989 legislative by-election, 96
  in 1995 municipal election, 112
Stoleru, Lionel, 125–126, 220
Suez campaign, 35, 37–38

Taguieff, Pierre-André, 163, 212, 214
Tapie, Bernard, 108
Teitgen, Paul, 38
Thatcher, Margaret, 76
Thomas, Albert, 142
Thorez, Maurice, 21
Tixier-Vignancour, Jean-Louis, 53–56, 169–173
Touton, Jacques, 91, 133
Toulon, 74, 112, 251, 263
Touraine, Alain, 253, 256
Tourcoing, 113
Touvier, Paul, 216
Trilateral Commission, 128, 221
Tristan, Anne, 218

UDCA. *See* Union de Défense de Commerçants et Artisans
UDF. *See* Union pour la Démocratie Française
UNEF. *See* Union National d'Étudiants Français
Unification Church, 193–195
Union de Défense de Commerçants et Artisans (UDCA), 27
Union pour la Démocratie Française (UDF), 73, 75, 133, 175, 199
Union National d'Étudiants Français (UNEF), 12
Union National des Indépendants Républicains (UNIR), 12
Union National Interuniversitaire, 193
United Nations, 128
UNIR. See Union National des Indépendants Républicains

Valla, Jean-Claude, 198, 212

Veil, Simone, 75, 126, 176, 214
Venner, Dominique, 47, 55
Vernet, Daniel, 93
Vial, Pierre, 213
Viarengo, Guy, 78
Vichy, 2, 16–17, 20, 54–55, 123,
    135–136, 150, 193, 229, 264
Vidal, Francette, 153
Villiers, Philippe de, 108–111, 179
Vitrolles, 112, 254

Wagner, Georges-Paul, 106, 129, 133
Weil, Patrick, 150, 154–155
Weil, Pierre, 171, 173
Williams, Philip, 31

Yahiaoui, Abdenour, 38
Yamgnane, Kofi, 102

Zeller, André, 44

Printed in the United Kingdom
by Lightning Source UK Ltd.
112708UKS00001B/223